Fifth Edition

Strategic Brand Communication Campaigns

Advertising Titles from
NTC/Contemporary Publishing Group

Advertising Principles: Choice,
Challenge, Change
   Bruce G. Vanden Bergh and Helen Katz

Advertising Media Planning, 5/e
   Jack Sissors and Lincoln Bumba

Media Planning: A Practical Guide, 3/e
   Jim Surmanek

Advertising Media Sourcebook, 4/e
   Peter B. Turk

Essentials of Media Planning:
A Marketing Viewpoint, 3/e
   Arnold Barban, Steven M. Cristol,
   and Frank J. Kopec

The Media Handbook
   Helen Katz

Which Ad Pulled Best? 8/e
   Philip Ward Burton and Scott C. Purvis

Strategy in Advertising, 3/e
   Leo Bogart

Creating and Delivering Winning Advertising
& Marketing Presentations, 2/e
   Sandra Moriarity and Thomas Duncan

Advertising Copywriting, 7/e
   Philip Ward Burton

Fundamentals of Copy and Layout, 3/e
   Albert C. Book and C. Dennis Schick

Copywriting by Design
   David Herzbrun

The Radio & Television Commercial, 3/e
   Albert C. Book, Norman D. Cary,
   and Stanley I. Tannenbaum,
   Revised by Frank R. Brady

The Advertising Agency Business, 3e
   Eugene J. Hameroff

NTC Business Books
4255 West Touhy Avenue • Lincolnwood, IL 60646-1975
800-621-1918 • Fax 800-998-3103
ntcpub@tribune.com • www.ntc-college.com

Fifth Edition

Strategic Brand Communication Campaigns

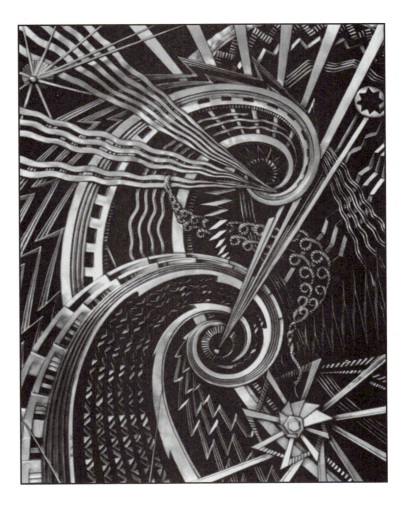

Don E. Schultz   Beth E. Barnes

NTC Business Books
a division of NTC/CONTEMPORARY PUBLISHING GROUP
Lincolnwood, Illinois USA

Acquisitions Editor: Lynn Mooney
Editor: Yvonne Zipter
Product Manager: Judy Rudnick
Art Director: Ophelia M. Chambliss
Cover design: Larry Cope
Cover image: Andrew Bordwin/Graphistock
Production Manager: Margo Goia
Production Coordinator: Denise Duffy-Fieldman

ISBN: 0-8442-2952-0

Acknowledgments/photo credits

Page 30	Courtesy Attorney's Title Insurance Fund, Inc.; agency: Kilgannon McReynolds
Page 41	Stock Montage
Page 81	Courtesy VDK Frozen Foods
Page 84	Courtesy United Airlines
Page 96	Courtesy Hyatt Hotels & Resorts
Page 222	Courtesy California Milk Processors Board
Pages 248–249	Courtesy Bristol-Myers Squibb Company
Page 260	Courtesy Mott's, Inc., and Nickelodeon
Page 268	Courtesy The Gillette Company
Page 279	Courtesy Hallmark
Page 281	Courtesy Oreck Corporation
Page 285	Courtesy HP Hood, Inc.
Page 286	Courtesy First Moments, Inc.
Page 289	Courtesy Frito Lay, Inc.
Page 293	Courtesy Unilever United States, Inc.
Page 295	Courtesy the ICEE Company
Page 303	Courtesy BMG Music Service
Page 304	Courtesy Oldsmobile
Page 307	Courtesy Mutual of Omaha
Page 313	Courtesy *VIBE* Magazine
Page 320	Courtesy Unilever United States, Inc.
Page 321	Courtesy Unilever United States, Inc.
Page 322	Courtesy Eprise Coporation

Published by NTC Business Books, a division of NTC/Contemporary Publishing Group, Inc.
© 1999 NTC/Contemporary Publishing Group, Inc., 4255 West Touhy Avenue, Lincolnwood
(Chicago), Illinois 60646-1975 U.S.A.

Brief Table of Contents

Contents

Strategic Brand Communication Campaigns

Strategic Brand Communication Campaigns

Contents

List of Exhibits

Strategic Brand Communication Campaigns Reviewer Panel

Joel Geske
Iowa State University

Nancy Mitchell
University of Nebraska

Thomas H. P. Gould
University of North Carolina

Doug Newsom
Texas Christian University

Norman Govoni
Babson University

Len N. Reid
University of Georgia

Kazumi Hasegawa
Emerson College

Elizabeth Tucker
University of Texas at Austin

Joe Bob Hester
Texas Tech University

Marc Weinberger
University of Massachussetts

Kevin Keenan
American University in Cairo

Janet Zipser Zipkin
San Francisco State University

Jim Maskulka
Lehigh University

Preface

When the first edition of this text was written in 1979–1980, advertising as a business function was finally starting to be formalized and codified. *Strategic Advertising Campaigns* was the first textbook written to describe the process of developing a cohesive approach to an advertising campaign. The goal was to take the student and the practitioner through the campaign development process, starting with the development and understanding of customers and prospects by using research and proceeding through the various steps in creating an effective and efficient advertising program: strategy development, creative execution, budgeting, media distribution, and evaluation. As more alternative forms of promotion were developed in the marketplace—such as sales promotion, public relations, and direct marketing—those forms of promotion were addressed in subsequent editions. In other words, all the changes that were made in the various editions of this text have been reflections of changes in the marketplace, consumers, technology, media, marketing, and advertising itself.

In our view, however, advertising is changing so dramatically today that the last edition of this text, which illustrated an inside-out versus an outside-in approach, is no longer relevant or appropriate. Advertising is and will continue to be a driving force in marketing and the marketplace, but advertising alone is simply not enough for most marketing organizations. It is not enough, that is, to assure success in a global marketplace in which competitors abound and consumers are increasingly knowledgeable. Even the concept of Integrated Marketing Communication, which was pioneered by us, cannot accommodate the changes that are occurring in the marketplace.

Advertising, as it has been defined, even in campaign form, cannot assure the marketplace success of products and services. Such success takes more than advertising, and it takes different forms of communication. While advertising is a key ingredient, it is not the only ingredient in a successful product or service. From the marketing viewpoint, it takes a solid product, a sound price, relevant distribution, and effective promotion. From a promotional standpoint, it takes more than media advertising—or even promotion or marketing—to be successful in the twenty-first-century marketplace. It takes a different view of the marketplace and a different approach to communication.

In our view, the critical form of communication in the future will be broader than simply advertising. It will be broader than what has traditionally been defined as a promotional mix. It must be broader and perhaps deeper than even marketing itself, which is rooted almost entirely in the concept of transactions and exchange. In the twenty-first century, it is the brand that will be important. It is, after all, the brand with which customers and prospects have relationships, not the advertising or promotion or merchandising or the like. It is the brand that communicates value to customers and prospects. It is the brand, in fact, that combines all the communication forms and activities that give products and services meaning. It is the brand that will drive the twenty-first-century marketplace, and it is brand communication that must therefore be planned and developed and executed by skilled communication experts.

The most apparent and major change to this edition of *Strategic Brand Communication Campaigns* is the emphasis on identifying and managing the contacts that a customer or prospect has with the brand, rather than simply managing the messages that the organization sends toward customers in the form of advertising, sales promotion, public relations, and the like. While those elements are important, they are simply the output of the organization. It is the customer or prospect who is responsible for determining the outcomes of those communication activities—that is, the responses in the form of sales or purchases or inquiries or advocacy or whatever. It is this change in focus—from what we as marketers send out or distribute to what customers or prospects receive—that differentiates advertising management from brand communication management. Brand communication management is much broader than advertising because it includes all the ways customers or prospects come in contact with the brand. That includes the product itself, packaging, channels, pricing, distribution and location, employees, and on and on and on. In short, brand communication is how the customer or prospect encounters the brand, and that comes in multiple forms and formats over a period of time. Thus, brand communication is much broader than marketing. It is broader and deeper than product promotion. It is the sum and substance of everything about the consumer and the brand and their relationship in the marketplace.

In addition, brand communication is not just outbound—that is, only those messages the organization sends out to customers or prospects. Rather, it is both outbound and inbound: whenever the customer or prospect comes in contact with the brand it is in an interactive format. Something occurs. Something is enhanced or destroyed or reinforced or learned about the brand. This is a major change in the way we have traditionally thought about marketing and communication. It is from a customer's standpoint rather than a marketer's view. And it is dynamic, not static. It is something that the brand and the customer create together and through which they interact. So while traditional advertising might have some impact on customers and prospects, it was and continues to be primarily an outbound activity: something the marketer wants to communicate to the customer. Brand communication, in contrast, is an interactive relationship between the two. It adds to and changes what the brand means, and it is generally at the discretion of the customer, not the marketer. In other words, it is the outcome, not the output.

To sum up, this text has made a transition from traditional advertising to integrated marketing communication to brand communication. *Strategic Brand Communication Campaigns* is the first book to take this next step in what is a logical progression. While the approach we take here is completely new, it is a natural extension of technology, the consumer, the marketplace, and the marketing organization. It is global. It is interactive. It is designed for the twenty-first-century marketplace. But it is not complete. As our communication systems evolve, as they increasingly reflect the change in communication, these approaches will have to be adapted as well. We see this as the first step in the development of formalized communication systems between buyer and seller that must occur in an increasingly interactive marketplace. A caution, however: all commerce will not become electronic. All communication will not become interactive. All marketing activities will not be designed simply to achieve a transaction or exchange. Nevertheless, all communication must be related to the brand and to the brand relationship between buyer and seller. Therefore, we will deal with how to achieve outcomes for the brand, not outputs about the brand. That, in and of itself, will be a major departure as we move from the twentieth-century marketplace. Join us for the ride. It should be fun.

Don E. Schultz
Northwestern University

Beth E. Barnes
Syracuse University

Introduction

Welcome to the Marketing

Communications Revolution

There is little question that we are in the midst of a marketing communication revolution. There have been massive and rapid changes in how and where and in what
ways people communicate, not just on a one-to-one level, but in the commercial
world as well. Where once a letter sent through the postal service was the primary
form of interpersonal communication, now electronic mail is delivered by a series of
computers linked by telephone lines and satellites around the world. Where once the
delivery boy sped court documents and business contracts and even advertising lay-
outs across city streets, now the almost ubiquitous facsimile machine transports
these kinds of documents. Where once couriers boarded steamships or airplanes to
assure delivery of replacement parts or architectural plans or financial documents,
today overnight delivery services such as DHL and Federal Express provide safe, se-
cure shipment to any part of the world, commonly in less time than it would take a
person to travel the same distance. Personal communication is becoming more personal, more direct, and easier, while impersonal communication is becoming more
prevalent, even invasive.

Similarly, other forms of communication, particularly media, are expanding.
Television is global. Radio is international. Newspapers and magazines are developing regional and local editions to satisfy the increasing demands of readers,
viewers, and listeners. The World Wide Web now links commerce throughout the
world, making distance an issue of the past. Speed is critical. Understanding is col-
lapsed into "sound bites."

In other words, communication, particularly marketing communication, is changing, but is it really changing that much? Certainly there are new techniques and

technologies. Electronics are everywhere but is *communication* really changing? Do people access, process, and store information or knowledge in new or different ways? Probably not—at least not significantly. Only the manner in which information is transferred between individuals or organizations has changed, though, in some cases, communicators seem to be reverting to methods used in days gone by. One could, for example, argue that e-mail is nothing more than instant letters or epistles created in an electronic format and delivered instantaneously. Likewise, conversations on cellular telephones are little different from face-to-face conversations except that they are carried out over long distances. Teenagers, for example, think nothing of picking up the phone and asking a friend the time of day, what they are doing, or how they are feeling. Again, the method of communication has changed, but not the nature of communication itself.

Over time, the emphasis has been primarily on developing mass communication systems whereby one could communicate with many. Newspapers and magazines achieve this in a delayed fashion. And we've developed instant electronic communication systems such as radio and television that allow events and activities to be communicated as they occur. But communication is now changing primarily from the one-to-many approach, on which mass media has heretofore focused, to the one-to-one communication permitted by the new technologies such as telephones, faxes, and e-mail. It is changing from a single message distributed to many listeners, viewers, or readers to individual messages delivered person-to-person through numerous types of new viewer- or listener- or reader-accessed media forms. Yes, communication is changing, but it is also remaining much the same—or perhaps even regressing to earlier times. This seeming contradiction is at the heart of our current conundrum: Is communication progressing to a newer and more sophisticated level or is it simply regressing to what we knew and did before? In this text, we will argue that we are likely going both backward and forward at the same time. Forward to the instant, personalized communication that the new technology offers. Back to forms of communication that have been lost in the mass media frenzy of the past fifty years or so. Forward to ways in which humans can conduct interpersonal communication almost anywhere in the world instantaneously. Back to ways in which people actually know the people they are communicating with so that they can transfer truly personal meaning and ideas and content. Forward to a time when individual communication means something unlike anything we've previously experienced in terms of communication. Back to the time when individual communication was taken for granted. And both forward and backward in the sense of communication truly meaning *communicating* with others.

Obviously, the change in communication form and function will continue to have an impact on mass media communication and, indeed, on all forms of communication. That, of course, includes the most extensive and perhaps global form of mass communication: advertising. Advertising *is* mass communication: one message to many people delivered through various forms of media. Singular concepts and ideas about products and services sent out in an attempt to influence the purchase and use of commercial products or services among a wide audience. Messages and incentives sent by marketing organizations to groups of people whom they believe might be most attracted to the product or service, wrapped, in many cases, around free entertainment to make the messages more relevant or attractive. Mass messages about products and services delivered through mass media.

That was advertising yesterday, and that is advertising today and will likely be advertising tomorrow. The question is, in the increasingly more personal world of communication, how, where, and under what circumstances does or should advertising fit in today's world of commerce? With the change of media delivery forms, will advertising become more or less relevant? Is there a place for advertising in this seemingly more personal and changing world of communication? And, if so, how and where does advertising fit? Those are questions all advertising professionals, academics, and even students find themselves struggling with now, and that struggle will undoubtedly continue into the twenty-first century.

Information Technology

Two major factors are fueling the communications revolution: information and technology. The shift in control of these two areas—from the marketer to the channel and ultimately to the consumer—is the reason for the upheaval in communications and therefore, marketing. For simplicity, we combine the concepts of information and technology, referring to them as *information technology* for the balance of this book.

Information technology is all those innovations, particularly electronic devices, systems, and processes that allow people and organizations to gather, store, manipulate, and use data to create information that increases the ability to communicate. In this sense, our primary focus will be on the forms of technology that can be used to transfer information that provides the basic function of communication. Using this concept, information technology would or could include, but would not be limited to, electronics such as computers, telephony, satellites, data storage in databases, and the like. In addition, we could include such traditional information or communication forms as printing, radio and television signals, and other well-known forms. Thus, in our definition, information technology is the basis for all forms of communication, both personal and impersonal, direct and indirect, commercial and not-for-profit.

Historically, information and technology have been the key elements in the marketer's arsenal. Marketers used these to identify, communicate, and—it was hoped—persuade customers to consider or to purchase a product or service. Information and technology have been the tools that organizations such as market research firms, advertising and promotion agencies, and media have mastered and made available to marketing organizations. Thus, while our focus in this Introduction is on marketing, information technology has generally been the tool kit used by all types of organizations to assist marketers in their quest to create transactions and exchanges with customers and prospects.

To understand the communication revolution and the shift of information technology, we discuss in some detail the history of marketing, and the impact experienced as a result of the shift of information technology. This sets the stage for our discussions in Chapters 1 and 2 of the twenty-first-century marketplace and how and why brands and brand communication are or will become the most important factors for most marketing organizations.

Carbon Paper, Slide Rules, Four-Function Calculators, and Marketing

What do these four things have in common? They were all developed, refined, and came to business prominence during the 1950s and 1960s. Marketing is the only one to survive almost intact. Carbon paper has been replaced by copying machines, slide rules by computers, and four-function calculators by electronic spreadsheets. Unfortunately, however, in most organizations marketing is still practiced in almost the same way as when it was developed and implemented some forty to fifty years ago. And therein lie many of the marketing and communication challenges faced today.

Unlike carbon paper, slide rules, and calculators, which have been replaced by newer, more relevant, and superior approaches and methodologies, the concept of marketing has not changed dramatically in the past fifty years. While many business practices and activities have evolved and grown, marketing is still focused on many of the same concepts, approaches, and techniques used fifty years ago. There are some who will argue that marketing has indeed evolved, but any change has been superficial and slow in coming. Most of the minor changes in marketing have been refinements of the basic concepts. While those concepts continue to work in some situations, they are, in too many cases, ill-suited for a rapidly changing, technologically driven global marketplace with sophisticated and experienced consumers. Simply put, the problem with current day marketing is that the concepts being applied were developed for a dramatically different marketplace than the one today and the one that will evolve rapidly in the twenty-first century. In the next sections, we illustrate what has happened to marketing and communication, and why these changes are impacting how marketing organizations can and should adjust to them in order to be effective.

The Development of Marketing Practice in the United States

With that rather grandiose title for this section, we move immediately to an explanation of how and why marketing theory and practice developed as it did over the past fifty years, particularly in the United States. To start, one must recall that most marketing and marketing communication concepts and activities we use today were developed in the United States during the years immediately following World War II. Several factors influenced those developments. First, the United States was the one major manufacturing economy that was spared the destructive forces of war. Unlike Europe and Asia, the U.S. consumer market emerged relatively unscathed. True, most manufacturing had been converted to the war effort, but that was quickly and rather easily returned to peacetime use to fill consumer needs. Thus, there were manufacturing facilities in place that could be and were quickly converted from one line of products to another. Second, there was a retail and distribution base on which to build marketing concepts and practices. That was supported by logistical systems that made the transport of the new products to national markets quite effective and efficient. Third, there were communication systems that could be used to inform and persuade consumers. Many of these had been developed during the war years and were readily adapted to consumer use. In short, the United States was the only country that had in place all the facilities and resources on which to build the principles of marketing, distribution, and communication. Thus, it was a relatively straightforward task to develop and apply the principles of mass marketing, mass distribution, and mass media. From that base, much marketing thought and practice has since been spread around the world.

The Development of the Four Ps of Marketing

In the late 1950s, Jerome McCarthy, then a professor in the business school at Michigan State University, published a marketing textbook that focused on what he called the management of the "four Ps of marketing": product, place (distribution), price, and promotion. This mnemonic device, stressing the management of the supposed four major functions available to the marketing manager, was quickly adopted by academicians and practitioners alike. They used the four Ps as the basis for developing and managing marketing programs. Thus, since the early 1960s, most marketing management focus has been on the proper development, allocation, and management of these four, supposedly controllable activities. Interestingly, although the marketing concept is said to focus on consumers and meeting consumer needs and wants, consumers are nowhere to be found in McCarthy's four Ps approach. The four Ps approach is oriented almost entirely toward what the organization wants to do and the tools available to accomplish those goals. As we will see later, it is this internal focus on the management and control of marketing activities, rather than on customers and consumers, that is creating much of the difficulty in the transition of marketing and marketing communication into the twenty-first-century marketplace.

During the 1950s and early 1960s, the primary goal of most organizations was to produce and distribute the tremendous flood of products and services that were then flowing from the converted plants and factories. The goal was to meet and fill existing consumer demand at a profit, not to develop marketing practices. The pent-up consumer demand created by the worldwide depression of the 1930s followed by the war years of the 1940s had created a marketplace of shortages. Consumers wanted and were willing to buy almost anything the manufacturers or service providers could develop. The "baby boom" of the war years provided the consumers. The rapidly expanding economic base provided the financial support. The technologies developed during the war years were converted to the consumer marketplace in the form of radically new products. And the rapidly expanding consumer workforce provided the fuel and funds to turn what had been a dormant U.S. consumer marketplace into an economic boom. Organizations responded. Mass production fueled mass distribution, which led to mass marketing, which was supported by mass communication. The primary tool used by marketing organizations was mass media advertising, which flowed from the development of radio and television. Consumers had common needs for products and services. Manufacturers could supply those needs. Thus, mass advertising was used to advise consumers of the availability of desired products and services. It was used to inform consumers about new products and concepts. It was used to homogenize the wants and wishes of the rapidly expanding consumer base. The United States became the birthplace of consumer marketing that was fueled by the U.S.-developed and perfected consumer advertising. Advertising was king, and marketing organizations responded by pouring more and more money into the media. That concept and approach survives to this day. Many marketing organizations apparently still believe that with enough money and sufficient media weight, almost any product or service can be "sold" to consumers.

The marketing and advertising concepts that were developed in the 1950s and 1960s worked well. Marketing, as it was practiced then, was powerful. Consumers responded to the availability of new and exciting products and to advertising that informed and advised. Everything was wonderful in the world of marketing and advertising, most marketers believed that was the way it would always be. But, changes that were afoot as early as the mid-1960s set the stage for the transition in which we find ourselves today.

When Advertising Was King

Mass production drove mass distribution, which required mass marketing. And mass marketing needed mass advertising to help shape the wants and desires of a rapidly growing consumer marketplace. Indeed, the development of media was directly related to the need by advertisers to find ways of sending messages to prospective customers. Newspapers were too local. Magazines were too slow. Marketers needed speed and space to reach the entire population. In fact, radio programming developed primarily, not to deliver information, but as a way to sell radio sets. Television was much the same, with programming structured to provide audiences that could be rented to advertisers. Advertising-supported media, particularly radio and television, were the first media to unite the country. They brought homogenization of culture, of taste, and, most of all, of products and services. Manufacturers were focused on mass production, on making similar products in great quantity at increasingly lower prices. That meant large homogeneous audiences were needed to absorb the increasing production that stemmed from economies of scale. Radio and television advertising provided the vehicles. In the United States in the 1960s, then, everything the marketer developed was working: mass production; mass distribution through growing retailing systems; mass promotion in the form of mass media advertising. The marketing and advertising concepts developed for those times are still the same ones we use today. Indeed, the need for a transition is hardly surprising when one recognizes that the marketing concepts and approaches that were designed for a different marketplace continue to be used today. But what brought about the changes that have occurred in the United States since the mid-1960s?

The Marketplace and Marketing in Transition

Shown as Exhibit I-1 is a chart that identifies the major changes which have occurred in U.S. marketing organizations since the mid-1960s. The chart illustrates the

Exhibit I-1

Marketplace in Transition

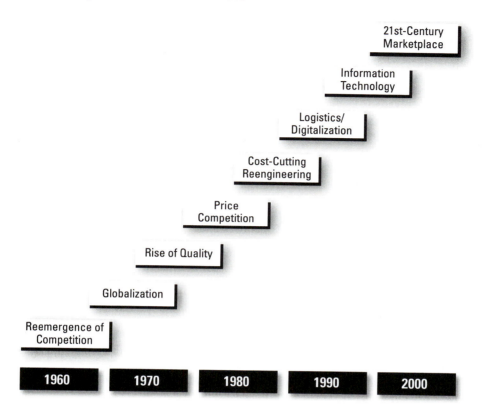

effects on U.S. marketers of the reemergence of competition in the early 1960s. Prior to that time, U.S. manufacturers dominated the world economy in many product categories. The problem, though, was that demand was so great that quality became a nonissue. The goal of the manufacturer was simply to produce the product, get it out of the plant, and get it into the hands of eager consumers. The focus was on speed and production capability, not on product quality. As we will see, U.S. manufacturers would pay the price for this production/distribution orientation later.

It was in this 1960s period that competition reemerged. As Germany, Japan, France, and the United Kingdom rebuilt and replaced their war-damaged production facilities, they reentered the marketplace. In addition, the low-labor-cost countries in the Asia–Pacific Rim such as Hong Kong, Singapore, Taiwan, and Korea, entered the market as well. U.S. marketers, because the North American economy was so dynamic, robust, and growing so rapidly, chose to focus on the domestic arena. Thus, while much marketing thought and practice developed in the United States, it had a strong domestic bent. That, as we will see later, is one of the challenges facing U.S. marketers today—converting from a domestic to a global view of marketing practice.

In the mid-to-late 1960s, the Japanese changed marketing forever. They introduced the concept of product quality through an approach called Total Quality Management or TQM. Recall that most U.S. manufacturers, following the war, had based their approaches on mass production and distribution: Get the product out of the plant and fix it when it broke. The Japanese concept of quality, which was actually introduced into that country by Edwards Deming, an American, totally changed the way consumers thought about and made product purchasing decisions. Where the U.S. organizations had focused on obsolescence, continuously introducing minor improvements and changes in products to encourage consumers to constantly replace, upgrade, or repurchase, the Japanese focused on major improvements that enhanced and improved product performance over the long term. The Japanese introduced this new focus on quality first in automobiles and then in consumer electronics, cameras, optical goods, and so on. Consumers responded and soon Japanese products became the category quality leaders and ultimately marketing leaders as well. By the simple concept of introducing product quality, the Japanese wrested market after market from the United States and changed the process of marketing.

By around 1975, marketers had another problem with which to contend. In the short twenty-year period from the mid-1950s to the mid-1970s, the domestic and global marketplace had gone from product shortage to product surplus. Technology had provided the means and manufacturing organizations had applied them to the manufacturing process. Many product categories became oversupplied. The development of manufacturing facilities in Asia and the Pacific Rim, where cheap labor, new manufacturing concepts, and eager workers provided the output, contributed to the glut of products. Aggressive global marketers, primarily from Japan, Hong Kong, Malaysia, Singapore, and Korea, moved quickly to distribute that output around the world.

At about that same time, global demand for products and services started to flatten, particularly in consumer products. The baby boom had reached its zenith and started to decline. Consumers had need for only so many refrigerators, televisions, automobiles, and the like. Many marketing organizations found that their marketing approaches, which were designed for a continuously expanding marketplace, stopped working. While the market was still expanding, its growth had slowed. Manufacturing had far outstripped demand. To make matters worse, the plants and factories were designed to operate at maximum output, to maximize economies of scale. To cut back on production would mean higher individual product costs, which consumers simply wouldn't accept. So, in many marketing organizations, the decision was made to attempt to build consumer demand. To most organizations, that meant price promotion. "Lower the price and more consumers will buy" was the idea.

Using basic economic theory, marketers quickly converted to a price promotion approach. They seemed to believe that they could price promote and price reduce their way to success. Thus, in the mid-to-late 1970s, marketing was characterized by price promotion, not product or benefit promotion. Marketers tried to lure consumers into purchase with coupons, discounts, deals, displays, and gimmicks. The truth was, however, that these were not just price promotions, they were also margin reductions. Soon, many organizations found themselves with the same costs, but lower margins and falling demand. Since all marketers were using the same price promotion approaches, one deal seemed to cancel out the other. It was a marketing stalemate played at increasing costs. The marketer's response? Reduce internal costs to improve margins.

In the United States and seemingly around the world, the 1980s were the decade of cost reduction and rationalization. Companies rethought their entire businesses. They called it "reengineering," which generally meant closing plants, laying off workers, reducing overhead, and attempting to get down to some core business, which they hoped to dominate. For marketing, this meant several things. For one, marketing was pushed into the background. Since marketing had come to mean price promotion, there was less and less interest in deals and discounts that simply reduced margins and provided no lasting marketplace advantage. For another, it meant that organizations turned inward, focusing on what they needed to do to become efficient, not on how to serve customers. They looked at how to reduce costs, not how to enhance customer relationships. Areas such as consumer research, customer service, research and development, and product improvements were slashed as organizations attempted to get down to what they considered essential elements to survive. In short, in the United States and in most of the rest of the world, the customer and consumer were reengineered out of the organization just as were many employees and production facilities. And because the focus of most organizations was inward and the customer was external, it was the customer who suffered.

Thus, we see marketing and communication—which had generally been given credit, often not deserved, as being the engine that drove the consumer marketplace in the 1960s and 1970s—being relegated to a less important role in the 1980s and early 1990s. Organization structure, staffing and production reduction, and rationalization were king. Marketing was a detail, and not a very important detail at that. Such was the situation as we entered the 1990s.

The Development of the Twenty-First-Century Marketplace

Starting in the mid-to-late 1980s, several major events came together to create what we call the "twenty-first-century marketplace." Most of these events were driven by information technology. While many of the elements had been in place for a number of years, it was not until toward the end of the 1980s that they began to come together. For our purposes, these included items such as Universal Product Codes (UPC) in combination with optical scanners that were located in retail stores. While originally designed to reduce the cost of product handling and errors in retail store check-out and to improve management of product inventories in supermarket warehouses, UPCs were quickly adapted to marketing tasks such as identifying the results and impact of promotional efforts, including price reductions and coupons. Computerized electronic data capture and storage was also used to develop frequent shopper programs in which customer purchases and responses were recorded and then stored in a database. In addition, new forms of communication and message distribution became available, such as cellular telephones, faxes, e-mail, and the World Wide Web. Indeed, in the past ten years we have seen a virtual communication revolution, which has had a tremendous impact on marketing activities.

The Development of Marketplace Power

The primary change in marketing and communication has been and will continue to be the result of transitions in information technology—which leads to our twenty-first-century marketplace concept. Historically, marketing organizations have controlled, or at least managed, most of the information technology in the marketplace. It is marketers who have had information about products and services, such as what could be manufactured and what could not. They have had information about consumers, their location, needs, and desires. They have had control of the marketing channels such as stores and retail locations. They have controlled price, determining how much to charge. In short, marketing organizations have been in control of the marketplace. Consumers have simply responded to, but have not controlled, the marketplaces in which they lived and operated. That marketer power is illustrated in Exhibit I-2.

This exhibit illustrates two types of marketplaces, one of which we call "the historical marketplace" (on the left). The historical marketplace is when the manufacturer or service provider is dominant. There, the organization controls the information about product and service production and availability, about consumer desires, and about prices and costs, as well as distribution and knowledge transfer about the product. In short, the marketing organization controls the market because it has mastered information technology. For example, take the recent release by Pfizer of the drug Viagra, a product for impotence. With a product that so many people seemingly want and need, all the pharmaceutical company had to do was to go to the news media and tell the story of the product's success against impotence. At the time of this writing, Viagra is selling for $8–$10 per pill in the United States and for as much as $40 per pill in Brazil. In other words, the pharmaceutical company (the marketer in this case) controls the marketplace. Pfizer controls the production, distribution, pricing, and communication. There is little need for advertising or promotion since knowledge of the product has quickly spread among those needing it.

In Exhibit I-2, we call this the historical marketplace because this is the fundamental method of marketing—that is, the marketing organization dominates the system by having a superior product and managing the various marketing activities in that system.

Alternatively, another marketing system is shown in Exhibit I-2. This has been labeled "the current marketplace." In this system, the distribution channels control the marketplace. Here, product manufacturers commonly all provide similar products

Exhibit I-2

Historical and Current Marketplaces

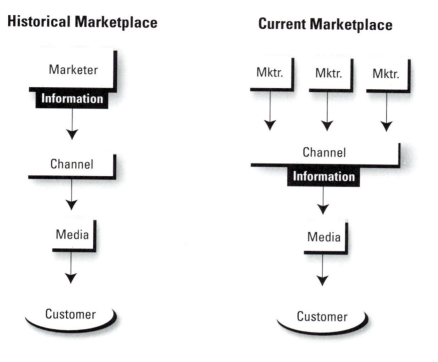

Historical Marketplace

Marketer

Information

Channel

Media

Customer

Current Marketplace

Mktr. Mktr. Mktr.

Channel

Information

Media

Customer

or services. They distribute those products and services through various forms of retail distribution channels. These distribution channels deal directly with the end users. In this marketplace, the channel member thus has more and better information and stronger relationships with customers and prospects than the manufacturer does. The channel controls this system. Because the channel members deal directly with consumers and end users, they therefore acquire and control all the needed marketplace information about customers and prospects, which they may or may not share with the manufacturer.

This is the type of marketplace in which many consumer and business-to-business products exist today. There is little product differentiation: the channel controls the information and has the relationship with the consumer or end user and, thus, has control of the marketing system. Examples of these types of marketplaces can be found among so-called retail category killers such as Wal-Mart, Toys 'R' Us, Home Depot, and CompUSA. The retailer or channel controls the distribution of products or services that manufacturers vend through their stores. Consequently, the retailer controls which products it will stock, the prices it is willing to pay the manufacturer, the types of promotion it demands, and the marketplace support it wishes. Retailers have the retail locations where consumers come to buy. They have information about what consumers want and are willing to buy. Information technology is, in this case, in the hands of the channel.

In these two examples (the historical marketplace and the current marketplace) information technology is in the hands of the marketing organization, whether it be the manufacturer or the channel. The manufacturer and the channel produce or provide the products and services consumers want. They have access to those consumers and prospects. They control and manage the marketing system from product and service availability through distribution and pricing and promotion. Consumers buy what the channels make available. Thus, channels control the marketplace.

The Rise of the Twenty-First-Century Marketplace

What we see happening today, however, is a shift of power in the marketplace from the marketer and channel to the consumer or customer. This is occurring primarily because of the shift in information technology. The twenty-first-century marketplace, as we envision it, is shown as Exhibit I-3.

The primary difference between the twenty-first-century marketplace and that of the historical and current is that the marketplace is interactive. Information and knowledge flow both ways: from marketer to consumer and also from consumer to marketer. Where the historical and current marketplace are controlled by the marketing organizations, in the twenty-first-century marketplace, that control will be shared with customers and consumers. The reason for this shift is easy to explain. Marketplace power is the result of access to and use of information technology—information about the marketplace and the technology to acquire or use that information. As the consumer gains more and more access to information, knowledge and technology, the power shifts from marketer or channel to consumer. The World Wide Web is the tip of the information technology iceberg and a small indication of what the twenty-first-century marketplace will be like. Using a computer and search engine, a consumer can now search the world easily and quickly for products and services. No longer limited by geography, retail locations, or lack of information about products or services, the consumer can learn about products, identify sources of supply and price, and determine delivery capability, all at the click of the mouse. As these types of systems develop, the consumer's power in the marketplace increases because information and technology provide access to resources that previously the marketer or channel controlled. Consumers can determine what they want to buy, search all available sources, and compare prices and alter-

Exhibit I-3

Twenty-First-Century Marketplace

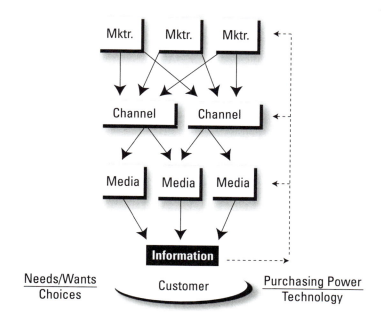

natives, and they can do that when, where, and using whatever methods they choose. It is this shift in information technology that is creating the new twenty-first-century marketplace and is changing the needs and requirements now confronting marketers. This is the transition that marketers must undergo. We discuss this new type of marketplace in more detail in Chapter 1. For the present, it is important to note where control of the marketplace resides and why, because that has much to do with marketing and communication development for organizations in the future.

It is the shift in information technology that demands a new view and a new approach to marketing and communication and that changes the way marketing organizations operate, how they relate to consumers and prospects, and how they develop and implement marketing and communication programs. It is here we believe the student of marketing and marketing communication should focus his or her studies for it is here where they will spend most of their careers. This is not to say that knowledge and understanding of the historical and current marketplaces are not worthwhile. They are. For one must understand the existing situations to prepare for the new. Also, as exciting and revolutionary as the new marketing and communication arenas may be, the existing ones will not simply disappear. Rather, they will adjust and evolve. The goal of this text is therefore to help the student who has developed an understanding of marketing, advertising, sales promotion, direct marketing, public relations, and other similar marketing communication tools to relate and use those tools in the twenty-first-century marketplace that we are now entering. As we proceed through this text, keep in mind that some organizations, some markets, and some consumers will adapt to the shift in information technology at different rates. Thus, a critical skill for the marketing and marketing communication practitioner is to recognize the current status of the marketplace, the consumer, and the marketing organization and to bring his or her knowledge and understanding to bear on the development of appropriate programs. The balance of this text is devoted to helping readers develop these skills.

The objective of this text is to present students with the knowledge and skills they need to prepare effective marketing communication campaigns. These campaigns must begin with a sound understanding of the marketing organization and its major asset, its brands. The concept of brand value will be explored and tools for estimating customer value will be presented. A strategy for creating an Integrated Brand Communication (IBC) program will be outlined and the components of this program will be described in detail: Consumer behavior, consumer research, budgeting, mass media, public relations, sales promotion, direct marketing, and media planning all come together in the effective campaign. Methods for measuring the effectiveness of the campaign will be described as well. Finally, a brief chapter on "Selling Management on the IBC Plan" has been included to help students overcome potential resistance to this new way of thinking.

Part 1

An Introduction to the Idea of Brands

1

Marketing and Communication in the Twenty-First-Century Marketplace

In the Preface and Introduction, we set the stage for the new marketplace of the twenty-first century, the arena for which we believe marketers and marketing organizations must develop communication programs now and into the future. In this chapter, we review the evolution and revolution driving this change. To cope with the required transition that marketers must make, we provide a tool called the *marketing diagonal*. The marketing diagonal concept can be used by marketing and communication planners to determine the type of communication program that should be developed. In order to provide a basis for the transition that is occurring in the marketplace, we start this chapter by continuing the discussion of how marketing organizations have traditionally competed.

How Marketing Organizations Compete

Exhibit 1-1 illustrates how organizations have traditionally competed in the marketplace. As can be seen, organizations have historically competed by product or service differentiation, through distribution and channels, or, most recently, through customer knowledge and focus.

Exhibit 1-1
How Organizations Compete

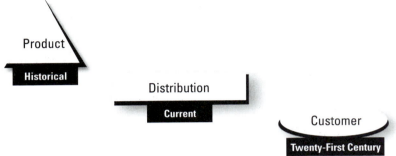

Competing on Product Differentiation

Many organizations have chosen to compete on the basis of differentiated products or services. The product differentiation approach was particularly popular in the developmental years of modern-day marketing. "Build a better mousetrap and the world will beat a path to your door" was the belief. Thus, organizations attempted either to develop new and unique products for the marketplace or to continuously enhance or extend their existing product lines. The organization's goal was to stay a step ahead of competition and, through this or that product advantage, find favor with customers and prospects. This product differentiation or product superiority approach was used by most organizations when current marketing concepts and approaches were being developed in the 1950s and 1960s.

Today, we find most consumer product firms still competing on the product superiority approach. They are continuously adding new ingredients, new formulations, new line extensions, new flavors or colors or styles—anything to differentiate the product or service from that of the multitude of competitors. Laundry detergents offer a good example of this approach. Procter & Gamble, for example, markets nine laundry detergents under the brand names Cheer, Tide, Era, Oxydol, Bold, Dreft, Gain, Ivory Snow, and Dash. Each detergent is designed to provide the same basic consumer benefit: to get clothes washed in an automatic washing machine clean. Yet, each product is unique in some way. For example, Cheer offers color guard. Tide promises to help keep clothes looking new. Era is the ultra power tool for stains. Likewise, Lever Brothers does practically the same thing in the detergent product category, marketing All, Wisk, and Surf, again differentiated by minor product differences that are believed to provide additional benefits to the purchaser.

Competing on Distribution Superiority

Alternatively, some organizations compete on distribution. That is, their primary marketing approach is to provide ease of access to their products or services. In many cases the products or services are similar, or at least they are perceived to be similar by consumers. Availability, itself, provides the competitive advantage. Little search effort is required on the part of customers, and prices tend to be approximately the same among the competing products or services. We see this type of competition for products such as gasoline, soft drinks, fast-food restaurants, and even snacks and candy bars. For example, Coca-Cola has chosen distribution as its major competitive differentiator. The goal of Coca-Cola is to be ubiquitous—always within arm's reach of a customer. Distribution occurs through vending machines, quick-serve restaurants, food stores, mass merchandisers, sports arenas, and so on. Whenever thirst hits a consumer, Coca-Cola wants its soft drinks to be there.

Other types of organizations use the same strategy, but apply it somewhat differently. For example, McDonald's has created a science to determine where to locate its restaurants. Each McDonald's restaurant is designed to be just the right distance from other McDonald's outlets. Site selection is very deliberate in order to meet the needs of hungry customers and prospects. Gasoline retailers make their site selection decisions in roughly the same way. As a result, in most U.S. cities the corners of major intersections are commonly populated by retailers of four different brands of gasoline, all vying for the consumer's patronage.

Competing on Customer Focus

As shown in Exhibit 1-1, the third traditional form of competition is that of consumer or customer knowledge, focus, or specialization. For the most part, service organizations and business-to-business firms have competed in this way, as have direct marketers. That is, the company develops a product or service that has particular appeal to a specific group of customers or prospects. For example, in the legal profession one can hire attorneys who specialize in tax law, others in corporate law, and still others in divorce or murder or injury claims. Each provides services to meet specific client needs. Dow Chemical is an example of a specialized business-to-business organization; in this case one that specializes in the development of various chemicals that are related to polyurethanes. Likewise, DuPont has focused on protective coatings and lubricants, while Arco Chemical has specialized in propylenes and styrenes. Each organization has identified specific manufacturers or processors who have need for its specific line of products. As a result, each works very closely with its customers to identify future needs, and then Dow, DuPont, and Arco develop specific products and services that will fill those needs.

Using Marketing Communication

For the most part, organizations have developed their marketing and communication programs based on how they have chosen to compete. For example, Procter & Gamble has relied heavily on product development and consumer advertising to advise consumers of the product differences among Tide, Cheer, and Oxydol. Mc-Donald's has used advertising and promotion to build consumer demand for its fast food, while Dow and DuPont have relied primarily on their sales forces or those of their distributors to bring their marketing story to customers and prospects. Consequently, each organization tends to define and manage its marketing communication programs based on how it has chosen to compete in the marketplace. Indeed, the marketing communication program is a critical element. The program must fit the audience the organization is attempting to serve and must be relevant in terms of reach and impact on customers and prospects.

Inherent in this selection of a marketing communication approach, however, is the idea that the marketer has control of the communication system with which it plans to compete. For example, P&G determines and defines what messages it will send to consumers, through what media, in what time frame, at what volume levels, and the like. The same is true of McDonald's. DuPont and Dow, of course, control their communication system by directing the efforts of their salespeople and the nature and level of sophistication of their sales presentations. In this way, each of these organizations, though they compete differently, has—or at least believes it has—control of its marketing communication systems. But how appropriate will approaches to marketing communication such as these be in the twenty-first-century marketplace we are now entering?

The Evolution and Revolution of Information Technology in Communication

Let us now turn to the shifts in information technology and then examine why and how they demand a transition in the way marketing firms develop and implement their communication programs.

Reprise of the Three Marketplaces

Exhibit 1-2 illustrates what we call "Marketplace Evolution and Revolution." Our focus now is to relate the historical, current, and twenty-first-century marketplaces to the marketing transition that we see occurring.

For the most part, these three marketplaces are dependent on and driven by information technology. To review, in the historical marketplace the manufacturing or marketing organization controls the information technology. Its control of information technology allows the marketing organization to also control the distribution systems, the media availability of product or benefit information, and, ultimately, the consumer or end user. The marketing organization determines the consumer need to be filled, as well as when, where, under what circumstances, and with what level of detail information about the product or service will be made available. This gives the marketing organization power in the marketplace. Consumers must find the information about products or services in order to make informed purchasing decisions to fill their wants and needs.

In the current marketplace, of course, this control of information technology shifts to the distribution channel. Channel members, because they are the conduit between the manufacturer and the end user, have control because they manage not only the distribution of those products or services, they also have information and access to both the marketer and the consumer. This central location and role allows the channel to control the manufacturers, the media, and, ultimately, the consumer. In making purchase decisions, the consumer is dependent on what the retailer makes available and on information the retailer provides about marketplace alternatives.

Finally, in the twenty-first-century marketplace, the customer will have most of the marketplace power. As discussed earlier, this comes because the access to information technology is shifted to the customer, who then uses that information to pit one manufacturer against another or one distribution channel against another. The customer has power because he or she has information, access to product data, the ability to compare prices and terms, and the choice of delivery channels.

An Interactive Marketplace

Perhaps the most relevant factor in the twenty-first-century marketplace is that it is interactive. As shown in Exhibit 1-2, both the historic and current marketplaces are one-way and outbound only. That is, the marketing organization, with its control of information technology, develops outbound messages and information about its products or services and attempts to deliver those messages and incentives to customers and prospects through its distribution systems and various forms of media. The same is true in the current marketplace, although it is generally the channel or the combination of the channel and the manufacturer who develop these linear, one-way, outbound communication programs.

As shown in Exhibit 1-2, the twenty-first-century marketplace will not be one in which one group or a combination of groups of marketers controls the information and communication. Instead, the twenty-first-century marketplace will be interactive. Marketing organizations, channels, media, and consumers will all share information and technology. They will create dialogues among themselves—not the traditional monologues of marketing organizations talking at or to customers and prospects. This major change is already starting to occur.

Driving this interactive twenty-first-century marketplace will be information technology in the form of databases, interactive communication systems such as the Internet and the World Wide Web, and new forms of marketing and communication channels in which buyers and sellers can communicate easily, effectively, and almost instantaneously. Already, we see some of this interactive marketplace in the Internet and Web. For example, today consumers can explore and compare products and services from all over the world. They can get instant replacement or product service for items they currently own. They can search innumerable databases for information about products or services to fill their wants and needs. Indeed, it is

Exhibit 1-2
Marketplace Evolution and Revolution

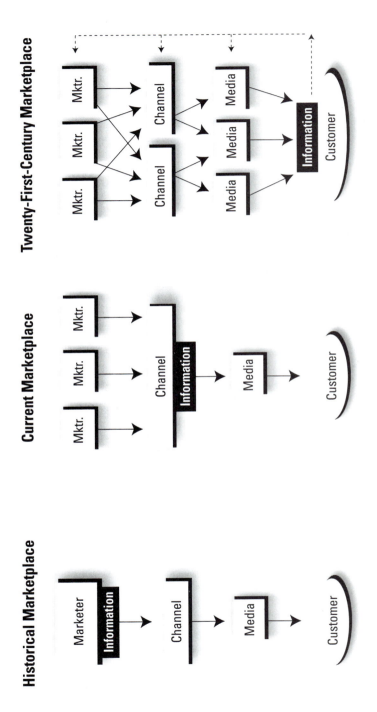

Historical Marketplace

Current Marketplace

Twenty-First-Century Marketplace

the shift of information technology from the marketer to the consumer that is creating many of the transitions that will characterize the twenty-first-century marketplace.

There Is Concurrent Evolution and Revolution—That's the Problem

Part of the problem for marketing organizations today is that they are being affected by both evolution and revolution. In some cases, their marketing organizations are slowly evolving, that is, they are moving from the historical to the current marketplace at a leisurely and identifiable pace. The marketing organization can recognize the changes occurring as information technology shifts to the channels or the customers. For example, in many business-to-business situations, marketers and their suppliers are now interconnected with electronic data transfer systems. In such a system, the organization that supplies parts and other elements to manufacturing companies has electronic data interchange systems that allow for continuous parts reordering, product design, new product development, and the like. These interconnected electronic systems replace much of the traditional communication between the organizations, such as sales calls or advertising or other forms of data interchange.

In other cases, however, the changes in information technology transfer are swift and often unrecognized by the marketing organization until it is too late. An example of swift and unwanted information technology transfer happened to an electronic scanner manufacturer with which we worked a few years ago. The manufacturer decided to embark on a major product upgrade. In considering what new features or elements consumers or end users might want, the manufacturer discovered that it knew little or nothing about who was actually using its electronic scanners. The company had been selling its units to systems integrators (organizations that wrote software that interconnected computers to the scanners), which, in turn, had been selling them as part of a unit, thereby making the optical scanner only one ingredient in the final system. In other cases, the manufacturer had been selling the scanners to value-added-retailers (VARs), who had been building other types of information systems for their customers, the end users. Thus, the optical scanner manufacturer had little or no information about how their scanners were being used, by whom, or for what purposes. Therefore, the manufacturer had little to go on when deciding how it might improve its product line.

In an attempt to learn more about its end users, the scanner manufacturer approached its systems integrator customers and its VARs to ask what types of organizations were using the scanners. They were quickly told that the end users were not the customers of the scanner manufacturer; instead, they were the customers of the integrator companies and the VARs. These groups refused to share the information about who was using the optical scanners, fearing that the scanner manufacturer would attempt to start selling directly to those they believed to be their customers. In short, the optical scanner manufacturer had shifted information and technology to the systems integrators and VARs, and so was operating in the current marketplace, not in the historical marketplace in which it believed it marketed. While the optical scanner organization was eventually able to get information about its end users, it did so at a high cost and with some resulting bad feelings with channel partners.

If a marketing organization has multiple products or markets in a number of categories or countries it can find itself faced with the challenge of operating in all three of the marketplaces illustrated in Exhibit 1-2 at once. For example, Product Line A may be in the historical marketplace, Product Line B in the current, and Product Line C in the twenty-first century. This is particularly difficult if the organization is accustomed to trying to develop and implement a single marketing approach across the organization and for all of its products. It becomes even more problematic for management when some managers are operating in one market and others in another. Centralized marketing systems are challenged, to say the least. For organizations operating globally, this is almost always the case. One country is well developed in terms of marketing and communication while others may be far behind. It is this need for "mix-and-match" marketing and communication programs that is one of the major challenges almost all organizations now face, or will face in the near future. Simply identifying the appropriate marketplace for marketing and communication programs becomes a true feat for marketers and communication planners.

Fortunately, there is a tool that can help the communication planner in determining what type of marketing and communication program needs to be developed. We discuss that next.

Using the Marketing Diagonal

An effective way to analyze and provide an understanding of what type of marketing and communication program needs to be developed is through the use of what we call the marketing diagonal, illustrated in Exhibit 1-3. The marketing diagonal illustrates the concept we have been discussing for some time, that is, the shift of information technology. As shown, information technology slides down a marketing diagonal from marketer or manufacturer to the channel and eventually reaches the customer or consumer. In other words, marketplace power shifts continuously as a result of information and technology being transferred down the marketing system chain. As this information technology shifts, power in the marketplace shifts as well.

The primary use of the marketing diagonal is as a marketing and communication planning device. By identifying where information technology currently resides, planners can then understand the type of competitive framework in which the organization exists. A historical marketplace-oriented communication plan developed for an organization that is competing in the current marketplace is likely to fail. Further, the organization should be able to estimate how quickly the information technology is sliding down the marketing diagonal. That estimate provides a time frame for the organization on the need to change its marketing and communication systems.

An Example of the Marketing Diagonal in Use

The marketing diagonal is relatively easy to use. First, the organization managers must identify where they believe they are on the marketing diagonal currently. That

Exhibit 1-3
The Marketing Diagonal

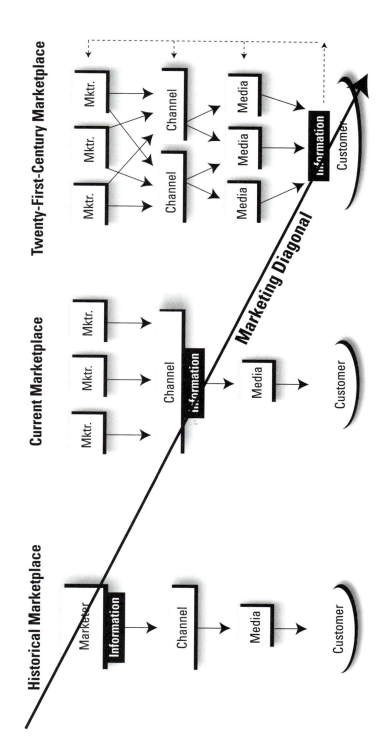

is done by simply marking on the marketing diagonal where they believe the organization currently stands in terms of information technology. In the historical marketplace, the marketing organization has most of the information technology and controls most of the marketing system. In the current marketplace, information technology resides with the channel and so on, as we discussed earlier.

After identifying the current marketplace location, managers then identify where they believe information technology will reside in the future. How quickly will the information technology slide down the marketing diagonal, or how quickly will information technology be shifted to the consumer or customer? This provides an organizational time frame, suggesting the degree of speed with which the organization must transition its marketing and communication programs. Commonly, in our consulting activities we have used a one-year, three-year, and five-year time frame for this information technology power shift.

Interestingly, in the organizations with which we have consulted, most managers have quickly agreed on the current location of information technology in their marketplace and in their organization. Further, they have been quite capable of estimating where and when information technology will shift down the marketing diagonal to the consumer. Thus, we have found that the marketing diagonal gives marketing and communication managers a simple and easy way to identify and express their estimates and beliefs about the shift of information technology as it will impact their organization.

A Real-World Example of the Marketing Diagonal

Attorneys' Title Insurance Fund, Inc., of Orlando, Florida, provides an excellent example of the marketing diagonal and its impact on an organization. The following case history describes how information technology has changed one organization and the impact it will likely have as we move forward into the twenty-first-century marketplace.

Background

In post–World War II America, Florida was a very different place. Pre-Disney Orlando had fewer than 50,000 residents and Florida had not yet been "discovered." Soon, real estate began to boom. As property prices increased, owners, lenders, and investors started demanding greater financial protection against title defects.[1] As a result of this demand, title insurance companies began expanding into the state. At first, these companies issued policies based on independent real estate attorneys' opinions about the state of the title, but then they retained their own counsel and built their own title plants (facilities at which records about properties were housed). Independent real estate attorneys, who had traditionally handled all real estate transactions in Florida, were facing a serious threat.

---

[1]Titles are the rights of ownership and possession of a particular property and/or the document that shows evidence of those rights. A title defect is any legal right to a property claimed by a person other than the owner.

Exhibit 1-4
Attorney's Title Insurance Fund, Inc. Advertisement

To protect attorneys' real estate practices from competitive encroachments, one Orlando attorney envisioned forming a title insurance underwriter organized exclusively by attorneys for attorneys. Florida attorneys who were active in real estate transactions could become "members" of this organization, with each member contributing part of the fee from real estate transactions to a statewide "fund." This fee would then underwrite issuance of a title insurance policy, coupled with a legal opinion. This vision soon became a reality. In 1948, Attorneys' Title Insurance Fund, Inc., better known as "The Fund," opened its doors as Lawyers' Title Guarantee Fund. Since its inception, The Fund has been like an advocacy group for attorneys, striving to keep them competitive and involved in real estate transactions.

The Fund Today

Today, The Fund is Florida's leading title insurance underwriter and title information provider. With approximately 6,000 members, The Fund receives almost 25 percent of all title insurance premium dollars in Florida.

In addition to issuing title insurance policies through its members, one of The Fund's primary services is providing title information, or data, on real estate in

Florida. For example, during a real estate transaction, the buyer or seller or both often employ an attorney to handle the real estate transaction. The attorney is required to conduct a title examination, which involves researching public records to uncover the legal history of the property, including names of previous owners, prior deeds, mortgages, court judgments, foreclosures, liens, and other matters that could affect the title to the property. This research is conducted to ensure that the seller has the legal right to sell the property and thus the ability to transfer a "clear," or unencumbered, title[2] to the purchaser.

Once the title examination is complete, a common practice in real estate transactions is for the buyer to purchase title insurance. Unlike car, homeowner, or life insurance, which all protect against future potential mishaps, title insurance safeguards against occurrences or events in the past. The purpose of title insurance is to protect against the possibility of hidden defects, which may not have surfaced even in the course of a thorough title examination. Some examples of hidden defects include lost or forged deeds, documents signed by minors, or clerical errors made at the courthouse. The Fund issues title insurance policies via one channel only—real estate attorneys who are members of the organization.

Historical Marketplace Organizations

Historically, real estate transactions were conducted and recorded on a county level. Title companies copied the legal records kept in the county courthouse and made them available for a fee to interested parties—attorneys, insurance companies, and lenders (such as banks and savings and loan associations)—when a property was changing hands. In other words, title companies held copies of the records on much of the real estate in a particular county or area of service. As a consequence, they could facilitate the title search and examination process, which was required in a real estate transaction.

A title search was a tedious and time-consuming task commonly performed by a clerk working through the records by hand. It required knowledge of the records, their whereabouts, and how the information could be synthesized quickly and completely. Since the title company housed all the property and transaction records, it controlled most of the market for this information in its service area. While there were competitors in the marketplace, generally there was one leading title company in each county that was successful simply because it had more complete records than its competitors and could, perhaps, offer better and faster service.

We could identify these local title companies of a half-century ago as being in the historical marketplace. They were the primary source of title information. Customers such as attorneys, lending companies, and real estate purchasers and sellers came to the title company because of legal and financial requirements. As a result, title companies didn't need to do much advertising or promotion, since those requiring their services would seek them out. Since they controlled the data, there

---

[2]Property is said to have clear title when the title has no problems or only minor problems that any well-informed and prudent buyer would accept.

were no channels or middlemen involved, unless one wanted to call the attorney a channel or middleman.

Consolidation and Concentration

To provide its members with tools to do business faster in a marketplace with rapid growth, The Fund began to computerize title information in 1973. The Fund consolidated information from localized, manual systems across Florida into one computerized title information network. Today, this on-line database called Attorneys' Title Information Data System, or ATIDS, gives members access to more than 100 million public records from thirty-two counties statewide, dramatically reducing the turnaround time for title searches.

Here, we see The Fund moving into the distribution or channel system that we call the current marketplace. In our example, the power in the marketing diagonal has moved from the historical to the current marketplace location on our chart. The Fund, by aggregating real estate data from a number of local title companies, has become a major marketer of title information itself, which, in turn, has strengthened its already strong position in the market as a title insurance underwriter.

Part of this movement on the marketing diagonal was driven by The Fund's desire to give its members a competitive edge by providing them with quicker access to data. In addition, advances in technology, which enabled The Fund to consolidate title information into a central database, brought about this movement. Through the early adoption of technology, The Fund had a virtual monopoly on computerized title information in Florida. As a result, members (as channels of information) were put into a stronger position in examining titles and issuing policies through The Fund. Clearly, power has shifted from the independent title company to The Fund. The Fund has opened distribution branches in all major Florida cities. The organization has multiple ways of providing information and actively promotes to generate use of ATIDS, its title information database.

Moving to the Twenty-First Century

One of the major challenges The Fund may face is the inevitable shift of information technology to the end user or ultimate purchaser of the property. Today, the primary purchaser of the data is still The Fund member. It is not hard to envision, however, that the ultimate consumer or user of the title information may become the ultimate purchaser of property (the do-it-yourself real estate purchaser, or others in the transaction such as the lender or mortgage company).

The shift from a paper-based to an electronic format for records, the ease with which a title search can be conducted, and the ebbing power of the attorney in the real estate transaction process are all converging on buyers and sellers in the title insurance industry. The Fund is entering the twenty-first century with radically different requirements than those it had only a few short years ago. And, as the transition of information technology continues to move from marketer (title company) to distribution channel (The Fund) to the ultimate consumer, the management of

The Fund may have to rethink their business model and the products and services they provide. It is indeed an interesting time at The Fund, and one that dramatically illustrates the impact of the marketing diagonal on one organization.

The Marketing Diagonal Changes How Organizations Compete

The value of the marketing diagonal is the way that it illustrates changes in how organizations compete. As has been discussed, historical marketers compete on product or service differentiation. As with the Pfizer product Viagra, if no one else has it, the marketer is in control and the information technology is not an issue. Current marketers, on the other hand, compete on distribution and channels. The frequent-shopper cards used in retail stores around the world, through the technology of purchase information capture, provide customer data to the retailers in the local area. Consequently, information technology has shifted the power from the large packaged goods companies who don't know their end users to the retailers who do.

Twenty-first-century marketers compete on knowledge and understanding of customers and prospects. By developing shipping software that allows a customer to print out his or her own airbills, order supplies, and track packages, Federal Express has used information technology to bind the customer to them and make it very difficult for their customers to switch to another service supplier. This benefits both the marketer and the user, but the user of the service feels in control of the process and has complete information.

Marketing on customer knowledge and information and by extension customer relationships is a dramatically different approach for many organizations. It changes the way they must think about and plan marketing and communication programs. It also forms the crux of our new approach to marketing communications planning.

The Demise of Product Differentiation and Distribution Advantage

Given the shift of information technology, most organizations already or shortly will find it difficult to compete on product differentiation or product or service superiority. Technology today allows competitors to replicate or duplicate almost any product improvement or enhancement in a matter of days, weeks, or, at most, months. Those product differences not protected by patents normally have a very short life cycle. The computer and software industries are good illustrations of this shift.

Companies that sell cereal products for children may spend over a year developing a new flavor or product line, doing taste tests, conducting focus groups, and building a brand program. Unfortunately, however, competitors have the capability and capacity to duplicate the new line or flavor almost instantaneously. The same is true in other product categories as well. Look how quickly competitors duplicate or replicate consumer products. For example, one of our associates spent almost eighteen months assisting a juice company in developing a new line of packaged drink products. Once the product was introduced in the marketplace, it was replicated by a competitor in less than four weeks. That included a similar product, knock-off packaging, similar advertising and promotion, and lower pricing—the whole marketing package. Needless to say, the first organization saw little profit from developing this particular new product line.

Keep in mind that product enhancement and improvement are not the only areas that can be quickly duplicated by competition, given current manufacturing and processing skills. Price changes, too, are instantly met. Look how quickly one gasoline marketing organization's price increase or decrease is met by its competitors just across the street. And, the same is true with distribution. One organization finds a new way to distribute or to bring its products or services to market and competitors quickly replicate—and sometimes even enhance—those distribution systems. Witness the major shift in how personal computers are sold direct by Dell and Gateway 2000.

The result of all this competitive capability in the technologically oriented marketplace of the twenty-first century will demand a new type of marketing approach and the rethinking of our marketing communication programs. The balance of this text will address developing communication programs for the twenty-first-century marketplace.

Competing with Brands and Communication

To review the common methods of competing, refer again to the Evolution and Revolution Chart shown in Exhibit 1-2 on page 22. If, indeed, product differentiation, pricing, and distribution are no longer viable competitive strategies as we have indicated in the preceding paragraphs, what strategy does that leave available to the marketing organization? Our answer: its brand and brand communication. While we develop this concept in greater detail in Chapters 2 and 3, a brief introduction is appropriate here.

For the most part, the primary competitive advantage most marketing organizations will employ in the twenty-first-century marketplace will be perceptual brand value. Not physical product differences, since those that are developed can be quickly replicated, as can price, distribution, and even promotion strategies. By extension, in our view, the marketer must compete at the customer level with brands, branding, and brand communication. While these are presently considered perceptual values, they in truth will be the most basic elements that the marketer can control and manage. Further, in an age of product and service confusion, tremendous competitive alternatives, information overload, and a global marketplace, it is our belief that the primary competitive tool the marketing organization will have will be its ability to create relationships with customers and prospects. That is commonly done through communication and branding.

It is clear from the Evolution and Revolution diagram in Exhibit 1-2 on page 22 that the interactive marketplace of the twenty-first century relies primarily on cooperation, relationships, and dialogue—not on marketplace control, marketer-only benefits, and monologues. As a consequence, the marketing organization must rethink, reanalyze, and remake much of its branding and brand communication strategies and tactics. While previously these had been useful tools for the historical and current marketplace organizations, they become critical to all marketing organizations in the twenty-first-century marketplace.

New Requisites and Requirements

We now preview the critical changes that the marketing organization must make, which will be discussed in more detail in later chapters. The first change is a new and more complete understanding of the brand and how the brand must be managed. The second change is the increased importance of customer and consumer data. As shown in Exhibit 1-2, the Evolution and Revolution diagram, customer and consumer information, though nice to have, is not critical to the marketing organization in the historical marketplace. If the organization could develop a product or service that filled some common consumer need and could properly differentiate that product or service from competitors, marketplace success often followed. Thus, in the historical marketplace the marketing organization needed only broad general information about customers and prospects who made up the marketplace. For example, knowing only basic demographics was commonly sufficient to develop and promote most consumer products. Indeed, most consumer product organizations still rely on these basic marketplace building blocks. So, while customer and consumer information was useful, it was not essential. At one time, every household wanted or felt that it needed a television set. Simply knowing how many households there were in the market, the income levels of those households, and whether they already had a television set was enough for most television marketers in the historical marketplace.

The same is true in the current marketplace. For the most part, retailers operate in a set geographic area. People are generally only willing to travel a certain distance to purchase various types of products. While there are, of course, differences between how far one will travel to purchase a gallon of milk versus the distance to buy a television set, marketers can estimate those parameters with some accuracy. Thus, the channel organization normally can estimate the number of likely prospects for most products or services simply by knowing how many people reside in the area, the consumption patterns for the product, and the income level of the households. Thus, manufacturers rely on their channels to provide simple measures of customer patterns so that marketing and communication programs can be planned and implemented appropriately.

In the twenty-first-century marketplace, the marketing organization must know a great deal about its customers and prospects. It must know its customers intimately in order to develop and manage dialogues. The marketing organization must have knowledge of their needs, wants, and desires and how those have been filled in the past. It must know whatever is relevant to the households or individuals that could become customers in the future. Without this degree of customer knowledge, the twenty-first-century marketing organization cannot successfully communicate with and influence customers and prospects.

The third critical change that the marketing organization must make concerns communication skills. As we move from product differentiation to distribution superiority to customer knowledge, the marketing organization must change the way it thinks about and manages its communication programs. Communication cannot be an afterthought, or simply a set of tactics used to generate customer or prospect interest. Instead, communication, particularly brand communication, must become one of the key skills of the organization. It will lead the organization, not simply support it. It will provide the strategic direction for the organization, not simply tactical support. It will be one of the primary competitive skills the organization must develop. We will explore this theme in more detail in Chapters 3 and 5.

Rethinking the Importance of the Brand

With this understanding of the evolution and revolution in communication and the shift of information technology, in the next chapter we discuss the increasing value of the brand, branding, and brand communication. Given our discussion of the new nature of marketplace competition, it is clear that the brand will be the key element in any communication program that an organization might develop.

Summary

Understanding who controls information technology, the marketer or the channel or the customer, is the key to marketing communications success. As more and more marketers face situations in which they cannot compete effectively on the traditional bases of product, price, place, or promotion, they will need to develop a better understanding of their brand from the customer's point of view. The marketing diagonal tool helps determine where the organization's brands are currently located and how quickly enhanced customer knowledge and understanding will be required in order to compete successfully in the twenty-first-century marketplace.

2

Brands and Branding

Brands, Branding, Brand Management, and Customers

Brands have been at the core of advertising and selling almost since time began. However, it has only been in recent years that we have begun to recognize brands and branding as critical ingredients necessary for marketplace success. Recall our discussion in Chapter 1 on modern marketing's development in the 1950s and 1960s. Most marketing emphasis has, for the past forty years, been focused on the management of the four Ps: product, price, place (distribution), and promotion. While branding has often been considered a part of the promotion mix, most organizations have placed much more emphasis and management attention on the functional areas of advertising, sales promotion, and public relations than on brands and branding. Thus, the management of the brand has often been a diffused task; everyone in the organization had a hand in it, but no one had total responsibility for it. As a result, while brands have been a major ingredient in the development and execution of marketing programs, they have often fallen victim to current tasks and activities that seemed to have higher priority.

As we discussed in the Introduction, there is little question that brands and branding will become increasingly important in the twenty-first-century marketplace. A brief history of brands and branding will set the stage for our premise that brands, branding, and brand communication must become the most valuable organizational skills a firm can develop to successfully compete in the years ahead.

A Seven-Paragraph Overview on Brands and Branding

The term *brand* or "brandr" comes from the ancient Norse word meaning "to burn."[1] The original term was developed to signify the source or maker or owner of a product or item. From that came the more common usage, the "branding" of cattle, horses, sheep, or other possessions. As commerce developed, *brand* came to mean the origin or source of a product or to differentiate the maker from others who produced like products, such as silversmiths, china and pottery makers, leather workers, and sword makers. Today, the brand is generally used to signify or identify the manufacturer or seller of a product or service.

Brands in the United States have a long and storied history. Perhaps the most famous use of the brand was in the great cattle drives of the middle nineteenth century. Since cattle were herded from the feeding grounds in the Southwest to the great cattle pens and distribution centers of the Midwest, owners needed some way to differentiate their cattle from herds belonging to other owners. In this way, a very colorful cattle branding system developed that continues to this day.[2]

In more traditional marketing, it is generally agreed that many of the modern concepts of brands and branding were formalized in the United States at the Procter & Gamble Company beginning in the late 1800s. Perhaps the most famous P&G brand is Ivory soap, which has been marketed under that brand name for over 100 years.[3] It was also P&G that developed the now popular concept of "brand management" in the 1930s.[4] This management approach to brands and branding has led to the formalization of many of the marketing, promotion, and communication programs used today by all types of organizations around the world.

In a legal sense, brands are protected by a wide range of laws that apply at both the state and the federal level.[5] There are even international conventions that protect the rights of brand owners engaged in international commerce.[6] Most of these legal approaches apply to the protection and maintenance of brand names, trademarks, colors, icons, symbols, and the like. They have commonly been developed to protect the brand owner from incursion by competitors. Thus, an organization can "own" and legally protect names and symbols that represent products and services vended by the organization.

Today, brands occupy a unique place in commerce. Brands can be bought and sold. They can be franchised or rented. They can be protected domestically and globally. Perhaps the greatest threat to a brand owner is the risk that the product or service that the brand owner has developed or marketed becomes the generic equiv-

---

[1]Ken Runkel and C. Brymer, "The Nature of Brands," in *Brand Valuation*, ed. Interbrand, PLC (London: Premier Books, 1997), p. 4.

[2]Paul Stobart, *Brand Power* (London: MacMillan Press, 1994), p. 1.

[3]David A. Aaker, *Managing Brand Equity* (New York: Free Press, 1991), pp. 1–5.

[4]Lynn B. Upshaw, *Building Brand Identity* (New York: Wiley, 1995), p. xiii.

[5]Runkel and Brymer, "The Nature of Brands," p. 4.

[6]Ibid.

Exhibit 2-1
Ivory Soap Advertisement

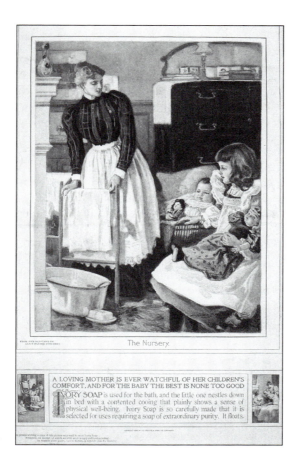

The Nursery.

A LOVING MOTHER IS EVER WATCHFUL OF HER CHILDREN'S COMFORT, AND FOR THE BABY THE BEST IS NONE TOO GOOD

IVORY SOAP is used for the bath, and the little one nestles down in bed with a contented cooing that plainly shows a sense of physical well-being. Ivory Soap is so carefully made that it is selected for uses requiring a soap of extraordinary purity. It floats.

alent for the product category. That is what happened to brands such as "cellophane" and "escalator." These brand names became so widely used and connected to the products they represented that they lost their protection as a brand. Companies who market brands such as Xerox and Scotch Tape fight ongoing legal battles to prevent their brands and brand names from becoming generic to the product category.[7] It is this legal protection of a brand name that encourages organizations to invest resources to develop and promote their brand in the marketplace. Therefore, the brand has value to the organization, because it is a legal entity that has marketplace value other than the sales it can generate among consumers.

[7]Jean-Noel Kapferer, *Strategic Brand Management* (New York: Free Press, 1992), pp. 166–169.

While the brand provides relatively little specific legal protection to the consumer or purchaser, most manufacturers and service providers are anxious to protect the value of their brand with consumers to generate ongoing sales. Thus, they often provide warranties, guarantees, or other similar protective legal devices to consumers to reinforce the quality, workmanship, delivery, or performance of their products and services. While consumers do have some forms of legal redress against manufacturers and marketers for shoddy merchandise, unfulfilled product promises, and the like, for the most part buyers still operate in the "caveat emptor" or "buyer beware" marketplace. As the consumer gains power in the marketplace, primarily through the shift of information technology, there is little question that brands increasingly will be required to support and justify legal claims that may be brought against them by unsatisfied or aggrieved consumers. The issues with tobacco are just one example of this type of situation.

Brands can survive and prosper even though the products and services they represent may change significantly or disappear altogether. Brands have value, which we propose is critical to organizations today in a marketing sense and will be increasingly so in the twenty-first-century marketplace. But brands have varying values, and it is a brand's value that underpins the brand's importance in the marketplace. For the brand communication manager, the value of the brand is one of the key ingredients in developing an effective brand communication program. Thus, the ability of the organization to build consumer value in the brand will truly be one of the major goals of brand communication in the twenty-first-century marketplace. In the next section we will help to clarify how brand value is built.

From Brand Death to Resurrection in Ten Short Years

Following "Marlboro Friday" in 1994 (the day Philip Morris, Inc., decided to reduce the price on their globally dominant cigarette brand, which caused a wave of selling in the stock market), *Advertising Age* predicted the death of traditional manufacturer brand names in the United States and a rapid decline in their value to the brand owners.[8] But, as Mark Twain once said, "the reports of my death have been greatly exaggerated."[9] Brands did not die in the 1980s, nor in the early 1990s; in fact, they have become stronger than ever. To understand why and how brands will, we believe, have even greater value in the future, it is necessary to understand why Wall Street and the media predicted their death in 1994.

What We Know About Brands

Interestingly, although brands and branding have always been at the core of the advertising and marketing communication disciplines and were part of the development

---

[8]Steve Yahn, "Death of Brands: Advertising's Grave New World," *Advertising Age*, May 16, 1994, p. 1.

[9]Samuel Clemens, Cablegram from London to a New York newspaper (June 2, 1897).

of modern marketing in the 1950s, very little was written or researched about them until the mid-1980s. While marketers and advertisers believed in the value of brands and their importance in differentiating their products and services from competitors, the subject received scant research attention, even from the academic community. What little was known about brands and branding generally was anecdotal or experiential information gathered by advertising agencies and their clients. Usually, the information related only to their specific brands, customers, and markets. Thus, there was little true knowledge about the subject of brands and branding in a general sense.

The idea of branding appears to have been taken for granted. Many advertisers seemed to assume that brand value occurred or was developed as a result of advertising campaigns and other promotional messages delivered to customers and prospects, commonly through various forms of media advertising. Further, it was apparently assumed that any organization could create and maintain a brand in the marketplace, given sufficient resources, although there were widely varying ideas about how this could or should be done.

Perhaps the first formal approach to developing a brand and brand communication came from the work of Trout and Reis[10] in the 1970s with their approaches to "positioning." From that start, our knowledge of brands and branding has continued to grow. Aaker developed his seminal book on brands and branding, *Managing Brand Equity*, in 1991.[11] Since that time, a number of other authors such as Farquhar,[12] Kapferer,[13] Jones,[14] and others have presented various approaches and theories on how to develop and build a brand.

Why Brands Became a "Hot Topic"

In the mid-1980s, brands became a "hot topic," not just in advertising, marketing, and communication, but in general business management and particularly in the financial community. This interest stemmed from two somewhat divergent factors.

1. **Overreliance by marketing executives on short-term promotional techniques.** As we discussed in the Introduction, between 1960 and 1980, the U.S. marketplace went from one of product and service shortage to one of market surplus. During that twenty-year interval, too many marketing organizations began to produce too many products and services for a maturing consumer marketplace. Thus, many marketing organizations moved from product and benefit promotion to price promotion and discounting in an attempt to hold market share, dispose of factory output, and generate short-term returns for the organization.[15]

---

[10]Al Ries and Jack Trout, *Positioning: The Battle for Your Mind* (New York: Warner, 1986).

[11]Aaker, *Managing Brand Equity*.

[12]Peter Farquhar, "Managing Brand Equity," *Marketing Insights*, Summer 1992, pp. 59–64.

[13]Kapferer, *Strategic Brand Management*.

[14]John Philip Jones, *When Ads Work* (New York: Lexington, 1995).

[15]George Belch and Michael Belch, *Advertising and Promotion*, 4th ed. (Boston: Irwin McGraw-Hill, 1998), p. 11.

From a promotional standpoint, starting in the mid-1970s, marketers increasingly switched from the promotion of product value to coupons, discounts, price-offs, and the like. Thus, some have argued, marketers drove down the value of the brand and created a price- and promotionally-oriented group of customers that exists to this day. Margins on brands declined, and many traditionally strong organizations found themselves in difficult financial situations in the mid to late 1980s. This situation led, as we illustrated in the Introduction, to much of the cost-cutting and reengineering that organizations initiated in an attempt to solve their margin problems. As we also saw earlier, when the organization focuses on reengineering and restructuring, commonly it turns inward. That is, it looks at what it can do to cut costs, reduce redundancy, and manage facilities. However, these internally focused programs often reduced customer and consumer understanding, service, and relationships as a by-product.

2. **Brand acquisitions by corporate raiders.** About this same time, financial organizations began to investigate the potential future value of brands and branded product manufacturers as possible acquisition targets. The basic approach these so-called corporate raiders used was to offer to pay far more than the supposed market value of the organization, take over, and thereby gain control of the organization's brands. Using such tools as "junk bonds" and "zero coupon" financial instruments, these corporate raiders offered to buy or acquire the stock of the organization at prices clearly far higher than the marketplace value of the organization's tangible assets. The goal of these corporate raiders was to acquire the brands and brand value that these organizations possessed, not necessarily the tangible assets that the organization controlled.[16]

Because brands generally provide long-term financial returns to the brand owner, the corporate raiders simply identified those organizations that had valuable brands but perhaps undervalued stock prices. They bought control or a controlling interest in the company, which allowed them to reconstitute the board of directors in their favor. They used long-term financial instruments that they assumed could be liquidated with the marketplace returns and income flows generated by the brands. Thus, the 1980s saw major management changes in many brand product manufacturing organizations such as RJR/Nabisco in the United States[17] and Hovis Rank in the United Kingdom.[18] Corporate raiders such as Kohlberg, Kravis, and Roberts, for example, simply took over the organizations, gained control of the brands and assets, and began to operate them much differently. In some cases, to help pay for the acquisition of the brand and debt service, the corporate raiders sold off assets and even some of the brands they bought. It was this new view of a brand as a corporate asset that changed much of the way we think about brands today.

The Concept of Brand Value

The ability of corporate raiders to take over brand organizations in the 1980s and early 1990s stems in part from the accounting principles used to value organizations

[16]Tom Blackett, "Nature of Brands," in *Brand Valuation*, ed. Interbrand, PLC, 2d ed. (London: Business Books Ltd., 1989), pp. 8–9.

[17]Ibid.

[18]Stobart, *Brand Power*.

The Changing Nature of Organizational Value

From Tangible to Intangible Assets

Assets of a firm are the probable future economic benefits that can be obtained or controlled by the organization as a result of past transactions or events. To be an asset, a resource other than cash must have three essential characteristics:

1. The resource must, singly or in combination with other resources, contribute directly or indirectly to future net cash flows.

2. The firm must be able to obtain the benefit and control others' access to it.

3. The transaction or other event that results in the firm's right to, or control of, the benefit must already have occurred.

Assets are recognized in the financial statement when (1) the item meets the definition of an asset (above), (2) the item can be measured with sufficient reliability, (3) the information about the item is capable of making a difference in user decisions, and (4) the information about the item is reliable.

Assets usually are classified on a balance sheet in the order of their liquidity (or nearness to cash) in the following manner:

- Current assets

- Long-term investments

- Property, plant, and equipment

- Intangible assets

- Other assets

Typically, financial managers speak of tangible and intangible assets in discussing the value of an organization. Tangible assets generally include land and buildings, plant and machinery, fixtures and fittings, trading stock, investments, debtors, and cash.

Intangible assets are special rights, grants, privileges, and advantages possessed by a business that can benefit future operations by contributing to the enterprise's earning power. Generally, intangible assets have no physical substance. These might include goodwill, patents, copyrights, trademarks, trade names, franchises, licenses and royalties, formulas and processes, and, increasingly, brands and publication titles.

The question of tangible or intangible assets is a major one for many organizations. In most cases, tangible assets can be listed on the balance sheet. Depending on the country and its accounting conventions, however, intangible assets, with the exception of goodwill, are not listed.

Many managers today argue that the real value of the organization is its ability to earn income and profits into the future. That potential is driven more by intangible assets such as brands, management and employee skills, and customer relationships than by tangible assets. Yet, intangible assets cannot be listed on the balance sheet when determining the value of a company.

In the 1980s, organizations were, for the most part, valued on the basis of their tangible assets in terms of their market value and stock price. Corporate raiders, recognizing the future income flows that brands and other intangible assets could likely provide, purchased the stock of companies at what were believed to be very high prices based on their book, or tangible, asset value. They were gambling that the income flows from the brands and other intangible assets would, in future years, make it possible to pay off their purchase price.

Today, increasingly, financial managers recognize that the value of an organization is not only its fixed tangible assets, but also its future earning potential. Thus, an organization such as Nike has few tangible assets, but very valuable brands that provide the organization with major streams of income. Yet, these brands, because they are intangible assets, cannot be listed on the balance sheet presently, at least in the United States.

Though brands are generally considered to be intangible assets, they provide much of the future income for the firm as a result of the relationship that customers have created with those brands. We see a curious and interesting conflict between accounting and finance and marketing and communication in terms of the value of the enterprise. Our traditional methods of valuing companies and organizations are changing as we move to a service-based economy in which brands and employee and management skills, rather than an organization's raw materials, manufacturing facilities, and distribution systems, determine the success of an organization.

Based on "A Dictionary of Accounting," edited by R. Hussey. Oxford, Oxford University Press, 1995[19]

in the financial community. Established accounting practices count only tangible assets in determining the value of an organization. In most cases, tangible assets include only those assets that can be converted to or have cash value, such as plants and factories, product inventory, land, equipment, and cash itself. Brands are and continue to be considered intangible assets of the organization. That is, because a brand has no immediate cash value, it is therefore considered intangible. Generally, the brand cannot be listed or carried on the organization's balance sheet. As a result, from a financial view, brands have little or no value. See the sidebar on tangible and intangible assets: The Changing Nature of Organizational Value.

Because brands generate income flows to the organization into the future and accounting generally looks backward to review what has occurred previously, the value of the brands the organization controls are generally listed as "goodwill" or "retained earnings" if they are found on the balance sheet at all. It is this intangible nature of brands that creates many of the challenges in brand communication budgeting and measurement, as we will see later.

Interestingly, while brands and brand value cannot be listed on the balance sheet in the United States, in England some new accounting standards now allow organizations to list on the balance sheet the value of brands they acquire externally from other organizations.[20] In other words, if an organization buys a brand from another

---

[19]Sidebar written by Steve Fowler.

[20]Jeremy Sampson, "The Nature of Brands," in *Brand Valuation*, ed. Interbrand, PLC (London: Premier Books, 1997), p. 175.

organization, it can be carried as an asset and listed and accounted for in financial documents. If, however, the organization builds the brand internally, it cannot show this value other than as an intangible asset of the organization.

This whole issue of brand value is undergoing serious financial and accounting scrutiny. Although changes may be imminent, for the present, brands in the United States continue to be regarded as intangible assets and consequently have somewhat nebulous value in the financial arena.

This new view of brands and branding that corporate raiders brought to the marketplace has changed many of the ways marketers and top management think about and develop brand programs. Brands do have value because they generally produce ongoing income flows into the future. Given that accounting practices don't recognize these future returns from brands, in many cases brand-owning or brand-marketing organizations may well be undervalued in traditional financial terms. It is this accounting anomaly that, as we will see throughout this text, provides many of the challenges brand marketers are facing.

What Is a Brand?

Before beginning a more detailed discussion of brand value and the sources of that value, it is helpful to review precisely what we mean by the term "brand." In addition, we need to consider some of the associated concepts that are related to brands and branding, such as brand messages, brand contacts, brand associations, and brand equity. All of these make up the brand relationships that are generally created through various forms of brand communication.

Brand Definition

There are numerous definitions of a brand. For example, the American Marketing Association defines a brand as:

> *A name, term, sign, symbol, or any other feature that identifies one seller's good or service as distinct from those of other sellers.*[21]

As is evident from this definition, the AMA suggests that the primary value of the brand lies with the seller or marketer. In other words, the brand provides differentiation from competitors and ownership protection in the marketplace. While this is obviously a relevant definition, it does not, in our view, accurately define the true value of the brand in the marketplace.

In our brand communication approach, the brand in the twenty-first-century marketplace is more than a "name, term, sign, symbol, or any other feature." For example, a young person wearing a pair of Nike Air-Jordans places much more value on the sneakers than simply what the name or the famous "Swoosh" symbol implies, or what the shoes could be sold for in the equity marketplace. Instead, we

---

[21]Peter D. Bennett, *Dictionary of Marketing Terms*, 2d ed. (Chicago: American Marketing Association, 1995).

Exhibit 2-2
Brand Relationship

argue, the brand has become a part of the relationship between the marketing organization, Nike, and the owner of the shoes, the consumer. The brand represents the bond between the buyer and the seller, as illustrated in Exhibit 2-2.

More than ownership, the brand brings marketplace meaning to the consumer. It represents what the consumer is and what he or she believes the brand provides to help reinforce his or her place in society. Thus, the brand is more than a name or a symbol or an icon—it's a relationship that only the consumer can create. We discuss this consumer behavior view in more detail in Chapter 6. For the present, it is important to understand that the brand has two forms of value: value to the marketing organization and value to the consumer. It is this differentiation that will be critical in developing brand communication programs for the twenty-first-century marketplace. A few explanatory concepts will help clarify our approach to brands and branding.

How Brands Are Created

Brands are created primarily through various forms of communication. Here, we use *communication* in its broadest sense; that is, communication is anything that helps transfer meaning from one person to another or from a product or service to the consumer. In this way, communication can be the form or value or quality of the product or service. It can include information about where the product or service is available, the packaging, and the price, either as currently suggested or in comparison to other competitive products or services. How the brand communicates can also include current users or consumers of the brand whom new users may see or hear about and consequently want to emulate. In other words, the communication of the brand is the total package of benefits, values, ingredients, physical forms, formal or informal messages, and the like that together provide meaning and benefit to the customer or prospect. Communication is every way in which the brand and its essence touches the customer or prospect.

From the view of the customer or consumer, the brand is a bundle of many forms, factors, functions, and contexts that give it meaning in the marketplace. This is illustrated in Exhibit 2-3. Thus, if the brand truly is an amalgamation of all the

Exhibit 2-3

How Organizations Deliver Brand Communication

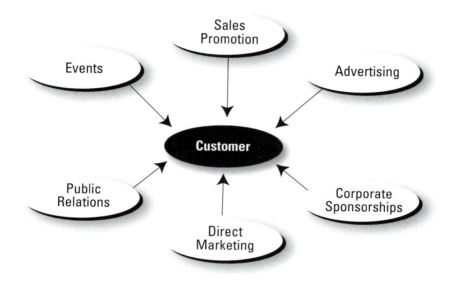

elements shown, that would suggest that brand communication certainly must be managed in an integrated fashion, and from the customer's view. Therefore, all elements that relate to the brand—not just the marketing mix, must be included as brand communication. We will further explain and illustrate this point throughout this book.

Because the entire organization is involved in the meaning and management of the brand, we include both internal and external brand communication. Indeed, the full range of communication must be aligned in order to provide a consistent view of the brand, what it means, how it relates to the customer and consumer, and, likewise, how they relate to it. Our view of brand management is illustrated by the aligned and integrated chart shown in Exhibit 2-4.

As shown, managing the brand means managing all the elements that go to create the brand. Initially, that would include the benefit or value the product or service provides consumers and how the sales and marketing organization thinks about and manages that benefit or value. It would include all the suppliers who provide input to the development and distribution of the product or service. It would include all internal employees and their activities that give meaning and value to the customer relationships that make up the brand. It would obviously include all external communication the organization sends to the marketplace to give a view of the brand and

Exhibit 2-4
External/Internal Alignment

Integrating the System, Not the Pieces and Parts

its meaning and value. All these factors make up brand communication management in our approach to the twenty-first-century marketplace.

Some Key Elements in Brand Development

Inherent in this very broad view of a brand and brand communication is the need to identify the various elements that can be used to help build and maintain a brand. In a sense, the elements listed below are additive; that is, one leads to or enhances the other to create the whole of the brand. While they are often viewed separately in the marketing organization, it is critical that they all come together, for when they do they form the brand, the brand meaning, and the brand essence, or what we will define later as consumer-based brand equity.

Brand messages are those concepts, ideas, icons, colors, symbols, and so on that the organization sends out or distributes to customers and prospects to give meaning to the product or service. Generally, these messages are designed to influence or persuade customers and prospects to consider, buy, continue buying, or recommend the product or service. Commonly, brand messages are delivered through various forms of advertising, sales promotion, direct marketing, public relations, and other planned and directed activities.

Brand contacts are more than brand messages. Messages are formalized by the marketing organization and are generally controlled by that group. Brand contacts, on the other hand, are all those image- or information-bearing experiences a customer or prospect might have with the brand in the marketplace. Exhibit 2-5 illustrates the concept of a brand contact.

As shown in the exhibit, here is how McDonald's might identify various brand contacts it has with customers. Brand contacts can range from planned advertising and promotional events to the McDonald's characters, the food, the ambiance in

Exhibit 2-5

Consumer Sources of Information

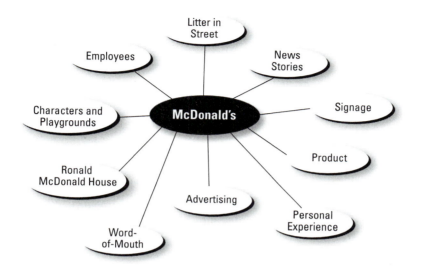

the restaurants and the service employees provide (both elements of personal experience), and even the cleanliness of the area around each McDonald's location. All of these aspects and many others serve to provide the customer or prospect with a framework by which he or she relates the brand to his or her situation.

We will use the following formal definition of brand contact: Any information-bearing experience that a customer or prospect has with the brand. Given this definition, a brand contact can positively reinforce current brand meaning or essence, destroy positive brand meaning, or create new brand meaning that can lead to different brand relationships with customers and prospects.

Brand Associations and Brand Networks Consumers structure brands in their memory and their lives through what we call **brand associations**. This simply means that to integrate the brand and the brand meaning into their mental structures, consumers use a system of associations or relationships with other concepts, ideas, and activities that make up their sum of experience. This association with other concepts and ideas is what allows consumers to develop brand and product meaning. The association process connects the brand in some way with what the consumer has already experienced or knows or feels or believes. Thus, a product such as Coca-Cola has associations such as thirst, cold, and refreshing. Further, it has associations with situations of usage—times when the consumer drank Coca-Cola. It is this associative nature of human memory that allows people to create the concept of a brand based on what we call the brand network.[22]

The *brand network* is simply the structure of the concepts, ideas, thoughts, elements, and other factors through which the consumer creates meaning for the brand. This idea of brand associations and brand networks will be critical in our development of brand communication programs later in this book. For example, knowing the brand associations that exist, or having an understanding of how consumers do or might be able to associate certain ideas and concepts with a product or service is the basis for all marketing and communication planning and implementation. Since consumers already know most brands, often they already have created the brand associations or networks that define the brand for them in their lives. Sometimes, however, it is the brand communication that the marketer develops and delivers that either reinforces or changes the brand meaning and value. For example, the association of Michael Jordan with Nike basketball shoes gave the brand a whole new meaning that has become richer and more complex with time.

Brand Equity The sum of all the brand messages, brand contacts, brand associations, and brand networks that the consumer creates in his or her mind to manage information about the brand is summarized in what is called *consumer-based brand equity*. The leading proponent of this concept is Professor Kevin Keller of Dartmouth College. Professor Keller has defined consumer-based brand equity as follows:

> *The differential effect that brand knowledge has on the customer response to the marketing of that brand. Equity occurs when the customer is familiar with the brand and holds some favorable, strong, and unique brand associations in memory.[23]*

While the brand obviously has value to the marketing organization, it is this consumer-based brand equity that is the true value of the brand. Earlier in this chapter, we stated that the true value of the brand comes from the consumer or end user of the brand. This person or organization or firm reaches down into a pocket or wallet and either implicitly or explicitly says, "The brand is worth this much to me. Here's the money." While there may be intermediaries involved in the purchase and use of the product, it is, in truth, the end user or consumer who determines the real value of the brand in the marketplace. This is why we agree with Professor Keller's statement:

> *There are two key points about brand knowledge:*
>
> *1. All types of organizational activities have an effect on brand knowledge. Changes in brand knowledge will impact such traditional measures as sales.*

---

[22]Peter F. Farquhar and Paul M. Herr, "The Dual Structure of Brand Associations," in *Brand Equity and Advertising*, ed. David A. Aaker (London: Erlbaum, 1993), pp. 263–77.

[23]Kevin L. Keller, "Conceptualizing, Measuring, and Managing Customer-Based Brand Equity," *Journal of Marketing* 57 (January 1993): 1–22.

2. *Long-term success of the organization's brand is affected by short-term marketing and promotional activities and experiences.*[24]

Customers or consumers create the brand for themselves, and their understanding of and experience with the brand are unique and individual. Thus, while the marketing organization might like to think otherwise, there is no single brand image or understanding for most products and services. Instead, there are literally millions of brand images and understandings and networks for a product, with the number depending upon how widely distributed the product is and how much it is exposed to the marketplace. In short, every customer who comes in contact with the brand has his or her own view of the brand and what it means to him or her.

This point that customers create the brand is an important one and deserves some additional explanation. What we know about how the human mind works and how memory is developed and stored has much to do with how brands are established and recalled by customers and prospects. Exhibit 2-6 illustrates the concept of a neural network.

The human brain works on the basis of chemical changes and electric impulses. Nodes, called neurons, continuously flash through the brain as we think. When two of these neurons meet, they generally form a loop in which memory is stored. Thus, the meeting of the neurons or nodes of Michael Jordan and basketball shoes created in the minds of many customers the loop we call Nike.[25] Since every consumer has different concepts and ideas about Michael Jordan and basketball shoes, the node or loop that the thoughts create, which we call the Nike brand, is unique to each person. An individual creates his or her particular brand image based on previous experiences and neurons and nodes. While Nike, the company, may well own the trade name, the lettering, the "Swoosh" symbol, and anything else that is used to make up the Nike brand identity, the company does not own the brand. The consumer owns the brand because he or she created it specifically for himself or herself. Although Nike provided many of the images and colors and words and pictures to help the process, the consumer finally created the Nike brand in his or her own mind.

This point about who creates and owns the brand is critical in our approach to brands, branding, and brand communication. If the consumer truly has created the brand in his or her own mind and therefore owns that brand image, then in order to be successful, marketers and marketing organizations must manage the brand from the customer's point of view, not just the organization's own view. The brand can mean only what customers and consumers will let it mean. Therefore, although marketing organizations may attempt to "position" a brand in the marketplace, that positioning success is determined by the acceptance or rejection of the marketers' ideas and concepts when they are related to what the customer or prospect already knows about the product or service. Brand communication programs can only enhance or add to the information consumers already have stored away about the brand. It is this history of the brand that determines much of the brand's future

---

[24]Ibid.

[25]Neural network cite.

Exhibit 2-6

How the Consumer Builds the Brand in Memory

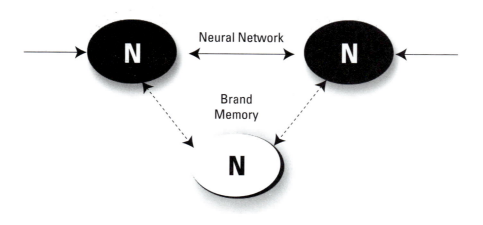

value. The concept of customer-brand equity is critical in the twenty-first-century marketplace and will play a significant role throughout this text.

Understanding Brand Value

It should be clear from our previous discussion that brands have or provide value for both the customer and the brand organization. To understand this brand value, however, it is necessary to understand the different values or valuation that the organization and consumer place on the brand.

Given the focus in the 1980s on the value of brands to the equity market, it is not difficult to understand why much of the research and study of brands and their value has been from the organizational, rather than the consumer, viewpoint. We seem to be more advanced in determining the equity marketplace value of a brand than the consumer or customer value. In spite of this inequity, we believe it is clear that the true value of a brand must rest with the consumer, not the owner or the financial manager of the brand.

In this section, we discuss two basic approaches to brand valuation—that of the financial community and that of the end user or consumer of the brand. We should explain here that when we speak of the consumer or end user, we include all forms of consumption in all types of markets. Thus, an organization buying raw materials to make a finished product is just as much an end user of those ingredients or raw materials as is the ultimate end user or consumer of the product or service. The organization derives its value from its finished product just as much as does the final or ultimate end user. Thus, for convenience, we use the term *consumer* to mean the person, organization, or unit purchasing and deriving value from the product or service. Further, it will be emphasized as we develop the theme that, while organizational value of the brand is important, the true value of the brand rests with the customer or consumer.

Organizational Value of the Brand

Most brand valuation approaches have focused on what and how an organization should value a brand if it were interested in either buying or selling that brand to another organization. Thus, most evaluation approaches focus primarily on the financial value of the brand in the marketplace.

This financial emphasis came directly from the equity marketplace of the 1980s in which there was much discussion and confusion about what a brand was or might be worth to either the buyer or seller of that brand. As discussed earlier, this confusion developed and continues today because of accounting conventions that classify the brand as an intangible asset to the organization. Since present accounting systems have no way of estimating future value, that is, they accommodate only past value and rely on valuations of tangible assets only, the valuation of a brand from an equity view has been difficult. Indeed, even the most accepted approaches are still criticized.

Today, most of the brand valuation approaches used in the purchase or sale of a brand have been developed by Interbrand, PLC,[26] a research organization headquartered in London. Interbrand has developed a brand valuation model that is based on seven factors ranging from stability to leadership to support. The Interbrand approach attempts to determine the net present value of a brand today based on its expected future earnings potential to either the buyer or the seller. A brief description of the Interbrand approach is explained in the sidebar, What's in a Name?

As widely used as are the Interbrand process and some of the competitive approaches developed by other brand-value organizations such as Young & Rubicam and Segal & Gale, their evaluation concepts provide only the organization value view of the brand. For example, note that in the Interbrand valuation model, customers or consumers are not included in the valuation. It is assumed that they will perform as the financial models suggest with or without marketing and brand communication. The problem, however, is that sometimes consumers perform as they are expected to and sometimes they don't. For example, the prediction of fads and fashions has been an extremely difficult task for most organizations. Thus, even the most complex and tested model still is just that—a model that is subject to the whims of the consumer. Thus, our focus on brand value is based primarily on the value the customer or end user—not just the equity marketplace—places on the brand.

---

[26]Raymond Perrier, *Brand Valuation* (London: Premier Books, 1997).

What's in a Name?[27]

What's in a name? Plenty, according to Interbrand, a company that provides specialized service in brand and corporate name development.[27] Through its method of brand scoring, Interbrand attaches economic value to this intangible asset.

Among the assets of a company—tangible assets, brands, and other intangible assets—the challenge of brand valuers, according to Interbrand, "is to identify what proportion of the earnings can be attributed to the brand." Depending on the nature of the business, a brand can account for a significant percentage of earnings, as in the categories of luxury goods, service, food, or beverage companies.

As Interbrand points out, accounting techniques vary when it comes to brand valuation. Historical financial results alone are not necessarily an accurate indication of future performance. Interbrand does use historical data, however, as a foundation for forecasting three-to-five-year brand valuations by discounting future cash flows.

Once the company has identified the proportion of earnings attributed to the brand, the next task is to assess the brand strength in order to accurately project cash flows. "The value of the brand reflects not only what earnings it is capable of generating in the future, but the likelihood of those earnings actually being realized." In order to determine that likelihood of future earnings, Interbrand has developed a seven-factor scale to determine a brand's "risk profile." The stronger the brand, the less risk in securing those future cash flows.

---

[27] Adapted from, and with quotes from, ibid.

Interbrand's Seven-Factor Brand Strength Analysis

1. **Market:** Brands in stable but growing markets are stronger than those in markets that are prone to obsolescence or trendiness. Maximum value ten.

2. **Stability:** Well-established, familiar brands have the advantage of existing customer loyalty. Maximum value fifteen.

3. **Leadership:** To the degree that a brand dominates a category and is able to influence its entire market, it earns high marks for leadership. Maximum value twenty-five.

4. **Internationality:** The strongest brands along this dimension have obtained a high level of acceptance in a number of international markets. When one of these markets proves unstable, these brands retain a strong base elsewhere. Maximum value twenty-five.

5. **Trend:** Brands that show consistent growth over time have proven their relevance to consumers as well as their ability to win share from competitors. Maximum value five.

6. **Support:** It's not just the amount of investment in the brand, but also the quality and the consistency of that investment which contributes to the brand's value. Maximum value ten.

7. **Protection:** Registered trademarks and other protections sometimes afforded by common law contribute to brand value, while the lack of such protection could preclude inclusion of brand value on the balance sheet altogether. Maximum value five.

A variety of marketing resources, from market research studies to advertising awareness reports to Nielsen data, is used to obtain the raw scores for each of the seven factors. While there is global branding, variation will occur from market to market, and so brand strength, or risk profile, is assessed market by market. According to Interbrand, this risk profile can be a useful tool, not only in forecasting brand value, but also in targeting areas for improvement from brand-to-brand comparisons.

The bottom line, according to Interbrand, is that its Brand Strength Analysis is not a measure of brand equity, but is merely one component of it. Rather, its primary focus is the assessment of future brand earnings. "Brand equity represents an assessment of the brand's influence from a *consumer* perspective while brand strength represents an assessment of the brand as an engine of profit from a *management* perspective."

Customer Brand Value

While organizations may be able to determine the value of the brand and its potential earning power and therefore set some type of acquisition or sales value for it in the marketplace, most of the real value of the brand truly resides with the customer or consumer. If the consumer does not value the brand, or if the customer value of the brand either increases or declines, then, over time, the value of the brand to the organization is sure to increase or decline as well. The ultimate marketplace consumer of the brand determines the value of that brand to him or her in competition with other marketplace alternatives and his or her own needs and desires. Thus, the task of the brand manager in our approach is to determine the current and future value of the brand to those ultimate users or consumers. As we have stated before, it is the consumer or end user who reaches into his or her pocket to pay what the consumer believes the brand to be worth. So, while the financial market may place a buy-or-sell value on the brand for a financial transaction, it is the consumer or customer who truly determines the value of the brand in the marketplace. We argue that, long term, this consumer value is the only one that really matters, for it defines the ultimate value of the brand.

In this text, consumer or end user brand value will consist of two parts: (a) the attitudinal or perceptual value, and (b) the financial value. This combination of values has made most consumer brand valuation schemes difficult to develop. We briefly discuss these two aspects of brand value to set the stage for a more complete discussion in Chapter 3.

Consumer Attitudinal or Perceptual Brand Value

As discussed earlier in this chapter, consumers create the value of a brand based on their own experiences. Brand networks, associations, and, ultimately, consumer brand equity contribute to the process of value creation. The value that a consumer places on the brand from previous experience, from brand knowledge, from marketplace activities, and from brand messages and contacts all go to make up the perceptual value of the brand. Also, as we discussed, brand value is different from one consumer to the next. No two consumers will likely value a brand in the same way since no two consumers will likely have created the same two neural combinations that represent the brand in their minds and memory. As a result, for the marketing organization to accurately determine the value of the brand in the marketplace, the firm must group together customers having similar beliefs, feelings, and perceptions about the brand.

There is little question that how customers feel about a brand determines how they will value the brand and, often, how they will behave in connection with the brand. We will expand on this attitudinal or perceptual value in more detail in Chapter 5. The important concept to understand at this point, however, is that brand value, while it may be attitudinally driven, does not always predict how a customer or prospect will perform in the marketplace. Thus, a consumer may hold the brand in high regard, may believe it has great value, and may even prefer it to other brands, yet purchase another brand when he or she enters the marketplace. One of the anomalies of consumer behavior is that often there is a major gap between how customers feel and how they behave. Thus, in our twenty-first-century marketplace approach to brand communication, we believe it is necessary to combine both attitudinal and behavioral consumer data and information about the brand to fully understand how the brand is valued in the marketplace.

Consumer Behavioral or Financial Brand Value

Over the past several years, behavioral data, that is, information on what consumers actually do in the marketplace, have become increasingly available. Stemming primarily from the use and improved capability of technology, such as computers and optical scanners, tremendous amounts of data can be captured, stored, and manipulated about actual consumer behavior in the marketplace. In database form, these data are available for a wide variety of product and service categories and are expanding daily. It is behavioral data that are the driving force in determining customer brand value.

Behavioral data began to emerge with the introduction and popularization of computers in business organizations. As it became easier and faster to capture and store data such as sales records and demographic and geographic data, organizations began to manage and massage those data over time. Early users of customer and consumer behavioral data were organizations such as book and record clubs, catalog companies, and business-to-business and service organizations. All quickly adopted the concept that behavioral data or, what the customer or consumer did, were the true value the customer placed on the brand. So, no matter what the customer said or how he or she felt, it was what he or she did that really mattered. For example, most of these organizations applied longitudinal data to customer behavior to predict future customer behavior. Since behavioral data record what has actually occurred in the marketplace, and these records can be used to determine financial value to the organization, there have been and will likely continue to be major shifts in how brands are valued.

Attitudinal data reflect how consumers feel and can be used in attempts to predict how they might behave in the future. Behavioral data tell what customers have done and provide a view of their financial value if they continue on that path in the future. It is the combination of these two types of data that is really critical in understanding and developing brand communication programs.

Combining Attitudinal and Behavioral Data to Determine Customer Brand Value

The increasing availability of behavioral data has created a major schism in the marketing and communication research and planning fields. Traditionally, most marketing and communication researchers have been trained as social scientists. Thus, they have been trained to use attitudinal data to understand customers and consumers. In contrast, direct marketing and financial analysts have been trained to use behavioral data in their work. Each is convinced that their approach is most accurate and useful in understanding how customers and consumers value brands. Each approach does have its strengths, but each also ignores some very important information in total. In the twenty-first-century marketplace, however, a combination of attitudinal and behavioral data will likely be required to truly understand how customers and consumers value the brand.

Given this understanding, the approach we will use in this text is somewhat forward-looking. That is, our premise is that the marketing organization must determine some basic financial value that customers and consumers put on the brand—not just their attitudinal value or even a value based on their past behaviors toward the brand. After all, the marketing group invests money to purchase brand communication programs that are then allocated against groups of customers or prospects. To justify this expense, the organization must have some idea of the financial returns that can be expected from these investments. Likewise, while having access to attitudinal data is useful, it has been difficult historically to connect changes in attitudes about a brand to actual marketplace purchases or returns. Thus, our approach in this text will be to base most of our brand valuation on behavioral data. We will use attitudinal data to explain the behaviors that we have observed in the marketplace. While this may be considered a somewhat radical shift from the research approaches used in the past in communication planning, we believe it will prove to be the rule, not the exception, in the twenty-first-century marketplace.

Focusing on Customer Brand Value

From the previous discussion, it should be clear that any financial investment in a brand communication program must increase or maintain the financial value of the brand among customers and consumers. In addition, if consumer value can be increased, the equity marketplace or stock value of the brand should rise as well. Thus, while both customer and financial brand values are important, we start first with the customer or consumer, for we believe the consumer is the primary base of brand value.

In Chapters 3 and 4, we will discuss in detail how financial brand value will be used in our new brand communication planning approach. These chapters also will provide the detail on the brand measurement system we have developed. It is now possible to relate investments in brand communication programs to financial returns to the brand marketer. In short, we will illustrate a closed loop brand communication program in this text. It is our belief that the brand communication planner should be able to determine how much should be invested in brand communication, and against what group of customers or prospects, with a fairly good idea of what will be returned to the marketing organization as a result of these investments. That's why we focus on brand communication rather than on advertising or sales promotion or public relations in this approach to developing marketing communication.

With this view of brands, branding, and brand value, we can now develop in Chapter 3 the basic approach to brand communication planning that we propose for the twenty-first-century marketplace.

Summary

The brand is the marketing organization's chief asset in the twenty-first-century marketplace. While we can control some aspects of the brand, the brand's true meaning and value come from the consumer. Brand messages, brand contacts, brand associations, brand networks, and brand equity are key concepts in developing our understanding of brands and our ability to manage brands effectively. Both attitudinal and behavioral data are needed to evaluate the brand from the perspective of the customer.

3

Building Brand Value

If the brand will be the organization's most valuable asset in the twenty-first century, the challenge for brand communication managers must be to build brand value for both the customer and the organization, but especially for the customer. And, as was discussed in Chapter 2, brand value must be built for the entire spectrum of the brand's customers, from end users to channels to employees to the financial community. Exhibit 3-1 illustrates this concept.

Too often, brand-building communication considers only one or two of the customer groups that the brand must serve. In our approach, the communication manager must consider, reach, and motivate all customers and prospects for the brand, no matter their location or their involvement. While this text focuses primarily on the external customers of the brand—the ultimate consumers or end users—the brand communication planner must always be thinking of how the approach being developed could be translated to other audiences as well. The goal is to understand and manage the impact of the brand communication program on the customer's view of the brand and its value.

The second important factor in developing effective brand communication programs is that, given the changes that have occurred and those to come in the twenty-first-century marketplace, communication must move from a supporting role in a marketing effort to a leadership role in the organization. Historically, product managers considered communication to be a secondary element in the marketing mix. Since their focus was on managing specific functions of marketing, they sometimes overlooked the fact that communication could be a key element in making those specific functions more effective. The Marketplace Evolution and Revolution

Exhibit 3-1
Building Brand Value Umbrella

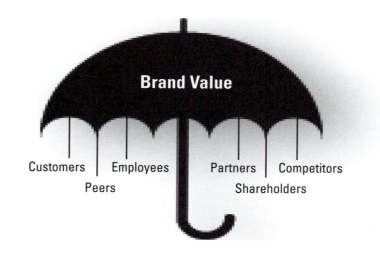

model in Exhibit 3-2 illustrates the changes that are occurring in marketing and communication and how communication will likely become the lead element in most marketing organizations in the twenty-first century.

As we illustrated in the Introduction, in the twenty-first-century marketplace the brand moves from being an identifier of a bundle of product features, pricing, and distribution to being the trust, quality, and relationship value that the customer is buying. Likewise, communication moves from being a supporting, tactical player to that of prime motivator in the purchase decision. The twenty-first-century marketplace is a marketplace of relationships, and the brand must provide the prime relationship between the marketer and its customers.

With these thoughts in mind, we can now start developing the framework for the preparation of a successful brand communication program.

Building Customer Brand Value from the Customer's View

Traditionally, marketers have looked to their product or service or the marketing elements such as price, distribution, or promotion as the primary methods of differentiating themselves from competition. Therefore, very commonly, marketing organizations have focused more on what competitors have done or are doing—their product offerings, their distribution systems, their pricing policies, their advertising messages, and the like—rather than trying to learn and understand what

Exhibit 3-2
Marketplace Evolution and Revolution

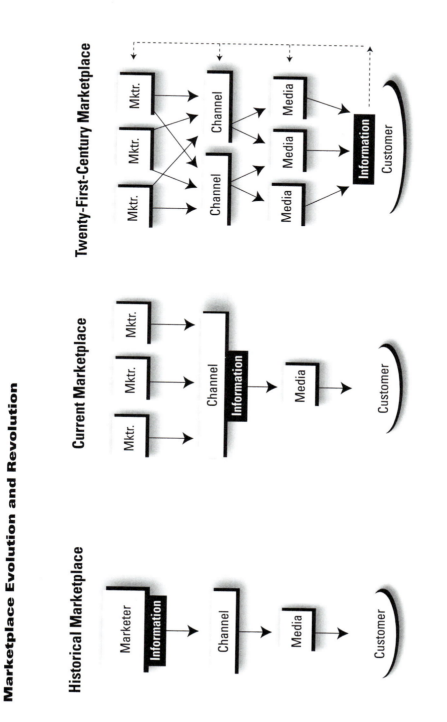

Historical Marketplace

Marketer (Information) → Channel → Media → Customer

Current Marketplace

Mktr., Mktr., Mktr. → Channel (Information) → Media → Customer

Twenty-First-Century Marketplace

Mktr., Mktr., Mktr. → Channel, Channel → Media, Media, Media → (Information) → Customer customers and prospects want or need to know about the brand and then providing it. Viewing competition as the driving force in the marketplace often distracts the marketing organization from what is truly the most important part of the equation, the consumer or customer. In our view, the primary thrust of brand communication must be to focus on the end user. Certainly, competitors are important, but they should not drive the organization's brand communication programs.

The best way to create effective brand communication is to look at the output or programs from the customer's view and in customer terms, not those of the marketing organization or the competition. We call this an "outside-in" approach, in contrast to the more common "inside-out" view of brand communication development that is used by many organizations. The outside-in concept is illustrated in Exhibit 3-3.

In Chapter 6, we go into considerable detail about how customers operate in the marketplace: how they make decisions; what factors they use to determine what they need and want, what they seek from marketing organizations; and how they process and store brand communication. Understanding our most valuable customers is the key to our brand communication approach. In every case, we start with customers or prospects, try to determine what they want and value, and then try to develop messages and incentive programs that will meet their needs. This customer-focused approach to developing brand communication programs builds value

Exhibit 3-3
Outside-In Planning

for the brand because it is what customers want to hear—not just what we as marketers want to tell them.

When we take this outside-in or customer view of the brand, we change a number of the traditional approaches to developing marketing and communication programs. We should note, however, that the changes we suggest are not because the previous practices of marketing and brand communication were wrong. On the contrary, the reason we suggest these changes is because the market has changed and consumers have changed and most of these changes have been driven by developed and developing technology. It is this superior technology that provides the basis for many of our recommendations. Following is a discussion of six changes that we believe are necessary in the primary areas of brand marketing and communication planning.

1. From Functions to Processes

For the most part, brand communication programs traditionally have been developed and delivered by functional specialists: experts in advertising, public relations, sales promotion, and direct marketing. While the total brand communication programs sometimes came together, often they did not. Thus, the customer saw one message in advertising, a separate unrelated incentive from sales promotion, a totally separate program in direct marketing, and so on. Most traditional approaches to developing brand communication programs have allowed or even encouraged each discipline to "do its own thing" or "do what it does best." Commonly, there have been broad guidelines, but the functional specialists developed their own special kind of execution and delivery of the brand message. At some point in the process, some attempt would be made to integrate these functional programs either under a common theme or with a common look, often called the "one sight, one sound" approach to managing communication programs.

In our brand communication approach, we take a much broader view, however. As illustrated in Exhibit 2-2 (p. 44), we attempt to bring all of the elements together by focusing on the customer first and always. We then align and integrate the entire organization to focus on the end user.

As the exhibit shows, the first step is to get the internal organization focused and directed. Then, external suppliers must understand what the brand means, how it relates to customers, and their suppliers' role in delivering brand value. Aligning and integrating the internal organization is next. That means making sure that employees, operations, customer service, logistics, and other groups know and support the brand as planned. Next come external communication programs. Commonly, here in the middle of the process is where most organizations start with external communication, and often they get no further. In our view, the entire organization must be aligned and integrated for communication to add value to the brand.

This approach provides a true brand communication planning process, avoiding a group of unaligned and uncoordinated functional elements pulled together simply for management approval. This move from attempting to coordinate a group of separate elements to a fully aligned and Integrated Brand Communication (IBC) program truly differentiates this approach from others.

2. From Transactions to Relationships

Generally, most organizations have measured their success in terms of transactions or exchanges—purchases or sales or unit volume. Given this, most organizations measured the success of their communication programs on number of units sold, share of market versus competitors', whether sales were up or down, number of new customers acquired, number of leads processed, and so on. In other cases, they used surrogate measures to determine communication impact. These measures included advertising awareness or brand recall or intent to buy. In the twenty-first-century marketplace, however, the goal will be to build ongoing, long-term relationships with customers—not simply to separate them from their money. Recall that our goal with a brand is to build a long-term relationship, not to generate only short-term returns. Do not, however, misunderstand our position. Sales must occur for the organization to survive, and there must be profit if the organization is to provide employment and if stockholders are to receive returns. So, although the goal of brand communication may be to build immediate sales, it must also be to build long-term customer relationships and to increase brand value.

Understanding the brand allows us to build a brand communication program to achieve these goals. Thus, in our approach, sales and relationships are not separated. They are the crux of the brand communication program.

3. From Monologue to Dialogue

As you will recall from our illustration of the twenty-first-century marketplace, brand communication must become interactive. As shown in Exhibit I-3 (p. 13), there must be a dialogue in which the customer can ask and receive information from any source, as well as listen to messages being sent by the marketing organization. This suggests that the marketing organization must be as good at listening to what customers and prospects want and need as it is in communicating with them on an outbound basis about product benefits or values. Each participant must talk, but, more important, each must listen and respond.

This is a somewhat radical change for most marketing organizations. Today we are trained to talk *at* customers, not listen to them. Most organizations have not developed their customer listening skills very well. We have spent our time developing more and better and less expensive ways of talking at customers instead of talking with them. In fact, most brand communication planners spend more time deciding what to say than they do determining what customers want to hear. It is this interactive nature of communication that will be critical in the twenty-first-century marketplace we are now entering.

4. From Tactics to Strategies

Today, most marketing and communication activities are tactical in nature. That is, they are regarded as things that the organization "should do" or "are nice to do" or "might be helpful sometime," but commonly they are not considered essential to the success of the organization or to the ongoing value of the brand. Examples of this abound. Advertising budgets are cut in the middle of the year if sales are not going well. New brand and branding approaches are delayed or put on hold while other, supposedly more important, decisions are taken. Brand communication is turned on and off year-to-year at the whims of management or as the financial situation of the organization dictates. Marketing and communication are tactical activities that the organization apparently does not value or whose contribution to the organization's success has not been demonstrated.

In many cases, it is the marketing and communication community that has created this tactical view of communication. We have failed to develop an effective method of measuring and evaluating the results of marketing and communication programs. We have hidden behind a cloak of creativity and attitudinal measurements. We have shied away from fiscal responsibility. Indeed, in many cases it is the marketing and communication manager who has asked for his or her discipline to be valued for its tactical, not strategic value. As the famous philosopher of the 1960s, Pogo, once said, "We have met the enemy and he is us!"

In the twenty-first-century marketplace, organizations will succeed or fail based on their success in allocating scarce organizational resources. Those who make the best allocation decisions, whether they be in new products, new markets, retention of existing customers, or new and better brand communication, will succeed. Marketing and brand communication must come to be regarded as strategic tools of the organization—not something added at the last moment to fill in a perceived hole or slashed if things aren't going well. This will necessitate a major change in the way organizations evaluate marketing and communication expenditures, which we will discuss next.

5. From Buying Communication Programs to Delivering Organizational Returns

Perhaps the greatest change needed in the development and implementation of brand communication programs as we move from the traditional to this new twenty-first-century view is the change of focus from what we buy to what we get back from customers, that is, from buying television time or coupon drops or corporate sponsorships or direct mailings to the return in terms of purchases and income flows and ongoing relationships. In brand communication programs, we value outcomes rather than outputs. In other words, we value customers' purchases that come back to the organization as a flow of income. In truth, the income flows are what we are trying to influence. We are investing in customers through brand communication, trying to increase, maintain, or find new flows of income from customers and prospects. That is the basis of brand communication—investing in customers to get returns or income flows. The advertising or sales promotion or direct marketing or an event we use are simply vehicles to communicate with customers and prospects to produce a return. Thus, the value of the communication program must be measured in terms of the income flows to the organization that it generates. As measures of the success of our communication programs, income flows demonstrate the amounts customers are willing to pay to purchase our brands to gain the values we provide. This approach will become clearer as we illustrate the actual planning process in Chapter 4.

Generally, most communication planning has focused on what we could or should buy to influence customers or prospects. We have developed very sophisticated approaches to buying all types of media, from television to print to outdoor to participation in the Olympics. Further, we have been just as involved in creating the messages and incentives that we deliver through print ads or outdoor boards or tee-shirt logo designs or even hour-long television specials. The primary focus has been on creating or buying or delivering the messages and incentives. That is, the emphasis has been on the output, not the outcome. This focus must change, however. In our view, bringing about this change is one of the major challenges to brand communication development.

The twenty-first-century brand communication marketplace requires us to focus on delivering outcomes and results and returns on investments to the organization. Fortunately, in a marketplace that is interactive, like the one just ahead, it will be much easier to measure the returns from brand communication programs. Customers will be more willing to advise us of whether we are providing the information and product that they need or want.

6. From Efficiency to Effectiveness

A corollary to the concept of the communication program's changing from buying to investing for returns to the organization is another new concept. The brand communication program must move from simply developing efficient ways of delivering brand communication programs to customers and prospects to effectively influencing customers and prospects so that we generate maximum returns on our communication investments.

Today, most functional communication approaches base their purchase of various forms and types of brand communication output on the basis of efficiency. Efficient distribution of the message is commonly the key goal in communication. Thus, media and promotional executives are continuously looking for less expensive ways of delivering messages and incentives. We gauge our communication programs on cost-per-thousand homes delivered or gross rating points or gross impressions. We emphasize delivering messages and incentives efficiently, not necessarily effectively. Therefore, most of our evaluation methods are based on how inexpensively the message or incentive was delivered, not whether it had any impact or effect on the customer or prospect. Today, we measure outputs. Tomorrow, however, we must measure outcomes.

In our brand communication planning system, we focus on effectiveness as well as efficiency. We are much more interested in whether our brand communication program had some influence on the customer or prospect rather than in our ability to deliver the message or incentive for the least expense. As we have discussed earlier, our goal is to create changes in behaviors, not just changes in attitudes or awareness of brand communication programs. Behaviors that result in sales and profit for the firm can be measured and evaluated. Further, the behaviors signify relationships—our critical brand element for the twenty-first century. Unlike traditional forms of communication measurement, which focus on attitudinal change or development, brand communication will be measured on how effective our messages and incentives were in influencing the customer or prospect to do something specific with regard to our product or service. To summarize, we want to achieve marketplace effectiveness, not just marketplace efficiency. In truth, when the marketing organization achieves effectiveness, in our experience efficiency generally comes along as well.

Having identified six changes from the traditional methods used, one might wonder how dramatically different from advertising, sales promotion, and other forms of marketing communication our brand communication planning is in practice. We explore the difference in the next section.

From Outputs to Outcomes—From Campaign Planning to Brand Communication Planning

The structure of an advertising or sales promotion or public relations campaign is generally based on an experiential formula that has been developed by an agency, consulting organization, or external supplier. That is, most of our planning methodologies have their roots in the advertising agency planning process. They have since been adapted to sales promotion, public relations, event, and trade show applications. Since advertising typically has focused on media-delivered messages on behalf of the product or service, this has become the de facto approach to message and incentive planning. While there are some strong points to the agency view, it is important to know that, increasingly, marketing organizations are attempting to develop their own planning process that better reflects the client's or marketer's view of the world.

In the following sections, we outline the new brand communication planning approach we have developed. To highlight the contrast between the agency planning and the brand communication approaches, however, we first review the traditional agency approach to planning. It is the approach that was used in the first four editions of the predecessor to this text, *Strategic Advertising Campaigns*.

Traditional Advertising Planning—A World of Specialists

In Exhibit 3-4, we illustrate the structure of the advertising planning process as it appeared in the third edition of *Strategic Advertising Campaigns*, published in 1989. As can be seen, while media advertising is the lead element in the process, other specialties such as sales promotion, public relations, and direct marketing, are included as parts of the advertising plan. Historically, however, advertising has been considered the lead element in the agency campaign. Sales promotion, direct marketing, public relations, and other functional activities were regarded as supporting tools to maximize the return on the advertising program. Likewise, if we were to look at a public relations plan of the same era, we would find public relations to be the prime element in the planning process, with advertising, events, and other activities being viewed as support for the PR program. It is this "lead element" approach that has

Exhibit 3-4
Advertising Campaign Planning Process

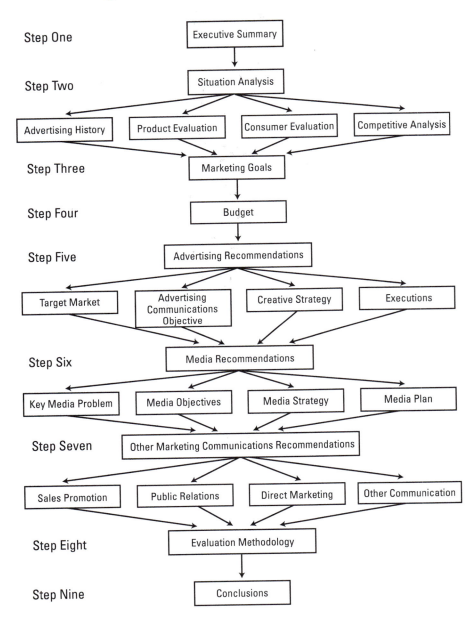

Step One	Executive Summary
Step Two	Situation Analysis
	Advertising History — Product Evaluation — Consumer Evaluation — Competitive Analysis
Step Three	Marketing Goals
Step Four	Budget
Step Five	Advertising Recommendations
	Target Market — Advertising Communications Objective — Creative Strategy — Executions
Step Six	Media Recommendations
	Key Media Problem — Media Objectives — Media Strategy — Media Plan
Step Seven	Other Marketing Communications Recommendations
	Sales Promotion — Public Relations — Direct Marketing — Other Communication
Step Eight	Evaluation Methodology
Step Nine	Conclusions

created, in our view, many of the brand communication planning difficulties of the past several years. This is because the functional specialty approach looks at brand communication from the view of the organization, not the view of the customer. Customers and prospects don't care if advertising leads or supports the brand. They don't care if public relations is the dominant functional activity or if that is played by sales promotion. They look only for information and value that serve their interests.

Unfortunately, around the world, this functional specialty as lead element is still the most current and widely used approach to brand communication planning. The focus of the communication planner is to coordinate and combine all the disparate brand communication elements into one coherent whole that can be delivered to the customer or prospect. The planner's objective is to orchestrate the elements into line—not to start with a coherent whole and then deliver the necessary pieces and parts to customers and prospects as they need or want them. As stated earlier, this traditional advertising planning approach is fraught with concerns over which type of communication should be dominant. Should advertising lead, and promotion be developed to support that advertising approach, or should public relations be the lead element, with advertising designed to support the PR? Whenever the focus is on the activity rather than on the customer or the outcome, generally issues about turf and power are soon to follow.

Start with the Customers or Prospects

In the brand communication planning approach that we propose, we start with the customer or consumer and work back to the organization. The reason for this change is simple: we want to view communication as the customer or prospect sees it—not as the organization attempts to distribute it. Exhibit 3-5 illustrates the concept.

As shown, customers and prospects don't distinguish between advertising and sales promotion, or between direct marketing and in-store displays, or even between advertising and distribution and pricing. They simply aggregate and store away mentally all the messages and incentives and brand contacts and product or service elements that they encounter. They then combine those with the new elements and activities to which they are being exposed. Finally, they try to form some basic opinion or feeling about the brand. Commonly, they simply say "I received or saw a lot of stuff from Sears or Kraft or IBM or Ford, and this is what it all means to me"! Commonly, they don't separate advertising from direct mail. They don't sit down and try to determine whether a magazine ad with a coupon is sales promotion or advertising. They don't spend time deliberating about whether an article they read in the newspaper was placed by a public relations agency or by a product placement agency. Instead, consumers simply take in the useful information, discard what is irrelevant, and process what is needed or wanted, putting that away with what they have stored up previously about the brand. Thus, any new brand communication is evaluated against what is already known, then either filed away in the mind or discarded. It is as simple as that.

We advocate this combined consumer view of a brand and brand communication, rather than the organizational or agency view of how the communication is created and delivered. We begin with the customer or consumer, looking at brand commu-

Exhibit 3-5
How Consumers See Marketing Communication

Customer Service

Product Design

Pricing

Direct Mail

Customer View of Marketing Communication

In-Store Displays

Distribution

Sales Promotion

Advertising

nication from his or her view. Given that consumers live in an increasingly complex, information-loaded world that is likely to become more so in the twenty-first century, consumers typically sift and discard their way through the communications, seeking to simplify the message.

Roll Up the Communication Disciplines

If the consumer sees brand communication simply as "stuff we got from the marketing organization," that indicates a need to overhaul the process of planning and implementing a brand communication program. If we want to plan from the customer view, we must think like customers and prospects. That is what a brand communication planning approach attempts to do. And that requires rolling up the communication disciplines we have so carefully created and crafted inside the organization and simplifying them to match the customer view. As shown in Exhibit 3-6, we have simplified our view and management of brand communication into two elements—messages or incentives.

As shown, we begin our brand communication planning process by looking at communication the way consumers view it. That is, the marketing organization is trying to either deliver a message or deliver an incentive to the customer or prospect.

Exhibit 3-6
Brand Communication Planning Matrix, Part 1

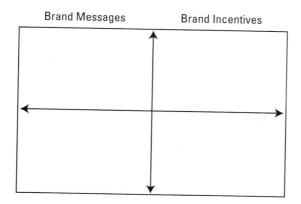

Brand Messages   Brand Incentives

From the consumer's view, this idea is quite simple: either the marketer wants the consumer to understand and store away something about its product or service, which would constitute a message, or the marketer wants the consumer to do something with regard to the product or service, generally within a specific time frame, which would be an incentive. Consumers can generally differentiate between these two behavioral marketing objectives: the organization wants to tell me something or the organization wants me to do something.

By the same token, most marketing organizations clearly know what they are trying to do with their brand communication programs. They, too, want either to tell the customer or prospect something or to get the customer or prospect to do something. With the brand communication approach, the marketing organization and the consumer or customer are in harmony. That is, both understand the goals and objectives of the brand communication program and both know what the outcome should or could be. Messages are things consumers process and store, either for future use or because they reinforce concepts or ideas that consumers already know. In contrast, incentives should be acted upon immediately, or at least in the reasonable future. Messages or incentives—that's the way consumers see brand communication. As such, this view must guide the way we plan and implement our brand communication programs.

The collapsing of the traditional forms of marketing and brand communication is not only reasonable and rational, it greatly simplifies the planning of brand communication programs from the view of the marketing organization. Today, arguments rage inside organizations about allocating budgets among advertising, sales promotion, and direct marketing activities. Functional specialists fight for turf, funds, and power using approaches and concepts that have little meaning to the customers whom they are supposed to influence. For example, if a print advertisement in a magazine contains a cents-off coupon, is it sales promotion or is it still advertising? If a sales promotion offer is mailed to a customer or consumer, does it suddenly become direct marketing? These are the confusing and often conflicting problems that communication managers face today. Fortunately, the new brand communication planning matrix brings the entire planning process into focus. Message or incentive? What is the organization trying to do? How is the consumer or customer supposed to respond?

One of the concerns of adopting this new approach is the question of what happens to the functional specialties. What happens to an employee who has spent his or her entire business career becoming the world's greatest living authority on cents-off coupons to housewives between the ages of eighteen and forty-nine? In the brand communication approach, he or she continues to be important and relevant, but does not drive the brand communication planning process. Rather, he or she is a supplier to the planner. The planner, then, must determine the strategy: choosing between delivering a message or an incentive. The choice of a cents-off coupon, for example, is a tactic. The question of whether messages or incentives are appropriate for brand communication planning is a strategic one. How that message or incentive might be delivered then becomes a tactical question.

The use of this message or incentive approach has great value for the planner from the standpoint of implementation. For example, once the planner determines that messages about the brand need to be delivered to customers and prospects, the tacticians are free to find a multitude of ways in which to deliver that message. For example, it could be delivered through traditional media advertising, or it might be communicated through an event, a public relations program, or even a sponsorship of something such as stock car racing. Indeed, there is no limit really to how and where and under what circumstance the message can be delivered. Further, having determined that a message is appropriate, planning is freed from the sometimes arbitrary view of the functional specialists.

Obviously, the delivery of messages or incentives implies some response to the brand communication program, whether short-term or long-term. A key element of brand communication is the determination of time frame for the program. That is, over what period of time will customers and consumers be expected to react? Our discussion of this issue follows.

Short- or Long-Term Response

By separating our communication activities into messages and incentives, we conceptually separate them into short-term and long-term activities. Messages are long-term, brand-building activities. Incentives are short-term, business-building activities. Marketing companies and consumers recognize that, but functional marketing and communication specialists who try either to stretch their activity or to minimize its effects to generate more budget or more support seem to ignore it. Advertising people, for example, argue that advertising has long-term, brand-building effects, yet they also make the claim that advertising has impact and generates sales response in the short-term. Likewise, sales promotion people know that their incentives are designed to generate short-term returns, yet they argue that sales

Exhibit 3-7
Brand Communication Planning Matrix, Part 2

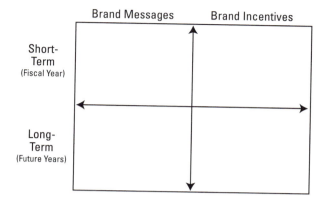

promotions have long-term value because they build brand equity with consumers. Actually, both groups may be right. It is quite possible that advertising can build short-term sales and that sales promotion can build long-term brand value. In fact, there appears to be considerable evidence supporting both of these nontraditional values. Given this blurring of accepted truths, marketing and communication planners cannot be constrained by the stereotypical, functional definitions that have grown up over the years. In the twenty-first-century marketplace, we must move beyond the approaches that were developed and accepted in the 1960s.

Having added short-term and long-term returns to our planning matrix, we have now developed a brand communication model that is useful and usable in the new brand communication marketplace we are entering. The complete matrix is shown as Exhibit 3-7.

As illustrated, our planning process requires that the brand communication planner determine whether brand communication messages or brand incentives are to be delivered to customers and prospects and whether those messages or incentives will be designed to achieve short-term or long-term brand communication goals. We classify all short-term activities as business-building, because they are designed to have an immediate impact on the brand's sales. We classify long-term activities as brand-building, because their effect will be on the brand's image and strength over time.

The brand communication matrix shown in Exhibit 3-7 offers the brand communication planner a new and unique view of consumers and options for the development and delivery of brand communication. To further explain the brand communication planning approach, two examples of how the matrix might be used are described in the sidebar, Messages and Incentives.

Messages and Incentives

Example 1: Van de Kamp's Grilled Salmon and Tuna

As the brand communication planning matrix illustrates, brand communicators have four types of brand communication efforts that can be applied, depending on the situation. Two are business-building: a short-term brand message and a short-term brand incentive. The other two efforts are brand-building: a long-term brand message and a long-term brand incentive. The advertisement/sales promotion for Van de Kamp's Grilled Salmon and Tuna shown in Exhibit 3-8 illustrates two of those alternatives. The original appeared in a free-standing insert (FSI) in a Sunday newspaper.

Short-term incentive

The primary purpose of this Van de Kamp's piece, as is the case with virtually all FSIs, is to promote an immediate sale of the product. In this case, the consumer is offered a $1.50 coupon redeemable for any two Van de Kamp's grilled salmon or tuna fillets. Coupons are a common means of generating trial for new products, because the price reduction reduces the consumer's risk in trying the product. (Coupons will be discussed in detail in Chapter 12.)

Short-term message

The FSI also contains some informational elements intended to launch the new product successfully. The piece signals clearly that this is a new product, that it can be prepared in fewer than twenty minutes, that the consumer does not have to do any actual grilling, and that there are four varieties of the product. For a fish-loving consumer, that may be enough information to persuade him or her to try the product. (Particularly when combined with the coupon.)

Long-term incentive

Van de Kamp's could offer coupons on each product package designed to generate repeat purchases.

Long-term message

The company could continue to introduce and promote new varieties of the product or develop a publicity campaign that touts the health benefits of eating fish.

The present strategy of combining a short-term message with a short-term incentive makes a great deal of sense for a new product, particularly one that will take up valuable space in the retailer's freezer case. Van de Kamp's needs to generate sales of this product quickly in order to hold on to that shelf space.

Exhibit 3-8

Van de Kamp's FSI

Exhibit 3-9
United Airlines "Rising" Advertisement

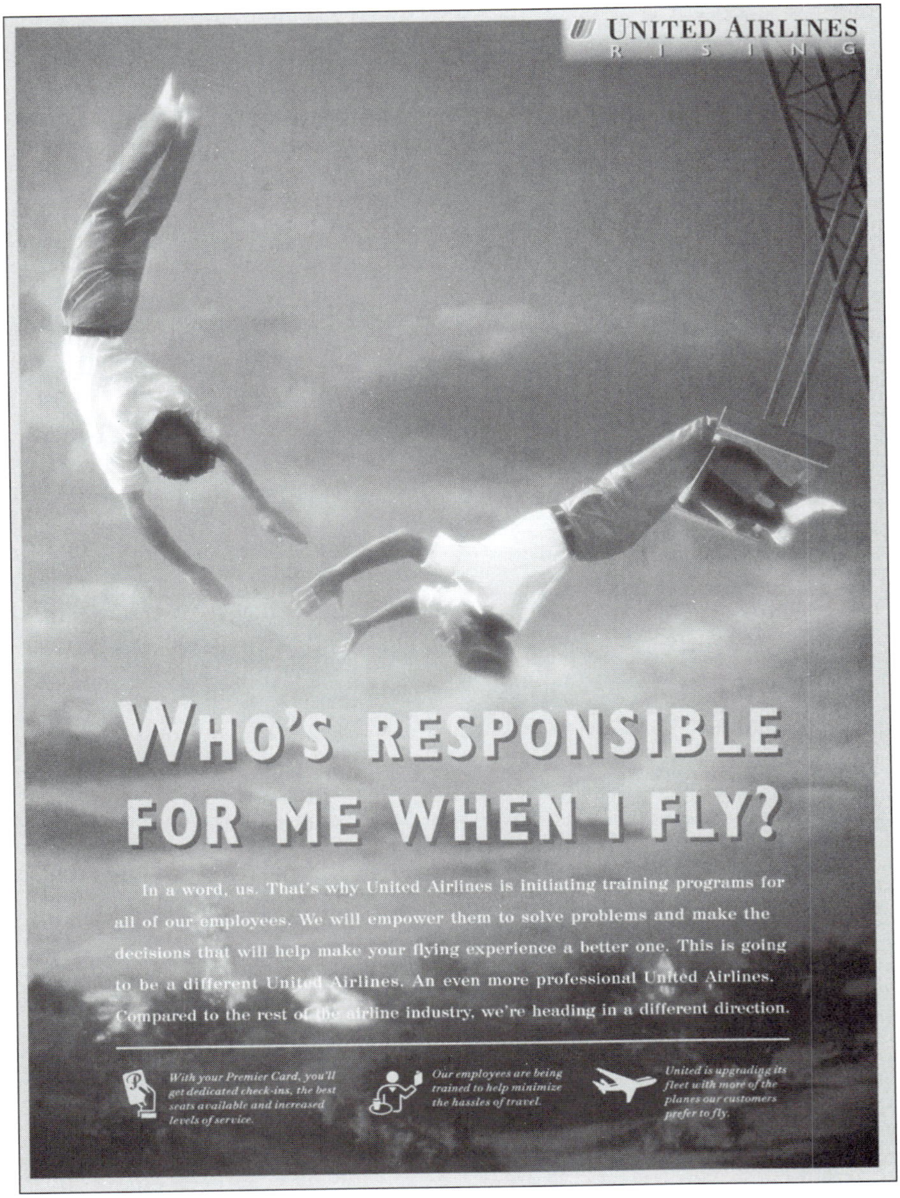

Example 2: United Airlines "Rising" Campaign

Airlines make use of both long- and short-term incentives.

Long-term incentive

United Airline's Mileage Plus program, which offers rewards and incentives for the airline's frequent flyers, is a long-term incentive intended to promote brand loyalty and passenger retention.

Short-term incentive

United, like other airlines, often runs short-term incentives in the form of reduced price tickets to particular destinations. This type of short-term incentive is often intended to reduce surplus seats on less-popular flights or to meet a competitive threat. For example, if a regional carrier added a new city to its route map, United might reduce prices on its flights into that same city to combat the new competitor.

And, airlines certainly make use of both long- and short-term messages.

Long-term message

Most traditional image advertising in the mass media is intended to convey a long-term message. United frequently runs television ads under the "Rising" theme that work to maintain United's high-quality image.

Short-term message

A series of magazine ads from United highlight increased flight availability in order to persuade air travelers to consider booking a flight on United.

Having established the need to view all brand communication activities from the consumer's point of view, we move next to a review of the entire IBC planning process, with particular attention to how we can use our knowledge of the consumer to develop IBC programs that are both effective and efficient.

Summary

Looking at the brand from the customer's view and developing customer-based communication requires six basic changes to marketing communication planning: (1) from functions to processes; (2) from transactions to relationships; (3) from monologue to dialogue; (4) from tactics to strategies; (5) from buying communication programs to delivering organizational returns; and (6) from efficiency to effectiveness. Understanding these concepts will help the planner look at communication decisions from the customer's view and determine whether brand communication should take the form of a message, an incentive, or both, and whether that communication should be designed primarily for short-term or long-term effect.

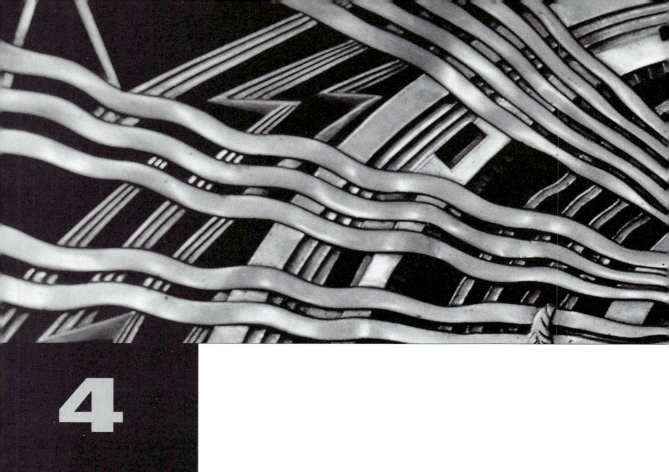

4

The IBC Planning Process and Estimating Customer Value

In this and the next chapter, a detailed, step-by-step approach for using the IBC process will be outlined. As discussed in Chapter 3, we have broken the entire development of an IBC campaign into three basic areas.

As shown in Exhibit 4-1, we start with customers and prospects. This requires that we identify those customers and prospects whom we believe are important. That decision is based on their current or future value to the organization. Once we know what a customer/prospect is worth or might be worth, we can develop our behavioral marketing objectives. Based on these objectives we can then determine the best method of influencing those customers or prospects—that is, either through messages or through incentives.

Clearly, one of the key elements in valuing customers or prospects is determining their net value to the organization. This is illustrated in Exhibit 4-2. First, we must aggregate or combine all those customers and prospects who are alike in terms of their purchase or use of the product or brand. Then, we must determine their "share-of-requirements," that is, the percentage of time our brand is purchased or used by the customer as a percentage of the total purchases the customer or prospect makes in the product category. For example, if the customer/prospect purchases four soft drinks per day and three of those are our brand, we can say we have a 75 percent share of that customer's requirements. The next step is to determine how much those four soft drink purchases are worth. In other words, how much did the customer pay to purchase those four soft drinks at retail? From that, we must subtract our cost of the product itself and the marketing that accompanied it. Those costs might include the dealer margin, advertising, general overhead, and so on. Thus,

Exhibit 4-1
Brand Communication Strategy Development

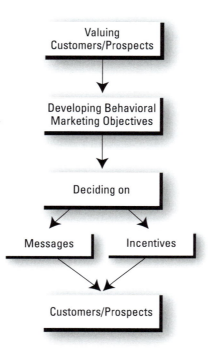

Exhibit 4-2
Customer Valuation

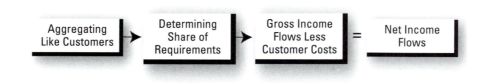

our result is how much net income the organization received from the sale of the four soft drinks. We call this the net income flow to the organization. It is important because it determines how many actual dollars the organization receives from each customer, which it can reinvest in new products, new plants, or equipment, or in hiring more people, or most important of all, for us, it determines how much might be available to fund a brand communication program.

On the following pages, we will delve into the IBC process in some detail. To orient ourselves to the structure and flow of the process, we show the entire process in Exhibit 4-3. While it looks complex and forbidding, it really is quite simple and rational.

The Brand Business Review

As shown in Exhibit 4-3, the first step in the IBC process is a complete brand business review. This simply means updating where the brand stands in the marketplace, its relationship with customers and prospects, the competitive framework within which it operates in the marketplace, any new or pending product improvements or developments, any new distribution systems or approaches being considered, and the like. Obviously, this review should include a look at the major areas of legislation, environmental questions or concerns, and government restrictions or regulation. In short, this is to be a total analysis of the current situation for the brand and any long-term or short-term factors that might impact the brand during the planning or implementation period for which the IBC plan is being developed. Additional concerns related to this review are discussed in Chapter 7. We have found that any attempt to develop an IBC program without fully understanding the brand, its customers, and the marketplace environment in which it operates generally is unsuccessful.

Assuming a thorough brand business review has been conducted, however, we now turn to what we know about customers and prospects. This information frequently is found in the database.

Understanding the Customer/Prospect Database

Databases have been around for many years. Most commonly, they have been referred to as customer files, purchase records, and sales records. Only recently, however, because of the development of more sophisticated, computer-assisted data processing methodologies, have they entered the broad arena of marketing and brand communication. As was discussed in the Preface, Introduction, and Chapter 1, information technology and the use of data are totally changing the way marketing and communication plans and programs are developed and conducted. IBC, as a process, is designed to take advantage of new technological advantages that give the organization better knowledge and understanding of its customers and prospects. There

Exhibit 4-3 IBC Five-Step Planning Process

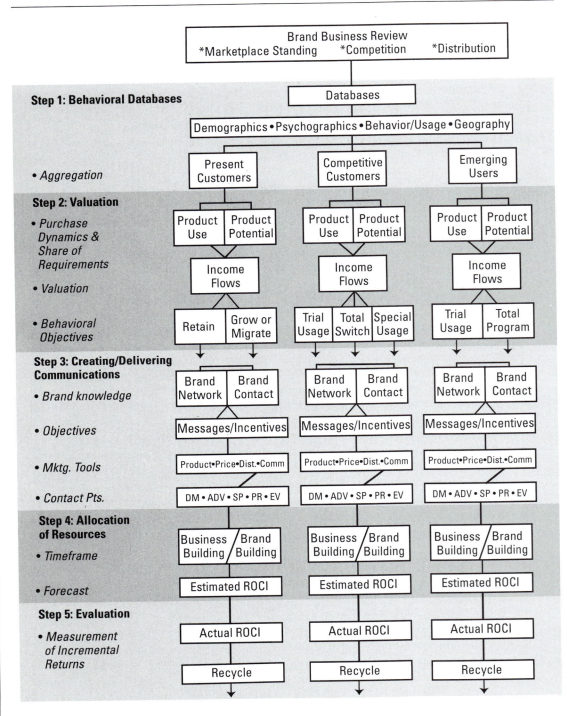

is little question that data and databases will drive all forms of marketing in the twenty-first century.

For our purposes, it is not necessary for the IBC planner to have great technical knowledge of how databases are constructed, organized, or maintained, although we provide an overview of some of those issues in a database sidebar. Rather, our approach will be primarily that of using the data that either are stored or can be developed from the database content. Thus, we view the database as a repository of customer information, not as a mechanical and technological monster to be tamed and mastered.

Marketing Database Content and Use

In most marketing databases, organizations have stored data and information about their customers and prospects. These data commonly consist of information about individual customers, households, and some prospects. The data may include, but not be limited to, information such as is shown in Step 1 of Exhibit 4-3. One type of data included in the behavioral database might be demographics—measurable data about customers, prospects, households, business organizations, or whatever is the relevant unit for the brand organization. These data commonly are used to explain or illustrate something about the relevant unit. For example, using our database we can say we know that Albert Turberville currently lives at 83 Ashworth Street, Maximum, Maine 00345, with his wife and two children. They own their home and one car.

A second category of information commonly included in a database is psychographics. These data indicate something about Albert and his interests. For example, we might have information stored that shows that Albert has a two-year-old, twenty-two-foot sailboat. We might also know that he is president of the Maximum Yachting Club. Further, we might also have data that show he is a member of both the Maximum Rotary Club and the Mid-Coast Toastmasters Club. Data of this type give us an idea of Albert's specific interests and how he spends his leisure time. While these data may have come from a number of different sources, they all can be included in (or, in database jargon, "appended to") Albert's file, which will give us a much better understanding of who he is, what he enjoys, how he spends his free time, and so on.

A third primary area of data we might have on Albert concerns his purchase of various products or services, particularly product categories. These data generally would come from panel data that Albert may have supplied to a research organization, agreed to share with a retailer in return for various forms of rewards, or were gathered by an outside source from any number of records and data sources. For example, from these purchase data we might know that Albert bought a new car three years ago and appears to do so regularly every four years. We might know when and where he bought his sailboat and the accessories he purchased at the same time. If we have access to retail purchase data such as frequent shopper programs at supermarkets, drug stores, or mass merchandisers, we might know that Albert buys motor oil at the drug store and auto tires from his favorite service station. Of particular interest to us as brand communication planners is Albert's purchase history—his purchase and use of products in our product category. For example, if we know that Albert buys motor oil for his boat and car at the chain drug store, we would also likely know what brand he buys, when he buys it, how often, and in what quantity. This is critical information as we start to determine the value of customers and prospects and to estimate or calculate their income flows to our brand.

While this is only a brief overview of the database, it should be clear to the IBC brand communication planner that the behavioral database is the key to understanding customers and prospects. The more data and the better the data, the better the understanding of the customer or prospect, and, thus, the more effective the brand communication plan.

Market or Customer Segmentation or Aggregation

It is useful to note here that the type of data we just described is the ideal. Generally, only those organizations that have ongoing, direct dealings with their customers, such as direct marketers, hotels, auto rental companies, travel agents, banks, and financial organizations, have access to so much data. Other organizations, particularly those who sell through various channels such as retailers and wholesalers, often have to rely on grouped or syndicated data that provide only generalized information about customers and customer groups and do not address individual customers or specific groups of customers or prospects. This lack of specificity is generally true even of frequent shopper data. Such data often are available by geographic area, such as a supermarket or drug store cachement area—the geographic area from which most shoppers come. Often, we do not have individual household data, or if we do, we cannot connect it to a specific household, but only to a generalized group. So, in spite of all the hoopla about "one-to-one" marketing and communication, in most cases and for most product categories, particularly consumer product categories, we must rely on aggregated data. These are data about groups of households or census blocks or the like. In the United States, there are few restrictions on how much or what type of data on customers and prospects might be gathered, captured, or stored by a marketing organization. With few exceptions (primarily in healthcare, video rentals, and some financial transactions), the marketer is free to build as extensive a database as possible. This is not the case in other countries. For example, in the European Union, data restriction laws clearly spell out what types of data can be captured, how they can be used, and how they can be shared among marketers. This is discussed in more detail in Chapter 13.

A database vastly improves our ability to recognize and understand customers and prospects, their needs and wants, and how we might serve them; however, if the organization does not have a customer database, various types of consumer research may be used to identify and learn more about present customers and prospects. The more commonly used types of consumer research are discussed in Chapter 7. As a rule, most of the pieces of information in a database are disaggregated. That is, they are kept at an individual or household unit level. Therefore, as illustrated previously, the data on Albert Turberville are likely stored as various bits and pieces in

Database-Driven Relationship Marketing

I. What Is a Database?

The database is a repository for information about customers and prospects. This information is the history of the relationship between the organization and the customer over time. The content of the database should be representative of all contacts and transactions between the two parties. One of the key elements of a database is that material must be stored so that it can be accessed and manipulated to generate information from which the marketing organization can make sound business decisions. This means the data must be captured and maintained so those who need to retrieve and analyze these data have access to them. If the data are not accessible and available to those in the organization who need to utilize them, the database is less useful and simply an expensive artifact. A database, then, is a tool with which customer relationships can be started, developed, cultivated, and maximized over time.

II. What Should the Database Contain?

As the history of the relationship a customer has with the company, the database must contain pertinent detail on what has happened over the course of that relationship. Information such as who, what, when, where, how often, and how much should be included. For example, when a customer calls their healthcare provider at an 800 number, he or she expects the organization to be able to look at a complete history of their dealings with the firm. The customer expects the organization to be able to serve him or her from that point and not need time to reconstruct the relationship.

Databases were traditionally transaction registers in which were stored data about where items were purchased, who purchased the items, the amount paid, and the date of the transaction. Now this amount and kind of information is often only the beginning of what is desired and required by organizations in order to communicate and manage customer relationships effectively and efficiently. Marketing organizations often are interested in collecting the following information:

- transaction/purchase history
- inquiry/response history
- distribution systems details/behaviors
- relationships among database members
- brand affiliations of the customer
- marketing and sales communication (brand communication)
- customer care and technical support calls and outcomes
- training/customer handling details and history
- demographics/psychographics/firmographics
- other relevant appended data

Of the list above, maintaining records of contact with the customer and responses to those outbound communications is critical. Another important aspect implicit from the above list is a dollar value measure for the customer. This information allows the marketer to understand the differences between good customers and bad customers and various customer groups. From this, sound communication programs can be developed. Obviously, the data needed in the database depend on factors such as the company's intended application for the data, the industry category, which critical variables influence purchase behavior, and other details that vary according to the unique situation faced by the organization. For example, if a consumer goods company selling hand soap, bath soap, dish soap, and laundry detergent is building a database of people who buy the complete product line, it probably is not imperative to collect data about their brand of television set or whether their kids play little league baseball. Rather, the goal is to accumulate data relevant to the customer and the product or service—information that can be used to develop more relevant brand communication programs.

III. Database Structures

The easiest way to think of a database is as a digital and therefore electronic compilation of data kept on a computer. Databases come in all shapes and sizes. In our experience, we still see many organizations who store data on card files, or in ledger books, or in the heads of salespeople or other key individuals. With the advances in technology, data can be acquired, stored, cleaned, and maintained at an ever decreasing cost. This is good, because the amount of data organizations capture continues to grow at an ever increasing rate. Desktop computers often are capable of managing data for 50,000 customers or more. And, with client server technology, a central repository of data can be accessed and manipulated as needed. In order to succeed in data-driven marketing, then, an electronic format that brings together the important data will be necessary.

There are two main types of database forms. One is the structured database that is based on flat, hierarchical, and network files. The other is the relational database. The main difference between the two types is that with a relational database one data element can be related to many other data elements. In contrast, the structured format has one data element related to only one other data element. Relational databases allow multiple elements to be connected through tables that facilitate access and reporting. While this is not a technical discussion by any means, it is important for the planner to know in what format the database is constructed to be able to know how the data can be manipulated. Although the technical expertise needed for a relational database is higher than for a structured database, the ongoing management and capability for more people to access and utilize the data make the relational database worth the extra expertise required. Whatever format is chosen, however, it is critical to begin database construction with a clear understanding of how the database will be used and what information is to be extracted.

The same is true of software. Most software packages will allow basic and ad hoc queries of the data. Most packages will allow reasonable access to the data for multiple personnel. Further, most software packages may be scaled according to changes in data requirements, adding capability as needed. Software packages such as Access from Microsoft allow extensive manipulation and query capability from a desktop personal computer, for example.

There are hundreds of vendors for both hardware and software. The database can be a huge investment, in the millions of dollars, or not so huge. Database costs depend on what is to be done, the amount of data currently available, and the budgetary constraints of the organization. It is also important for business units or divisions of large companies to choose a platform that will be compatible across divisions, so that when the need to combine the data becomes clear, the data will be in a similar form and can be combined readily.

IV. How the Database Is Utilized

The database should contain all the data necessary to manage the customer relationship over time. One of the key uses of the data is to evaluate customers, usually according to their value to the organization. With this information, marketers can better allocate finite resources to the most important groups with the highest return.

Another use of the database is to understand the potential of various customer and prospect groups. For example, if there is a group of customers whose profiles mirror best customers, then some investment can be made to assist the prospect group to reach its potential. Share of requirement analysis, for example, focuses on the portion of a customer's spending the organization currently receives, as well as his or her total spending. Using that information, the marketer can send brand communication to specifically build customer or prospect purchases of a particular product or category.

Marketing strategy can be driven by database analysis. When various customer groups are known and valued in some way, the marketer is then able to develop specific behavioral objectives, strategies, and tactics that also facilitate resource allocation over time. The database allows marketing strategy to be developed based

on differences between customers, rather than treating them all the same way.

When contact and response information is captured and analyzed, measurement of the various programs is also facilitated. This ability to determine the return on the brand communication turns the database into a tool that can pay for itself. It also allows the organization to learn over time which tactics work and how programs can be enhanced in the future. Databases can be used for many purposes. Some creativity is necessary to determine the best uses for each organization. However, even if the database is used only to evaluate or value customers and allocate resources to best customers and prospects, generally it is a worthwhile investment.

V. Privacy Concerns

Businesses and people are receiving more and more communication than ever before. There is concern that organizations know too much. The Direct Marketing Association has a phone number people can call to request removal from all mailing lists. The critical issue for marketers is to give the customer a reason to share the information. There must be a quid pro quo. In other words, the customer receives additional value, better service, more targeted communication, or some similar benefit, but there must be some reason to share personal or organizational information. We look at privacy issues in greater detail in Chapter 13.

VI. Examples

Hyatt International Hotels

Traditionally, hotels have gathered large quantities of data about guests, but have not been very good at utilizing that information to build or maintain guest relationships over time. Hyatt International has, over the past four or five years, spent considerable time combining datasets from various sources to gain increased understanding of guests and their behavior. Data from the Food and Beverage area has been combined with data from the Rooms records to understand the total value of a guest. For example, one guest stays for three nights in a basic room, orders room service, eats in the restaurant for lunch and dinner, and frequents the minibar. That guest's value is substantially different from someone who stays in a similar room for three nights and never uses any of those options. Hyatt is then able to manage both types of customers to maximize their value to the hotel and other hotels in the chain. Communication investments can be made, or adjusted, based on the additional knowledge. Various targeted messages or incentives can be utilized to maintain or enhance the customers' behavior over time.

Exhibit 4-4
Hyatt Hotel Advertisement

Pioneer Hi-Bred

From the agribusiness industry comes a good example of using data and databases to sell and manage customers over time. Pioneer Hi-Bred, a seed company, has built a database that contains both customer/farmer and syndicated crop information, down to the individual farmer level for the whole of the United States. Pioneer is able to tell the farmer how his farmland produced last year, how it compared in yield to national and regional averages, and what the expected yield might be during the current season based on regional weather forecasting, soil conditions, and a number of other factors. This information allows the salesperson to provide substantial value for the farmer, all from a laptop that can be opened up on the kitchen table of the farmer's house.

As is evident from the examples above, beyond basic transactional data, the database must contain data pertinent to the relationship between the marketer and the customer. Databases must provide the information that enables the organization to develop and maintain profitable customer relationships over time.

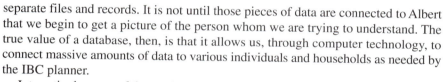

separate files and records. It is not until those pieces of data are connected to Albert that we begin to get a picture of the person whom we are trying to understand. The true value of a database, then, is that it allows us, through computer technology, to connect massive amounts of data to various individuals and households as needed by the IBC planner.

Interestingly, most of the marketing information that has been developed over the past fifty years or so has been aggregated data or market-level data. Most marketing organizations know very little about specific customers or prospects. Instead, their basic source of knowledge is at the product sales or industry usage or category development or geography level. Thus, most of the marketing analysis done today is an attempt to disaggregate these data so that effective marketing and communication programs can be developed. For example, let's look at the automobile category. Category data include all sales of all makes and models of automobiles sold. This could include new cars, used cars, pick-up trucks, and sedans. To be able to develop an effective and efficient marketing and communication program, however, these data have to be broken down in some way so specific marketing and communication programs can be developed. We marketers have developed very sophisticated segmentation methods and approaches in an attempt to understand various groupings of customers. Ironically, today marketers spend literally millions of dollars trying to break down aggregated data that were originally disaggregated. The reason this occurs is that marketing companies generally rely on outside organizations to gather and provide industry data. These organizations combine data from many sources and provide total records of sales or product purchase. The A. C. Nielsen Company and Information Resources, Inc., are examples of these types of industry aggregators. They take sales data from statistically valid samples of food stores and then project them to the national market. Marketing companies then try to break down these aggregated data to understand their own brand or market or geography.

Marketing organizations deal with aggregated data when they start to develop marketing and communication plans. Thus, we speak of the canned peas category or the women's clothing category or newspaper readers. These combined figures don't tell us very much about the consumers themselves, though, so we spend inordinate amounts of time and money trying to find like groups or segments of consumers so that we can speak to them directly and relevantly.

With databases, marketers do just the opposite. We try to aggregate or bring together like-behaving customers into similar groups based on some relevant behavior. Hence, the approach in the IBC process is to aggregate up individual customers into markets, not break down to the level of the individual user. Exhibit 4-5 illustrates the concept.

As shown, traditional marketers try to break down total markets into relevant groups for directed marketing efforts. In the IBC process, since we start with individual customers or prospects and we know something about their behaviors, our job is to aggregate those customers in some way that will provide economies of scale in marketing and communication programs. Suppose, for example, that a brand communication program was needed for a five-star hotel. If all persons labeled A in Exhibit 4-5 were frequent hotel guests at five-star hotels and all persons labeled D practically never stayed in a five-star hotel, it would be easy to see the value of this aggregation scheme. Indeed, the real value of the database is the opportunity to aggregate customers and prospects in any manner that makes marketing and communication more relevant to the customer or prospect and more efficient for the marketing organization. This capability of aggregating customers and prospects leads us to Step 2 of the IBC Planning Process shown in Exhibit 4-3. The focus here is on valuation.

Identifying and Valuing Customer Groups

The database gives us the capability of aggregating individual customers or customer groups into like-behaving units, providing a meaningful way for identifying those groups of customers or prospects for our IBC efforts. We take customers or groups of customers who have shown behaviors we would like to influence and identify and value them for specific IBC programs.

In the IBC process chart in Exhibit 4-3, we aggregated customers and prospects into three groups: present customers, competitive customers, and emerging users. Present customers, of course, are those who primarily purchase their category needs from our company or use our brands. Competitive customers buy in our category, but fill most of their needs with competitors' products or services. Emerging users either are just entering the category or they have no specific product or service preference at this point. This is the most basic aggregation scheme for most IBC planners, but many more elaborate schemes can be devised. For example, rather than aggregating

Exhibit 4-5
Market Segmentation/Aggregation

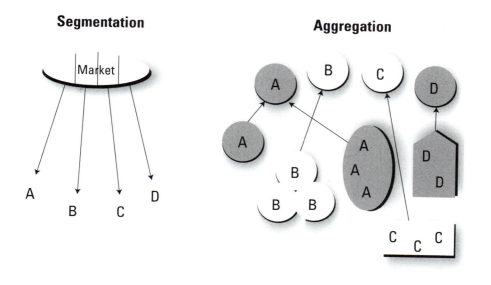

customers by product usage or brand loyalty, we might classify them by where they purchase the product: food or drug stores, mass merchandisers, discount operations, convenience stores, and so on. Or, we might aggregate customers and users on when they buy: beginning of the season, midseason, end-of-season, or final sale only. In other words, IBC planners can aggregate customers and prospects in any number of ways that might provide insight into their relationship with a brand or the potential for their relationship in the future.

One additional note of explanation should be given about the classification or aggregation scheme shown in the IBC process chart in Exhibit 4-3. The identification of present customers and competitive customers is somewhat arbitrary. Unless the product or service is unique or only an occasional purchase, such as an automobile or home or boat or other long-lasting durable good, most consumers buy from a range of suppliers. They split their business among several brands. True, there are some customers who are 100 percent brand loyal, but they tend to be the exception rather than the rule. Thus, to use the labels "present" and "competitive" meaningfully, some distinction must be made between them. Generally, we use the share of requirements filled by the customer to differentiate between present and competitive types. For example, if customers give 60 percent or more of their business to our brand, they are labeled as present customers. Likewise, if they give 60 percent or more business to our competitors through purchases of their brands, we give them the label of competitive customer. Obviously, depending on the product category, these percentages may vary, but for most frequently used or purchased consumer products, we have found that these purchase classifications, based on a 60 percent threshold, work.

Determining Share of Requirements or Purchase Dynamics

If we know enough or have sufficient data about customers and prospects so that we are able to classify them in terms of their purchasing of our brand versus those of competitors, we should be able to determine their share of requirements. That is, we should know what share of their total purchases in a category goes to us and what share goes to our competitors. This is the next phase in the process.

Determining Share of Requirements

As shown in Exhibit 4-3, our first goal is to determine or define our brand's share of the total category usage by the customer or group of customers. The optimal way for this to be done is on an individual or household basis. Often, however, when specific household or individual data are not available, we can use estimates or extrapolations to provide this value. The intent is to somehow determine the number of units or dollar value of our brand that the customer is presently buying and the share that it comprises of their total purchases in the category.

One question in determining product purchases is, of course, the length of time over which the measurement is to be made. This will depend on the product or service and its use or consumption by buyers. For example, knowing the present product purchase for an automobile in a three-month time frame is not nearly as important to an IBC planner working in that category as it is for a planner working in the soft drink market. Thus, some relevant time frame must be established for the determination of the product purchase category. Commonly, this is related to a purchase or usage cycle.

What to Measure

The second question concerning purchase dynamics is determining what is to be counted as a purchase and how that might be defined. Historically, marketers have used units or volume as measures of product purchase. However, our experience has been that while these measures are useful, they are not terribly helpful in understanding the actual value of a customer or group of customers to the organization. For example, heavy users in a product category often are very sophisticated buyers. That is, they expect and accept promotional offers. They are willing to negotiate. They are willing to stockpile products at low cost and warehouse them in their home or business to use as needed. In other words, just because a customer buys a large amount of the product or uses the service on a regular basis does not mean he or she is profitable or has great value to the marketer. Sheer volume of use does not necessarily mean profitability for the marketing organization.

For that reason, we have found it best to use income flows—the dollar amount the individual or group pays for the brand product or service. By using income flows, we are not as concerned about unit volume as we are about income to the organization. Thus, an occasional purchaser who buys at full price might be more financially valuable than a customer who generates twice as much volume but buys only at reduced or sale prices, uses coupons or discounts with every purchase, and demands substantial amounts of service from the marketing organization.

We should also point out that these income flows must be calculated or estimated in terms of actual dollar returns to the brand organization. If the consumer is buying through retail channels or through other types of distribution systems, those margins or costs must be discounted from the actual price the consumer or customer pays. Our analysis must be at the "net to the marketer" level. In other words, it should determine the amount of income flow that actually comes back to the marketing organization that could then be invested in new or additional future IBC programs. This "net to the marketer" aspect of the analysis is critical, as we will emphasize in future sections.

Determining Relevant Customer Value

In terms of income flows, "net to the marketer" has several ramifications. It means that the brand marketer actually is working with true customer worth or value, not some surrogate. Since we are investing net organizational dollars to develop and implement an IBC program, we must work at this level to be able to determine or define our marketplace success. Commonly, many marketing and communication managers estimate or calculate only the gross or total returns to the brand from their efforts. That is, they are interested only in growing the top line or gross income of the brand.

Sophisticated direct marketers have chosen to estimate the value of a customer or group of customers with a recency-frequency-monetary (or RFM) value analysis, as shown in Exhibit 4-6. We illustrate how this concept can be adapted for all marketers, because it defines the true value of customers and prospects, not just gross income flows. As shown, the direct marketer values a customer based on recency, that is, how recently a customer purchased. The idea here is that the more recent the purchase, the more valuable the relationship between the customer and the brand. The second element of the analysis is the frequency with which a customer purchases, that is, how often purchases are made during a given time period. Obviously, the more times a customer purchases, assuming all purchase levels have the same value, the more valuable is the customer. The third element of the RFM analysis is the monetary value of the purchase. Large purchasers generally are more valuable than customers making small purchases. Finally, when recency is measured against frequency and then evaluated against monetary value, a complete understanding of the customer can be determined. This same approach can be used for almost any type of customer in almost any product category. Of course, adaptations will have to be

Exhibit 4-6
RFM Analysis

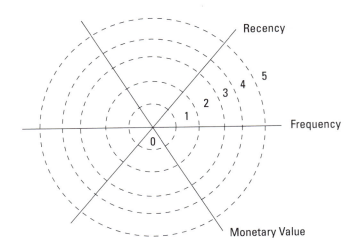

made for type of product or service being offered, but usually the RFM analysis will help give a fairly accurate representation of the top line value of a customer or group of customers.

Note, however, that the RFM calculation determines only the amount of income the brand organization has generated from that customer or customer group. As with any marketing activity, costs are always incurred in serving customers. For that reason, in order to determine the "net returns to the organization," one must deduct the costs of the customer management activities. Exhibit 4-7 illustrates what some of these costs might be.

Typically, there are three major costs in obtaining and serving customers. As shown in Exhibit 4-7, these are acquisition costs, migration/service costs, and retention costs. Acquisition costs, or the cost of initially obtaining a customer or customer group, might include various types of solicitation or distribution, such as discounts to wholesalers or retailers, advertising, credit checks, setting up the customer account if ongoing purchases are to be made, and bad debt. Migration/service costs might include premiums and incentives to build customer sales or entice customers to continue purchasing. This category also could include, for example, customer service and technology support. Finally, retention costs are those to maintain a customer and prevent him or her from defecting to competitors. These might include frequent shopper programs, thank you notes, and information booklets.

Using this approach, we can then estimate the costs of serving customers by adding our acquisition costs, migration/service costs, and retention costs and determining the total for each customer or group of customers. When we subtract that cost

Exhibit 4-7

Valuation Analysis

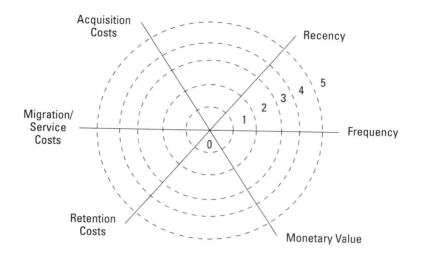

total from our income flow generated by the RFM analysis, we have a fair idea of what our net income flow from a customer or group of customers might be. This gives us at least some idea of our "net-to-the-marketer" income flow that can be used to develop new IBC programs.

By determining the current income flow from a customer or group of customers, we can then move to the next major step in the IBC process, that of setting behavioral marketing objectives. In that step, we start to develop specific plans to influence the behavior of various customers or groups of customers. As we described in some detail previously, we use a cascading approach. First we set objectives. Next, we develop strategies that are followed by message or incentive decisions. These then result in the actual brand communication programs to be executed in the marketplace. Knowing the value of customer or prospect groups is critical to this strategy decision. For example, it is obvious that the marketing and communication objectives developed for a group of present users of our product or service will likely be dramatically different from those we develop for a group of competitive users, and certainly different from those for a group of new or emerging customers. A simple example of that point is illustrated in Table 4-1.

Shown above is a decile ranking of customers for a major resort hotel for a one-year period. These are actual data that have been disguised for this text. (A decile ranking simply aggregates all customers into ten equal groups.) In this case, we have aggregated customers from highest dollar spending in the hotel to lowest. This is done to give us some idea of the value to the hotel for specific groups of customers based on their visits over the previous year.

Table 4-1 ▸ **Decile Ranking of Resort Hotel Customers**

% Rank	No. of Guests	Cume. No. of Guests	Total Revenue ($000s)	Cume. Revenue ($000s)	% of Total	Min. Spend	Average Spend
10%	1,942	1,942	$13,501	$13,501	57.5%	$2,322	$6,952
20	1,942	3,884	3,257	16,758	71.4	1,248	4,677
30	1,942	5,826	1,987	18,745	79.9	843	1,023
40	1,942	7,768	1,402	20,147	85.9	613	722
50	1,942	9,710	1,045	21,192	90.3	468	538
60	1,942	11,652	790	21,982	93.7	348	407
70	1,942	13,594	602	22,584	96.3	278	310
80	1,942	15,536	487	23,071	98.3	226	251
90	1,942	17,478	349	23,420	99.8	100	180
100	1,942	19,420	40	23,460	100.0	0	21

19,420 $23,460

30% of Customers = 80% of Total Revenue

This decile analysis is very revealing in terms of understanding various groups of customers and their importance to the hotel. It provides us with a better view of how we might develop marketing and communication strategies to impact the customers' future behavior. A decile analysis can be done using any number of variables such as, in this case, number of visits to the hotel, or number of nights stayed, or value of room spending. We chose to use total revenue since the IBC planner was interested in increasing total revenue for the hotel. That would, of course, be based on the total amount spent by customers over the period, not just by visit.

The decile analysis for the resort hotel illustrates several important points. A relatively small number of guests are terribly important to the success of the hotel. As can be seen, 10 percent of the guests in the measured year accounted for over 57 percent of the hotel's total revenue. Thirty percent of the guests accounted for nearly 80 percent of the total revenue generated by the resort hotel for the entire year. Thus, we see Pareto's famous 80/20 rule, or at least a version of it, at work here.[1] Pareto's rule is simply that a relatively small number of customers generally account for a disproportionate amount of the organization's business.

The minimum spend and the average spend provide views of the dramatically different value of individual customer decile groups. For example, at this resort, the top value group, the top 10 percent of guests during this year, averaged spending nearly $7,000 in total, while the lowest spending group of guests averaged only $21. The lowest-spending group brought practically no income to the hotel

---

[1]Garth Hallberg, *All Consumers Are Not Created Equal* (New York: Wiley, 1995), p. 27.

(apparently they were on passes or vouchers), while the minimum spend among the best guests was over $2,000.

From this simple decile analysis, it is clear that some groups are simply more valuable than others. In the case of the hotel, the top three decile groups are tremendously more important than the bottom three decile groups. Also, it is apparent that some of the decile groups have much more value opportunity and growth potential than others. And, it becomes clear there are some decile groups that simply don't deserve much marketing or brand communication investment or attention. Simply put, it is quite unlikely that some of the bottom deciles would ever return a sufficient amount of income to offset the cost of a marketing or communication program. Of course, other conclusions or inferences could be drawn from this simple decile analysis about the development of behavioral marketing objectives and the resulting IBC communication objectives and strategies. The point is clear, however. Not all customers are alike, and certainly, in this case, not all customer groups are equally valuable. This points out one of the major disadvantages of traditional marketing and communication planning, and that is developing programs for the "average customer." In this case, an "average customer" for the resort hotel simply doesn't exist, and developing marketing and communication programs to meet the expectations or needs and wants of the greatest number of customers may well be irrelevant to the most valuable customers who keep the resort hotel in business. From this analysis, it is clear that we need separate marketing and brand communication objectives for specific groups of customers. One shoe certainly will not fit all these customers or customer groups.

With this view of customer value, we can now start to develop our specific marketing and brand communication behavioral objectives.

Setting Behavioral Marketing Objectives

Once we know the value of a customer or customer group, we can start to determine what objective or objectives we might set for that person or group. For example, based on our review of the total revenue of the hotel above, we might determine that there is little way we can increase the spending of the top two decile groups. They are likely bringing us the maximum amount of revenue that we can expect. Thus, we might set our marketing objective for these decile groups simply as retention, that is, make sure they are satisfied and keep them coming back. That behavioral marketing objective decision—customer retention—would then lead us to our communication objective or objectives. We might, for example, determine that the best thing to do with the top group of customers is to thank them for their patronage through letters, personal visits, and other courtesies. Thus, our communication program would be built around this retention objective.

Alternatively, for decile three, the group that spent just over $1,000 on average, we might decide to try to increase their patronage of the hotel by encouraging them to make another visit. Or, we might try to increase their spending in the hotel while they are with us. This marketing objective could be implemented by a number of strategies, such as offering various types of incentives. For example, for this group we might offer a special weekend holiday package; we know they spend a great deal while they are at the hotel, and an additional visit would likely be profitable. Or, we might consider some type of offer for this group when they are next in the hotel, such as a special dinner or "two-for-one" golf green fees. In other words, we can have multiple behavioral marketing objectives for various groups of customers. Since we know who those customers are and their value, we can vary our marketing and communication programs to fit those various objectives.

Referring to our IBC planning process chart from Exhibit 4-3, the first part of which is reproduced here for reference as Exhibit 4-8, we can see that there are likely two behavioral marketing objectives for present customers, three behavioral objectives for competitive customers, and perhaps two or three behavioral objectives for emerging users. We should note, those objectives listed are not the total of what might be done and should not limit the IBC planner. These objectives are used only as examples. The creative IBC planner will doubtless develop other more relevant behavioral marketing objectives for his or her customers and prospects.

To illustrate the process, we briefly review the possible behavioral marketing objectives for each of our three customer groups below. We will use the resort hotel example as our base.

Present Customers

Since our data consist primarily of existing customers, that is, customers who have visited the hotel during the past year, we obviously know more about these customers and their behavior than about the other groups. As outlined above, there would appear to be two basic marketing strategies for present customers: to retain them, or to grow their value in the future. In our example above, we suggested a retention program for the top decile group and perhaps a growth strategy for the third decile group. Obviously, these decisions must be made based on more than the decile analysis that is shown here, but the concept should be clear.

There is a third strategy that might be used with these present customers, which is to migrate them to more profitable returns to the resort hotel, or, in other words, to move them up in value to the hotel, but not necessarily through additional stays or longer visits. Instead, we might do this by encouraging them to use more profitable facilities in the hotel. If, for example, after further analysis we find a group of customers in deciles three and four who always request the largest double room and then request a crib or roll-away bed for their children, we might suggest they move up to a junior suite or perhaps take adjoining rooms. This would provide more value to the customer and would also provide more income to the hotel. The same approach could be used if we were to determine that some group of guests continuously used the hotel swimming pool but didn't visit the spa. Since we know they like the water, we might encourage them to visit the spa and try the sauna or whirlpool facilities. More pleasure for the guest, more income for the hotel, and both groups win with this type of marketing and communication objective.

Exhibit 4-8

IBC Planning Process, Steps 1 and 2

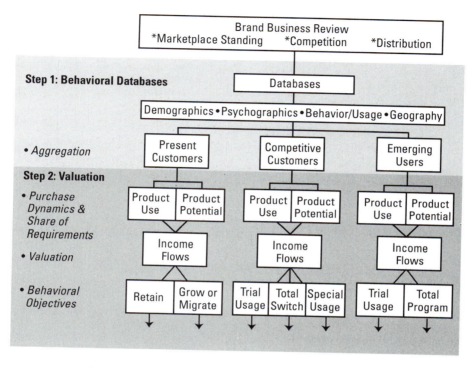

While these are just a few of the marketing strategies that can be developed from a simple decile analysis, they should give the IBC planner an idea of what is possible.

Competitive Customers

While strictly speaking, we do not have enough data in the simple decile analysis to determine who is a competitive customer, that information could likely be determined either by a guest survey or through appending data from other sources to the files of the individual customers whom, in the case of the resort hotel, we know by name.

For purposes of illustration, let's assume we have identified a fairly large number of customers in deciles four and five as being occasional visitors to our hotel, but who spend most of their holidays at competing resorts. We know from the decile analysis that they are customers we would like to retain and encourage to visit more frequently, since they all spend at least $1,000.

On the IBC planning chart, we show three potential marketing strategies for competitive customers: trial usage, total switch, and special usage. Each is illustrated below.

Trial usage generally is meant to persuade competitive customers to try the product or service for which the IBC plan is being developed in the belief that once they have tried the product or service, the customers will be satisfied and likely become regular customers. In the case of the resort hotel illustration above, this is likely not an appropriate marketing objective, however, since the guests we have in our database already have visited the facility. But it could be used if we had some new or interesting or innovative facility that these previous guests had not experienced. For example, if we had just completed a new set of cabanas around the pool, or just opened some new guest cottages around the golf course, this trial strategy might be appropriate.

The second strategy shown is *total switch*. This means that we would hope to convert the visitors who are customers of competitive resort hotels, winning them over from those properties to our facility. Depending on what we know about the guests, that could be feasible. For example, if we know that the guests enjoy golf, we might persuade them to play golf more regularly at our facility rather than the course at another resort that they visit. This might be done through any number of brand communication messages or incentives.

The third behavioral objective for competitive customers is *special usage*. By that, we mean that our objective might be to encourage competitive resort users to visit our hotel more frequently because of some special activity, event, or facility that we offer. For example, if the group of competitive guests we identify always spends the Memorial Day holiday visiting a resort, we might encourage them to make our hotel their regular Memorial Day retreat. Of course, there are multiple ways in which this behavioral objective might be achieved. We will discuss and illustrate some of them in the following sections and chapter.

Emerging Users

The final group shown in our partial IBC Planning Process chart in Exhibit 4-8 are those customers who are just coming into the category. In the case of our resort hotel, these would likely be young people or couples who have just become affluent enough to begin visiting resort hotels. Or, perhaps, the emerging users are retired couples, or those whose children have reached the age when a resort might appeal to the entire family. Alternatively, these could be people who have just taken up golf or tennis or swimming or another activity that the resort offers. As can be seen, these customer alternatives go far beyond traditional demographic and geographic analyses that are commonly used to classify customers and prospects. They are based on behaviors, that is, on how people act in the marketplace. That is why an IBC approach is so much more powerful in the marketplace than the traditional marketing approaches used in the past.

As shown, there are two alternatives that might be considered: trial usage and total brand program. The case of trial is self-explanatory, that is, we would simply like to persuade emerging users to visit the resort hotel and experience the facilities. The total program objective simply means we would like to immediately convert these emerging users to regular customers. As might be imagined, each of these behavioral objectives would require a different strategy. Getting people to visit a resort hotel one time is vastly different from convincing them to become regular guests. That, of course, is addressed in the marketing strategy and the brand communication objectives that follow in the next chapter. For the present, however, it should be clear that different behavioral objectives require different marketing strategies and different brand communication objectives.

Of course, these examples of behavioral strategies are tied very specifically to the resort hotel illustration we used. For other types of products or services, these might change dramatically. The appropriateness of a strategy depends upon the product or service, the customers or prospects who are to be communicated with, the goals and objectives of the marketing organization, and so on. From the resort hotel example, however, the reader should have a reasonably clear understanding of how to set behavioral objectives in an IBC approach.

Summing Up Behavioral Marketing Objectives

Although not explicitly stated, behavioral objectives in an IBC approach have to do mostly with growing or maintaining income flows from customers. As shown in the resort hotel example previously, in each case the goal of the IBC communication planner was either to increase or to maintain the flow of income from a customer or customer group. Again, this differentiates IBC planning from traditional marketing or communication planning. IBC planners focus on the financial returns that the organization would receive as a result of the marketing and brand communication program or programs. By determining the customer's financial value, planners know how much is appropriate to invest in a brand communication program tailored to a given group of customers. This approach also gives us a clear path for measuring the success of a program and for determining how we might improve it in the future.

Understanding Incremental Value or Returns

The concept of incremental value or incremental income flows is simple. All existing brands currently have some level of business activity. That is, they are generating some level of income flow from customers, or else they wouldn't exist in the marketplace. The incremental income flow idea is that brand communication should provide additional (incremental) returns to the firm beyond those that are currently being generated. Exhibit 4-9 illustrates this concept.

The x axis in the exhibit is the time the particular measurement is being made. On the y axis, we show the volume that has resulted from sales to consumers during that time period. This measure can be in whatever units the organization is using as the basis for measuring its success, such as dollars or market share points, for example. As shown, line A is the current value of customer income flows to the organization. This is what current customers are returning to the organization as a result of its present marketing and communication efforts. While we have shown this as a flat line, in truth these flows of income vary with time period, efforts on the part of the

Exhibit 4-9
The Concept of Incremental Value

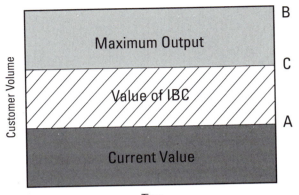

company, or as a result of competitive activities. For the sake of illustration, we have shown a level line representing the average income flow from the customers.

Line *B* at the top of the chart is the maximum output possible by the organization, or the maximum income flow from customers that the organization could expect. If the organization is in manufacturing, for example, maximum output would represent the capacity of the various plants available. If it is a service business, maximum output represents the total amount of services the people employed could provide. Thus, Line *B* actually represents the total capacity of the company or the total income flows it could expect from customers and prospects if it achieved all its goals.

Line *C* represents the new volume or customer income flow that might be achieved as a result of an investment in a brand communication program. The difference between current income flow and what might be achieved with an investment in a brand communication program is thus incremental value to the brand and the organization. In Exhibit 4-9, this incremental value is represented by the crosshatched area. Without the brand communication program that is being contemplated, income flows equal to Line *A* would be expected from customers and prospects. With the application of the planned brand communication program, however, income flows equal to Line *C* would be achieved. The difference between Lines *A* and *C* represents the "incremental income flow" to the company—the measure of success for the brand communication program.

Given this picture, it is easy to see how the brand communication program might be valued. If the cost of the brand communication program is less than the incremental income flow to the organization, we would generally call this a successful investment of the organization's resources. If, however, the firm did not get back as much as it invested in the brand communication program, then the program might be considered a failure. In reality there are many situations in which the immediate income flow return does not offset the initial cost of the program, but this serves to demonstrate the concept. The company invests money in a brand communication program to achieve additional returns. An IBC program should return more than it costs if the firm is to grow and prosper. This basic view of incremental returns must strongly influence the development and evaluation of any brand communication program.

In summary, there are generally three basic behavioral objectives for a brand communication program among present customers:

- retain income flows from a customer or group of customers;

- grow or increase the flow of income from a customer or group of customers;

- migrate a customer or group of customers through the product or service portfolio that the brand organization offers.

For competitive customers, our goals might be to:

- generate trial usage;

- try to achieve a total switch to our product or service;

- develop some type of special use or reason to buy.

For emerging customers, goals might be to:

- generate trial usage;

- encourage new customers to purchase our total program.

As can be seen, our goal with all customers and prospects is never to lose a customer but to gain their initial trial and then move or migrate him or her from one product or service to another as needs or wants change.

From this view of behavioral objectives, we can move on to the next steps in the process. Those flow from this first section and are described in detail in Chapter 5.

Summary

This chapter reviews the initial stages of the IBC process, which is based on the concept of managing customer income flows. The IBC process begins with the brand business review, followed by analysis of the customer/prospect database. (For organizations without a database, any available information on current customers and likely prospects would be analyzed at this point.) A market or customer segmentation/aggregation scheme is then developed for targeting purposes. The value of each chosen customer group is determined in terms of dollar value to the marketing organization, including an analysis of share of requirements based on income flows. This makes it possible to set behavioral marketing objectives, which will vary widely depending on whether present customers, competitive customers, or emerging users are being targeted.

5

Converting Customer Knowledge into IBC Programs:

The IBC Strategy

We are now ready to move on to setting brand communication objectives and strategies. Once these are set, we will then need to develop specific communication programs and activities to achieve those objectives.

Cascading Objectives and Strategies, Incremental Value, and Closed-Loop Systems

In the IBC approach to marketing communication we use a formalized method of developing brand communication programs. That is, each step is the basis for the next step until we have a complete program. This is not to say that creativity in the communication arena is not essential, but the creativity is focused on achieving specific business objectives. We start with the objectives, which lead to strategies. Strategies lead to message or incentive alternatives. Message or incentive decisions lead to specific programs and activities that will be carried out in the marketplace, directed at selected groups of customers or prospects. Thus, the process of developing the IBC program creates a cascade: from objectives flow strategies, which provide the impetus for decisions on messages or incentives, which then lead to specific tactical executions in the marketplace. Throughout the process of brand communication development, the focus remains fixed on the customer.

Understanding Objectives, Strategies, Programs, and Tactics

Objectives are the broad goals the organization wants to achieve. But objectives must always be developed within the context of customer value. If there is no value for the customer in the organization's achieving its objectives, then, over the long term, the program will fail. Value for the customer must always be kept in mind as brand communication programs are developed.

Organizational objectives generally relate to some type of financial goal, the "scorecard" that businesses use to determine their success.[1] For some organizations, their objective for a brand communication program might be to increase or maintain total revenue from the brand—that is, to increase top-line sales. Alternatively, other organizations might have an objective to increase market share, or, in other words, the share of volume that the brand enjoys in its category. Often, organizations seek to improve their bottom line, or the net returns to the company. This last goal is a common objective because increased net returns would allow managers to add production capacity, hire additional employees, or reward shareholders with higher dividends. Thus, a company with a bottom-line objective is not so much interested in growing sales as it is in growing profits.

Whatever the objective of the organization for which the brand communication program is being developed, it is critical for the planner to understand that objective. Until the broad objectives of the organization are known, the brand communication planner simply can't develop effective programs. While all IBC programs are generally designed to focus on customer income flows, those must be balanced against the goals of the organization.

We should also note, objectives of organizations change over time, depending on the focus of the management. Thus, while past brand communication programs may have tried to grow top-line sales or total sales volume, changes in the market, changes in the goals of management, or even changes in the general direction the organization wants to take in the future all could affect the objectives of the brand communication program currently being planned. It is therefore vital that the brand communication planner know what the IBC program is to achieve to be able to develop an effective program.

Objectives are achieved using strategies. In fact, strategies flow from objectives. For example, if the goal of the organization is to increase total sales volume or increase income flows from customers, that can be done by acquiring new customers, persuading present customers to buy more of the same product, developing add-on sales of other products or versions of the brand to existing customers, and so on. Strategies are broad views of how the objectives might be achieved or the alternatives the organization might follow. Hence, when we speak of IBC strategies, they will generally focus on customers and customer income flows or prospective customers and their potential income flows.

---

[1]Don E. Schultz, Stanley I. Tannenbaum, and Robert F. Lauterborn, *Integrated Marketing Communications: Putting It Together and Making It Work* (Lincolnwood, Ill.: NTC/Contemporary Publishing, 1993).

Messages or Incentives?

The decision of whether to develop messages or incentives or both (discussed in Chapter 3) provides the basis for the actual marketplace communication programs to be developed and executed. For example, if the decision is made to use a message approach with present customers, there are many ways to execute and deliver those messages. We could deliver a message through something in or on the product package, through traditional media forms such as television commercials or print ads, or through nonpaid media using public relations or publicity programs. Likewise, there are many ways to deliver an incentive: through a frequent shopper program, a cents-off coupon in the store, or even by giving away a baseball cap with each unit purchased. Regardless of whether the choice is message or incentive, however, the IBC planner must know and understand the organization's objectives, pinpoint which customers or prospects are involved, determine the influence on income flows the program is to have, and then—and only then—develop effective communication programs to achieve those goals.

Note that in the IBC approach, we start with the broad objectives of the organization and match those against the customer base or potential customer base for the brand. This helps us define strategies that could be executed against the various customers or prospects. It is only toward the end of the planning process that we start to develop specific, tactical, functionally oriented communication programs. IBC is more about objectives and strategies than it is about specific communication tactics. Our belief is that if we know the customers and prospects well enough, we will be able to develop communication programs that will influence their behaviors. Thus, in the IBC approach, we attempt to be "functionally neutral." In other words, we try to select or develop the most appropriate communication program—not simply start with an advertising idea or a PR approach. In doing so, we avoid the historical baggage of functional activities such as advertising or direct marketing or public relations and all the restrictions and conflicts they involve.

Developing an IBC Program

One of the most important concepts in IBC, as we discussed in Chapter 4, is the goal of determining the financial value to the organization of an investment in brand communication. This financial valuation is what differentiates IBC from other forms of functional marketing communication programs. We seek to manage and measure the financial impact of our communication programs, not just the attitudinal impact. This change is critical as we move into the twenty-first-century marketplace.

Historically, most advertising or communication planners have been interested primarily in determining the communication effects of their activities. That is, they have focused on whether and when attitudes, feelings, or opinions of customers and prospects changed as a result of an advertising or communication program. This focus happened because in the early 1960s most advertising and communication managers moved away from any type of financial value for communication.[2] Since that time they have studiously avoided being held financially accountable for their communication investments, other than for attitudinal returns. Later in this section we will explain why this occurred and the impact it has had on how organizations value marketing and communication.

IBC has a different focus, however. While we believe that consumer attitudes, feelings, and opinions are important, we maintain that they are not as financially valuable to the organization as are behaviors—what people actually do in the marketplace (what they buy, how they spend their money, where they shop, what effort they are willing to make to obtain the brand, and so on). Less significant, at least to the brand organization, is what consumers say and feel. As has been shown in numerous consumer behavior studies over the years, consumer actions speak much louder than words, especially when it comes to generating income flows. Since the organization spends money to develop and deliver brand communication messages and incentives, the return to the organization must be in financial terms as well. Money out for a brand communication program; money back to the firm as a result of that investment. It's as simple as that.

To illustrate how the IBC approach differs from traditional advertising or public relations or sales promotion planning, we first set the stage for how communication objectives have been set historically. We will use traditional advertising planning as the model.

Attitudes as Surrogates for Behaviors

Marketing organizations have almost always been interested primarily in sales and volume results. That's their scorecard, or how they determine whether they are succeeding in the marketplace. Certainly, rational managers of organizations would not invest in something they didn't believe would provide some sort of a return. Indeed, finite resources dictate that spending money must result in some return, or the company will simply run out of resources. Yet, how can the value of an advertising or public relations or sales promotion program be measured? That question continues to plague most marketing organizations.

This difficulty in measuring the results of advertising or public relations or sales promotion programs hasn't always been so challenging, however. In the not-too-distant past, measuring the impact or effect of advertising was a simple matter. The advertiser placed an ad in the local newspaper, or printed up circulars for distribution in the community, or plastered posters on the walls of buildings or fences. Messages were simple: "Buy my product," "Visit my store," or "Come to my circus." Obviously, if people bought or visited or came, the communication program had worked. If there was no response, the advertiser's money had been wasted. Dollars

---

[2]Don E. Schultz and Anders Gronstedt, "Marketing and Communication as Organizational Investments," *Marketing Management* (Fall 1997).

out for the ad; dollars back in increased sales. (Note: This is the basic concept behind incremental returns, as we discussed in Chapter 4.)

As we moved from the historical marketplace to the current marketplace, it became harder for an advertiser to determine what worked in the marketplace and what didn't. The marketplace held lots of messages, lots of consumers, and lots of competition, but few ways to tie specific results to specific advertising or public relations or other promotional programs. This problem was exacerbated by the advent of mass marketing, mass distribution, and mass media. By the 1950s, mass marketing and mass communication were the rule rather than the exception for many large advertisers.

In 1961, two men attempted to explain the impact and effect of advertising, primarily television advertising, in light of all the marketplace changes. One an academic and the other a market research executive, Lavidge and Steiner developed the model of a hierarchy of effects to explain how advertising worked in the marketplace. The hierarchy attempted to illustrate how consumers might respond to advertising exposures seen through mass media. This attempt to explain advertising effects was particularly important in a mass market in which mass media and mass advertising were being used, and where direct results, in terms of customer purchases or income flows, were most difficult to relate. A stylized version of the Lavidge and Steiner hierarchy appears in Exhibit 5-1.

As can be seen, Lavidge and Steiner hypothesized that exposure to advertising messages, delivered through the media, moved a consumer or group of consumers

Exhibit 5-1

Lavidge and Steiner Hierarchy of Effects: The Traditional Advertising-Based View of Communications

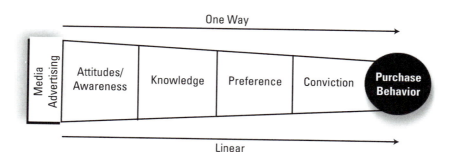

Acting on Consumers

along an attitudinal continuum. The continuum they hypothesized was that consumers went from basic unawareness through a series of steps to, finally, product purchase. The premise was that the continuum stretched from simply knowing the product or service existed to the actual purchase behavior. That is, consumers moved through a series of measured steps in this hierarchy, and thus their progress on the way to purchase could be measured and movement determined.

First, consumers become aware of the product or service. They then learn something about it. From their knowledge, they develop a positive attitude toward or preference for the product or service among other alternatives. The following step is conviction—a decision to purchase that specific product or brand when the occasion or opportunity arises. The final step in the hierarchy is actually purchasing the product.

As shown, it is further assumed that prospects (the hierarchy of effects model seems to ignore present customers, although these provide most of the income for existing brands) move through this process at some type of measurable pace as a result of exposures to advertising or other forms of marketing communication. In the hypothesis, it is assumed that the hierarchy of effects is a linear, one-way process. That is, the prospect is always gaining more information or being more effectively persuaded based on the level or volume of advertising or communication. There is no turning back. There is no deviation. Always forward, always more likely to buy, and always as a result of advertising or marketing communication. Those are the basic premises of the hierarchy of effects model.

This approach to explaining how advertising and, thus, marketing communication works was developed in 1961 and has been widely accepted around the world. This is in spite of the fact that many researchers[3] have been unable to find evidence of this hypothesis or even to demonstrate that this is the sequence or process that consumers use in the real world. Nonetheless, the hierarchy of effects model has become the basis for almost all forms of advertising media planning and measurement in the world today. The value of advertising and marketing communication, it is widely believed, is to move prospects along the hierarchy of effects continuum.

Also in 1961, the Association of National Advertisers (ANA) published a book by Russell Colley titled *Defining Advertising Goals for Measured Advertising Results* (DAGMAR). That methodology was based on the hierarchy of effects and hypothesized many of the same approaches and results as proposed by Lavidge and Steiner. Today, the DAGMAR process for measuring advertising and other mass communication marketing approaches is widely used and advocated by marketing researchers, marketing organizations, and their agencies. Old concepts are difficult to change. Sidebars further explain and illustrate the hierarchy of effects model and the DAGMAR approach.

The basic premise of the hierarchy of effects model is that education leads to attitudes that lead directly to behaviors. That is, if the marketer can inform customers or prospects about product features and benefits, that will change those customers' attitudes or opinions or feelings to ones more favorable to the product or service.

---

[3]Larry Light, *The Trustmarketer's Road to Enduring Profitable Growth* (Stamford, Conn.: Coalition for Brand Equity, 1993), pp. 19–21.

A Model for Predictive Measurements of Advertising Effectiveness

Lavidge and Steiner's Hierarchy of Effects Model

Lavidge and Steiner hypothesized a basic model that was intended to provide one approach to the measurement of advertising effects. Their premise: Advertising is not always and should not always be measured by sales results. Advertising has some immediate effects and more long-term effects. Consumers don't turn into "convinced purchasers" from "disinterested individuals" in a single leap.

Lavidge and Steiner proposed that consumers progress along a series of mental steps that ultimately lead them to purchase the product. Advertising is a force that moves consumers up the steps. The seven steps are as follows.

1. At the foot of the steps stand potential purchasers who are completely unaware of the existence of the product or service in question.

2. Closer to purchasing, but still a long way from the cash register, are those who are merely aware of the product's existence.

3. Up a step are prospects who know what the product has to offer.

4. Still closer to purchasing are those who have favorable attitudes toward the product.

5. Those whose favorable attitudes have developed to the point of preference over all other possibilities are up still another step.

6. Even closer to purchasing are consumers who couple preference with a desire to buy and the conviction that purchase would be wise.

7. Finally, of course, is the step that translates this attitude into actual purchase.

Obviously, all potential purchasers may not move through all the steps in similar time frames. The hypothesis: The greater the psychological and/or economic commitment involved in the purchase of a particular product, the longer it will take to entice consumers to move up these steps, and the more important the individual steps will be.

Advertising helps to create awareness and knowledge, develop liking and favorable attitudes or preferences, and, finally, produce the action of purchasing. Advertising research can determine which steps are most important, how many people are at each step at any given time, and which people on which steps are important to reach. Over time, measurement can be done on how long it takes for consumers to move between steps and how many advertising exposures are needed to expedite the process.

These measures provide a basis for global attitudinal measurements and for specific image measurements, as well as a methodology for correlating the two.

Source: Robert J. Lavidge and Gary A. Steiner, "A Model for Predictive Measurement of Advertising Effectiveness," *Journal of Marketing*, vol. 25 (October 1961).

Chapter 5

Defining Advertising Goals for Measured Advertising Results (DAGMAR)

Defining Advertising Goals for Measured Advertising Results is an outgrowth of a study initiated by the Association of National Advertisers, Inc., in the spring of 1959 to investigate the needs and questions regarding advertising that were considered to be most pressing to its membership and others in the general management of leading companies. The book is devoted to a course of action to assist further in building the effectiveness of advertising and in measuring advertising results.

The first step in advertising management is to define the objectives. The final step is to measure the achievement of those objectives. The information needed to define advertising goals includes: merchandise (What are all the important benefits of the products and services we have to sell?), markets (Who are the people we want to reach?), motives (Where do they buy or fail to buy?), media measurements, and messages (What are the key ideas, information, and attitudes we want to convey in order to move prospects closer to the ultimate aim of a sale?).

Next, we need an assessment of who buys the product. Information could include past and current industry sales data, forecasts of industry sales, and competitive share of market estimates. Such data are vitally important to advertising planning.

Then we need to determine why they buy. Some critical areas of inquiry include buying habits and characteristics, and buying motives and influences. After this comes a determination of what the message is. This is the heart of the advertising and includes an answer to the question, "How do we best present our product in a manner that will make prospective customers favorably disposed toward buying it?" An examination of the type of media used is important in this analysis.

Next we need a buying attitude benchmark. If we first know where consumers are, we can better judge what to do and how to do it.

Measured advertising results refer to the systematic evaluation of the degree to which the advertising succeeded in accomplishing predetermined advertising goals. Categories of evaluation can include audience research, media research, and copy research. To measure results we must determine the stage of commercial communication that the advertising has achieved. The five stages are unawareness, awareness, comprehension, conviction, and action.

We must then measure the penetration of the key advertising message. This involves an evaluation of not only the message but also the media used, the benchmark against which it is measured, a postadvertising survey, and an economic evaluation of the advertising.

A good question to ask at this point is, "Can the impact be measured?" If the answer is no, chances are the communication objective has not been clarified. If the answer is yes, then advertising performance needs to be tracked. Companies with well-organized, long-range advertising research operations continually conduct studies of share-of-mind, message penetration, and product usage. Using independent consumer cross sections (panels) and other research techniques, "trend lines" can be established to show changes in consumer knowledge and other measures.

It is important to remember during this process, however, that measurement is not an end in itself. It is only a means to an end, which in this case is more productive, more profitable advertising.

Source: Russell H. Colley, *Defining Advertising Goals for Measured Advertising Results*, (New York: Association of National Advertisers, Inc., 1961).

Then, sales and income flows will likely follow. Unfortunately, that premise has been difficult to prove either through research or in the marketplace. Indeed, this construct is being increasingly challenged by current research, based on actual consumer behavior in the marketplace.[4]

It is important to acknowledge that when the hierarchy of effects and DAGMAR approaches were developed, there was little computer technology available. It was difficult, if not impossible, for marketers to track consumer behavior in the marketplace. Since they couldn't actually measure the behavioral impact and effect of their marketing and communication efforts, managers accepted as surrogates for actual marketplace measurement the hierarchy of effects model and the premise that attitudes lead to behaviors. Today, with the increase in technology and the ability to capture, store, manage, and manipulate vast amounts of data, including actual consumer purchase behaviors, we can move to more relevant measures of how all forms of brand communication work in the marketplace. In the case of IBC, customer income flows are the measures of communication effectiveness.

More Relevant Communication Measures: Behaviors and Income Flows

As should be clear, the IBC approach is to relate, or at least to correlate, the firm's investments in marketing and communication with the actual financial returns the organization receives as a result of those investments. We call these returns "income flows." They are incremental dollar returns to the marketing organization as a result of the investments made in brand communication programs. We use income flows because they are the most direct link between consumer expenditures and returns to the firm. Additionally, income flows are clear, concise, and easily related to brand communication investments. We discuss the use of income flows in the next section.

Income Flows as Values

There is little question that consumers use and value brands. How else can we explain a consumer's willingness to purchase logo-laden clothing and to wear it conspicuously on all sorts of occasions, thus identifying the person with the brand and, in essence, becoming a walking billboard for the brand? For years, researchers have been trying to understand how consumers value brands, what benefit they get

---

[4]Schultz and Gronstedt, "Marketing and Communication as Organizational Investments."

from them, why they are so important to certain groups, and so on. The under-standing of brand value is most complex. Indeed, it is a separate subject unto itself and would require volumes to properly discuss.[5],[6]

So, how can the brand communication planner determine how individual customers and consumer groups value the brands they buy and use? Quite simply, it can be done through the measurement of income flows. Customers vote on and define brand value with their wallets. When a consumer buys a brand, he or she defines the value he or she puts on the brand. Without fancy calculations or complex research, we have a simple, but valid measure of brand value: the brand is worth exactly what the customer is willing to pay for it. And, since we can now commonly measure what brand consumers buy over time and how much they are willing to invest in that brand, we have a running record of how brand value for various groups of consumers changes over time. By using this income flow approach, the brand planner doesn't have to explain why or how the consumer defined the brand value, for, in many cases, even the consumer doesn't know or can't articulate why he or she preferred one brand to other alternatives. Thus, we take the customer's or consumer's purchase behavior as the relevant measure.

The use of income flows as the basic IBC planning and measurement tool in the process raises two questions: What about attitudinal measures and their value in the IBC approach? and How can we measure income flows among individual consumers and, more importantly for the brand communication planner, among relevant groups of customers and prospects?

What About Attitudinal Data?

For those who have studied or been exposed to traditional consumer behavior courses or research, the use of income flows to measure consumer behavior may sound like blasphemy. The common complaint is: "The developers of IBC are trashing attitudinal data" which has been the stock-in-trade of most advertising and communication managers. While we do challenge the present use of attitudinal data, our approach is not to simply dispose of attitudinal research of customers and prospects. Instead, it is to use attitudinal data in a different way. Rather than using attitudinal data to try to predict what a consumer might do, which has proven to be extremely difficult, we take advantage of the increasing availability of behavioral data in the form of purchase records of consumers from scanner panels, frequent shopper programs, and customer-contributed data, and we now know what consumers actually have done.[7] The challenge is to determine *why* consumers behaved as we observed. This is where attitudinal data are most helpful. If we know the behavior and can then identify the underlying attitudes that may have influenced that

[5]Kevin Lane Keller, *Strategic Brand Management: Building, Measuring and Managing Brand Equity* (Upper Saddle River, N.J.: Prentice-Hall, 1998).

[6]David A. Aaker, *Building Strong Brands* (New York: Free Press, 1996).

[7]Don E. Schultz, "Maybe They're Both Right or Maybe They're Both Wrong: Determining How Brand Communication Works in the Short- and Long-Terms" (paper presented at the Advertising Effectiveness Research Forum, London, March 17, 1998).

behavior, we should have the most powerful marketing and communication process of all—behavioral explanation. An example will help illustrate the concept.

Patty Cox, a sixty-three-year-old widowed retiree, recently needed to buy a new clothes dryer. She knew that she wanted to buy a particular brand, but was not sure from which retailer she would buy. After checking the Yellow Pages for a list of retailers selling her desired brand, she immediately eliminated one of the retailers from consideration, checked prices at three others located near her home, and made her purchase at the store with the best price of the three. When she reported to her daughter what she had done, she was asked why she hadn't checked the price at the fourth store, which the daughter believed had competitive prices and a better delivery policy than the store at which Patty bought the dryer. Patty replied, "I would never buy anything there. I shopped there once and they wouldn't sell me an appliance that was on display, even though it was the only one they had left. And, they charge very high interest on their credit card purchases." Patty's daughter told her that those things were no longer true of the store, even if they had once been, but Patty was adamant. Her negative opinion of the store explained her behavior—she would not even consider shopping there.

With this new approach of using attitudes to explain behaviors, we next illustrate how we might measure consumers' behavior and convert that into an estimate of income flow to the organization.

Measuring Consumer Income Flows

Understanding and measuring income flows from consumers requires longitudinal data. That is, we need observed behaviors of consumers over a sufficiently long period of time so that we can understand what is a normally purchased brand, what is an occasional purchase, within what price range the consumer will buy the brand, through what types of locations the brand will be purchased, and so on. Often, the problem with understanding who is a customer and who is not has occurred because marketing organizations have tried to measure the impact of an advertising campaign or a sales promotion activity or a public relations event in a very short time frame. Thus, many marketers have mistaken a single purchase occasion for a brand commitment or an instance of a specific brand switch as brand loyalty or brand preference. Only by viewing consumer purchase behavior over some reasonable length of time can the marketing organization and the brand planner really identify who is a customer, who is a prospect, who is a brand-switcher, and so on. That generally comes from somehow measuring over time consumer purchase behavior that results in income flows. As we discussed in the previous chapter, this is most easily handled through a database. We can now illustrate the basic premise of the process—a closed-loop communication system.

Using Closed-Loop Systems

The basic difference between an IBC process and those of other marketing and communication planning approaches such as an advertising campaign, a sales

Exhibit 5-2

The Closed-Loop Process

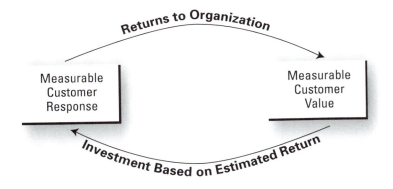

promotion event, or a public relations activity is the use of a closed-loop process. At the start of the loop, the planner knows the value of a customer or consumer group before the brand communication program is planned. Based on that valuation, a rational decision can be made as to how much should be invested in that customer or customer group in the form of a brand communication program. That should provide some estimate of what return might be expected. If that return can be estimated, then the planner should be able to identify what type of communication tactic should be employed to favorably influence the behavior of that customer or group of customers toward the brand. Then we can estimate how much we would be willing to invest to change or reinforce those behaviors. Finally, with the database, we can measure returns to the organization. This represents the completion, or closing, of the loop, as shown in Exhibit 5-2. Additionally, if we know these customers or consumers well enough so that we can measure their income flows, we should have a fairly good idea of how to influence them in a favorable manner with a brand communication program.

Building on your understanding of the three important concepts of objectives cascading to strategies, income flows, and closed-loop systems, we now move to the actual IBC strategy development process.

The IBC Strategy Development Process

The nine-step IBC strategy development process is shown in Exhibit 5-3. This process takes the closed-loop system discussed above and converts it into a series of questions to be answered by the brand communication planner. We will review each step.

Step One—Customer Definition

Knowing which particular group of customers or prospects we are trying to influence is the essential first step in the IBC process. That's because the knowledge base, perceptions, and, most important, the behavior of a current user of our product or service are very different from those of a person using one of our competitor's products, or those of a person not currently using any product or service in our category. We cannot begin to plan how to develop our IBC program until we have a clear idea of who we will be talking to, and until we have a sense of the brand volume or market size of that customer or group of customers.

As you might guess, we advocate developing separate strategies for each customer group of concern. That may mean the brand communication planner will be tasked with developing and implementing a variety of plans, but we believe that such an approach will generate much greater returns than a one-size-fits-all strategy that ignores important behavioral and attitudinal differences among current customers, competitive users, and prospects. However, we should note that the planner may well find similarities in brand perceptions across customers and customer groups, making it possible to aggregate groups for improved efficiency in message delivery through the mass media in areas such as advertising and public relations.

Further, while for purposes of explanation we deal here only with the broad distinctions of current, competitive, and nonusers, each of those groups could be (and, in many cases, should be) further subdivided based on behavioral differences. Some current customers are more valuable to us than others: loyal users versus occasional users, for example. The more precisely the IBC planner is able to describe the customer group of interest, the stronger the resulting communication strategy is likely to be.

We also need to look at *how* this group buys and uses our product (or, for groups who are not current users, how they use whatever product they are currently using to meet their need). Is it something they buy on impulse, or a purchase they plan for in advance? Is there a particular type of store (or catalog or Web site, etc.) where they prefer to buy the product, or is that a consideration? Is it a product they think about often, or something that comes to mind only when we remind them about it through some form of marketing communication? Understanding how the product is bought and used will help us think about the product as the consumer sees it.

After defining the consumer segment of interest in terms of their current behavior with regard to our product or service, we need to look at what else we know about this group. Here, we turn to more traditional ways of defining targets, including demographic and psychographic information. We need to know as much as possible about the customer or prospect so that we can develop a thorough understanding of who they are, how they live, and what kinds of interests they have. This information will help us develop messages and/or incentives that will be relevant to them, and to which they will be receptive. Demographics, psychographics, and so forth can help to enhance our understanding of the

Exhibit 5-3
IBC Strategy Development Process

Step One—Customer Definition

1. What is the customer group we want to communicate with? (current customers, competitive users, new/emerging users, etc.)

2. What does this group buy now? How do they buy and use the product(s)?

3. What do we know about the consumers in this group? (demographics, lifestyles, psychographics)

Step Two—Customer Behavior

1. What income flow does this group generate to the category? To our product?

2. What is our share of requirements from this customer group?

3. What is the current value of this customer group? What is their potential value?

4. How does this group perceive the products in the category?

5. What is the key group insight?

Step Three—Customer Strategy

1. What is our strategy for this group? Grow? Retain? Migrate? Capture? Trial?

2. Given this strategy, what is the competitive frame? Why?

3. What do those competitors now communicate to the consumer?

4. How are the competitors perceived by the consumer?

5. How is competition likely to retaliate against our strategy?

Step Four—Investment Strategy

1. Review the current value of this group to our brand.

2. How much are we willing to invest in brand-building activities against this group?

3. How much are we willing to invest in business-building activities against this group?

4. What is the time frame for this investment?

---

customer or customer group and aid us in explaining their current behavior with regard to our brand.

Step Two—Customer Behavior

Having defined the group we want to communicate with, the next step involves thinking about how the customers interact with our product (or with the category, in the case of people who are not current users of our product or if we are marketing a

Step Five—Communication Strategy

1. Do we need to deliver a message or an incentive (or both) to this group?

2. If a message, what is the strategy for this group (grow, retain, etc.)?

3. If an incentive, should it decrease the product's price or increase the product's value to the consumer?

Step Six—Delivery Strategy

1. Which marketing communication technique(s) should be used to deliver the message and/or incentive? Why?

2. Which message/incentive delivery systems are most relevant to this communication strategy?

3. Which message/incentive delivery systems are consumers in this group most receptive to?

Step Seven—Action Objectives

1. What action do we want the consumer to take as a result of the communication? (Trial? Increased usage? Request more information?)

2. What main point do we want the consumer to take away from the communication?

Step Eight—Desired Perceptual Effect

1. What will be the business-building effect of the communication? (That is, the impact within one year?)

2. What will be the brand-building effect of the communication? (The impact beyond one year?)

Step Nine—Evaluation

1. How will we assess the short-term impact of the communication?

2. How will we assess the long-term impact of the communication?

3. What type(s) of research will be needed in the future to further develop the communication strategy? Why?

new product). We start this step by looking at the income flow this customer group generates for the category as a whole and our brand in particular. That leads to an examination of this group's share of requirements related to our brand. In essence, this is a measure of the group's relative loyalty to our brand—do most of their purchases within the category come to us, or are they spending more of their money on competitive brands?

Another part of this step is customer valuation. How much is this group currently worth to us, either as individuals or aggregated across the group? How much could they be worth if we were able to increase their purchases of our product? Finally, how does the group's income contribution to our product compare to their contribution to the category as a whole? (Unless the target group purchases our product exclusively, their overall contribution to the category will be greater than their contribution to our brand.) Recall our detailed discussion of customer valuation in Chapter 4.

Having identified the value of this group, we then need to think about how the people in this group perceive the products in the category. In other words, why do the people hold their current value? Do they regard the brands in the category as all being interchangeable, that is, at parity? Or are there a couple of brands that are seen as being superior to the rest of the category? What product attributes are considered most important or desirable? How do the different brands compare on those attributes?

One of the most critical determinations at this stage is the identification of the key group insight. In her book *Hitting the Sweet Spot*, Lisa Fortini-Campbell describes the sweet spot as "the place in the consumer's mind where you make a connection between a consumer insight and a brand insight."[8] Finding the sweet spot opens the door to generating consumer response, because our communication will be addressing issues and ideas that we know are important to consumers. So, what's the key that motivates this particular group as far as our product or service is concerned? What do we need to talk about in order to be relevant to this group? We discuss issues related to how customers take in and process brand information in more detail in Chapter 6, and we look at some of the ways to determine consumers' attitudes toward our brand and those of our competitors in Chapter 7.

Step Three—Customer Strategy

Now that we know who our target is, what they think about the category in general and our brand in particular, and how much they are worth to us, we can turn to developing the strategy to influence the group. We start by determining what our basic goal should be. For current users, we might want to increase their usage by having them buy our brand more often. This would be a growth strategy. Or, we might just want to hold on to their business at their current level of spending, which would be a retention strategy. For a competitive user group, we might develop a migration strategy to move them to our brand. Note that whatever the strategic decision, it is a behavior-based strategy that we are developing. Steps One and Two dealt with identifying and understanding current behavior; Step Three brings us to either behavior reinforcement or modification.

The chosen strategy helps to determine the competitive frame. Which other brand or brands will be trying to communicate with this same consumer group? What messages and/or incentives are they currently offering this group? How does our target segment perceive these competitors? Are they seen as being at parity with us? Superior to our brand? Of lesser value than our brand? This analysis will help us un-

[8]Lisa Fortini-Campbell, *Hitting the Sweet Spot* (Chicago: Copy Workshop, 1991), p. 16.

derstand how our messages and/or incentives are likely to be perceived in comparison to those of the competitive brands.

Finally, we need to try to anticipate how our competitors will respond to our brand communication program. If we offer a price-cut incentive, are they likely to match it? How quickly? If we focus on a high-quality message, will they talk about their own quality, or perhaps try to denigrate our brand in their communication? Or, is it more likely that they will ignore our efforts and continue with their current communication programs? Obviously, competitors are likely to react more aggressively to our approach if we're trying to take their customers away than if we're focusing on our own users. By anticipating competitive reactions, we can plan ahead for how we will respond, rather than being forced into merely reacting.

Step Four—Investment Strategy

Each of the strategic possibilities that come out of Step Three has investment implications. And, each option likely has both a brand-building (or long-term) component and a business-building (or short-term) aspect. In Step Four, we first review the current value this customer group holds for us, because that helps us determine how much we are willing to invest in that customer group. That's an important distinction: we're investing in customers, in either maintaining or improving our relationship with them. Once we determine the size of the overall investment we're willing to make, we then allocate that investment to marketing communication efforts.

We state how much we are willing to invest in both types of communication activities, as well as identifying the relevant investment time frame. This is quite a departure from traditional marketing communication strategy approaches, which often treat budgeting as totally removed from communication strategy. But, since the amount of money available to spend usually determines what kinds of messages or incentives we are able to develop and deliver, we believe that investment considerations are a critical component of any strategy development process. We talk about investment strategies and budgeting in Chapter 8.

Step Five—Communication Strategy

We now come to the heart of the IBC strategy, the decision of what to say or offer in order to obtain the desired behavior. This is where we decide whether we need to provide a message to the group, or offer them an incentive, or some combination of the two. If we determine that a message is needed, that message must relate to the selected behavioral strategy. A growth-related message, for example, might focus on new uses for the brand, since this would encourage increased usage. A retention message might emphasize brand quality to reinforce current usage patterns.

If we decide that an incentive is needed, we need to determine whether the incentive should reduce the price of the product or add value. If our strategy is to attract competitive users, and we are higher priced than the competitive brand, a price reduction might be needed to get a competitive user to try our brand. On the other hand, if our brand is already comparably priced, a relevant premium offer might be the key to gaining trial from competitive users. This step of the IBC process sets the stage for the selection of marketing communication techniques and other tactical considerations.

Step Six—Delivery Strategy

In Step Six, we determine how to communicate the message and/or incentive to the target group. This is where we decide on what mix of marketing communication techniques should be used: advertising, public relations, sales promotion, direct marketing, personal selling, event marketing—whatever we think the target group will be most receptive to. We will look at each of the major forms of marketing communication in more detail in subsequent chapters, discussing their strengths as either business-building or brand-building approaches. Advertising is covered in Chapter 9, public relations and event marketing in Chapter 10, trade sales promotion in Chapter 11, consumer sales promotion in Chapter 12, and direct response and interactive advertising in Chapter 13.

After identifying the broad technique(s) to be used, we next look at the specific delivery systems that are most relevant to our strategy. For example, if our goal is retention, direct mail advertising to our current customers might be an effective approach. Or, perhaps we should use the product package as a delivery device. The other important aspect here is consumer receptivity: Does this group read direct mail? Are they likely to look closely at the product package? Or is there some better way to reach them? Do we know which magazines they read regularly? If so, perhaps we should try to get some publicity coverage in those publications. Message delivery considerations are discussed in detail in Chapter 14. The choice of message delivery systems will necessarily be related to customer value. For a customer group with comparatively low value to us, messages might be limited to package information, whereas we might be willing to invest in much more expensive direct marketing activities for a high-value customer group.

Step Seven—Action Objectives

What do we want the people in our target group to do once they've received our message and/or incentive? Step Seven begins to get into accountability issues. What specific action do we want the group to take? Should they purchase our brand the very next time they visit the store? (That would be a business-building approach.) Or, do we want them to *consider* purchasing our brand the next time they go to the store, or simply to change their attitude toward our brand? (That would be brand-building.) We need to think in terms of income flows here, determining the potential income flow associated with different types of action goals.

We also need to state what we want the consumer to take away from the communication. Is there a particular aspect of the brand he or she should remember? A specific new use? A comparative claim related to a competitive brand? The message(s) and/or incentive(s) that are developed from the IBC form will need to be evaluated against this main point, so it's important to agree on it in advance to guide the creative process.

Step Eight—Desired Perceptual Effect

If we think of Step Seven as concerning the effects of our communication on the target group, Step Eight looks at the effects of that communication on our brand. If all goes as planned, what will our sales or market share be one year from now? What kind of return will we be getting from investment against this customer group? What will the new income flow be? If we are working on a retention strategy, we would expect those measures to remain stable. If the strategy calls for growth, sales and income flow should be higher in a year.

We also need to consider the longer-term effect of the proposed communication program. Will it have an impact beyond the current planning period? While this sort of effect is more difficult to predict and to measure, it is important to try to estimate it. We know that certain types of marketing communication have a lasting impact on consumers, and therefore must be assessed in a longer time frame than one year. We discuss appropriate evaluation approaches in Chapter 15.

Step Nine—Evaluation

This final step spells out how the effects of our communication program will be assessed. What types of short-term measures will be used? For example, will we rely on sales measures alone, or will we also survey members of the target group? How will we measure income flows and determine whether those are acceptable? We also need to determine how we will assess long-term effects. As we discussed earlier, measuring attitudes can help us understand behavior. What kinds of research should we conduct (and when should we conduct it) to help us better understand this target group so that we can improve our future communication efforts?

An example of a completed IBC form is shown in the sidebar. This will help you see how to apply each of the IBC strategy development steps in practice.

The Role of the Account Planner

In a growing number of U.S. advertising agencies, the responsibility for either preparing the IBC strategy form or at least providing much of the needed information falls to the account planner. While account planning is an approach developed in the traditional advertising setting, it fits very nicely with the IBC approach we are advocating. That's because the account planner has the job of representing the consumer within the planning process.[9]

Account planning came to the United States from England, where it has been used since the late 1960s.[10] It resulted from growing marketplace complexity, and

[9] Account Planning Group, "What Is Account Planning?" (www.easynet.co.uk/apg/whatis.html).

[10] Ibid.

Example IBC Strategy for a Replaceable Computer Component

The brand in this example is a replacement part for a computer printer. Customers typically buy this type of product three or four times a year. The product is sold through retailers. There is limited brand loyalty in the category, and a great deal of price promotion and discounting goes on. There are four primary customer groups: loyal buyers, switchers, new users, and problem buyers. The IBC strategy shown in this example is for the loyal group.

Step One—Customer Definition

1. What is the customer group we want to communicate with? (current customers, competitive users, new/emerging users, etc.)

Loyal customers in either small offices or who work out of home offices. We want to retain their current business.

2. What does this group buy now? How do they buy and use the product(s)?

Loyals currently give us about 60 percent of their purchases in this category. They tend to be heavy users of their computer printer, and, as a result, they tend to buy the product more frequently than the average purchaser. They are very interested in consistent quality.

3. What do we know about the consumers in this group? (demographics, lifestyles, psychographics)

They are primarily college graduates who work full-time in professional, managerial, and sales positions. A significant portion of this group have a home office where they spend many of their working hours, explaining their heavy printer use. Most are between twenty-five and fifty-four years of age; there are slightly more men in the group than women. Most of our loyals don't have a great deal of leisure time; when they do have some time off, they like to travel. Many are big fans of spectator sports and follow their local pro, minor league, and college teams.

Step Two—Customer Behavior

1. What income flow does this group generate to the category? To our product?

Their income flow to the category is $1,009.80. At their current level of use, our brand gets 60 percent of their category business, giving us an income flow of $600.00.

2. What is our share of requirements from this customer group?

Our share of requirements from this group is 60 percent.

3. What is the current value of this customer group? What is their potential value?

The current value of this group is $600.00 in income flow and $151.47 in contribution margin. If we are able to retain their business given market condition estimates, we will retain the current income flow. As this group is vulnerable to competitive efforts, retention is an important goal.

4. How does this group perceive the products in the category?

Loyals view our brand as being slightly higher in quality than other products in the category, but they view several other brands as offering acceptable quality. They switch brands for special promotions and tend to purchase our brand when there is no promotional activity in the category.

5. What is the key group insight?

Consistency of quality is essential. Our product is an integral part of these people's work-related activity, and they count on it delivering as promised. That said, they're not averse to saving some money on another brand that offers acceptable quality.

Step Three—Customer Strategy

1. What is our strategy for this group? Grow? Retain? Migrate? Capture? Trial?

We want to retain these loyals at their current 60 percent share of requirements level.

2. Given this strategy, what is the competitive frame? Why?

The competitive frame is the other brands in the category that loyals consider to have acceptable quality. In particular, our competition is those brands that offer periodic price promotions, because it's those price deals that most often prompt our loyals to buy a brand other than ours.

3. What do those competitors now communicate to the consumer?

Decent quality and reliability, widespread availability (these brands are available from the same retailers who sell our product; like us, these brands also allow consumers to buy over the Web), and, during promotional periods, "bargain" prices.

4. How are the competitors perceived by the consumer?

They are seen as being of slightly lower quality than our brand, but as being acceptable. During nonpromotional periods, these brands are generally priced slightly lower than our brand, but the perceived higher quality of our brand is enough to offset the price difference. But, when these brands significantly undercut us during their promotional periods, the difference in price becomes enough to get our loyals to switch over.

5. How is competition likely to retaliate against our strategy?

The competition is not able to match our quality level; if they were, it would have happened by now. It's doubtful that competitors will increase the frequency of their price promotions, or the degree of price reduction.

Step Four—Investment Strategy

1. Review the current value of this group to our brand.

Current net contribution is $151.47; if we chose not to invest against this group, net contribution will drop to $121.18 because share of requirements would fall to 48 percent.

2. How much are we willing to invest in brand-building activities against this group?

This group bases its brand perceptions almost exclusively on product performance. Our brand-building investment against this group comes in the form of continued product research and development.

3. How much are we willing to invest in business-building activities against this group?

We are willing to invest $18.00 of the current net contribution in business-building activities against this group. This will drop their contribution to $133.47, but will retain their share of requirements at 60 percent.

4. What is the time frame for this investment?

The time frame is the 2001 calendar year.

Step Five—Communication Strategy

1. Do we need to deliver a message or an incentive (or both) to this group?

Both—a message that reinforces our highest-category quality positioning in order to keep our name in front of the loyals between purchasing occasions, and an incentive to provide a price reduction on our brand once during the year. (This incentive is a continuation of our current approach.)

2. If a message, what is the strategy for this group (grow, retain, etc.)?

Retention. We are not willing to increase our price promotion incentives over current levels, and it is therefore essential that we continue to communicate our superior quality in order to retain loyals at their current share of requirements.

3. If an incentive, should it decrease the product's price or increase the product's value to the consumer?

Our product is already seen as providing good value. A once-a-year price promotion is a means to reward the loyals for their business and to keep our product from being perceived as overpriced.

Step Six—Delivery Strategy

1. Which marketing communication technique(s) should be used to deliver the message and/or incentive? Why?

Our quality message is best delivered through advertising and our Web site, as these are the locations where loyals are accustomed to seeing our message. Since our goal is retention, consistency of marketing communication activities is a good way of reinforcing current behavior. The norm in the category is to deliver incentives in-store at the retailer, with featuring in the retailer's own advertisements. Again, this is where loyals expect to see price promotions.

2. Which message/incentive delivery systems are most relevant to this communication strategy?

In addition to our established Web site, print advertising in computer and general business magazines is most relevant to loyals. These are the places where they look for information on computer-related products. Most of our retailers also rely on print advertising, most often in the business section of newspapers.

3. Which message/incentive delivery systems are consumers in this group most receptive to?

When it comes to computer and home/office-related purchasing decisions, loyals are most receptive to print media. They look to computer and business publications to keep them up-to-date on developments in office technology; the products that advertise in such publications benefit from the association with authoritative editorial. On a local level, the business section of the local newspaper is seen as a useful adjunct to the national media.

Step Seven—Action Objectives

1. What action do we want the consumer to take as a result of the communication? (Trial? Increased usage? Request more information?)

We want loyals to continue to give us 60 percent of their share of requirements. We want them to maintain their current buying behavior.

2. What main point do we want the consumer to take away from the communication?

Our brand continues to yield the highest quality in the category, offering solid price/value.

Step Eight—Desired Perceptual Effect

1. What will be the business-building effect of the communication? (That is, the impact within one year?)

Loyals will continue to give our brand 60 percent of their share of requirements.

2. What will be the brand-building effect of the communication? (The impact beyond one year?)

Loyals will continue to perceive our brand as having the highest quality and therefore being their preferred brand in the category.

Step Nine—Evaluation

1. How will we assess the short-term impact of the communication?

Trend analysis of purchasing among loyals; are we still getting 60 percent of their category purchasing?

2. How will we assess the long-term impact of the communication?

We will continue to conduct attitudinal tracking surveys yearly to measure loyals' quality and value perceptions of our brand.

3. What type(s) of research will be needed in the future to further develop the communication strategy? Why?

Continue to develop and update our customer database to accurately track share of requirements and loyals' responsiveness to our brand's price promotion. Also, continued investment in product research and development to insure that we maintain our quality edge in the category.

from an increased emphasis on brand image. While traditional agency researchers were able to collect and analyze data on customers and prospects, they served primarily as consultants on strategy development. Account planners, on the other hand, use research to better understand consumers. The account planner is the "person who is charged single-mindedly with understanding the target audience and then representing it throughout the entire advertising development process."[11]

This emphasis on knowing and understanding the customer and prospect obviously fits with what we have said about the IBC process. One more reason that the account planning orientation matches our approach is that, unlike the traditional advertising researcher who often merely provides a measurement service, the account planner "has a line responsibility to insure the advertising is relevant and motivating to the consumer—ultimately accountable for its effectiveness."[12]

[11]Jane Newman, "What Is the Client Relationship to Account Planning?" (www.apgus.org/2_2a.html).

[12]Ibid.

Part 1

Summary

The IBC strategy development process provides a framework for planning brand communication efforts incorporating the concepts of cascading objectives and closed-loop systems. The IBC strategy development process is based on identifying current behavior and setting objectives based on behavioral goals. The process does not ignore the role of attitudes in decision making, but it places attitudinal considerations into a behavioral context. This is very much in keeping with the increased use of account planners in advertising agencies, because the planner's goal is to bring greater consumer awareness and understanding to the advertising development process. That requires an emphasis on behavior and the underlying factors that drive behavior.

Part 2

Understanding Consumers and Their Relationship to Brands

6

Consumer Behavior and Information Processing

The preceding chapters have set the groundwork for the IBC process for planning brand efforts. We now look at the key elements of the process in more detail. We begin by examining how consumers take in and use brand communication information. As we have already pointed out, understanding customers is the key to effective brand communication. We will look first at how customers behave in the marketplace, then attempt to explain this behavior through an examination of information processing.

Behavior in the Marketplace: Supermarket Shoppers

Supermarkets are fertile ground for researchers seeking to understand consumer behavior, and grocery stores are ideally suited for observational research. As discussed in previous chapters, the availability of scanner data has provided researchers with a wealth of information on who buys which products and under what conditions. These behavioral data offer us insights into how people buy. While the supermarket shopping experience is not directly comparable to all buying decisions (for one thing, most people tend to shop for groceries far more often than they make other purchases), it is probably the best example of behavior in the current marketplace. (Recall from the Introduction that in the current marketplace the retailer has the power, which is certainly the case concerning products sold through supermarkets.

Retailers own the scanner data, so they own the information marketers need to better understand customers.)

Shelf Shopping

In a landmark study, Peter R. Dickson and Alan G. Sawyer made a comprehensive examination of in-store behavior of supermarket shoppers, with particular emphasis on consumers' perceptions of product prices and how consumers use pricing information to make brand decisions.[1] The researchers stationed observers/interviewers in stores to watch consumers choose brands of coffee, toothpaste, margarine, and cold cereal. The observers recorded the amount of time shoppers spent in the product display area, how many different brands and sizes of products they picked up, and the brand they finally chose. Once consumers had selected a brand, they were stopped by the interviewer and asked to answer some questions. If they agreed, they were paid a dollar for their time; less than 1 percent refused.

In the interview, consumers were asked the price of the item they had just selected and whether that was the same price they normally paid. Next, each shopper was given a card showing three different shelf labels. They were asked which label was the right one for the brand they had chosen. The results of Dickson and Sawyer's study reveal some surprising aspects of consumer behavior. On average, shoppers spent less than twelve seconds at a product category display. Further, 85 percent picked up only the brand they selected for purchase, and 90 percent picked up only one size of that brand. In addition, 58 percent of the shoppers reported that they had looked at the price of the brand they chose, either out of habit or to help make their purchase decision. (In the group that didn't check the price, most said it was because "price was not that important.") Just under half of the shoppers did know the exact price of the product selected. Also, 21 percent refused to estimate a price, while 32 percent reported a wrong price. On average, the wrong price was off by 30 cents!

A total of 802 shoppers were interviewed across four different stores. Of those 802 shoppers, 570 (71 percent) chose a brand that was not being offered on some price promotion. Of those who did buy a promoted brand, most claimed that the price was lower than it actually was.

In discussing the implication of their findings, Dickson and Sawyer pointed out that supermarket shoppers seem to know much less about product prices than marketers might expect. The authors suggested a need to use something beyond a simple shelf label to get attention for price reductions. In fact, Dickson and Sawyer urged manufacturers and retailers to offer smaller price reductions and to use the money saved to promote those price reductions at the point of purchase.

Promotion Signals

Dickson and Sawyer's recommendations on the use of point-of-purchase reminders of price reductions are borne out by findings from another study on in-store behav-

---

[1]Peter R. Dickson and Alan G. Sawyer, "The Price Knowledge and Search of Supermarket Shoppers," *Journal of Marketing* 54 (July 1990): 42–53.

ior. The promotion signal study, conducted by J. Jeffrey Inman, Leigh McAlister, and Wayne D. Hoyer of the University of Texas at Austin, found that point-of-purchase material and in-store displays signal a special price to consumers.[2]

The Texas researchers grouped consumers on the basis of their "need for cognition," or their need to have information before making brand decisions. When presented with a promotion signal, such as a display or a special shelf tag, those consumers less interested in getting information were more likely to choose the signaled brand even without an actual price reduction. For this group of consumers, it was not the size of a price reduction that determined purchasing behavior so much as the presence of a promotion signal.

Brand Buying over Time

Researchers at Northwestern University examined eighteen months of supermarket scanner data to try to understand consumers' behavior in regard to purchasing spaghetti sauce. This study was funded by the Advertising Research Foundation (ARF), which provided scanner panel data gathered by Information Resources Inc. (IRI). In a scanner panel, households are recruited to take part in ongoing data gathering. Households that agree to participate are given their own identification card, which is scanned each time they shop at the supermarket. In addition, a metering device is attached to their television set to record when the TV is turned on and the channel to which it is tuned. The information in the database included purchasing data (brand[s] purchased, package size, price paid), in-store data (which brand[s] had special display space in the store and which brand[s] were featured in the store's own advertising), and television opportunities-to-see (OTS) data. The OTS data recorded when the households in the study had their television sets turned on and tuned to a channel that aired a spaghetti sauce ad. This is classified as OTS rather than viewing because we can't be certain that a household member was sitting in front of the television when the commercial aired.

The researchers looked at data on 223 households. They looked first at each household's purchasing behavior during a thirty-six-week base period. Each household was classified into one of six user groups: nonbuyers (households that bought no spaghetti sauce during the thirty-six weeks), one-time buyers, light buyers (households that bought spaghetti sauce twice during the thirty-six weeks), switchers (households that bought spaghetti sauce three or more times, but bought only one brand less than 75 percent of the time), Ragú loyals, or Prego loyals. The two loyal groups were made up of households that bought spaghetti sauce three or more times during the thirty-six-week period, and who bought the specific brand 75 percent or more of the time.

The researchers then tracked these same households' purchasing behavior across the next year. They broke the remaining fifty-two weeks of data into four thirteen-week quarters and looked to see if a household remained in the same user group during each quarter, or whether their spaghetti sauce usage changed. For example,

[2]J. Jeffrey Inman, Leigh McAlister, and Wayne D. Hoyer, "Promotion Signal: Proxy for a Price Cut?" *Journal of Consumer Research* 17 (June 1990): 74–81.

did the households classified as nonusers during the base period ever purchase spaghetti sauce? Did a Ragú-loyal household remain loyal to Ragú?

The results provide a great deal of information about consumer behavior and the role of mass media advertising. Brand loyalty was found to be very important in this category, because the loyal buyer group was very resistant to competitive advertising and promotion. That is, it took a great deal of effort by Prego to get a Ragú-loyal buyer to switch, and vice versa. In fact, the researchers found that the competitive brand would need to be advertised twice as often as the other brand in order to get a loyal buyer to make an exception and buy the advertised brand. In general, mass media advertising appeared to cancel out competitive activity where current buyers were concerned. And households originally classified as nonbuyers were more likely to buy spaghetti sauce during periods when there was a greater than usual amount of spaghetti sauce advertising being aired.

Based on their findings, the researchers concluded that mass media advertising helps retain brand-loyal customers; reminds light users of the product category, thus encouraging them to buy more often; influences brand switchers (switchers tended to trade off between brands with similar levels of advertising); brings new users into the category; and holds current users at a lower cost than sales promotion (loyal users will buy their preferred brand whether or not a price incentive is being offered).

Taken together, the three studies discussed here show that consumer decision making is not always the result of a systematic process. Indeed, many decisions are made quickly, without a great deal of time being devoted to comparing alternatives and evaluating brands on multiple criteria. Decisions can be affected by in-store activity, such as displays and promotion signals, and by advertising; however, much decision making appears to be by force of habit. To begin to understand this type of behavior, we need to look at how customers take in and process information on brands.

Consumer Decision Making

John A. Howard identified three types of buyer behavior,[3] as shown in Exhibit 6-1. His approach takes into account the fact that consumers move through decision making at different speeds, depending on the particular situations in which they find themselves.

Before looking at Howard's model in detail, however, we briefly review what happens at each stage of the decision-making process.

- **Problem Recognition** Whenever there is a difference between the consumer's actual situation and what he or she would like it to be, problem recognition occurs. It can happen under a variety of circumstances. It can be simple: "Oh, I'm just about out of toothpaste. I'd better get some more." Or it can be sparked by an advertising message: "That new brand of fat-free cookies sounds like it might be good. Maybe I'll buy some

[3]John A. Howard, *Consumer Behavior: Application of Theory* (New York: McGraw-Hill, 1977).

Exhibit 6-1
The Howard Model of Consumer Decision Making

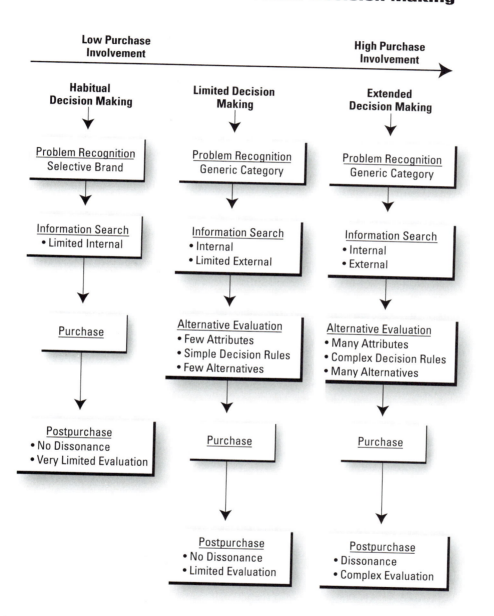

next time I'm at the store." Unfortunately, brand communicators often have a hard time predicting just when problem recognition will occur. One person may run out of toothpaste tomorrow, whereas his or her next-door neighbor might have enough to last for several more weeks. This predictive difficulty is the reason that many advertisers feel they have to advertise frequently, if not constantly. That way, the message will always be there when problem recognition starts the decision-making process.

- **Information Search** Once a problem has been identified, the question of how to solve that problem arises. At the information search stage, the consumer looks for input to help make the decision. That input comes in two forms: internal and external. Internal search involves a quick check of information stored in memory, which we'll discuss in detail later. External search involves looking outside. It may include asking friends and family for advice, checking the latest issues of *Consumer Reports*, looking through a specialized magazine, or simply paying more attention than usual to brand communication efforts.

- **Alternative Evaluation** The information search stage may identify several different means of solving the problem. During alternative evaluation, the possible solutions are compared. At this stage, consumers typically decide what sorts of trade-offs they're willing to make. For example, compact disc player A may have more features than player B, but it also costs $100 more. Am I willing to pay the extra price for more features, or is player B good enough for my needs? At this point in the process, brand communication may play an agenda-setting role. That is, advertisements for or publicity stories featuring the different brands may establish which features are most desirable. Alternative evaluation is guided by past experience with and knowledge of the product or category as well as input from others (family, friends, or salespeople, for example).

- **Purchase** After evaluating the alternatives, the consumer comes to a decision and takes the action that will solve the problem. Generally, that action is buying the brand that came out best among the alternatives. However, other factors can come into play. The store may be out of the preferred brand, so the next-most-preferred brand is bought instead. Or the consumer receives a coupon for a less-preferred brand, and the price difference is enough to move that less-preferred brand to most-preferred status.

- **Outcomes** The final stage of the decision-making process comes when the consumer evaluates the completed purchase. Was this the right decision? Does the brand live up to expectations? (Those expectations can be generated by past experience or created by brand communication—the risk of making a product sound too good to be true.) Whether the outcome is satisfaction or dissatisfaction, that information gets stored in memory to be used the next time a decision has to be made.

In the Howard model, the most complicated form of decision making is termed Extensive Problem Solving (EPS). Here, consumers are dealing with a product category and brands that are new to them, such as buying a home for the first time. Because of the newness of the situation, consumers want a great deal of information before making a decision, leading to a relatively lengthy decision-making process with considerable time spent at each step. In EPS, consumers not only have to evaluate the various brands against each other, but they must first determine the appropriate basis for that evaluation. Because consumers perceive more risks in such situations (including social risk, physical risk, and monetary risk), such decision making often is described as *high involvement*, since the consumer invests a great deal of time and effort in the decision.

In Limited Problem Solving (LPS), consumers are faced with a new brand in a familiar product category. An example might be buying a new CD player to replace a model that's no longer available. Here, consumers want some information on the new brand so that they can evaluate it against familiar brands. The decision-making process will be quicker than in EPS, but it will still involve some consideration of brand attributes. The consumer must determine how the new brand measures up to the brands that he or she has used in the past.

In Routinized Response Behavior (RRB), the consumer is familiar with both the product category and the brands within that category. Because of the level of familiarity, there is little information search and evaluation, and decision making occurs quickly. Often, the consumer simply repurchases the brand bought last time, as is the case with many package goods such as toothpaste, shampoo, and soft drinks.

Howard argues that in all three problem-solving processes, consumers rely on brand concepts they've formed in their minds. Those concepts are based on choice criteria, or standards for judging competing brands within a product category. An evoked set of brands emerges from the choice criteria. This evoked set is the two or three brands the consumer is willing to buy out of the overall group of brands. In other words, at this point, some brands already have been eliminated as possible choices because they don't meet the consumer's criteria. Howard's research suggests that most consumer evaluations are based on three or four criteria.

The three processes (EPS, LPS, and RRB) suggest very different strategies for brand communicators. For example, if our strategy is to hold on to current users, then our target market is likely to be using RRB processing. We need to reinforce their behavior, perhaps by rewarding them for continued purchasing through a sales promotion continuity program. We would also want to make sure that nothing happened to cause our customers to reevaluate their purchasing decision due, for example, to distribution problems and price increases.

What if we have a new brand trying to enter an established category? Remember, in LPS, consumers evaluate a new brand by comparing it to the brands with which they're familiar. We would need to provide sufficient information, through advertising or product publicity or on our Web site, to help consumers make those evaluations. Depending on the product's characteristics, we might also want to suggest some evaluative criteria.

In an EPS situation, much information is needed, and the emphasis needs to be on education. For example, Digital Music Express, a cable-delivered digital music system, faced the problem of convincing cable subscribers to add Digital Music Express to their monthly cable package. The system offers thirty channels of music programming, each channel specializing in a different musical genre. There are no commercial interruptions and no disc jockeys.

One of the first issues Digital Music Express had to address was competitor identification. There are no direct competitors: An individual cable system will carry only one digital music package. However, there are many indirect competitors, including radio, cable music networks such as VH-1, and home stereo systems, to name a few. As a new way to get access to and listen to music, Digital Music Express had to educate consumers both on what the system offered and how it compared to traditional alternatives. Clearly, this EPS situation is far more complex than the purchase reinforcement RRB situation discussed earlier.

The results of the in-store studies discussed at the beginning of this chapter seem to reflect primarily RRB-type decision making. Since little information search or alternative evaluation takes place in this low-involvement process, does that mean that there's no role for brand communication efforts to influence these types of quick decisions? Research by Richard E. Petty and John T. Cacioppo suggests otherwise.

The Elaboration Likelihood Model

Petty and Cacioppo's Elaboration Likelihood Model (ELM) is shown in Exhibit 6-2. This model outlines two routes to persuasion—a central route and a peripheral route.[4] The central route involves careful attention to brand communication messages and stringent evaluation of those messages. Here, the message receiver (the consumer), weighs carefully the claims being made in an advertisement, a salesperson's spiel, or any other form of brand communication and makes a conscious judgment on whether to believe the information contained in the message.

The peripheral route is unconscious message processing. Here, the receiver pays little attention to the arguments in the message itself, but may look to other cues such as the credibility or knowledge of the source of the message. So, under peripheral processing, information in a brand communication message may enter the consumer's memory without much effort or thought on the consumer's part. Recall the earlier description of the effectiveness of promotion signals. Those shoppers who assumed that a brand on display was being price promoted were using peripheral route processing.

Which route will be followed in a given situation? Petty and Cacioppo argue that there are two key predictors. In order for a message receiver to follow the central route, that receiver must (a) be motivated to process the message and (b) have the cognitive ability to process the message. The motivational aspect is related to the idea of involvement discussed earlier. While an advertiser might be concerned that a consumer following the central route would be more likely to disagree with or discount the advertising message, if attitude change does occur as the result of central processing, that change in attitude is likely to be a stronger influence on subsequent behavior than any attitude change resulting from peripheral route processing.

---

[4]R. E. Petty and J. T. Cacioppo, *Communication and Persuasion: Central and Peripheral Routes to Attitude Change* (New York: Springer Verlag, 1986).

Exhibit 6-2
Elaboration Likelihood Model (ELM)

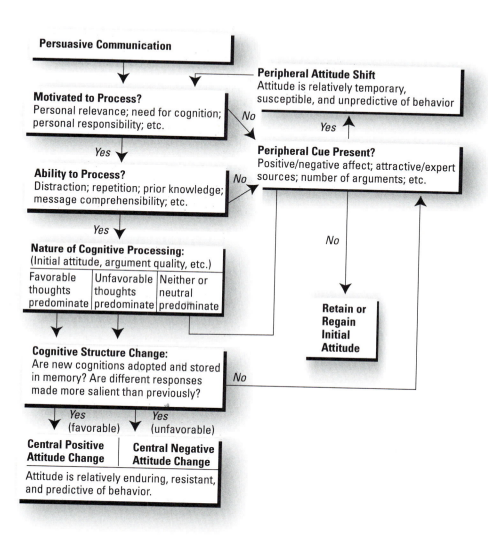

Source: R. E. Petty and J. T. Cacioppo, *Communication and Persuasion: Central and Peripheral Routes to Attitude Change* (New York: Springer Verlag, 1986).

Exhibit 6-3

Interpersonal Communication Model

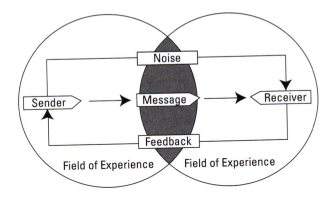

Source: Adapted from Wilbur Schramm and Donald Roberts, eds., *The Process and Effects of Mass Communication* (Urbana: University of Illinois Press, 1971).

Message Reception and Comprehension

We now examine the basic processes of communication. Exhibit 6-3 is a very basic communication model. Though greatly simplified, it represents the manner in which all forms of communication take place, from interpersonal discussion between friends to mass communication messages delivered by satellite. It is based on the idea of stimulus and response. In this model, there are five key elements: a sender, a receiver, a message, a feedback loop (the means through which the sender knows the receiver got the message), and noise. Noise is all those things that might prevent the sender from getting the message to the receiver or the receiver from obtaining the message from the sender. A critical part of the communication model is the overlap in the two *fields of experience*. This overlap is the basis for a relationship between the sender and the receiver. Their common experiences (*the shaded area*) are what really allow communication between the sender and receiver to occur. Without a common basis for understanding, it is very difficult for the sender and receiver to communicate. In brand communication research, one of the primary tasks is to understand what these common fields of experience are—to find out what the marketer and the consumer have in common, how the consumer thinks about the marketer's products or services, and how the marketer provides for the consumer's wants and needs.

How do consumers access and process advertising and other forms of marketing communication in the current marketplace? Exhibit 6-4 illustrates how traditional

Exhibit 6-4

How Advertising Communicates

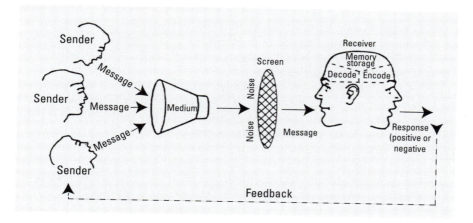

Source: Don E. Schultz and Stanley I. Tannenbaum, *Essentials of Advertising Strategy*, 2d ed. (Lincolnwood, Ill.: NTC Business Books, 1989), p. 32.

advertising and other marketing communication messages are taken in and stored by consumers. Commonly, there are multiple senders of advertising messages trying to reach the same consumer. All of these messages are sent through some form of media, which includes both traditional delivery systems such as television or magazines and other communication forms such as employees of the marketing organization, news stories about the brand, or even word of mouth. The important point is that there are multiple senders all trying to reach and influence the same consumer through multiple media. As the illustration shows, there is noise in the channel. In some cases, this noise comes from outside, but increasingly, as more and more marketers attempt to communicate with the same consumer, the noise may be generated simply by a very large number of messages.

An important resource for the consumer to control the flow of messages and keep from being inundated by the sheer volume of communication is his or her *perceptual screen*. The perceptual screen is nothing more than the consumer's ability to focus attention on a specific item, event, or activity and successfully screen out all other sensations or experiences. (The perceptual screen is related to the motivation to process in the ELM model.) It is the screening process that allows us to deal with the increasingly complex world in which we live. The perceptual screen also allows the consumer to quickly sort through incoming information or materials and identify those that are important. It is used to both screen and select available information and experiences.

Important to the concept of the perceptual screen is the idea of encoding and decoding messages. All communication is the result of sending or receiving coded sensations. In other words, all sounds, colors, tones, illustrations, odors, sizes, and so on are in some type of code. One of the key ingredients in the success of any brand communication message is for the receiver or consumer to get out of the coded brand message exactly what the sender intended. Through the perceptual screen, we are constantly looking for patterns or elements we understand. If there is no pattern, or if the receiver does not understand the code used, the message will not be accepted and no communication will result.

Once the consumer sorts through the codes and patterns the marketer has developed, he or she can identify the type of information the sender is transmitting and determine whether the material is to be processed. If it is processed, either it is dealt with immediately or, in the case of much advertising, it is stored away for later use. There might, for example, be an immediate response to a television direct marketing advertisement. The advertiser offers a four-disc set of Motown hits for a certain price. The consumer sees the advertisement, decides to buy, picks up the telephone, calls the toll-free number, and orders the set. The message is delivered and the consumer responds—a successful transaction for both parties. In this case, the feedback loop from the consumer is the call to the toll-free number and the placing of the order.

In many brand communication situations, however, the consumer's decision is not immediate. Quite often the consumer is not in the market for the advertised brand, is not in a position to buy at that particular moment, or perhaps has just made a purchase and satisfied the immediate need. In these instances, assuming the advertised brand is of interest to the consumer, the advertising message may be stored away for later use.

How Consumers Store Information

Because most brand communicators do not assume that consumers will act or react immediately to their messages, it is important to understand how information is processed and stored in the mind of the consumer. Exhibit 6-5 is a simplified illustration. We are constantly scanning our environment, looking for patterns in sounds, sights, smells, and so on. This helps us understand what is going on around us. As shown in the model, incoming sensations are subject to a scanning process through which we take in only those patterns that have some meaning or experience for us. Commonly, we screen out those we don't understand. An obvious example is language recognition. If you speak English, the sounds uttered by other English-speaking persons have meaning and are therefore likely to be accepted. Sounds uttered in Chinese or Hindi often have no meaning to an English-speaker and are easily rejected.

The scanning process involves one of the two forms of memory. Short-term memory is essentially a holding area in which we put recognizable patterns while we access long-term memory for more complex and detailed information with which to connect it and give it meaning. Short-term memory is, indeed, short-term and quite limited. For example, most people can't remember something as simple as a seven-

Exhibit 6-5
Information Processing Model

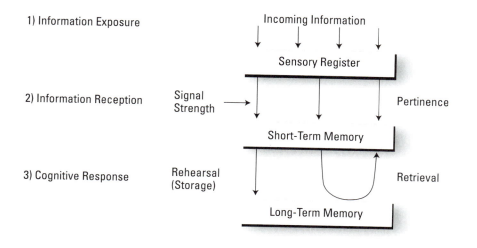

1) Information Exposure

Incoming Information

Sensory Register

2) Information Reception

Signal Strength → Pertinence

Short-Term Memory

3) Cognitive Response

Rehearsal (Storage)   Retrieval

Long-Term Memory

digit telephone number the first time they hear it. There is no space to store it and no way to relate it to anything in the long-term memory.

Long-term memory is believed to hold the entire history of the individual. Everything we have ever experienced is stored there. And it is stored in a unique way in the form of nodes and networks. One node may contain the basic element of a particular concept, but the node is related, enhanced, and connected to other nodes throughout the brain. Therefore, upon seeing a picture of Mickey Mouse, we automatically connect other nodes to it. These might include such things as Walt Disney, the Disney Store, the Disney Catalog, a visit to Disney World, a birthday, or a parade. This node and connection process, called *spreading activation*, makes every person different. The experiences are different, the connections are different, the relationships are different. It is important to understand this when developing brand communication campaigns that aim to establish various forms of brand contacts.

Try this experiment. First, think of Apple Computers. What images come to mind? Do you see the Apple logo? Do you see a computer, graphics, what? The images you see are stored in your memory and are connected to the node you call Apple Computers. Now think about IBM. Do you see the striped IBM logo, the color blue, the headlines about earnings losses at IBM? The connections you make to Apple and IBM are unique to you. No one has the exact same experiences with either company.

The concept of brand uniqueness in the eyes of the consumer really starts to get to the heart of why the brand belongs to the *consumer* more than to the marketer. The marketer only assists in building unique brand images in the minds of thousands, millions—even trillions of consumers around the world.

How Consumers Use Brand Information

Information is stored in the mind in three ways.

1. Objects are related to their *attributes*. For example, when we think of a particular product we attach to it any number of attributes. Toothpaste, for example, comes in a tube. It has a certain flavor, a certain color, and a certain texture.

2. Objects are related to *other objects*. For example, toothpaste is related to toothbrushes, dental floss, a bathroom, and so on.

3. Information is *stored over time*. Through our storage system, commonly called memory, we are able to move backward and forward in time. Often, we can recall what we were wearing at particular events. We can recall what was served at a special holiday meal. This ability to store and retrieve information over time explains why people remember and relate specific experiences to brands. It illustrates why it is so difficult to get people to forget bad experiences with one brand or why they generally expect only good experiences from another.

These three forms of information storage all contribute to brand knowledge. Brand knowledge has two primary components, brand awareness and brand image, as shown in Exhibit 6-6.

Brand Awareness

Consumers recognize, recall, and associate the name, symbol, color, package, advertising, and other factors relating to a specific brand to which they have been exposed over time. Brand awareness is the simplest form of brand knowledge. It relies primarily on the relationship of multiple pieces of visual and aural data to the overall perception of the brand. To succeed, it requires that the consumer be able to call up, generally from long-term memory, the physical elements and forms of the brand and relate them to all these elements.

Brand Image

Brand image is created primarily through brand associations. The consumer relates the brand to other concepts, both favorable and unfavorable. Through brand association, the brand comes to mean something to the consumer. It may fill specific needs or otherwise take on a certain value. The stronger, more favorable, or more unique the brand associations are, the less likely they are to be easily copied or transplanted by those of competitors.

These nodes of interrelated knowledge about brands have received a great deal of attention from consumer researchers, who attempt to map out the associations within consumers' minds through looking at schemas and scripts. As defined by J. Paul

Exhibit 6-6
Brand Knowledge

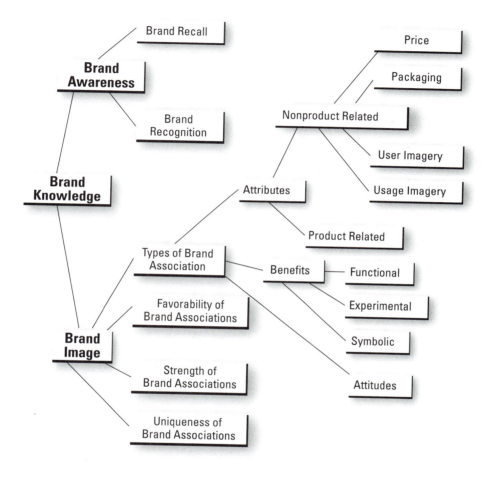

Chapter 6

Peter and Jerry C. Olson, a schema is "an associative network of interrelated meanings that represent a person's declarative knowledge about some concept."[5] Since declarative knowledge deals with a person's mental representation of information, each schema is a group of linked material tied to a particular issue. As mentioned in Chapter 2, we call these brand-related schemas *brand networks*. Exhibit 6-7 shows an older consumer's possible brand network for milk.

---

[5]J. Paul Peter and Jerry C. Olson, *Consumer Behavior and Marketing Strategy*, 3d ed. (Homewood Ill.: Irwin, 1993), p. 68.

Exhibit 6-7
Brand Network for Milk

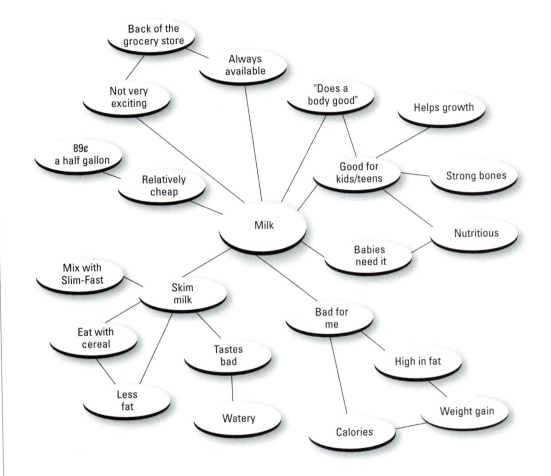

As you can see, this brand network contains a variety of information about milk: who it's good for (babies, children, teens), how it relates to this consumer ("bad for me"), uses for the skim variety ("eat with cereal," "mix with Slim-Fast"), and information related to purchasing the product ("always available," "89 cents a half gallon," "back of grocery store"). There is also some advertising-related information ("milk mustache," "Got Milk?"). While an actual brand network might be more complex with more interrelated information than this example, this gives an idea of the brand network concept.

As brand communicators, we need to find out what the brand networks for our product look like. What kinds of ideas, images, and feelings do consumers associate with our brand and with competitors' brands? Identifying the most common linkages can help us to determine whether there are problems with how our brand is perceived, tell us what sort of imagery will be most effective in our marketing communication efforts, and help us better understand how our brand differs from competitive brands as far as consumers are concerned.

Related to schemas is the concept of scripts, defined by Peter and Olson as "associative networks of knowledge that contain procedural knowledge."[6] Scripts are our understanding of how to do things: how to buy a particular type of product (at a specialty store, through the mail, only with a coupon), how to obtain a particular service, and so on. As with schemas, if we as marketers can begin to understand the scripts associated with purchase and use of our type of product, we may be able to identify problem areas that inhibit our ability to hold on to current customers and attract new buyers.

Evaluating Information Through the Judgment Process

The way we gather, develop, associate, and relate brand information is influenced by the *judgment process*. Under the central route to persuasion, when we see information about a product or service, we immediately try to connect that information to what we have stored away. We test or judge new brand contacts against what we already know. "Yes, this new information fits with what I know." "No, it doesn't fit." At this point, we decide whether we will take in the new information or material and connect it to what we have stored away, thus changing our knowledge of the brand, or whether we will reject the information. For example, Bozell's "Where's Your Mustache?" campaign for milk used celebrities to try to communicate the message that milk has important health benefits for adults, not just for children. (An advertisement from the "Where's Your Mustache?" campaign is shown in Exhibit 6-8.) Under the central route to persuasion, consumers would compare that information to what they had stored in their brand network for milk, and decide whether the message was believable. However, if a particular consumer's response to the milk message took the peripheral route instead, judgment of the message would likely be based more on the consumer's reaction to the particular celebrity than on the informational components of the message itself. In either case, the new message (milk is good for adults) would be judged against existing brand knowledge (milk is important for children).

The judgment process makes it difficult to develop and plan brand communication programs. While the marketer might have very valid reasons for sending out messages that are in conflict with what his or her brand has been in the past (we call this approach *repositioning*), it is consumers who finally determine whether they will accept or reject the new messages the marketer is sending. Interestingly, the milk

---

[6]Ibid.

Exhibit 6-8
"Where's Your Mustache" Advertisement

producers chose not to rely solely on the celebrity appeal of the "Where's Your Mustache?" campaign. Instead, they paired those persuasive messages with a television and outdoor advertising campaign developed by Goodby, Silverstein, which asked consumers, "Got Milk?" "Got Milk" used situations (having just taken a mouthful of peanut butter when the phone rings, for example) and other products (Hostess cupcakes) most consumers would already associate with milk to drive home the importance of always having milk on hand. The combination of campaigns helped to stop a downward trend in milk consumption.

A final point about the information processing model in Exhibit 6-5 is that message information and storage can be accomplished in two ways.

1. The marketer can get brand communication stored or acted upon by increasing the *volume* or *amount*. That, typically, is what advertisers have done. They have increased the number of messages or media weight, they have tried to be more "creative," they have tried to be more pervasive, they have tried to be everywhere. Or, they have tried to be louder, more strident, or more invasive to get consumers to accept and store advertising messages.

2. The marketer can, as shown on the right-hand side of the model, be more *pertinent*. Consumers will typically take in, store, and use information that is relevant or important to them. This is another of the major changes that is going on in brand communication. As the marketplace becomes more crowded or cluttered, it is necessary for brand communicators to make their messages more pertinent to their customers and prospects. To create relevant messages, then, marketers need to know more about consumers, to understand them better. Increasing relevancy of the message increases the chances that the consumer will process the message using the central route, which means that he or she will evaluate claims with much more attention than would otherwise be the case.

This change—from increasing the level or amount of brand communication to becoming more pertinent—is one of the major forces in brand communication today. How can we learn to be more pertinent? One way is to conduct research among our current customers and prospective customers. Research is the focus of the next chapter.

Summary

We learn more from observing consumers' behavior than from questioning them about their attitudes. The ways in which consumers take in brand information and use it to make purchasing decisions are designed to simplify the decision-making process. By understanding the basic process of communication, we can better design IBC programs to influence any target, be it current users or prospective users.

7

Researching the Relationship Between the Consumer and the Brand

The previous chapter looked at what we currently know about how consumers view brands and brand decision making. This chapter discusses where and how to find information on consumers and how to use that information in putting together the IBC program.

Secondary Research

The first step in any plan is to review information that is already available, whether from the company's own historical records or from syndicated or library sources. This is secondary research. Some key sources of secondary research data are discussed below.

Measures of Reported Behavior

Two major sources of syndicated secondary data on consumer behavior are the Simmons Market Research Bureau (SMRB) and Mediamark Research, Inc. (MRI). Both companies deal in reported behavior, that is, they gather data annually through extensive consumer surveys in which respondents are asked about their geographic and demographic characteristics, buying behavior, and media usage behavior. The surveyed consumers are reporting on what they *have done*, and marketers who use this information then assume that future behavior will follow past behavior. Both companies make their data available in both multivolume book and CD-ROM formats

Table 7-1   **SMRB "Items Ordered by Mail or Phone"**

	Ordered by Mail or Phone in Last 12 Months			
	Total U.S '000	A '000	B % Down	C Across %	D Indx
Total adults	187747	98529	100.0	52.5	100
Males	90070	42228	42.9	46.9	89
Females	97676	56301	57.1	57.6	110
Principal shoppers	115901	62869	63.8	54.2	103
18–24	23951	10761	10.9	44.9	86
25–34	41492	21928	22.3	52.8	101
35–44	40678	22707	23.0	55.8	106
45–54	29045	16769	17.0	57.7	110
55–64	21263	11448	11.6	53.8	103
65 or older	31318	14915	15.1	47.6	91
18–34	65443	32690	33.2	50.0	95
18–49	122143	64885	65.9	53.1	101
25–54	111215	61404	62.3	55.2	105
35–49	56701	32195	32.7	56.8	108
50 or older	65603	33644	34.1	51.3	98
Graduated college	37353	23885	24.2	63.9	122
Attended college	39301	22003	22.3	56.0	107
Graduated high school	73139	38567	39.1	52.7	100
Did not graduate high school	37954	14074	14.3	37.1	71
Employed males	62041	29990	30.4	48.3	92
Employed females	53100	33683	34.2	63.4	121
Employed full-time	99735	54837	55.7	55.0	105
Employed part-time	15406	8836	9.0	57.4	109
Not employed	72606	34856	35.4	48.0	91
Professional/manager	32308	20647	21.0	63.9	122
Technical/clerical/sales	35568	20890	21.2	58.7	112
Precision/craft	12562	5676	5.8	45.2	86
Other employed	34704	16460	16.7	47.4	90
Single	41125	18693	19.0	45.5	87
Married	111354	63515	64.5	57.0	109
Divorced/separated/widowed	35268	16321	16.6	46.3	88
Parents	61860	34616	35.1	56.0	107
White	159985	88240	89.6	55.2	105
Black	21570	8308	8.4	38.5	73
Other	6191	1981	2.0	32.0	61
Northeast—census	38611	20303	20.6	52.6	100
Midwest	45021	26057	26.4	57.9	110
South	65246	33969	34.5	52.1	99
West	38869	18200	18.5	46.8	89
County size A	76945	37788	38.4	49.1	94
County size B	55516	29913	30.4	53.9	103
County size C	27293	15097	15.3	55.3	105
County size D	27993	15731	16.0	56.2	107
Metro central city	58084	27380	27.8	47.1	90
Metro suburban	88940	48435	49.2	54.5	104
Non metro	40722	22713	23.1	55.8	106

Table 7-1

SMRB "Items Ordered by Mail or Phone" (continued)

Ordered by Mail or Phone in Last 12 Months

	Total U.S '000	A '000	B % Down	C Across %	D Indx
Top 5 ADI's	42410	19705	20.0	46.5	89
Top 10 ADI's	59256	28419	28.8	48.0	91
Top 20 ADI's	81977	41528	42.1	50.7	97
Hshld. Inc. $75,000 or more	26297	16149	16.4	61.4	117
$60,000 or more	43694	26299	26.7	60.2	115
$50,000 or more	61638	37472	38.0	60.8	116
$40,000 or more	83714	49983	50.7	59.7	114
$30,000 or more	110173	64231	65.2	58.3	111
$30,000–$39,999	26459	14248	14.5	53.8	103
$20,000–$29,999	28910	14264	14.5	49.3	94
$10,000–$19,999	29666	13008	13.2	43.8	84
Under $10,000	18998	7026	7.1	37.0	70
Household of 1 person	23989	10952	11.1	45.7	87
2 people	61625	33405	33.9	54.2	103
3 or 4 people	75459	39860	40.5	52.8	101
5 or more people	26674	14311	14.5	53.7	102
No child in hshld.	113318	58090	59.0	51.3	98
Child(ren) under 2 years	13676	7179	7.3	52.5	100
2–5 years	27475	14548	14.8	53.0	101
6–11 years	35656	19918	20.2	55.9	106
12–17 years	34050	19210	19.5	56.4	108
Residence owned	129490	73387	74.5	56.7	108
Value: $70,000 or more	80885	48502	49.2	60.0	114
Value: under $70,000	48605	24885	25.3	51.2	98
Residence rented	52590	22410	22.7	42.6	81
Daily newspapers					
Net one day reach	115376	63096	64.0	54.7	104
Read only one	94811	51200	52.0	54.0	103
Read two or more	20565	11896	12.1	57.8	110
Weekend/Sunday newspapers					
Net one day reach	132219	73133	74.2	55.3	105
Read only one	119704	65661	66.6	54.9	105
Read two or more	12515	7473	7.6	59.7	114

How to Read SMRB

For the demographic group of 18–24-year-olds:

Total U.S. = There are 23,951,000 18–24-year-olds in the United States.

Column A = There are 10,761,000 18–24-year-olds who ordered items by mail or phone in the last 12 months.

Column B = Of all adults who ordered items by mail or phone in the last 12 months, 10.9 percent are 18–24 years old. (10,761/98,529)

Column C = Of all 18–24-year-olds, 44.9 percent ordered items by mail or phone in the last 12 months. (10,761/23,951)

Column D = An index number comparing 18–24-year-olds' mail and phone ordering behavior with all adult behavior. The 86 index means that 18–24-year-olds are 14 percent less likely to order items by mail and phone than adults in general. (44.9/52.5)

(SMRB's computerized system is called "CHOICES"; MRI's is known as "MEMRI.") The computerized versions allow planners to develop customized cross-tabulations for more detailed target market identification.

Table 7-1 shows an excerpt from the direct marketing category in SMRB's 1994 *Study of Media and Markets*.[1] The specific product category is "Items Ordered by Mail or Phone in the Last 12 Months." Based on the responses to SMRB's survey, 52.5 percent of all adults reported having ordered items by mail or phone in the last year, with females being more likely to have purchased in this way than males (57.6 percent of females versus 46.9 percent of males). The SMRB data also indicate that twenty-five- to forty-four-year-old adults make up the largest portion of people purchasing in this fashion; 22.3 percent of purchasers were twenty-five to thirty-four years old, while 23.0 percent were thirty-five to forty-four years old. Other characteristics common to those purchasing items by mail or phone are that they are employed full-time, live in the South, and have household incomes of $30,000 or more.

In addition to the geographic and demographic data shown in Table 7-1, both SMRB and MRI collect information on media usage across a wide variety of media types and vehicles. The aggregate information on items ordered by mail or phone is also broken down into different types of items, such as auto accessories and children's books. In other product categories, data are available for specific brands. Using SMRB or MRI data, a planner can look at the characteristics of people who report having used the product in the past and then develop a description of a potential target audience based on these data. If the planner does not have access to other kinds of data, SMRB and MRI are invaluable starting points for developing a customer profile.

One important point to keep in mind with SMRB and MRI: The data are based on self-reports. The participating consumer fills out a booklet with page after page of questions about buying behavior over varying time frames: the last year, the last ninety days, the last month, the last week. Obviously, there's some potential for confusion in the reporting, and, in some product categories, there are also potential problems related to social desirability. This factor does not mean that the value of SMRB or MRI data is questionable, only that self-reported data are just that—self-reported, with the potential for human error.

Measures of Actual Behavior

To avoid the human error problem, the marketing planner can sometimes go to the source: records of actual purchasing and product usage behavior. The best source for such information is the company's own database. But if the marketer doesn't have a database, or has only recently started to develop one, there are other sources of actual behavioral data, a few of which are discussed next.

---

[1]Simmons Market Research Bureau, *Study of Media and Markets*, vol. P11 (New York: Simmons Market Research Bureau, 1994).

Information Resources, Inc.

IRI http://www.infores.com gathers a wide variety of purchasing data. Among its services are the following:

BehaviorScan Testing among 2,000–3,000 panel members in each of seven markets. Used to test new products and changes to marketing mix elements, including television advertising, price, sales promotion efforts, etc.

InfoScan Weekly scanner information from a sample of grocery, drug, and mass merchandise stores. Allows manufacturers to see both base sales and sales increases due to promotion. Sample includes over 3,000 grocery stores in sixty-four markets, 550 drug stores, and 288 mass merchandise stores. InfoScan Census provides similar analysis for all stores with scanners (12,000+ grocery stores and 7,800+ drug stores).

InfoScan Household Panel Sixty thousand households who use a special ID card on each shopping trip in order to have their purchasing data recorded. Fifty-five thousand households use ScanKey, an in-home scanner, to record all purchases regardless of store type.

Database America

Database America http://www.databaseamerica.com is one of a number of companies that collects information from a variety of sources and then makes that compiled data available to marketers to match against the consumers in their own database. Database America's consumer information database contains information such as home ownership, income estimates, occupation, vehicle ownership, credit card ownership, and ethnicity for over 165 million people in 95 million households.

Claritas

Claritas http://www.claritas.com offers a number of products, the best known of which is PRIZM, a market segmentation system that places every U.S. neighborhood into one of sixty-two clusters defined on the basis of demographics, psychographics, and behavior. Table 7-2 shows an example of one of the PRIZM clusters.

Claritas, Database America, and IRI are just a few examples of the many syndicated sources available that report on actual consumer behavior. While it's true that many product categories are not yet covered by these types of data, the applications seem to be increasing daily and provide a valuable source of information for the IBC planner. In most cases, client companies are subscribing to these services, meaning that clients now have the tools available to become experts on the consumer. That's an important shift because consumer expertise was traditionally the realm of the advertising agency. Agency-based planners must make an effort to become familiar with the new types of syndicated information that are becoming available.

Table 7-2	**PRIZM Cluster: Exurban Blues**			
Nickname	New Homesteaders	Middle America	Red, White, & Blues	Military Quarters
Demo-graphic caption	Young Middle-Class Families	Midscale Families in Midsize Towns	Small Town Blue-Collar Families	GIs & Surrounding Off-Base Families
Cluster number	37	38	39	40
Percent of U.S. households	2.0%	1.2%	2.3%	0.5%
Predominant adult age range	35–54	25–34, 35–54	35–54, 55–64	25–34, 35–54
Key education level	Some College	High School	High School Grade School	Some College
Predominant employment	White-Collar	Blue-Collar	Blue-Collar	Service White-Collar
Key housing type	Owners Single Unit	Owners Single Unit	Owners Single Unit	Renters Multi-Unit 2–9
Lifestyle preferences	Own a powerboat	Go bowling	Rent family/kid videos	Vote in elections
	Have a new car loan	Have $100K+ in insurance	Obtain life insurance thru agent	Have veterans life insurance
	Drink frozen orange juice	Shop at Montgomery Ward	Own a gas grill	Have avg. long distance bill $26+
	Listen to country radio	Watch daytime TV	Listen to early morning radio	Listen to religious/gospel
	Read outdoor life magazines	Read parenting/outdoor magazines	Read fishing/auto magazines	Read hunting/men's magazines
Socio-economic rank	Middle (26)	Middle (33)	Middle (35)	Lower Middle (40)
Race/ethnicity	W	W	W	Mix

Other Secondary Sources

There are a number of information sources available to the planner. As we sort through material, we must look for anything that might help us to better understand how consumers feel about our product and anything we might be able to use in developing an IBC strategy.

Company Records or Company Marketing Intelligence

The prime source of information for a brand normally consists of such documentation as sales records, product shipments, and customer reports. The amount of information that is gathered and stored by a company and that can be useful to the IBC planner is amazing. Fortunately, many companies in today's marketplace recognize the value of such data and are making an effort to house them in accessible databases. The key to obtaining and using existing company information is a clear, concise description of what is needed and what form it is needed in. If the needed information can be adequately described to the accounting or financial people, it usually can be obtained.

Previous Company Research

In many cases, a great deal of information can be taken from previous research studies conducted by the company for reasons other than advertising. This information may consist of consumer data, product tests, distribution information, and pricing tests. In some instances, the information is held in the marketing department; in others, it may be found in a research department or even in the sales organization.

Trade and Association Studies

Many trade journals and associations conduct surveys of their readers and collect data about their particular field or industry as part of an ongoing service. Many trade associations develop quite sophisticated data and information for their members; these data may be available if the advertiser company is a member of the group. In many specialized or limited fields or activities, the trade association may be the only source of market and/or marketing information.

Locating these data and determining their accuracy are the major obstacles to their use. This information (not including information collected by the government) has been gathered for a purpose and usually has been funded by some organization. Care should be taken in analyzing the data-gathering method, sample size, and age of the information when it is being used for a research base. Most marketing research texts have excellent lists of sources of this information. Additional sources are available at most libraries, through various trade organizations, and over the Internet.

Census and/or Registration Data

One of the most overlooked sources of information about markets and consumers is the data developed or gathered by various governmental organizations. Federal, state, and local governments are particularly good sources of data on almost any subject. The federal government publishes information through the Census Bureau on such topics as population, housing, retail trade, wholesale trade, service industries, manufacturers, agriculture, and transportation. In addition, states publish census data on such factors as population, retail sales, income levels, and employment. Even cities and counties issue census data on population trends and projections, income, economic and planning studies, traffic counts, and demographic factors. Virtually any large library can provide most types of census data; in addition, the Census Bureau's Web site http://www census.gov contains a wealth of easily searchable information. Because new census material is constantly being published, a thorough study of existing information should be made before additional research is undertaken.

Libraries and Universities

The library can quickly become one of the planner's best friends. Magazine and newspaper articles can be the source of important information on market trends and competitive activity. Sometimes, company executives will give a reporter information that would otherwise be treated as a state secret, so a quick trip to the library is always a good starting point. The search process is easier today than it has ever been, thanks to CD-ROM technology. There are a number of business information databases available, including ABI-Inform, Info-track, Dow Jones News/Retrieval, NEXIS, Wilson Businessdisk, and Compact Disclosure. And the consumer press must be included in the search; the *Reader's Guide to Periodical Literature* is another available on-line information source. Most of these services operate in the same way: The researcher types in a key word or words (such as a company name, product name, or subject), and the system searches the database for citations containing that word. The computer generates a list of citations, which may contain an abstract of the article in addition to the author, title, source, and date. Some systems, such as UNCOVER, even provide an option for having a copy of the article faxed to the researcher within a few days (the user provides a credit card number for payment). The point is that it is easier than ever to check the media for information on a product, its customers, and competitive activity.

The Internet

Today, the Internet and the World Wide Web are many researchers' first stop on a hunt for information. Many companies maintain Web sites that provide background information on their products and services. In addition, there are Web sites dedicated to helping searchers find information, such as The Virtual Reference Desk http://thorplus.lib.purdue.edu/reference/index.html and Research-It! http://www.iTools.com/research-it/research-it.html. And, as we'll see later in this chapter, market researchers are also using the Internet as a means to *collect* information on consumers.

Miscellaneous Sources

The supply of data sources for the IBC planner seems almost endless. Individual companies, market research organizations, and others often gather and publish data on various industries and consumer categories. The same is true of advertising and marketing consultants, advertising agencies, and so forth. A quick check of the telephone book and a few calls can often turn up additional sources or leads. Current marketing and research journals are among the best sources of information. This will often turn up leads, particularly when a bibliography is included. In short, data usually are available. It takes only a bit of investigative interest and creativity to turn up the leads and the material.

Using the Information

Information gathering is only the first step in the research process. The second and much more critical step is using that information to make business decisions. Think about it: In a new business pitch in advertising, the competing agencies are frequently given the same information. Winning the account depends on what each agency is able to do with that information, what insights each is able to draw from it. Reporting isn't enough; analysis is what's essential. To illustrate the types of inferences that may be drawn from the data, we now review the four components of the brand business review. Keep in mind that the purpose of the brand business review is to study and interpret the current market situation, not just to report what's going on. Exhibit 7-1 lists specific points to be covered in each section of the brand business review.

Company and Product History

Suppose that our review of secondary data turns up the fact that our product was the company's main profit source last year. What does this tell us? It could mean that the company will do whatever it takes to support this product, including increasing spending on marketing communication activities. On the other hand, it might mean that the profits generated by this product are used to fund other products currently in development or that have been newly introduced, in which case the company probably won't be willing to divert any of those profits into increased promotional support. Which is the case? We must look deeper: Have spending levels changed over the past few years? If so, what's the trend? How has the company responded to competitive threats? How long has this brand been the profit leader? While the company and product history section of the situation analysis may be brief, it can provide us with insight into how our marketing communication recommendations are likely to be received.

One very important element that can come out of a review of company and product history is the product's current status in the marketplace. Identifying the brand's position is particularly important when it has varying levels of sales or penetration in markets across the country. Advertising and marketing people use a system of indices to illustrate the standing of the product in various markets: a category-development index (CDI) and a brand-development index (BDI), both of which are computed against the all-commodity volume (ACV) in the particular type of market. The calculation of these indices provides convenient numbers that help identify the best markets or the proportional percentage of distribution for individual products or services. All-commodity volume gives the total amount of sales in a given category. For products sold in food stores, for example, all food store sales would comprise the all-commodity volume. Because a small number of food stores often generates a large share of total food store sales, it is possible to achieve a high percentage of ACV distribution in a disproportionately small number of stores.

If total sales of canned tuna fish in Tulsa are 2,000 cans per month, that would be the ACV, or total number of cans of tuna sold. Further assume that each supermarket chain's sales by month were as shown in Table 7-3. The ACV is 2,000 cans of tuna

Exhibit 7-1
Considerations for a Brand Business Review

Company and Product History
Product/brand background
Past marketing communication budgets
Past marketing communication themes
Patents/technological history
Significant political/legal influences
Current creative theme
Current problems/opportunities
Major events/activities in coming period
Relevant marketing data (sales, share, etc.)

Product Evaluation
Comparison to competition
   features
   ingredients
   uses
Changes to product
Consumer perceptions
Price-value relationship
User satisfaction
Distribution
Retailer perceptions
Packaging/labeling
Brand name equity
Ancillary services
Consumer problems
Unique features

Consumer Evaluation
Demographic profile
   occupation
   marital status
   head of household
   race
   education
   age
   household income
   presence of children
   social class
   other characteristics
Psychographic profile
   VALS (Values & Lifestyles)
   SMRB/MRI data
   other lifestyle
Behavioral profile
   consumption level
   where used
   attitudes toward product
   loyalty

Competitive Analysis
Direct competition
Indirect competition
Competitive marketing communication
   spending
   themes
Retailers' perceptions
Consumer perceptions
Strengths/weaknesses

fish sold each month. Yet, these sales are not equally divided among the chains in the market or among the individual stores. For example, Chain A has only twelve stores, yet sells 850 cans of tuna per month—an average of 70.8 cans per store per month. On the other hand, Chain D has twenty-three stores and sells 154 cans per month, or an average of 6.7 cans per store per month. Closer examination probably would show that sales by individual stores within a chain are not equal either. Some stores may sell a lot of tuna, while others sell almost none.

A company that markets tuna obviously wants to get as wide a distribution as possible to take advantage of its advertising within the Tulsa market. By obtaining distribution in Chains A and B, whose twenty-eight stores account for only 14.8

Table 7-3	Sales by All-Commodity Volume Index		
Chain	**Number of stores**	**Number of cans of tuna sold**	**Percent of ACV**
A	12	850	42.5
B	16	420	21.0
C	19	180	9.0
D	23	154	7.7
E	4	103	5.2
All others	116	293	14.6
Total	190	2,000	100.0

percent of the 190 stores in the market, a marketer would have distribution in stores doing 63.5 percent of the ACV. This instance is not at all unusual. In some product categories, 60 percent or more ACV distribution can be achieved in less than 30 percent of the retail outlets across the country. This is particularly true in the many markets dominated by one or two supermarket chains.

Category- and brand-development indices are calculated in a similar manner. For the CDI, total sales of the category may be indexed against sales for a certain geographic region or type of store. In a product category such as soft drink mixes, for example, the CDI may be quite high in the Midwest, say 130 (average = 100), while somewhat lower in the Southwest, say 89. Here, the CDI calculation is based on the percentage of total sales that occur in each geographic region.

The BDI is the comparison of brand sales in the particular market indexed against total product sales calculated on a geographic or other basis. In the earlier example, Brand X might have a BDI of 125 in the Southwest, indicating that sales are very good in that region. This, however, would be offset to a certain extent because the CDI for that area is rather low. The use of these shorthand indices helps to better identify the present sales or potential market for a brand or category. They are widely used by commercial research organizations.

A major factor in any market analysis is the sales trend for the category and the brand. Trend lines that show patterns of sales over several years are developed. Five-year trends are usually best because frequently there are wide fluctuations in the marketplace over one- or two-year periods. Trend lines are especially important for products that have shown consistent growth or decline for a number of years. Being able to spot trends can be very helpful in planning the campaign. Scanner data have proven especially helpful in mapping the effects of sales promotion activity on product sales.

Product Evaluation

Marketers need to know the product or service inside and out to be able to market it effectively. Has it changed over the years? How do consumers feel about it?

How do channel members feel about it? What sort of equity comes with the brand name? Is the product priced appropriately for the value consumers receive? In particular, we must keep an eye out for any potential problems. If articles in consumer magazines refer to a product as the "premium" brand, it suggests that the price is on the high side. If retailers are stocking the product on lower shelves or giving it comparatively few facings, it's a signal that the product's a slow mover. We also need to look closely at the signals being sent by the current marketing communication program. What kind of image, if any, is being projected? Is that the image we really want? Remember, it isn't enough to just look at the advertising campaign. We must also consider publicity efforts, sales promotion offers, direct marketing activities, and so on.

Consumer Evaluation

Consumer evaluation often is the heart of the brand business review. Who buys and why do they buy? Take a product such as Hamburger Helper. Data from SMRB and MRI tell us that Hamburger Helper users are relatively downscale consumers. Their household income is fairly low, as is their education level, and they tend to be in multiperson households. When we think about that information in terms of the product, we realize that these people aren't buying Hamburger Helper to produce fine gourmet meals, but as a way of stretching their grocery dollars so that they can get a relatively complete meal out of a pound or so of ground beef. That's an important insight into the role the product plays in their lives, and it requires us to move beyond the information on the printed page (or the computer screen).

An important first step in considering consumers is defining whether our interest will be in current users of the product, users of competitive brands, or people not currently using the product category. As shown in the diagram in Exhibit 7-2, we can see that the total market is contained within the outer circle. Inside this broad category market circle are the three basic groups toward which marketing communication activities can be directed. Circle N includes those persons not presently using a product in the category; these are nonusers. Consumers in Circle C are predominantly users of competitive brands. Circle E comprises consumers who predominantly use our brand.

All of the consumers in these groups are very mobile (as indicated by the arrows). For example, some consumers move from the nonuser category to become users of competitive brands, while others move to become users of our brand. Our present customers also switch between our brand and those of our competitors. The market is quite fluid. Table 7-4 illustrates some of the alternatives the IBC planner might consider in choosing which group(s) of consumers to target.

When we're limited to self-reported secondary data, it's sometimes hard, but certainly not impossible, to develop a psychographic profile of users. Since SMRB and MRI can give us media usage information, we can use those data to gain some insight into consumers' lifestyles. For example, the following is a list of magazines that indexed at 150 or above (an index of 100 indicates average usage) in an SMRB report on a particular product:

Exhibit 7-2

Potential Purchaser Model

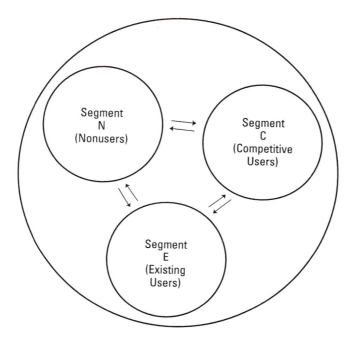

Barron's

Conde Nast Traveler

Eating Well

Entrepreneur

Financial World

Golf Digest

New York Times Magazine

Tennis

Vogue

What consumer insights can we draw from this list? Certainly, there are some indications about income level and age, but we would already have this information from the demographic data in SMRB. What psychographic characteristics can we infer? For one thing, this is a relatively active group. Its members like to travel and are interested in individual sports. They also believe in spending their money wisely.

Table 7-4 Objective/Market Group

Objective	Market Group
Increase total number of customers	Entire market
	Segments N and C
Increase total demand for product category	Entire market
Rekindle interest in a mature product	Entire market
	Segments N and C
Rediscover former users	Entire market
	Segments N and C
Attract nonusers of the category	Segment N
Attract users of competitive brands	Segment C
Maintain current sources or use	Segment E
Increase usage rate	Segment E
Increase frequency of use	Segment E
Increase variety of uses	Segment E
Reduce time between purchases	Segment E

These are useful insights for developing a marketing communication plan, particularly since the product in question is casino gambling. This is a profile of adults who have visited a casino more than twice in the last year![2] The heavy casino user is a bit more sophisticated than we might have thought, right? That's a psychographic insight based on secondary data.

Competitive Analysis

Competitive analysis is second only to consumer evaluation in terms of its importance in the planning process. To begin, exactly who are our competitors? We can't limit our consideration to direct brand competitors, or we may miss valuable opportunities. Instead, we need to think about the product like the consumer does. What other products can replace it? For example, if our product is a chain of frozen yogurt stores located in shopping malls, chances are our chief competition isn't other yogurt retailers (there's usually only one in each mall). Instead, it's more likely that consumers are choosing between us and other quick-service food sellers in the mall. That means that our competitors may include, among others, hot pretzels, cookies, and Orange Julius drinks.

Once we've identified our competition, we must look at how they're promoting their products. Where are they advertising? What benefit(s) are they emphasizing? What kinds of sales promotion offers are they making? What are they doing in terms of product publicity? Equally important, why are they doing these things? If the pretzel shop down the concourse is running a continuity program in which shoppers get a free pretzel after twenty purchases, the store is trying to encourage repeat business. If we're advertising primarily on television and one of our competitors is putting most of its money into magazines, it may be trying to stretch a smaller bud-

[2]Magazine data taken from *Study of Media and Markets*, vol. P9, pp. 416–417.

get. If our product is sold through grocery stores and one competitor seems to be getting all the prime shelf space without much consumer advertising, chances are it's putting a lot of money into trade sales promotion incentives.

We need to know what the competition is doing for two reasons: to know what we're planning against, and to anticipate how our competitors are likely to react to a change in our strategy. If we know their products and strategies as well as we know our own, we'll be able to plan more effectively.

Extrapolation of Data

Although it is sometimes true that data often exist for products or services currently being marketed, and that the real task is to determine what data are needed and how they might be gathered, this is not always the case. For example, even though the product may have been on the market for a long time, the planner may decide to develop a new strategy, advertise to another consumer segment, or suggest another use for the product. In such cases, if the use is new and the consumer purchasing group isn't fully established, specific market, usage, or consumer data may not be available. This is where the IBC planner really gets to take a creative approach toward research, converting existing data into usable information for another area. This technique is called *data extrapolation*; it is a very common practice in advertising and marketing research and should not be overlooked by the planner.

For example, assume the planner's brand is in the coffee category. A newly developed technique removes coffee acids without removing the caffeine. The resulting new brand tastes much smoother than other brands on the market. Of course, smooth taste is important to many coffee users, but the planner doesn't have much of a description of users of other brands. However, he or she can develop a profile of prospective new users from existing market information by extrapolating existing data.

The planner starts with people who have demonstrated that they dislike black coffee, which seems to indicate that there was something about the coffee taste they didn't like. What do people add to their coffee to change its taste? Some add cream or nondairy creamers, some add sugar. The assumption can be made that people who use nondairy creamers don't like the taste of black coffee. In other words, they may be looking for a smoother-tasting coffee. Because people use sugar for many purposes in addition to changing the taste of coffee, cream or creamer users might provide a better clue as to who prospects for the smoother-tasting coffee might be. The nondairy creamer market is large; the information on who purchases and uses nondairy creamers should be readily available. Obviously, not all users of nondairy creamers are prospects, but the planner can estimate a logical number who might be—that is, he or she can extrapolate a market for a smoother-tasting coffee.

This is just one way existing market data can be used to develop information that would be helpful in the planning of an effective IBC program. The extrapolation of data is limited only by the ability and creativity of the person seeking the information.

Types of Primary Research

Even the most thorough review of secondary information often leaves questions unanswered, particularly in terms of consumer behavior issues. When this is the case, the planner needs to supplement the secondary information with primary research. *Primary research* is original research carried out to gather specific information about the problem being studied. Primary research studies are appropriate for both existing and new products, and the information that follows applies to both.

Four general types of primary research are used in marketing communication planning: *qualitative or exploratory*, primarily used to better define the problem, the market, or the consumer; *quantitative or descriptive*, the most widely used type of research in planning; *experimental*, widely used in new product research, consisting of both laboratory and field tests in which a cause-and-effect relationship is sought; and *tracking or performance evaluation*, often used to evaluate the effects of a program (see Chapter 15).

No matter which type of primary research is used, data are usually gathered either by observation or by survey research. In observation data gathering, consumers or users are observed as they shop, evaluate products or services, make purchasing decisions, or are otherwise involved with the product or service under study. Survey data gathering entails either asking a number of customers or prospects questions about products or services or having them keep a diary of their purchases, product use, or other measurable activity.

Qualitative or Exploratory Research

Qualitative research is undertaken when the information needed is directional or diagnostic. Such research is usually done with fairly small groups of people, and the sampling is conducted on a quota or availability basis.

Definitive conclusions usually cannot be drawn from qualitative research. Instead, an attempt is made to get a general impression of the market, the consumer, or the brand. Two types of qualitative research are especially helpful in the exploratory stages of the brand communication campaign. These are intensive data gathering and the use of projective techniques.

Intensive Data Gathering

The informal research approach consists of gathering information or data through discussions with interested groups or individuals, such as consumers, prospects, and retailers, who have knowledge about the product or service. An excellent source of information is often the sales force, whose members are in direct contact with consumers and retailers.

Conducting focus groups or doing individual "depth interviews" are more systematic and formal methods of data gathering. The first approach, the focus group, is a discussion group made up of six to ten members of the target market for the product being studied. A trained moderator guides the group members through a series of product-related topics. For example, the researcher might be interested in learning about consumers' uses of the product category, attitudes toward his or her brand and competitive brands, and reactions to proposed changes to the product. The group setting often leads to more involved discussions than might occur in a one-on-one interview. Focus groups are one of the most widely used types of marketing communication research.

Creative researchers are developing new ways to conduct focus groups among targets that are often difficult to recruit for traditional groups. For example, telephone focus groups are frequently used to conduct research among teenagers. Telephone focus groups save both time and money, and teenagers not only are willing to participate but often are more forthcoming with information than in a traditional face-to-face group where there might be a stronger sense of peer pressure.[3] The Internet is also being used increasingly for focus groups. In one approach, participants who fit the target market profile are recruited to enter a chat room, where they type in their opinions on topics raised by the focus group moderator. One appeal of Internet focus groups is that participants of different ages, genders, and ethnicities all can take part in the same discussion; the norm in traditional focus groups is to keep the group membership as homogeneous as possible.[4]

The "depth interview" is conducted in a way similar to the focus group, except that interviews are done on an individual basis. Respondents are asked to discuss the product, the problem, or the situation. By asking carefully structured questions, the interviewer tries to probe the deeper feelings of the respondent rather than simply exposing surface opinions, which may be readily offered.

Both focus groups and depth interviews are best carried out by a trained researcher. Untrained persons may obtain general information through focus group discussion, but errors may creep in, or the group may be inadvertently led to a false conclusion unless the person directing the questioning or analyzing the data has had adequate previous experience with this form of data gathering.

Projective Techniques

Many forms of projective techniques may be used. All have the same basic approach: The person being interviewed is asked to involve himself or herself in a situation or experience in which he or she "projects" feelings and experiences about the product, brand, or problem set up by the interviewer. The assumption made in these projective techniques is that the person being interviewed, by involving himself or herself in a situation, will disclose underlying feelings, thoughts, and desires about the problem or situation that might not otherwise be revealed in direct questioning.

Projective research projects can take many forms, from word association ("What comes to mind when you hear the word Kellogg's?") to role playing ("You are serving breakfast to your seven-year-old son and nine-year-old daughter. What do you give them to eat?") to sentence completion ("People who eat Kellogg's Corn Flakes are _____."). Only skilled, experienced researchers are capable of

---

[3]Tom McGee, "Getting Inside Kids' Heads," *American Demographics*, vol. 19 (January 1997).

[4]Brad Edmondson, "The Wired Bunch," *American Demographics*, vol. 19 (June 1997).

developing successful projective research instruments and interpreting the results. If this methodology is contemplated, a commercial research organization should be consulted.

Qualitative or exploratory research should be used by the planner in the first stages of campaign development. Qualitative research is generally inexpensive; it can be done with small numbers of consumers, with selection based on a quota or availability sample. This type of research is often conducted to determine general trends in order to identify areas that need further exploration.

Qualitative research may be sufficient to answer the planner's questions. The information gathered, however, because of the nonprobability sampling methodology, is subject to wide variations in reliability and validity. If qualitative or exploratory primary research is to be used as the basis of the program, this limitation should be referenced in the communications plan.

Quantitative or Descriptive Research

Quantitative or descriptive research usually is primary research. The results can be projected to various portions of the market universe, and the laws of statistical probability can be applied to lend support to, or cause rejection of, the findings. Whereas qualitative research is used primarily to give direction to the marketing communication planner, quantitative research is used most often in choosing between alternatives or in decision making. The two most common methods used to gather quantitative data are observation and survey.

Observation

In quantitative research, the activities or habits of persons in the marketplace are observed either personally or through some mechanical means, such as with scanner panels. Historical data are gathered according to what the given person was observed doing or had done in the past; the data are used both to assess past behavior (and the reasons for it) and to predict future behavior. Observational research is used heavily for products targeted at children; researchers spend hours watching children interact with family members and peers both at home and away from home.

Another form of observation is the so-called pantry check made in consumers' homes. Pantries are checked to determine the various brands that have been purchased and the amount of product on hand. By correlating this observed information with the demographic characteristics of the respondents, the present users (or general target market) for the product can be identified.

Observation can be very helpful to the planner. However, collecting enough observations to generate conclusive answers to research questions can be quite an expensive undertaking.

Survey

Survey research is the most common method of primary research data gathering used for marketing communication programs. As the name implies, data are obtained through a survey of present or prospective consumers of the product or service. The usual goal is to obtain information necessary to develop a profile of the target audience or to determine the most effective message to be used.

Survey research methodologies differ according to the method of data gathering employed. The most common forms are personal interviews, mail surveys, consumer panels, and telephone interviews. As with focus groups, the Internet is increasingly being employed for surveys as well.

Personal Interviews. Personal interviewing may take many forms, ranging from traditional door-to-door canvassing to intercepts in shopping malls and laundromats or outside food and drug stores. The key to success in personal interviewing is to find situations in which respondents have the time available to answer questions, a very precious commodity in today's marketplace. The usual data-gathering form is a series of questions, scales, evaluations, or other devices that allow the respondent to express his or her ideas, concerns, or opinions. Interviews in the home may last an hour or more; interviews with persons interrupted while shopping, such as in a mall intercept, must usually be kept to five or ten minutes (although longer interviews are possible if appropriate incentives are offered). There is literally no limit to the type of data that can be gathered. In each case, the result depends on the kind of information desired and the situation in which the interview occurs.

The primary advantages of the personal interview are the opportunities to probe, to ask follow-up questions, and to use examples or samples of the product or communication material. The major disadvantages are the extremely high cost of personnel and diminishing consumer cooperation, particularly in door-to-door calls.

Mail Surveys. Much useful information can be gathered through a mail survey. Respondents tend to give more complete answers because the interview is relatively anonymous. Respondents can also answer questions that require access to data that might not be readily available in a personal or telephone interview (company financial information, for example, in a business-to-business survey). Because no interviewer is there to give directions, the questionnaire form must be made as easy to follow as possible, with primarily closed-end questions, that is, questions for which a list of possible answers is supplied or made available. The questionnaire may be any length and may cover almost any subject.

Data gathering by means of the mail questionnaire is relatively inexpensive. The main costs are for the mailing list, the questionnaire form, and postage. A nominal reward is sometimes included in a direct mail questionnaire to encourage response.

Mail questionnaires ordinarily have a fairly low return rate. A 30–40 percent response to a mail questionnaire is considered normal. Obtaining a return of 60–70 percent is exceptional. All results, however, depend on the product interest, the quality of the questions, and the mailing lists.

Consumer Panels. Preformed or existing panels of consumers have long been used for research data gathering. A number of commercial panels, such as National Family Opinion, Inc. (NFO), offer services that may be purchased.

Data gathering from consumer panels has the same disadvantage as do mail surveys in terms of time required. Response rates, however, often reach near 100 percent because the panels are established groups and are rewarded for participation. However, it is important to keep in mind that panelists answer many research questions during the course of a year, so there may be some danger of panelist wearout.

The major advantage of panel data gathering is that the information obtained is more complete and more detailed. The panel is accustomed to furnishing information through questionnaires and tends to be quite cooperative. Based on total research expenditure, cost per response by a panel is usually lower than in most other types of interviews.

Telephone Interviews. Telephone interviewing throughout the country can be done from a central location that provides complete control over the interview. Costs of telephone interviews are relatively low compared to other forms of data collection, and when time for data gathering is considered, this is probably the lowest-cost research method.

Telephone data-gathering usage has increased as samples have been improved. Originally, telephone samples were limited to persons whose names were listed in telephone directories. Newer systems of random digit dialing now make all connected telephones part of the sample frame, and every telephone home is a potential respondent, including the approximately 20 percent or more with unlisted numbers.

Telephone interviews are excellent for obtaining a relatively small amount of information from a large number of people. Because contact is by voice, only certain types of questions may be asked. Questions that require visuals or thorough understanding of a complex question are not practical. A telephone interview may last for as long as twenty minutes with many closed-end questions. Telephone respondents may provide information they would not ordinarily give in a face-to-face interview because the telephone offers a certain amount of anonymity.

The major advantages of telephone interviews are low cost, a complete sample frame, the ability to call any geographic area, and very rapid data gathering and reporting. Moreover, the telephone is the only practical method of conducting a coincidental survey—a study that is conducted at the same time marketing communication efforts are appearing.

Telephone surveys do have disadvantages, however. Answers usually must be shorter and not as in-depth as those obtained through other methods. There is no opportunity to use props or other materials that might help explain the questions or to display package designs, advertisements, or other items that the subject must see in order to respond. And, as more companies engage in telemarketing of products and services, consumers are often suspicious of telephone use for "research purposes only," reducing response rates.

Internet Surveys. While use of the Internet to gather survey data is still in the experimental stage, those researchers who have used this method claim that it is the least expensive way to conduct a survey. Further, it offers fast turnaround time. Among the benefits of this survey method are that respondents volunteer to participate, indicating their interest in the survey topic. And, since respondents pick the time when they complete the questionnaire, they may have more time to think about their answers than in other methods.

Internet surveys are particularly appropriate for technology issues and situations in which the population of interest is very specifically defined. However, there are important drawbacks to this research method. Internet samples are not random samples, so results cannot be projected to the larger population. In many cases, the researcher has little control over who answers the survey and little opportunity to verify the respondent's demographic information.

Experimental Research

Experimentation is a type of laboratory or otherwise controlled research in which a cause-and-effect relationship is sought. Strict controls are employed so that the variable that causes the effect can be identified. Experimentation is used only on a selective basis, because it is very difficult to control all marketing variables.

The most common form of experimental research is the use of a test market for new products or new marketing communication programs. Two or more individual markets are matched as closely as possible according to such marketing variables as population, category sales, and household income. Using these matched markets, a communication program is run in one market or set of markets and not in others. Then the results are observed. An alternative method is to use differing programs in a given set(s) of markets and to observe the differences that result. A third method is to use media weight tests. Here, varying levels of media promotion are used in matched test markets. Again, because other variables are held as nearly constant as possible, the influence of the media can be evaluated in terms of such effects as changes in attitude, awareness, and sales.

Experimentation is often an expensive method of obtaining information because the effects may not be immediately observable. However, it is widely used for new products, for example, to test the viability of the product on a small scale or to test various advertising or marketing alternatives prior to a major national introduction.

Sampling for Data Gathering

The success of any research design depends on the sample selected for data gathering. The major objective is to make sure that respondents to be interviewed are representative of the entire target population. It is important to determine who is to be sampled, the procedure to be used for sample selection, and the size of the sample.

Sample Frame

Persons to be interviewed must be representative of the target population. If the planner wants to learn about cat food, for example, then cat owners should be interviewed. In marketing communication research, this is done through screening questions such as, "Do you or anyone else in your household own a cat?" Those who do not have a cat would not be included in the study; they would automatically be screened out of the sample.

The research sampling frame for a marketing communication study can be easily defined. It may be as broad a frame as "all women from eighteen to forty-nine years of age with children under twelve years of age in the home," or it might be as restrictive as "those persons in the state of Nebraska owning iguanas." The sampling frame depends on the type of specific data to be gathered and a general idea of the information sought. A common definition of a sample frame is "present users of the product category or brand."

The key point in a sampling plan is to describe the sample universe clearly and concisely. If this is done at the outset of the project, no confusion will arise as to whether an individual selected for interviewing is qualified.

Sample Selection

There are two basic sampling techniques. *Probability samples* are those in which every known unit in the universe has a known probability of being selected for the research. For example, if the universe were defined as drugstores in the city of Des Moines with sales in excess of $1,000,000 annually, a complete list of stores could be developed from various sources, such as tax receipts and licenses. Knowing the names and locations of all the drugstores in Des Moines that fit the qualifications makes possible the development of a probability sample such that each store has a known chance of being selected. The results from research conducted using a probability sample can be projected to the larger population from which the sample was drawn.

Probability samples are used when the number of units to be measured is fairly small; a complete list of the items in the universe exists (such as all drugstores in Des Moines); and the need exists for precisely measuring the risk of sample error. Because of these conditions, the use of probability sampling in advertising and marketing research is generally limited, unless the universe can be very precisely defined.

A *nonprobability sample* does not provide every unit in the universe with a known chance of being included in the sample frame. If, in the earlier example, the restriction might be relaxed from stores doing over $1,000,000 in sales in Des Moines to simply those drugstores in the city that are high volume and located within easy access of major roads, this would not be a probability sample. It would be a nonprobability sample because not all high-volume drugstores would be included in the sample frame. For example, large stores that might qualify in every other respect might not be located near a major road, or might not be considered high volume by the researcher, and so on.

Although their results cannot be projected to the larger population, nonprobability samples are widely used in marketing communication research because no listing of the complete universe is available in many categories. Such samples are also used when the costs for a true probability sample are prohibitive because (1) the population members are widely dispersed geographically; (2) only a general estimate of the data is needed; (3) there is a possibility of obtaining a larger sample with a decrease in the magnitude of error; and (4) the nature and size of the bias can be estimated fairly accurately.

The primary reason for the popularity of nonprobability sampling in marketing communication research is simply the costs of obtaining data, in terms of both money and time. Once again, the IBC planner is faced with the cost-benefit trade-off.

Planners are usually willing to trade some validity and reliability to avoid the large costs entailed in developing a true probability sample.

Sample Size

One of the most difficult tasks in planning or evaluating primary research is determining the sample size required to achieve a given level of confidence. Statistical techniques are available for developing confidence levels of probability samples. The problem becomes more complex with nonprobability studies because the true universe usually is unknown.

A number of rules of thumb exist that are helpful to the IBC planner for determining sample sizes. Although they lack precision, such rules do give general approximations of sample sizes for various types of nonprobability studies. In intensive data gathering, such as depth interviews or focus groups, most ideas or answers concerning a product or service will be verbalized after the first thirty or so persons have been interviewed. This happens because most consumers have the same basic, general ideas about various products and services. Therefore, after about thirty persons have answered, repetition of the major ideas begins to mount rapidly. Similarly, interviews with 100–200 users of products or services, given a standard questionnaire in a limited geographic area, will tend to indicate the general attitudes of the population. After 100 interviews, reliability tends to mount as more and more respondents give the same answers to the questions being asked. For a regional study covering several cities or a few states, a sample of 300–400 qualified respondents is normally considered to be sufficient. A sample of 1,000–2,000 qualified consumers, selected according to a probability sample, will generally reflect the opinions and feelings of the national population on most subjects. Although these sample sizes are only estimates, they have been proven to the extent that only in unusual circumstances will major errors occur.

Problems

Four major problems usually are encountered with sample respondents: not-at-home, refusals, respondent bias, and interviewer bias.

Not-at-home and refusals create more problems in a probability sample than in a nonprobability one. For a group to constitute a true probability sample, the actual persons selected in advance must be interviewed. Obviously, this is not always possible. Steps must be taken, therefore, to select a large enough original sample so that substitutions for nonrespondents can be made without destroying the representative makeup of the original sample.

The biases of both respondent and interviewer are most difficult to control. Respondent bias usually appears when the person is truly anxious to assist the interviewer, and thus the respondent gives answers that do not reflect his or her true feelings. In some cases, in an attempt to appear knowledgeable, respondents give answers to questions on which they have no information.

Interviewer bias usually comes about when the interviewer, through either the question itself or the manner in which it is asked, indicates the type of answer that would be most acceptable or is generally regarded as "correct." The planner should be aware of the bias problem, particularly if the sample is small, if the interviewers are not professionally trained, or if the interviewers or respondents have strong feelings about the particular subject under study.

Evaluating Research

While research and research methods are important to the IBC planner, often it is just as important or more so to be able to judge existing or just-completed research. In many instances, the planner will not actually be doing the research. Instead, the research data may already exist or may be furnished either by the agency, the advertiser, or a research organization. In those cases, the ability to judge, evaluate, and extract information from the research studies is vital. If the planner doesn't have an understanding of research, how it is done, or the basis for sample selection, for example, he or she is in a very precarious position. He or she must rely totally on whoever analyzed the research to be accurate in interpretation and conclusions. A better situation would be for the planner to have a basic understanding of how to evaluate research studies so that he or she could be sure of the research base.

Criteria for Evaluating Research

In any type of research, the key question is whether results provide solid evidence on which to base marketing communication decisions. Knowing the answer to this question is especially important for the planner who may be proposing a new or unique approach. The crucial questions concern (a) how the research was or should be done, (b) how the research should be reported, (c) how the public (respondents) should be treated, and (d) how the business of research should be conducted.

A group of thirteen associations concerned with conducting marketing-related research has developed the "Research Industry Coalition Statement of Professional and Ethical Standards for Marketing, Opinion, Media, and Related Research." It is shown in Exhibit 7-3. Adherence to these standards should guide the design of any marketing communication research study, as well as the evaluation of previously conducted work.

Limitations of Research

Finally, here are a few caveats to keep in mind considering research. Any research study provides only a snapshot of attitudes and opinions at the time the study was conducted. While consumer attitudes may be relatively enduring, they can change due to a variety of factors. When market conditions change, results of previous research studies may no longer be relevant.

In addition, research does not provide definitive answers to questions—it provides only guidance for decision making. Also, research adds both time and monetary costs to the design of a marketing communications program.

Exhibit 7-3
Research Industry Coalition Statement

Research Industry Coalition Statement of Professional and Ethical Standards For Marketing, Opinion, Media, and Related Research

Properly conducted, research has great value to its sponsors and to the public, as citizens and consumers. The value rests, in the end, on the intelligence, creativity, and technical skills of research practitioners and, most critically, on their integrity and ethical standards.

No code can cover all of the ethical issues for research activities. But, regardless of the technique or the nature of the problem, certain rules describe good research practice. The rules relate to:

1. How research should be done
2. How research should be reported
3. How the public ought to be treated
4. And how the business of research should be conducted

What follows are recognized standards for good practice in each of the four areas.

1. How research should be done

    • Have well defined, clearly stated objectives—and an honest purpose.

    • Follow an orderly research approach and methods appropriate to the objectives.

    • Collect information carefully, to minimize bias or distortion.

    • Provide data representative of a defined population or activity and enough data to yield stable results. (Projectability may not be a relevant standard for qualitative research or other exploratory, experimental and observational studies.)

    • Critically examine the collected information. Process and refine it. Analyze it thoroughly. Search it for meaning.

    • Check and verify each step in the research process.

2. How Research Should be Reported

    • Present the results understandably and fairly. Fully report the relevant findings, including any that may seem contradictory or unfavorable.

    • Separate any conclusions from the factual findings. Be sure the conclusions and the findings are consistent.

    • Describe how the research was done, in enough detail that a skilled researcher could repeat the study. (If any trade secrets or other procedures are not disclosed, these should be identified, with a statement that the research cannot be replicated independently.)

(more)

Exhibit 7-3
Research Industry Coalition Statement (continued)

- Explain the applicability and the limitations of the research and provide information users need to judge for themselves the usefulness of the research and its quality.

3. How the Public Should be Treated

- If research is meant to represent the public and its thinking, make certain that what is said is justified by the research design, the sample and the findings.

- Avoid wasting the time or goodwill of the public. Treat with respect those who are asked to give information. Free respondents from embarrassment and pressure. Recognize as absolute the right to refuse or terminate participation.

- Assure the privacy of respondents. Do whatever is necessary to keep collected information anonymous. In the verification of information, protect the identity of respondents from outside disclosure.

- Avoid undisclosed observation or recording of the participants in research, except for internal quality control or in places where observation by strangers or monitors is expected.

- Unmask those who disguise as research their efforts to get money from people or influence their thinking.

4. How the Business of Research Should be Conducted

- Be highly principled and rigorously fair in all business dealings. Treat this research and its practice with the respect due a responsible and professional activity.

- Accept only those assignments that can be reasonably completed with the time, skills and resources available.

- Compete for research assignments on competence and value, not with secret deals or illicit financial arrangements.

- Claim only legitimate academic degrees, clients and other qualifications.

- Protect the confidentiality of anything learned about a sponsor's business. Honor the sponsor's rights of ownership and access to the research they have purchased.

- Give sponsors the right to validate research done for their use. Welcome professional review of any research released outside of the sponsoring organization.

- Challenge any badly done or dishonest research. Defend good research that is attacked unfairly.

Underlying each set of standards—for how research should be done, how it should be reported, how the public ought to be treated and how the business of research should be conducted—are four basic principles:

- Do good research, for an honest purpose
- Describe it clearly and report it objectively
- Represent the public well; guard its interest and its privacy
- Be professional and fair in doing business

These principles cover the most basic of the responsibilities of those who do marketing, opinion and related research. They are the ethical foundation for research practice.

This statement is endorsed by the following associations:

Advertising Research Foundation

American Association for Public Opinion Research

American Marketing Association

American Statistical Association

Association for Consumer Research

Council of American Survey Research Organizations

Market Research Council

Marketing Research Association

National Association of Broadcasters

National Council on Public Polls

Newspaper Association of America

Qualitative Research Consultants Association

Society for Consumer Psychology

Despite these limitations, research that is properly and responsibly done can be valuable to marketers. With the background provided in this and previous chapters on the status of the marketplace today, the IBC planning process, and basics of consumer behavior and research, we now turn our attention to specific components of the IBC plan. We begin in Chapter 8 with budgeting considerations—communication investment strategies.

Summary

The IBC planning process should always begin with a thorough review of existing data. Secondary research can help to answer many of the questions in the brand business review. To develop a comprehensive understanding of current customers and prospects, primary research probably will be necessary. Various forms of qualitative and quantitative research can be used to study the target audience. Careful attention must be given to how the research is designed, conducted, and analyzed in order to derive valuable insights from the study.

8

Developing Communication
Investment Strategies

Traditionally, one of the most difficult tasks in developing a marketing communication program has been the determination of the budget. There are several reasons for this difficulty, all seemingly inherent in the process.

Connecting Spending to Returns

As was discussed in Chapter 5, most marketing communication activities have relied primarily on the measurement of the impact of communication effects. That is, the programs have been designed to develop increases in awareness or changes in attitude or message recall or other attitudinal effect. (Remember our discussion of the hierarchy of effects and DAGMAR measurement methodology from Chapter 5.) While very sophisticated research techniques have been developed to measure these attitudinal changes that occur as a result of communication programs, it has been quite difficult, if not impossible, to relate attitudinal change to actual consumer behaviors such as purchases or brand switching or, as we advocate, income flows. Thus, since the marketing organization is spending dollars on marketing communication programs and measuring attitudinal response—which can't be tied to consumer behaviors and therefore to dollar returns—it has been almost impossible to relate spending to returns. And, if you don't know how much you will get back for what you spend, then it is most difficult to determine how much you should spend or invest in a marketing communication program.

From the senior manager's view, unless we can relate outgo to income, the most logical approach would be to spend as little as possible, or to use some type of allocation process that assured that any spending would be an amount the organization could afford and an amount from which no returns would be necessary for the organization to continue to operate. That thinking pretty much summarizes what has been done in terms of advertising, sales promotion, and public relations budgeting. Direct marketing is, of course, a bit different. If you don't send out any promotional messages, no orders will come back in. So, DM is a special case. To cope with this marketing communication budget problem, management assumes the marketing and communication funds are a sunk cost and, while they would like to get some type of return, they don't really expect one.

Marketing Communication as an Expense on the Balance Sheet

In line with this management view of marketing communication as something which is very difficult to measure from an accounting standpoint, marketing communication allocations are almost always taken as current period expenses, not as corporate investments. This simply means that the organization treats all marketing communications as an expense item in the current fiscal year and simply disregards whether it gets any return from the expenditure. Commonly, returns from communication programs to the organization do occur, but they come back in as sales or income. Since those are separate functions, they are assumed to be unrelated to the communication investment. So, unlike the association of ingredients with manufacturing or of labor with providing a service, communication—being unconnected to any returns—goes unrecognized by the organization as generating any results.

Short-Term Versus Long-Term Returns

To complicate matters further, many marketing and communication programs, while they are taken as current period expenses, often generate returns over the long-term, perhaps for multiple fiscal years. For example, Hyatt International Hotels has developed a promotional program to build visits and bookings for their hotels during their traditionally slow periods of November and December and April and May. The promotional programs to support these events are conducted during the spring and fall in advance of the actual offer. In the spring, Hyatt promotes the special activities and events for the fall period and vice versa. Since Hyatt operates on a calendar fiscal year, investments made in spring 1999 could be recognized as bookings in fall 1999 if the process were organized to do so. However, promotional investments made in fall 1999 would not show any returns until spring 2000, therefore spanning two fiscal years. Presently, because of accounting rules, there is no way for Hyatt to apportion their fall 1999 promotional expenditures against spring 2000 returns, thus the short-term/long-term problem.

While both the Hyatt promotional programs just described are relatively short-term, that is, they are expected to generate results and returns to the organization within six to nine months, other communication investments that an organization makes may not show results for several years. For example, in building a brand, there commonly are delayed communication effects. Customers who are exposed to the marketing or communication programs may not be in the market for the product or service for several years, or they may wait many months to change their purchasing habits. Often, this is called the "lagged effect" of marketing communication, that is, it takes time for the activity to have an impact in the marketplace. These lagged effects create major budgeting and return problems for organizations since, as the result of existing accounting rules, there is no way to account for what might or could happen in the future. Thus, while short-term returns within the organization's current fiscal year could be tracked, connected, and related to the expenditure, those returns such as brand building that occur over several years are difficult to tie to the expenditure that produced them. We will see more of this in Chapter 15 when we discuss the evaluation of brand communication programs. There, we will suggest some new methods that will help to overcome this short-term/long-term problem.

The Mystery of the Creative Product

Perhaps the greatest complicating factor of how much to invest in a marketing communication program is the lack of the manager's ability to predict what will work or generate results in the marketplace, either in terms of sales or communication effects. For example, the promotion that McDonald's ran with Beanie Babies as a premium was a runaway success. Further, the Beanie Baby craze has continued over several years. In contrast, several other premiums tied to movies have not fared nearly as well, even though they were promoted just as aggressively. For example, Nike was not the first sneaker marketer to use an athlete as its spokesperson, but Michael Jordan has been an incredible boost to Nike sales. Some advertisements and promotions are hugely successful and generate substantial returns, while others simply fade quickly into history. Unfortunately, marketing managers are not very good at predicting the impact or effect of a creative product. Therefore, it is most difficult to determine in advance how much should be spent in support of a particular campaign or activity.

In addition, there are other influences that can affect a marketing manager's ability to determine an appropriate marketing and communication budget. Among them are the general economic climate in which the communication program may occur, the history and past success of the product or service in the marketplace, the attitudes of management about the importance of communication in the success of the organization, and the type of channels or distribution through which the product or service is sold. So, given the difficulty of measuring marketplace results for marketing or communication program investments, most organizations have simplified their budgeting approach to the absolute minimum. The methodologies that management uses generally rely on rules-of-thumb or historical precedent. In the next section, we discuss some of these rather simplistic budgeting approaches that are still common in the marketing world. Further, these will provide a comparison to the investment approach that we recommend for a brand communication program.

Traditional Methods of Marketing Communication and Advertising Budgeting

Following is a brief description of the most popular budgeting approaches used for advertising and marketing communication today. We will contrast these approaches with our brand communication investment approach later in this chapter. Note that all of these approaches consider advertising or marketing communication to be an expense with little expected return. There is no feedback loop in the budgeting process, nor is there any built-in measurement tool. Hence, it is assumed that the goal of the advertising or marketing communication program is simply to distribute messages or incentives to prospects, with little thought to what the impact might be or the return that might be generated.

Advertising or Marketing Communication to Sales (a/s or Percentage of Sales)

The sales revenue for the coming budget period is estimated. Either the past or current sales year may be used. From this, a fixed proportion is allocated for advertising or marketing communication. For example: the average factory price of a case of goods is estimated to be $9.00. The sales forecast is that 900,000 cases will be sold. The allocation ratio to sales is set at 7 percent (a/s = 7 percent). The advertising or marketing communication budget is, therefore, $9.00 × .07 × 900,000, or $567,000.

Although the percentage-of-sales method is quick, easy, and accepted by many firms, it has an inherent weakness. When sales are good, the budget increases. When sales are bad, expenditures are reduced. The basic principle at work is that marketing communication is a result of sales, which is contrary to the belief that advertising or marketing communication should generate sales.

Advertising or Marketing Communication to Margin (a/m)

The gross margin for the brand or company is estimated for the next budget period. A fixed proportion of this margin is allocated for advertising and marketing communication. Sometimes, profit is used in place of margin, and sometimes, the previous year is used as the base. For example, assume the gross margin for marketing communication in Ferd's Foods is expected to be $2.72 per case. If we estimate that we will sell 5,000,000 cases of Ferd's eggrolls and that we are willing to spend 18 percent of our gross margin on marketing communication, the budget would be established at $2.72 × .18 × 5,000,000, or $2,448,000.

Per Case Allowance (Case Rate)

Unit volume is estimated for the coming year. This volume can be in any form of units; it need not only be in cases. (It is also possible to use either a past or the current year.) A fixed sum per unit is allocated for marketing communication. For example, assume the organization was willing to invest one half of the entire contribution margin for each case of Ferd's eggrolls in the coming year. In this example, assume that is $2.60 total or, at 50 percent, $1.30. We will estimate 3,500,000 cases will be sold. Therefore, the marketing communication budget is $1.30 × 3,500,000, or $4,550,000.

Other Allowances

A fixed sum per unit may be allocated for marketing communication. The units can be almost anything—the number of households in an ADI, the number of retail outlets stocking the brand, the number of automobiles estimated to be sold, and so on. For example, based on average sales per store, an organization believes it can profitably allocate up to $150 per store per year for marketing communication. If we were to allocate that amount for all 30,500 supermarkets doing in excess of $2,000,000 per year in sales, our advertising and marketing communication budget would be $150 × 30,500, or $4,575,000.

Inertia

The budget from last year is simply extended for the coming year. In other words, "if it ain't broke, don't fix it." For example, if $4,500,000 was allocated for advertising and marketing communication last year and the company or brand had a successful year, the coming year's budget would be set at $4,500,000. The assumption here is that something is working for the brand or company. It might well be the advertising or marketing communication, so don't change it.

Media Inflation Multiplier

The media budget for the past year often is used as the base. An estimate is made of what increases in the media budget are likely to be required as compared with last year. This percentage increase is used to increase the budget for the coming year. For example, the working media budget for the past year was $5,000,000. Media costs are estimated to increase by 15 percent for the coming year. Therefore, the budget would be set at $5,000,000 × 1.15, or $5,750,000.

Competitive Comparisons

Using this method, advertising and marketing communication expenditures for the total category in which the brand or company competes are first determined. Then competitive advertising or marketing communication expenditures are estimated. Relating share of market, share of units, or other factors to the share of advertising or marketing communication, a ratio is established. From this, the planner then seeks to achieve a "share of voice" or share of advertising that is, in general, equal to the share of market that the brand holds. For example, if it is determined that total advertising expenditures in the eggroll market are estimated to be $50,000,000 and Ferd's has a 15 percent share of market, then Ferd's advertising budget would be set at $50,000,000 × .15, or $7,500,000. In some instances, the share of voice is set higher than the share of market in the belief that it is necessary to overspend in the category to achieve growth. One of the most well-accepted approaches is that developed by J. O. Peckham using Nielsen data. From his studies, Peckham found that to hold market share, the marketer should spend at the same level as share of market. To gain sales, it was necessary to spend at 1.5–2.0 times market share. In this way, the industry rule-of-thumb for determining spending was established.

Fixed Amount

Often, this approach is called "management decision." Management sets the amount to be spent on advertising or marketing communication. The planner's only task is to allocate available funds. The management decision may be the result of past experience, estimated effects of advertising and marketing communication, financial requirements, or simply a management control tool. In any event, the allocation may have everything or nothing to do with the needs of the brand in the marketplace. However, it is management's prerogative to set budgets of this sort.

Modeling

Some marketing organizations and their agencies, using past advertising spending experience and brand or company sales data, have attempted to relate advertising and sales in some sort of model. The model itself relies on mathematical equations that attempt to relate the past advertising expenditures to product pricing, distribution, market share, and, eventually, sales. The goal is to develop a model that explains the relationship among the various elements and that enables the modelers to forecast future results.

Task or Objective and Task

This method is essentially the one in which specific advertising objectives are set first and then determinations are made as to how to reach those objectives. The budget is the result of identifying the advertising or marketing communication activities that will be needed to reach the objectives and then estimating a cost for those activities. The sum of those costs then becomes the budget. Obviously, adjustments must be made because it is unlikely that most brands or companies can afford the cost of reaching all their objectives. Therefore, the objective and task method is essentially one of adjustment and negotiation to reach a point at which the set objectives can be met with a budget that the company or brand can afford.

An example of the objective and task method: The company wants to increase trial of its brand of cat food. Previous television schedules had used a 65 reach and a 3 frequency against the target market. As a result of some market tests, it was found that increasing the reach to 70 and the frequency to 4 against the cat owners generated the desired trial. Because the previous television schedule had cost approximately $3,000,000, the new budget was set at $4,000,000 to make possible the new reach and frequency media goal. An estimate by the media department indicated that it would cost an additional $200,000 to achieve these 70 reach and 4 frequency goals in the selected markets. Therefore, using the objective and task method, the brand communication planner would either (a) have to allocate the additional $200,000, (b) reduce the number of television markets, (c) lower the reach and frequency requirements, or (d) see if the sales goals for the brand could be adjusted.

The Transition of Information Technology

The transition of information technology, which was discussed in Chapter 1, has much to do with the increasing difficulty of budgeting investment levels for brand communication programs. Exhibit 8-1, which also appeared in Chapter 1, demonstrates the effect of change over time on the market.

When the marketer controlled the marketing system, as illustrated in the historical marketplace, it was a much easier task to determine the marketing communication investment level. Who did the marketer want to reach, what media alternatives were available, what form of communication would be used, when would the communication be delivered, and with what frequency? Thus, the marketer could decide what he or she wanted to do and could have a fairly clear idea of the funds required to do it. The goal of the marketer, of course, was to be as efficient as possible. The more messages or incentives that could be developed and delivered at a given cost, the better.

Marketing communications in the current marketplace, while a bit more complex and expensive, is still the same outbound system. The marketer, still somewhat in control, determines what messages and incentives need to be sent to the consumer and the channel and what level of investment might be required. The major challenge in this system has been, and continues to be, determining what marketing communications elements need to be purchased and what their cost is. Efficiency continues to be important; consequently, the marketer will try to negotiate lower prices on media, promotional materials, and so on.

In the twenty-first-century marketplace, an outbound system is replaced with interactive communication. Ongoing dialogue with customers and prospects creates major changes in the way brand communication programs can be delivered and budgeted. No longer does the marketer dictate the nature of the communication. Now the marketer must consider what the customer wants to receive and under what conditions. As a result, an organization must scrutinize thoroughly all of its investments in brand communication. The idea of a fixed percentage of sales being allocated to brand communication seems somewhat archaic in the interactive, brand-dominated, consumer-driven marketplace of the twenty-first century.

In the following pages, we outline a brand communication investment approach to determining how much an organization should invest in marketing and brand communication activities against specific customers or prospects. It is an outside-in

Exhibit 8-1
Marketplace Evolution and Revolution

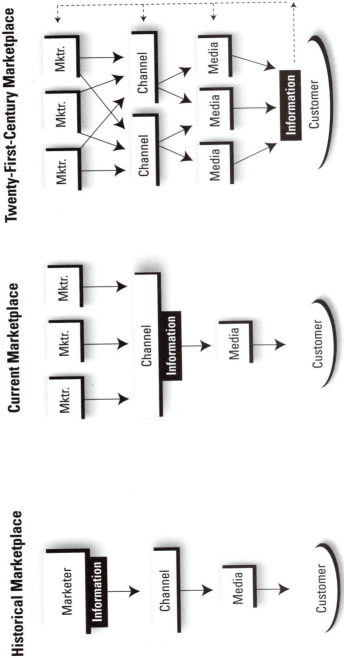

Historical Marketplace

Marketer → Information → Channel → Media → Customer

Current Marketplace

Mktr. / Mktr. / Mktr. → Channel → Information → Media → Customer

Twenty-First-Century Marketplace

Mktr. / Mktr. / Mktr. → Channel / Channel → Media / Media / Media → Information → Customer process based on the responses the planner expects to achieve. It is a financial approach as well, looking not just at what the organization might invest in brand communication, but at the cost of achieving the results that are expected. It is designed to look at both the short-term and long-term results the organization seeks. Finally, it assumes an interactive, ongoing brand communication process that is characterized by dialogue with consumers and prospects.

To lay the groundwork for this new approach to brand communication investment (notice we do not use *budget* or *spending* or *allocation*, for we consider brand communication to be an investment), we first describe a few basic financial concepts on which the process is based. We then illustrate the "outside-in" customer investment concept and follow that with a description of the actual investment decision approach.

Basic Financial Concepts Underlying Investments and Returns

The amount of money an organization is willing to invest in a brand communication program is, in general, directly related to how much management believes communication can affect income flows from customers and prospects. Thus, some companies in a given industry will invest heavily in a brand communication program while others allocate almost nothing for that purpose. The decision about how much to invest is based on management's belief in the likelihood that brand communication can help to achieve the overall goals of the organization.

Brand communication money is spent to achieve one or a combination of three basic organizational goals:

1. assist in optimizing profits;
2. assist in optimizing top-line dollar sales or unit volume;
3. assist in optimizing market share.

Each of these objectives is achieved by increasing or retaining customer or prospect income flows through sales and purchases. Let's look at the impact of these objectives on how brand communication investment might be made.

Sometimes the company objective may be to achieve some combination of these three goals, but most often one of the objectives is uppermost. This is critical for the brand communication planner to understand. If the goal is profits, the focus of the brand communication program likely will be on current customers, to retain and grow their business. This is simply because it generally costs less to grow an existing customer than to obtain a new one. Therefore, lower expenditures with higher returns help the bottom line. If the goal, however, is top-line sales or market share, brand communication should be used to gain new customers. In other words, invest to acquire customers. Their purchases will generate immediate sales and volume. Too often, planners overlook an important fundamental: the brand communication program must be aligned with overall corporate and management goals. As these examples of differing brand program focus illustrate, the objectives of management and the uppermost goal of the brand communication program must be in sync.

The Concept of Marginal Economic Returns

The concept of brand communication as an activity that can help achieve profits or sales or market share goals is often based on the economic concept of marginal returns on investments. The idea of marginal investment and returns is simple. The organization should continue to invest in any business activity as long as the return on the investment is greater than the investment itself. In other words, as long as the organization gets back more than it puts in, it should continue to put more money or funds into the activity. But what happens when the organization invests dollars in marketing communication and gets back attitude change? Attitude change is not a return on investment from the balance sheet standpoint: It can't be related to the money invested. Hence, there is no identifiable marginal return to the organization from a marketing communication investment.

Although the concept of marginal returns is simple, the allocation and evaluation process, particularly for traditional marketing and marketing communication programs, becomes quite difficult. First, in the case of marketing communication, allocations are made to several activities, such as advertising, sales promotion, direct marketing and events, and public relations. Each is treated separately and each is assumed to have some impact on the success of the product or service in the marketplace. So, how does an organization determine how much investment to allocate to each of these marketing activities? Assuming that the various available promotional activities do not all provide the same return, either a decision has to be made as to which activity should be funded and which should not, or some method of allocation must be found. Obviously, in an organization where each activity is funded and managed separately, this competition for funding creates major turf, power, and budgetary questions. Each manager wants more funding for his or her activity and each tries to prove that his or her activity is the most valuable to the organization. This dilemma is one of the major reasons for converting to a brand communication approach. It is the brand that is important to the organization because it is the brand that the customer buys, not the advertising program or the public relations event or the sales promotion premium. Taking a holistic view of brand communication solves many of these allocation problems, as we will demonstrate later.

In addition, management asks a second question: What is the return from the communication investment and how can we measure it so we know how much to invest now or in the future? Again, we return to the major issue of communication effects. As long as the organization measures only communication effects, that is, attitude change or awareness or recall, and is unable to connect those to sales or income flows returned to the organization, most budgeting systems have little value. A percentage of last year's sales or an estimate of this year's profits then becomes just as good a means of budgeting as any other. Thus, we are convinced that to determine how much an organization should spend on brand communication, it must have some way to measure what it can get back from that investment. We therefore focus on a measurable scorecard of investments and returns: customer income flows.

The third issue is how to measure returns. Simply measuring gross returns can be misleading. To accurately determine the return of brand communication investments, one must look at incremental returns, that is, what the brand communication investment generated that would not have occurred without that investment. As was illustrated in Chapter 4, the concept of incremental returns is key to determining not only the organization's return on its brand communication investment, but also the appropriate level of investment to be made now and into the future. The concept of incremental value is illustrated in Exhibit 8-2.

The organization in the illustration has an ongoing business: it has customers who generate income flows for the organization. Further, most organizations have some limit on the amount of business they can handle. In the case of a manufacturer, it is the number of units the plant can produce. For a hospital, it is the number of beds it has. For an airline, it is the number of seats on its planes. And for a consulting organization, it is the number of consultants it employs and the time they have available. In other words, there is generally some maximum output for almost any type of endeavor.

Between the current value level and the maximum output of the organization, there is a level of opportunity. It is at that level of opportunity where brand communication spending has an impact. How much additional business, or incremental revenue, can the organization obtain by spending against customers and prospects? This is the true value of brand communication investments, or, returns generated that the organization would not have obtained without the brand communication investment. This is what we call incremental returns to the organization.

Exhibit 8-2

The Concept of Incremental Value

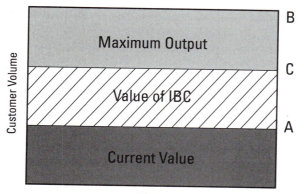

Of course, there is another side to the incremental revenue return to the organization as well. In the model, it is assumed that sales will continue at the present level without further investment. Often, however, this is not true. Customers move, their lives or businesses change, competitors become more aggressive, technology advances, and so on. Thus, the organization is continuously gaining and losing customers. Increasingly, as organizations learn more about this "most valuable customer," brand communication funds are invested in retaining existing customers. Therefore, there is often another goal of brand communication: retention of present income flows. This means that one can also consider how much the organization should invest simply to keep the business operating as it is today—not just to grow it now or into the future. It is the concept of marginal revenue on which we base our approach to brand communication budgeting and measurement of returns.

To further explain brand communication budgeting for the twenty-first-century marketplace, two other concepts are needed. One is the idea of inside-out versus outside-in, and the other is the closed-loop process. We take them in turn.

Inside-Out and Outside-In Communication Planning

As you might suspect by now, one of the major areas of change in how brand communication programs will be developed is the manner in which funding or investment levels are determined.

Inside-Out Approach

In the traditional historical marketer-driven marketplace or the current channel-focused approaches, funds are allocated on the basis of anticipated sales or expected profits of the organization. In other words, marketing communication budgets are designed to support the sales or channel efforts that would create the sale. Therefore, in organizations in which the sales force and heavy personal selling have been very important (for example, in business-to-business or professional services) marketing communication has never been very important. Product superiority, led by face-to-face selling, was believed to be the key ingredient, so the emphasis was on product features and sales activity, not the communication program.

In other areas, particularly those in which the manufacturer or marketer sold through channels (current marketplace in Exhibit 8-1), marketing communication has been more important but not vital to the organization. In these cases, marketing communication has been thought of as a way to support the retailer or the sales force in their efforts to influence the final or ultimate consumer. Obviously, if the channel doesn't actively support the product or service, then the likelihood of consumers or end-users being attracted to or continuing to use the product or service is limited. For example, even in consumer-oriented organizations selling consumer package goods, 50 percent of total promotional investments are made in trade promotion, not consumer advertising.

In both these systems, sales were estimated in advance, or sales goals were set internally for the brand, the product line, or even the organization. Communication was then set as a percentage of those estimated sales or profits. As illustrated in Exhibit 8-3, the marketing communications budget was derived from the sales estimate. Therefore, if sales estimates or margins went down, marketing communication spending had to be cut since it was a result, not a driver, of sales. It was a cost of doing business or supporting sales, not something that contributed to building sales or profits.

In the traditional inside-out approach to budgeting, marketing communication was not expected to contribute much, if anything, to returns. Therefore, it was treated as an expense, not as an investment with potential returns. That concept is illustrated in Exhibit 8-3.

Since sales or volume or profits were set in advance, most top corporate managers assumed marketing communication could do little to influence those goals. Thus, the

Exhibit 8-3
Typical "Inside-Out" Planning

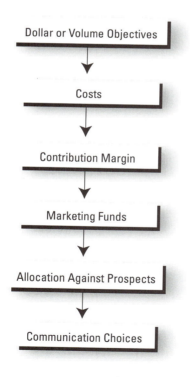

process of budgeting was focused primarily on trying to determine the most efficient amount to allocate to advertising and marketing communication, rather than seeing those as activities that might actually drive the business forward.

Outside-In Approach

In the brand communication investment approach, the view is entirely different. When we start with customers and identify their needs and wants, we can generally determine fairly accurately their value to the organization, or how many units or dollars worth of the product or service they buy now and more accurately estimate how much they might need to buy in the future. Knowing customers' present value (how much they currently buy) allows us to identify their potential or future value. Consequently, we can better estimate the value of particular brand communication programs to influence their purchases or usage decisions. We then could compare the costs of a particular communication program against the estimated return and determine whether the customer would be a viable investment for the organization. We call this an outside-in approach, and it is illustrated as Exhibit 8-4.

As can be seen, in this approach we start first with customers or prospects and work back to the organization. By beginning with customer value, we have a much better idea of what we would be willing to invest in that customer or customer group to generate or maintain future income flows, since we know that customer's value to the brand and to the organization.

Exhibit 8-4
"Outside-In" Planning

In brand communication investment planning, we look first at the current worth of our entire array of customers and prospects and value them according to dollars, units, profits, or the like. From that valuation process, we can then determine how much we might invest in them to generate future returns. In short, we look at "dollars out" in the form of brand communication programs and we evaluate results on the basis of returns resulting from those brand communication activities.

In this outside-in brand communication process, investments are made in customers, not in marketing communication activities. In other words, we invest in customers and prospects through various communication forms such as advertising or sales promotion or public relations—not in the tactics and techniques themselves. Advertising, sales promotion, events, and so forth never return anything to the organization. It is only customers who return something in the form of increased or continued sales or trial or other income-generating activity. This is a key point to remember in the brand communication approach: we invest in customers, we don't invest in "communication stuff." Advertising and direct marketing and public relations are simply ways we are investing in customers and prospects—they are not ends in and of themselves.

The Closed-Loop Investment Process

A key element in brand communication investment determination is the use of a closed-loop process. As we discussed earlier in Chapter 4, this closed-loop process has much to do with our new ability to invest to gain returns, rather than simply buying various forms of marketing communication and hoping that we were having some type of influence on customers and prospects. The closed-loop process we use is illustrated in Exhibit 8-5.

Exhibit 8-5
The Closed-Loop Process

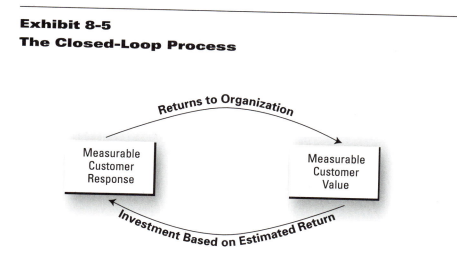

The closed-loop process is directly related to the outside-in approach we have just discussed. That is, it is based on the premise that today most organizations can value customers, customer groups, and even prospects on the basis of the value they currently have and their potential for the future. That is the basis for the evaluation of customers on an outside-in basis.

As we have discussed throughout this text, technology is primarily responsible for the development and implementation of our new approaches to viewing brand communication as a corporate investment, not a corporate expense. With databases, we can now capture, store, and manipulate data about millions of customers in terms of their purchases from not only our organization but often from our competitors as well. This ability to manage customer behavior records allows us to understand customer value currently and to estimate their value in the future. By knowing current value and having some idea of future value, the planner can invest in brand communication programs to generate returns—not just buy communication activities.

Returning to the closed-loop process in Exhibit 8-5, it is clear that if we know the current value of a customer, particularly in dollars at the contribution margin line, we can fairly quickly determine how much we might be willing to invest to either retain that customer, grow him or her, or perhaps migrate him or her to another product or brand line. (The contribution margin is simply the profit that an organization achieves on the sale of a product or service after cost of goods, distribution, marketing, and general administrative expenses have been deducted from gross sales. Commonly, it is the profit before income taxes.) Some examples will illustrate the point.

Present Customer Value

The first step in determining investment levels is to determine the financial value of a customer or prospect. Obviously, if we have historical records on customers, this is not a difficult task. If we have only generalized estimates of the value of customer groups, however, the task becomes somewhat more difficult but not impossible. As you will recall, in Chapter 7 we discussed the research technique of extrapolation, that is, extending or estimating customer value from other information. We might, for example, know only that $10,000 worth of our product was sold in Market A during the previous six months. From that information we can likely estimate who might have purchased those products, and from that, we can estimate or extrapolate the value of individual customers or perhaps customer groups. Therefore, while it is ideal to have exact individual or household data, in many cases, estimates or extrapolations will suffice for our budget-setting needs.

Potential Value or Income Flow

To invest in a customer or customer group we also need to know or estimate the value of the customer in the future. In other words, we need some idea of the potential value of the customer, which we might influence as a result of an effective brand communication program. We calculate this potential value through share of requirements, or the amount of the total requirements that a customer might have in our category as defined by our share of those requirements. An example will help illustrate the point.

Assume you are a Bank A customer. You have a checking account at Bank A, an auto loan, and a safe deposit box. From the view of Bank A, you are a fairly good customer since you use three of its services. But you also have a Visa card, an investment account with a brokerage house, a home loan, and a savings account at Bank B at which you used to do business but never got around to closing out accounts when you moved two years ago.

From the view of Bank A, you have potential to increase your deposits, roll over your auto loan, and retain your safe deposit box rental. Bank A's share of your banking requirement needs is only 30 percent because you are giving 70 percent, via the Visa card, investment account, home loan, and savings account, to Bank B. If Bank A could simply get you to convert to its Visa card and switch your savings account over to it, then it might account for 60 percent of your banking and financial needs. In other words, Bank A could double its business with you simply by capturing a greater share of the banking you are currently doing, or improving its share of your requirements.

Thus, to understand fully how much Bank A would be willing to invest in you as a customer, it must know not only your present value, it must also have some estimate of the share of your total banking requirements it has as well. This knowledge is key to determining how much an organization would invest in brand communication against a customer or set of customers.

Estimating Investment Levels

Once the marketing organization knows the value of a customer or group of customers or prospects, it can then determine how much it would be willing to invest in growing, maintaining, or retaining that customer. Let's continue the bank example from above. Assume that Bank A has identified you as one of its key customers. Let's say that through the analysis of its customer data, Bank A has determined that you are worth $500 net to the bottom line each and every year it keeps you as a customer. In other words, based on the income flows you generate through the auto loan, checking account, and safe deposit box rental, after the bank deducts its costs, you are worth $500 to Bank A each year.

Now the brand communication planner asks, "How much would or should Bank A invest in brand communication to keep you as a customer?" You're worth $500 per year to Bank A. How much would you invest? Five percent, that is, $25? Or, maybe a flat $50 per year? Or, using one of the other traditional budget-setting approaches, maybe Bank A wants to send you four brochures, seventeen television commercials, and four newspaper ads, all of which would total $116. How much should Bank A invest in you?

From an economic standpoint, Bank A could afford to invest up to $500 (your net total value to it during the year) in brand communication programs and still break even. That is, Bank A would get back in income flows just what it spent against you to retain you as a customer. That's right, Bank A could invest $500 to keep you as a customer, not grow your business at all, and still break even.

However, if Bank A wanted to get a 20 percent return on its investment in its customer, it could spend only $400 on brand communication ($500 value × 20 percent = $100; customer value of $500 less the brand communication investment of 20 percent or $100 = $400). If, on the other hand, Bank A wanted to make a net return on you of 50 percent, it could invest only $250 in brand communication, and so on.

If this is truly the case, why haven't marketing organizations used this approach before? Why apply the percentage-of-sales or management judgment or per unit allocation approaches? The answer, of course, lies in technology. Only since about the early 1990s have we been able to capture, store, and manipulate the data every organization already has. The data make this approach possible. So, it is technology that allows us to develop the new brand communication approach, and it is technology that makes obsolete many of the traditional ways we have planned, developed, and implemented traditional marketing communication programs, particularly budgets and investments.

Share-of-Requirements as an Investment Decision Tool

Another key element in the brand communication investment approach is the share of requirements. If we know the value of a customer, in your case, $500 per year to Bank A, then the assumption is that we should develop some investment strategy that suggests the amount the bank should be willing to invest in its customers. So if we valued customers only on their current value, every $500 customer would receive the same allocation. That idea is good, up to a point. The differentiating factor then becomes potential value based on share of requirements.

Let's assume your college roommate and you use Bank A. Further, let's assume that currently you both are worth $500 to the bank, that is, both of you generate ongoing income to Bank A of that amount. To Bank A, you and your roommate look exactly alike. You're both worth $500. You went to the same school (maybe even had the same major). You're the same age. Shouldn't Bank A be investing about the same amount of its brand communication resources in each of you? The answer is no, and for a very good reason. Earlier, we determined that Bank A had about 30 percent of your banking business. In total, you are worth about $1,650 in banking services to everyone in the market. Your roommate, however, is very conservative. She doesn't believe in credit cards and doesn't carry one. She pays cash for everything. She tends to spend every penny she makes on clothes, cosmetics, and a lavish lifestyle, and she has no investments at all. In other words, Bank A has about all the business that she is going to give any bank. That is, Bank A has about 100 percent of her business already. Given this, from the current view of Bank A, you and your big-spender roommate look alike. Though the same in current value, you have much more potential for Bank A in the future than does your roommate. If you were Bank A, then, how would you invest your brand communication funds? Quite probably, Bank A will spend the least it can on brand communication to retain your roommate and will spend a disproportionate amount on you since you have substantial potential. Thus, in terms of brand communication investment, Bank A must be able to discriminate between good customers and bad, good prospects and bad, and good investments and bad.

In summary, the brand communication investment approach starts with customers or prospects and determines their current value. Then, the customer or prospect's share of requirements or potential future value is determined. From that, the marketing firm makes an investment decision on how much to invest in that customer or customer group based on the experience it has had with the customer or the expected future value the customer might have. It is closed-loop and it is based on returns, not expenditures.

Obviously, there are other factors that will influence the investment decision of the organization—chiefly, the plan to deliver either messages or incentives to customers and prospects. The investment decision is driven to a great extent by what the planner believes will be needed to influence the customer or prospect to be addressed. For that decision, we will need some functional expertise. That follows in the next several chapters.

Summary

The outside-in communication investment process for IBC planning relies on assessments of current and potential customer value. Companies determine how much to spend on any given customer or prospect based on that individual's return potential. This is a far less arbitrary approach than traditional methods of marketing communication budget allocation, and it ties marketing communication activities directly to the results they generate.

Part 3

9

Brand Building

Mass Media Advertising

As the title of this chapter indicates, mass media advertising is most often viewed as a type of brand-building communication. Advertising agencies generally classify its effects as more long-term than short-term. However, current research by John Philip Jones indicates that often there is significant immediate impact on sales from advertising efforts, and that, in fact, long-term effects of advertising are generally the result of successive short-term effects.[1] Along with public relations activities (discussed in the next chapter), mass media advertising is one of the most effective ways to get brand messages out to large audiences fairly inexpensively.

The authors' experience suggests that mass media advertising performs a number of useful functions that affect both the short-term (business-building) and long-term (brand-building) success of the brand. For example, mass media advertising helps to retain brand loyal customers who are often willing to pay a higher price for the brand. Further, advertising holds those users at a lower cost than would be the case with sales promotion activities. Mass media advertising also helps to bring new users into the product category (though not necessarily to the advertised brand) and to increase purchasing among light users. In addition, advertising influences the brand choices of customers who switch brands on the basis of sales promotion activities: switchers tend to move among brands with similar levels of advertising, rather than switching across all brands in the product category. Finally, mass media advertising also strengthens the manufacturer's hand with retailers, because brands

---

[1]John Philip Jones and Margaret H. Blair, "Examining 'Conventional Wisdoms' About Advertising Effects with Evidence from Independent Sources," *Journal of Advertising Research* 36 (November–December 1996): 37–59.

that are well supported with advertising tend to command better profit margins and more shelf space than brands that lack such support.

Advertising should be regarded as the marketing communication technique best suited for creating and enhancing the brand's overall image and positioning in the marketplace. Advertising is often viewed as the creator and the sustaining element of brand identity, providing an umbrella under which more narrowly targeted types of marketing communication can be developed for specific customer groups. Because we have invented new and more sophisticated techniques to get messages to consumers, one of the biggest problems most marketing communication planners face today is getting the consumer's attention in an extremely cluttered media marketplace. The big question the planner must ask in developing advertising executions in support of the overall brand image is: What can I say and how can I say it so that my message is important enough for the consumer to pay attention to it, understand it, and react to it?

The answer to this question separates the excellent planner from the one who is only average. That is, to achieve excellence the planner must truly understand the person he or she wishes to reach with the advertising. In other words, the planner must have customer insight. He or she must be able to empathize with the consumer in order to solve his or her problem by means of the product or service. Both the problem and the solution must be clearly and concisely stated so that the consumer receives the message and is able to act on it easily. The next step, then, concerns the execution or presentation of the sales message.

Enhancing the Strategy with a Strong Execution

What to say is one of the most important decisions in a brand communication campaign. Indeed, other decisions simply reinforce that decision. But also important is the advertising execution, or how the brand communication strategy is communicated to the prospect. In general, a sound strategy will succeed regardless of the execution, because if what is said in the advertising is of benefit to the prospect or solves a prospect's problems, some response usually will occur. However, if the strategy is presented in an interesting, exciting, and memorable way, it is more likely that larger numbers of prospects will respond quickly to the advertising message. Thus, to qualify this position a bit, although the "what to say" is vital, the "how to say it" can prove to be the difference between a successful campaign and an outstanding one.

Here's an example. Quaker Oats Company's Life cereal was first introduced in 1961. After several moderately successful attempts to sell this new nutritional, ready-to-eat cereal to different target markets, Quaker Oats and its advertising agency at that time, LaRoche, McCaffrey & McCall, developed the basic strategy of promoting Life cereal as "the nutritional cereal that tastes good." After a few years and several different advertising executions, this strategy emphasizing nutrition and good taste had started to generate consumers' interest in Life cereal. Although sales were growing, the product was not an overwhelming success.

Then, in early 1968, sales of the cereal took off. That growth was due directly to a new advertising execution. Specifically, it was due to a television commercial known simply as "Mikey" that was developed by the Doyle Dane Bernbach agency. The strategy emphasizing nutrition and good taste did not change; the execution did. The "Mikey" commercial immediately caught the attention of ready-to-eat cereal buyers and users, and Life began its sales climb. The decision to feature taste in the advertising started the cereal on the road to success. The translation of that strategy through the "Mikey" commercial provided the impetus to make Life cereal a major winner. Some twenty years after the "Mikey" commercial first appeared, it was still winning new customers for Life cereal.

The "Big Idea"

Great advertising campaigns, particularly those brought about by great advertising executions, usually are the result of what is termed a "big idea." As with the "Mikey" example, the big idea often is very simple, but it brings a realism, an understanding of the marketplace, and an empathy with the target market that makes the advertisement jump off the page or television screen and into the life of the reader or viewer.

Through a series of simple but highly memorable executions, Goodby, Silverstein & Partner's recent "Got Milk?" campaign for Dairy Management does a marvelous job of reminding consumers why and when they should drink milk. Billboard ads feature larger-than-life photos of foods that just taste better with milk: a peanut butter and jelly sandwich, cupcakes, Cookie Monster's beloved chocolate chip cookies. The only copy is the question "Got Milk?" Likewise, television spots present situations in which doing without a glass of milk is simply unthinkable. In one, a man gets a phone call from a radio station conducting a contest. He knows the correct answer to the contest question, but he can't give it because he's just taken a big bite of a peanut butter sandwich and is out of milk.

The campaign was originally developed for the California Milk Processors' Association as part of a larger national effort to turn around a decline in milk consumption. The advertising proved so effective on the West Coast that it was licensed to Dairy Management for use nationwide. "Got Milk?" fits all the characteristics of the Big Idea described above: it's simple, realistic, and speaks to situations with which the target market can easily identify. An example from the "Got Milk?" campaign is shown in Exhibit 9-1.

How to Develop a Big Idea

As stated earlier, a big idea in an advertising campaign generally is quite simple. For example, demonstrating how the product complements a variety of everyday foods is not conceptually very difficult. Yet, commercials such as "Got Milk?" are considered to be quite creative, and the people who conceive such ideas are regarded as some of the best in the advertising business. They're successful not just because they are creative, but because they have used *controlled creativity*. As a result, these advertising

Exhibit 9-1
"Got Milk?" Advertisement

executions not only get attention, they get the sales message across. Most of all, they convince the consumer that the product really does provide a competitive benefit.

So how does one go about coming up with a really great idea that will turn a sound strategy into a winning advertising campaign—a "Mikey" or a "Got Milk?" That is usually the result of *ideation*, or the generation of ideas. Can anyone learn to generate ideas—to come up with new and exciting concepts and approaches that will grab the attention of the audience and drive the sales message home in an interesting and effective way?

Although there are some people who seem to have an innate gift for generating ideas, almost anyone can be taught to develop sound advertising executions. In fact, a big idea usually is more the result of perspiration than inspiration. If we use a sound, logical, proven approach as preparation for generating ideas, the ideas will come. Not all will be of the caliber of a "Got Milk?" of course, but they will be exciting advertising ideas that grab consumers' attention.

Basic psychological literature on creativity comes from several theories. All attempt to explain creativity and how it occurs. These include the psychoanalytic theories of Freud, Kris, and Kubie; the Gestalt theories of Wertheimer; the association theories of Mednich; and the composite theories of Koestler, Gruber, and Hadamand. All have contributed something to our understanding of how the human mind works and how people generate new approaches, new concepts, and new solutions to old problems.[2] Although a thorough review and explanation of theories of creativity are beyond the scope of this book, four particular concepts and techniques should prove helpful in understanding how ideas come about and in generating effective ideas for advertising.

---

[2]Thomas V. Busse and Richard S. Mansfield, "Theories of the Creative Process," *Journal of Creative Behavior* 14, no. 2 (1980): 91–103.

James Webb Young's *A Technique for Producing Ideas*

The best-known and perhaps most widely accepted method of developing advertising ideas is that proposed by James Webb Young, a creative executive with J. Walter Thompson advertising agency. Young developed his concept of idea generation in 1940. It has been widely quoted and discussed since that time. In summary, Young suggests that a "new idea is nothing more or less than a *new combination* of old elements." Young, in his book *A Technique for Producing Ideas*, suggests five specific steps for creating new combinations of old elements:

> First, the gathering of raw materials—both the materials of the immediate problem and the materials which come from a constant enrichment of your store of general knowledge.
>
> Second, the working over of these materials in the mind.
>
> Third, the incubation state, where something besides the conscious mind does the work of synthesis.
>
> Fourth, the actual birth of the idea—the "Eureka! I have it!" stage.
>
> And fifth, the final shaping and development of the idea to practical usefulness.[3]

Young's formula sounds very straightforward. Perhaps a few words of explanation will illustrate the process better.

Gathering Raw Materials

Young suggests that there are two types of materials to be gathered, the specific and the general. Specific elements and information are directly related to the product or service to be advertised. The general materials are all those things about life and events that a person gathers by living and being interested in the things around him or her. Because all ideas are simply new combinations of old elements, obviously the more elements available for this combining procedure, the greater the possibility of developing a combination that can be truly fresh and effective.

Working over the Materials in the Mind

Young likens the ideation process to chewing food, that is, masticating the materials for digestion. We start by turning over in the mind all the materials. Young says, "[You] take the different bits of materials which you have gathered and feel them all over, as it were, with the tentacles of the mind. . . . [F]acts sometimes yield up their meaning quicker when you do not scan them too directly, too literally." In other words, look for the meaning, not the absolute facts, in the combinations.

---

[3]James Webb Young, *A Technique for Producing Ideas* (Lincolnwood, Ill.: NTC Business Books, 1975), pp. 53–45.

The Incubation Stage

"In this third stage you make absolutely no effort of a direct nature. You drop the whole subject and put the problem out of your mind as completely as you can." In other words, turn the problem over to the unconscious mind; let it do the work. It is here that new combinations, new processes, and new meanings generally occur.

The Birth of the Idea

According to Young, "Now, if you have really done your part in these three stages of the process, you almost surely experience the fourth. . . . Out of nowhere the idea will appear. . . . It will come to you when you are least expecting it." That is, there is no explanation of how the new combination of old elements comes about; it simply occurs as a result of the first three steps. That's the mysterious, always exciting part of the process.

The Final Shaping and Development of the Idea

Once more, quoting Young, "[This is] the stage which might be called the cold, grey dawn of the morning after." Not every idea is complete. Often, it requires work and/or adaptation to make it fit the situation. At this stage, Young suggests many good ideas are lost simply because the idea generator wasn't patient enough to go through this final adaptation process—this final shaping of the raw idea into a really big idea.[4]

Arthur Koestler's "The Act of Creation"

Although Young's method has worked for many successful advertising people, it is not the only way to develop a big idea. Arthur Koestler's concepts of how ideas are developed and created are not directly related to advertising, yet they have had much influence on how people believe the mind works. Koestler's basic notion is the idea of *bisociation*. That simply means a new idea often occurs when two thoughts collide and combine. He describes it more fully as occurring when two frames of reference ("matrices") coincide. The coincidence or collision of these matrices results in a combination previously not thought of. In other words, two rather common concepts, thoughts, situations, or even events, when brought together through bisociation, result in a new and original idea. In fact, Koestler describes it as being "an act of liberation—the defeat of habit by originality."[5]

We need only look at various advertising executions to see how Koestler's bisociation concept works. It's in the "Mikey" commercial, "a nutritional cereal that tastes good."

---

[4]Ibid., pp. 30–54.

[5]Arthur Koestler, *The Act of Creation* (New York: Macmillan Co., 1964), p. 96.

David Bernstein, author of *Creative Advertising*, provides an excellent example of Koestler's concept of bisociation. The following example, one used successfully in Europe, illustrates how ideas come into conflict and create a new idea.

PROPOSITION

Lowenbrau is very expensive but it is the best quality beer you can buy. The Lowenbrau proposition gives you little to work on. If there were a "product plus"—an ingredient, strength or price advantage—an idea would be easier to arrive at. . . . If you were launching the first ever German beer on the domestic U.S. market, you could simply state that fact. . . . But if you accept that premise in this case you end up with a headline such as:

"Lowenbrau—supreme quality"
or
"Lowenbrau—when only the best will do"
or
"The mark of excellence"

And so on. Ad nauseam (which is a good name for this sort of advertisement). Brian Palmer has a favorite all-purpose headline for this proposition. "Preferred by those who like it best." It has the merit of sounding impressive and being totally acceptable to Weights and Measures Inspectors. . . . To return to the Lowenbrau proposition . . . and the idea.

IDEA

"When they run out of Lowenbrau, order champagne."

OBSERVATIONS

1. The idea re-presents the proposition. It says that Lowenbrau is a top quality beer without saying, "Lowenbrau is a top quality beer."

2. The idea is a relationship. The product has been associated with another, more accepted, symbol of quality. The association, moreover, justifies the price.

3. The idea is a reversal of normal thought processes. Instead of the beer being an acceptable alternative to champagne, it suggests the reverse.[6]

As Bernstein demonstrates, two ideas that were normally thought not to be related and even in conflict have collided and produced another, even more compelling idea. That's how bisociation leads to the birth of ideas.

---

[6]David Bernstein, *Creative Advertising: For This You Went to Oxford?* (London: Longman Group, 1974), pp. 86–88.

Edward deBono's "Lateral Thinking"

Edward deBono, in his book, *Lateral Thinking for Management*, defines *vertical thinking* as follows:

> *Vertical thinking is traditional logical thinking. It is called vertical thinking because you proceed directly from one state of information to another state. It is like building a tower by placing one stone firmly on top of the preceding stone; or like digging a hole by making deeper the hole you already have.*[7]

He contrasts vertical thinking with *lateral thinking*. Lateral thinking generally can be considered to be "discontinuity" or "change for the sake of change" thinking. Perhaps the best way to explain lateral thinking is to contrast it with the more traditional, or vertical, thinking that most of us practice. DeBono gives several examples.

1. Vertical thinking is selective; lateral thinking is generative.

2. Vertical thinking moves only if there is a direction in which to move; lateral thinking moves in order to generate a direction.

3. Vertical thinking is analytical; lateral thinking is provocative.

4. Vertical thinking is sequential; lateral thinking can make jumps.

5. With vertical thinking, one has to be correct at every step; with lateral thinking one does not have to be.

6. With vertical thinking, one uses the negative in order to block off certain pathways; with lateral thinking, there is no negative.

7. With vertical thinking, one concentrates and excludes what is irrelevant; with lateral thinking, one welcomes chance intrusions.

8. With vertical thinking, categories, classifications, and labels are fixed; with lateral thinking, they are not.

9. Vertical thinking follows the most likely paths; lateral thinking explores the least likely.

10. Vertical thinking is a finite process; lateral thinking is a probabilistic one.[8]

In short, lateral thinking seeks to explore relationships among elements, situations, events, or activities to generate new and unique ideas. These relationships are necessarily simple because we tend to think in patterns or in some sort of self-organizing system. Although these thought patterns are highly advantageous in

---

[7]Edward deBono, *Lateral Thinking for Management* (New York: American Management Association, 1971), p. 4. Copyright 1971 by the American Management Association. All rights reserved. Reprinted by permission of the publisher.

[8]Edward deBono, *Lateral Thinking: Creativity Step by Step* (New York: Harper & Row, 1970), pp. 39–46. Copyright 1970 by Edward deBono. Reprinted by permission of Harper & Row publishers.

dealing with the myriad rather mundane activities necessary to survival in our environment, they tend to inhibit the development of new approaches or concepts. Lateral thinking attempts to break out of these self-organizing thought patterns to look at new, unexplored relationships. In summary, deBono describes lateral thinking as follows:

> The purpose of lateral thinking is the generation of new ideas and escape from the old ones. The need for lateral thinking arises from the patterning behavior of the mind which is not good at restructuring ideas to bring them up to date and allow full use of available information. The traditional habits of thinking are very effective at developing ideas but not very good at restructuring them. Lateral thinking is designed to supplement traditional thinking and especially to introduce discontinuity that is necessary for restructuring ideas. The basic process of lateral thinking is the escape from old ideas and the provocation of new ones. The ideas generated by lateral thinking are selected and developed by traditional thinking methods.

The principles of lateral thinking could be summarized as follows:

1. Recognition of dominant or polarizing ideas.
2. The search for different ways of looking at things.
3. The relaxation of the rigid control of vertical thinking
4. The use of chance and provocative methods in order to introduce discontinuity.[9]

DeBono lists several methods that can be used to stimulate lateral thinking and to break the vertical thinking pattern, including (a) generate alternatives to present situations; (b) challenge present assumptions; (c) innovate; (d) suspend judgment for a period of time; (e) reverse a common approach; (f) develop analogies for the situation; and (g) brainstorm.[10] The intent of this method, then, is to use nontraditional, lateral thinking patterns, turn an idea upside down, and look at it in a different way.

William J. J. Gordon's Synectics

William J. J. Gordon has developed a creative thinking training program that is associative in nature. Called *Synectics*, it is based on forcing metaphor (lifting an idea out of context and using it in another context to suggest resemblance to some other concept) and analogy (an indication of form, process, or relationship that explains steps and procedures).

Gordon bases his approach on three types of analogies. The first, *direct analogy*, is a metaphorical comparison between a key element of the problem and a rough similar concept in a new context. In the second, *personal analogy* is developed by

---

[9]deBono, *Lateral Thinking for Management*, pp. 50–51.

[10]Ibid.

trying to empathize with the problem, for example, trying to imagine how an umbrella would feel opening in a storm. The third approach is called *compressed conflict*, in which new ideas are created by combining two word descriptions that contradict each other, such as "delicate aggressor."

The Synectics exercises are built around a simple logic formula: "A is to B as C is to what?" As the foundation of analogical thinking, it becomes creative by using free association to stimulate the wildest possible connections.[11]

Judging Advertising Executions

In most cases, the IBC planner and the advertising copywriter are probably not the same person, although in agencies that practice account planning, the planner and creative team will work closely in developing executions. Often, however, a brand manager or advertising manager for a manufacturer may be directly involved in the development of the advertising strategy, but dependent on the advertising agency creative personnel or, perhaps, creative people in his or her own organization to provide the actual physical translations. Similarly, in a traditional advertising agency, an account executive or other manager may have a large part in developing the strategy but rely on the creative department to translate that strategy into the actual advertisements. In any case, how does the IBC planner evaluate the executions, that is, determine whether advertising translations will be effective? How can the planner recognize a big idea? Is there a way to assure that what is presented will work in the marketplace?

A list of guidelines or checkpoints that have proven effective over the years follows. Use these guidelines to make sure that the advertising really is on target and does what it is supposed to do in the campaign. Remember, however, with one exception, these are simply guidelines, not rules. Sometimes there is a reason for bending the guidelines, and the good planner is receptive in those instances.

Is the Advertisement on Strategy?

This sounds like a simple evaluation for the IBC planner to make, but often it's the biggest problem with a campaign. The strategy is planned to say one thing and the advertising ends up saying another. Study the IBC strategy first. Then look at the advertising execution. If the execution doesn't translate the strategy, toss out the execution and start over, no matter how cute, clever, or exciting the actual advertisement, commercial, poster, or whatever seems to be. The first and guiding rule is that the advertising must say what it set out to say in the strategy; the execution must follow the strategy, without exceptions. (Actually, this is the only guideline mentioned previously that should be regarded as a rule.)

---

[11]Adapted from Sandra E. Moriarty, *Creative Advertising: Theory and Practice* (Englewood Cliffs, N.J.: Prentice-Hall, 1986), pp. 4–5.

Will the Execution Appeal to the Right Audience?

A great deal of time has been spent defining and locating the target market for the advertising message. The question now, assuming the ad is on strategy, is, "Will this execution appeal to that group of people?" If the answer is no (or even only maybe), toss out the ad and start over.

If we really know our target market, we should have a strong idea of whether a specific execution or interpretation of the strategy will appeal to it in terms of layout, style, grammar, music, tone, and so on. The execution should fit the audience. (This is another instance in which the account planner's detailed knowledge of the target market should prove invaluable.)

Does It Speak from the Marketer's or the Consumer's View?

Is the advertisement written from the marketer's or the prospect's viewpoint? One good check of an advertising execution is simply to ask, "Does this ad help the prospect buy, or does it simply try to help make a sale?" There's an enormous difference between those views.

Is the Execution Clear, Concise, Complete, and Convincing?

A big problem with many advertisements is that the writer often assumes the prospect knows (or cares) as much about the product as the writer does. When this happens, the reader, listener, or viewer is often left far behind. So, first, the advertisement must be clear. Is it easy to follow? Are all the benefits listed and supported? Is the advertisement complete? Is there anything important left out—anything the target market might need to know or have in order to make a decision in favor of the product or service advertised?

Also, the advertisement must be convincing: If the prospect never saw another advertisement or commercial for this product or service, would he or she know enough about how to buy and where to buy so that a sale could occur? If the answer is no, this is the time to make necessary changes.

Does the Execution Overwhelm the Message?

A common failing of many advertisements, but of television advertisements in particular, is that they succeed in getting themselves—not the brand—remembered. When this happens, usually it is the result of the advertising execution simply overwhelming the advertising message. The layout, color, or animation, for example, is so outstanding that it totally overshadows the message the advertiser is trying to get across. Remember, the advertising is there to sell or influence the purchase of a product or service. If it can entertain, amuse, thrill, or even bring a tear, wonderful.

But the primary job of advertising is to sell a product, a service, or an idea. Don't let the execution get in the way.

Is There a Call to Action?

Surprisingly, a great deal of advertising does not ask for any commitment from the viewer, reader, or listener. No effort is made to make the sale, no attempt is made to get some action or commitment from the prospect. Remember that the purpose of advertising is to persuade someone to do something he or she isn't doing now. That something can be a brand-building change of opinion, a mental pledge to consider the product at the next buying opportunity, or a business-building trial of the product. Regardless, all advertising should be designed to get some sort of response. After all, if the advertisement doesn't ask directly for the desired response, that response probably won't come.

Are You Proud Enough of the Advertisement to Show It to Someone Close to You?

Is this piece of advertising something to be proud of, something we would want our names on if ads were signed? If not, start over. Advertisements we aren't proud of rarely gain the response we want, particularly from the target market. Consider that people don't like to buy from rude, crude, or pushy salespeople. If advertising is to succeed, it must make friends of prospects and customers. Does the execution accurately reflect us and the brand? If not, change it now.

Pretesting Advertising Executions

Once the IBC message strategy has been executed into advertisements, the next logical question is whether the advertising will achieve the objectives set for the campaign. To determine how well the advertising communicates the sales message and if it will be effective in the marketplace, many major advertising elements and most proposed advertising campaigns are pretested in some way. There is an inherent belief in the value of pretesting advertising, perhaps because of the traditional difficulties encountered in measuring advertising effectiveness after the fact. There is, however, debate over how this testing should be done. Many practitioners argue that unless the testing system is acceptable, pretesting is not worth the time or effort, and experienced judgment is better.

To Test or Not to Test

The discussion of whether to pretest advertising continues to be heated. Most creative people are opposed to pretesting. They argue that a creative idea can't be subjected to ranking or numbering. Furthermore, because advertising is considered a form of creativity, they believe advertising pretesting stifles the creativity. On the other hand, clients and advertising executives are hesitant to invest millions of dollars in an advertising campaign with only their own intuitive guidance as to how effective the campaign might be. The controversy may never be resolved; nonetheless, there are five very good reasons to pretest or evaluate advertising prior to its use in the media or as a part of the final campaign.

To Prevent Disaster

In general, advertising pretesting gives only a limited amount of information, but that information can be very important. The primary objective is to determine whether the advertising campaign is an absolute disaster; that is, will the proposed advertising actually drive people away from the brand? Advertising pretesting is usually quite reliable in meeting this objective.

To Test New Approaches to Old Problems

Most advertising campaigns submitted for pretesting are for existing or established products. In those cases, the advertiser usually knows how the previous advertising has performed, or at least has some idea of what effect it had on consumers. Thus, there is a standard against which new advertising can be measured to determine if it is more effective, delivers the sales message more clearly or more efficiently, is better understood, or is more relevant than that done previously. If, for example, it was found that the new advertising was actually less effective, the advertiser would make changes prior to any major investment in the campaign or perhaps simply revitalize the present campaign.

To Evaluate Alternative Methods of Communicating the Brand's Sales Message

As is the case in any sales situation, several things can be said in several ways to communicate the benefits of the brand or to present the brand's solution to the consumer's problem. Some ways will be better or more effective than others. Usually, however, it is impossible to tell which way is best without actually trying the alternatives out with consumers. Therefore, the success of a new campaign isn't simply a judgment that can be made by the advertising's creators, by the IBC planner, or even by an account planner with comprehensive understanding of the consumer. Rather, the advertiser needs to try the proposed alternative creative approaches with consumers to get their reactions and see which alternative works best. Pretesting, no matter how effective, can't identify what the single best approach may be, but it can identify the best of the alternatives being tested.

To Determine How Well the Advertising Achieves Its Objectives

The pretest gives the planner an opportunity to see how well the proposed advertising campaign performs in terms of the objectives that have been set. If, for example, the major objective of the campaign is to generate brand name awareness among category nonusers, that can be measured in the pretest. If the advertising doesn't perform well, changes can be made. Thus, pretesting advertising provides a preliminary measure of how the advertising might perform in the marketplace to achieve the message objectives that have been set for the campaign.

To Improve the Proposed Advertising Before It Is Used

Obviously, the planner wants to use the strongest, most effective advertising possible in the campaign. The pretest provides an opportunity to identify any unforeseen weaknesses and correct them before the actual campaign. Not only can the advertising be improved, but major savings in production costs may result as well.

In summary, perhaps the best view of why advertising pretesting should be used and what it is all about is provided by Alan Hedges, a market researcher in England:

> We too often speak of testing advertising (a term which should be struck from all our vocabularies) as if we were submitting the piece of film or print to a testing machine (which happens to be made up of consumers) which will accept or reject it; just like the quality control process at the end of a production line which rejects items which are over or under weight, or whatever it may be.
>
> This is a very misleading way of looking at creative research, and one which I believe is responsible for a good deal of the misdirected activity which we find in this field. We are not testing the advertising since we do not have, and cannot have, any such machine. We are studying consumers in order to gain some better understanding of the way they are likely to react to stimuli of different kinds, the stimuli being advertisements or advertising ideas. Since both the stimuli and the repertoire of possible responses are highly complex (and since the research situation is a very unusual one), we know that we cannot make any precise and simple formulation of what a given advertisement will achieve—but we can improve our understanding to the point where we are better able both to produce relevant and effective ideas and to judge when we have a campaign which is adequate for our purposes.
>
> Therefore advertising research should seek to enrich our understanding of the way a particular advertisement is likely to affect people.[12]

When to Pretest

It is best to test any advertising at the earliest stage possible—usually at the message strategy development stage, at the time when the central benefit or key message to be communicated to the consumer is being identified. Unfortunately, however, much advertising pretesting occurs farther down the line, after copy has been approved, television commercials bid and sometimes even produced, and the battle lines drawn

---

[12]Alan Hedges, *Testing to Destruction* (London: Institute of Practitioners in Advertising, 1974), pp. 36–37.

between those who believe the advertising sound and good and those who think it can be improved. In general, advertising can be pretested at four basic stages: the concept stage, the message strategy stage, the rough stage, and the stage at which the advertisements are finished.

The Concept Stage

The most basic measurement of the value of a brand is often taken at the concept stage. Although concept testing is not an actual advertising testing technique, it is widely used for new product ideas or suggestions and new approaches for existing products. Thus, it is often the first step in the development of an IBC campaign.

The concept statement is a few sentences that outline to the consumer the attributes, uses, and advantages of a product or brand. Frequently, the concept statement is accompanied by an illustration or picture of the product as it looks or will look when produced, or of the problem solution it might provide. The combination of this illustration and the accompanying descriptive statement is called the *concept board*. It is used to help the consumer visualize what the product might be or might do.

More than one concept statement can be developed for the same product, and the alternative concepts can be tested against one another. For example, two concept summaries for the same product might read as follows:

Concept A: A home computer that can run a wide variety of software. Hundreds of programs are already available and more are being written daily to provide you with a broad range of options.

Concept B: A home computer that thinks like you do. Keys are labeled in clear language and programs operate in a sensible fashion. You won't have to spend months trying to decipher every command.

As you can see, each concept focuses on a different set of product attributes. The concepts would be tested against one another to see which is most attractive to prospective consumers, helping the IBC planner determine the more effective message strategy.

The IBC Strategy or Message Strategy Stage

The message strategy is the basic sales idea. This statement is a summation of what the message component of the IBC approach is supposed to communicate to the consumer. It is the real "heart" of the message portion of the campaign. Therefore, it is vital that this statement is sound, believable, relevant, and persuasive to the target consumer; otherwise, the advertising (and other message communication elements, such as public relations) is certain to fail no matter what else is done.

The message must offer the consumer a benefit or provide the solution to a problem. Often the message strategy is pretested in the form of a promise statement, such as the following designed to appeal to competitive brand users:

> *The Grumman American airplane gives you superior fuel and speed efficiency compared with similar models from Piper, Cessna, and Beechcraft.*

For pretesting purposes, the statement may be written in a form that provides a summary of the offer: "If you buy this brand, you will get this benefit, or it will solve this problem." The statement is often accompanied by an illustration of the product or the benefit offered to help the consumer visualize the offer.

The goal of most message strategy pretesting is to determine the strongest of several alternative sales messages that might be used with the brand. Therefore, the message strategy testing should take place very early in the development of the campaign.

The Rough Stage

The most common stage at which advertising is pretested is in a rough form—one stage prior to final production. The newspaper or magazine advertisement is done most often as a computer comprehensive, using scanned-in art to approximate the final visuals. For radio, a rough recording without full sound effects might be used. Television usually is tested in the form of a storyboard that may be shown to the respondents in its rough art form or photographed in some way to illustrate what is going to take place in the commercial. Many commercials are put into rough storyboard form and then transferred to sound on a video called an *animatic*. The sound and storyboard illustrations can be synchronized so that they represent a very rough version of the final commercial. These animatics may be either very rough or close to finished commercial form, depending on the method of testing to be used.

Generally, roughs are used when testing alternative ideas, such as benefit statements or strategies. Also, they may be used to test various executions of the same strategy to see which one best communicates the sales message.

The Finished Advertising Form

The pretesting of finished advertising is done primarily by large advertisers for major campaigns, and it is a fairly common practice for them. The form used is the finished print ad or commercial in almost exactly the same form that the consumer would actually see, should the campaign be approved for release. The most common reason for pretesting finished advertising is that many sales messages and advertising executions, particularly those that make use of image or mood, cannot be totally or accurately rendered except in final form. Thus, the argument is made that only a finished ad or commercial can truly elicit what the consumer's actual response to the advertising might be.

Most of the syndicated services that pretest advertising use a finished commercial or print ad for testing. Although testing finished advertising is much more expensive than testing at the earlier stages outlined, it is often required with certain types of campaigns.

Although the preceding discussion might have made it seem that advertising pretesting in various forms is an either-or situation, it is not. In fact, some advertisers pretest their message strategies and advertising at all of the stages mentioned. This is particularly true for campaigns being developed for new products, or when major changes are planned for existing products. The pretesting scheme should be developed and implemented by the planner just as the other parts of the campaign are. Budgets for this pretesting must also be set and included in the overall plan.

What to Measure

Obviously, what is to be measured in the pretest is often determined by the form or the stage at which the message strategy or advertisement will be tested. For example, with product concepts, it is difficult to test much more than varying levels of appeal. With finished television commercials, however, it is possible to test several things, including understanding, recall, and information communicated. Thus, the planner should determine in advance what is to be pretested, when, and in what form.

Measuring Against Objectives

The first rule of any advertising pretesting is to set objectives for the measurement. In other words, it must clearly be stated what is being measured and what the objectives of the test are. If the importance of varying new product concepts is to be measured, the real objective is to determine if the product as described will actually solve consumer problems or offer strong enough benefits to generate trial. On the other hand, if the objective is to measure the effects of a rough commercial, totally different objectives may be set for the advertising, such as implanting the brand name, communicating the sales message, and building knowledge of the product. Therefore, the advertising pretest should reflect the objectives of the advertising campaign. If the objective is to build awareness of the brand name in the marketplace, then the advertising should be evaluated on the basis of how well it communicates the brand name, not on how well the spokesperson is remembered. A simple rule: The results of the pretest should be measured on the same basis as the objectives that have been set for the campaign.

Effects Measured

In 1991, the Advertising Research Foundation (ARF) released the results of its "Copy Research Validity Project." This ambitious study, built on results from interviews with thousands of consumers, was designed to determine which copy testing methods and measures yielded the best predictive ability. The project showed that copy testing does work; that is, ads that test well also sell products in the marketplace—the ultimate test of any advertisement. The results suggest that pretests should use multiple measures to evaluate executions. Although the study found that all copy testing measures in common use have value, some measures emerged as better predictors than others.[13]

1. Persuasion. A question designed to measure the persuasive power of an execution might be asked as follows: "Based on the commercial you just saw, how would you rate the brand in the commercial on an overall basis using these phrases?" The consumer then chooses from phrases ranging from "Excellent" to "Poor." In the ARF study, the average overall brand rating generated from this type of question was an excellent predictor of commercial effectiveness.

2. Salience. This measure was a particularly strong indicator of market success when asked in a "pre/post" situation. That is, consumers were asked a salience question both before and after exposure to a test commercial; an increase in salience after commercial exposure was characteristic of successful executions. A sample salience measure is "When you think of margarine [product category], what are all the brands you can think of?" The first brand mentioned is considered to be the most salient.

3. Recall. Uncued commercial recall emerged as one of the best predictors in the ARF project. Memorable advertisements work to sell products. "What commercials do you remember seeing during the program you just watched?" would be a measure of uncued recall. (Cued recall would involve asking whether the respondent remembered seeing a commercial for a particular brand of product. As such, it is a much weaker measure.)

4. Communication. Communication measures go beyond simple recall to explore what elements of an execution are remembered. Correct recall of the situation in the advertisement and the message's main point were also good predictors of marketplace success. Main-point communication can be tested using a question such as: "Of course, the purpose of the commercial was to get you to buy the product. Other than that, what was the main point of the commercial?"

5. Commercial Reaction. One of the most interesting findings that emerged in the project was the importance of execution likability. Consumers are more likely to buy products that are advertised in likable executions. Likability can be measured in a number of ways, including asking consumers how strongly they agree or disagree with the statement "This commercial was one of the best I've ever seen."

6. Diagnostics. Like communication measures, diagnostics explore consumers' feelings about specific aspects of the advertising execution. In diagnostic testing, consumers are asked how strongly they agree or disagree with opinion statements about advertisements. The ARF findings suggest that consumers are more likely to respond to ads that tell them new things about a product, that tell them how a product works, and that allow them to learn something.

---

[13]Russell I. Haley and Allan L. Baldinger, "The ARF Copy Research Validity Project," *Journal of Advertising Research* 31, no. 2 (April/May 1991): 11–32.

Pretesting Hazards

While pretesting can indeed help to point out advertising problems earlier in the development process, some basic rules of thumb on the hazards of *any* form of pretesting should be pointed out.

1. Pretesting judges only the best of the lot tested. Any pretesting procedure gives one the opportunity to find the best of those advertisements being tested—not the best of all possible approaches. If all the advertisements being tested are quite poor, only the best of the worst will be selected, not the best possible approach.

2. Pretests should be realistic and practical. Although it is always tempting to ask consumers to make many evaluations in a pretest, keep in mind what consumers can and can't judge from the advertising being shown them. They can't, for example, tell whether an advertisement will turn the brand's sales around or whether it will generate the level of awareness or comprehension the planner is seeking. Respondents can tell only what the advertising does to them and how they react.

3. Try to prevent respondent prejudice. One of the most difficult tasks in advertising pretesting is preventing respondents from becoming "advertising experts." This simply means that respondents have a tendency to judge advertising by offering improvements rather than responding as consumers. When this happens, the opinions given are often worthless. Although "advertising expertise" is a difficult problem to overcome, efforts should be made to limit respondents' opinions and comments to their proper role as consumers of products and services, not as creative directors.

4. Campaigns can't be tested. All advertising pretesting is for individual advertisements in a given situation. Consumers can't tell what the effect would be of multiple exposures over time or how differing executions for the same strategy might affect them when coupled with other marketplace activities. Remember, individual advertisements are being tested, not a campaign.

5. Recognize the inherent problems in pretesting. Some common situations often occur in advertising pretests. These involve the problems arising from the difference in viewing advertising in a controlled setting as compared with normal viewing. For example, advertisements with negative appeals usually score poorly in pretests but are sometimes successful in the marketplace. Similarly, advertising that is entertaining, humorous, or light usually scores very well in advertising pretests, although it may not perform as well in the normal media channels. Finally, "hard sell" facts about the brand usually score the lowest of all on pretests. Yet, there is ample evidence that hard sell advertisements and commercials may be most effective in communicating with the intended audience. Certain types of advertisements may also score well depending on the specific pretest measure used (commercials with music, commercials with a great deal of action, and so on). It is important to keep these problems in mind when evaluating the results of a pretest.

Pretesting Results

One of the most difficult things to accept in advertising pretesting is the result. Much work has gone into the development and formulation of the campaign, much research has been done, long hours have gone into developing appeals, and yet a group of fifty consumers in a period of only a few minutes can totally reject the entire premise of a campaign. One's natural reaction is to seek another jury, to find another group who truly understands the campaign.

Unfortunately, although results of pretesting are only directional, they may uncover major flaws in the thinking and planning of a campaign. If that is the case, accept the truth. Determine, if possible, exactly what went wrong. Learn why the theme or appeal is weak or has little potential.

Most of all, learn to accept the fact that not every campaign will test well, not every campaign idea is a winner. If the pretest should prove that the campaign is a poor one, certainly an attempt should be made to determine why. But a vendetta against the "dummies in the market" who don't understand the campaign is the fault of the planner, not the respondents. Although it is often one of the most difficult parts of advertising development, one must accept such results as a guide for improvement.

Summary

Mass media advertising can be used for both business-building and brand-building efforts, although the latter is its generally accepted role. Advertising often creates the image-building umbrella that supports other communication efforts that may be directed at more narrowly defined audience groups. Successful advertising campaigns result from creative idea generation backed up by various types of research used to assess the communication effectiveness of the advertisements.

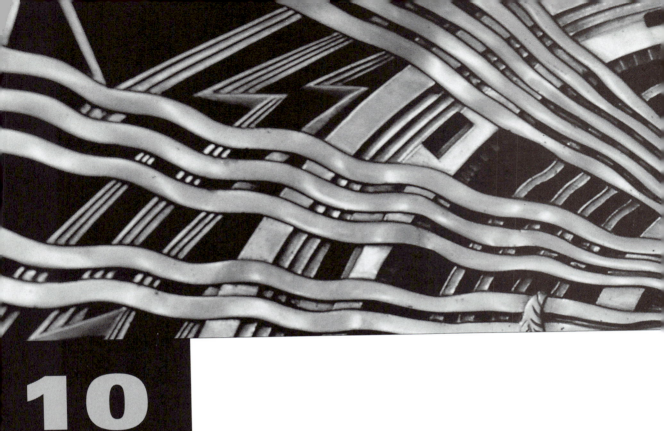

10

Brand-Building

Public Relations

What Is Public Relations?

Public relations is arguably the broadest of the marketing communication disciplines, involving a wide range of activities and specializations used to deliver corporate and brand messages. Public relations has been defined as "the management function that evaluates public attitudes, identifies the policies and procedures of an individual or organization with the public interest, and executes a program to earn public understanding and acceptance."[1] Public relations has developed from efforts specifically focused on selling products and services to a corporate advisory role. As a result, virtually all public relations activities are best classified as long-term, brand-building options. In the introductory section of this chapter, we explore the scope of public relations before turning to a look at specific public relations activities associated with brand communication.

Models of Public Relations

Grunig and Hunt[2] identify four models of public relations, all of which still exist to one extent or another in today's marketplace. The first model, most closely identified with P. T. Barnum, is the *press agentry/publicity* model. Characterized as

[1]H. Frazier Moore and Bertrand R. Canfield, *Public Relations: Principles, Cases, and Problems*, 7th ed. (Burr Ridge, Ill.: Irwin, 1977), p. 5.

[2]James E. Grunig and Todd Hunt, *Managing Public Relations* (New York: Holt, Rinehart & Winston, 1984).

propaganda, this type of public relations is focused on sending out strongly positive messages about the product, service, or organization, with little effort to strike a balance between puffery and fact.

The second model is the *public information* model, which is associated with the early public relations practitioner Ivy Lee. This form of public relations focuses on educating the public about organizations and issues; there is much greater emphasis on truthfulness than in the press agentry/publicity model. But, like the former model, public information is a one-way flow of ideas, from company to public, with little effort to conduct research to assess either message content or effectiveness.

The third public relations model is the *two-way asymmetric* model, developed by Edward L. Bernays (often referred to as the father of modern public relations). This model has persuasion as its chief goal, and relies heavily on research designed to monitor and evaluate public attitudes on issues.

The final model is the *two-way symmetric* model, also associated with Bernays but further refined by educators and professional leaders. This model focuses on building understanding between organizations and their publics through the use of research intended to evaluate what misunderstandings exist and how they might be cleared up.[3] As will be seen later in this chapter, both of the two-way models are important aspects of successful public relations efforts today.

Public Relations Roles

Another way of looking at the scope of public relations is through consideration of the different roles public relations practitioners play. Broom and Smith[4] have identified five roles commonly seen in the public relations industry. The *expert prescriber* conducts research to identify and solve client problems. The *technical services provider* is a specialist in an area such as writing, graphics, or production. The *communication process facilitator* acts as a professional mediator or moderator for the organization and its various publics. The *problem-solving process facilitator* helps organizational clients apply accepted processes for solving public relations problems. Lastly, the *acceptant legitimizer* provides support and approval for client decision making. Each role is important; which is most appropriate for a particular public relations decision depends on the specific nature of the problem. For example, if it's time to begin developing next year's annual report to company shareholders, the technical services provider is probably the person to call. If, on the other hand, management and employees are having major disagreements over communication issues, a communication process facilitator might be needed.

The Excellence Study

Over a ten-year period from 1985 to 1995, the International Association of Business Communicators (IABC) Research Foundation sponsored an extensive examination

---

[3]Summarized from ibid., table 2-1, p. 22.

[4]Glen M. Broom and George D. Smith, "Testing the Practitioner's Impact on Clients," *Public Relations Review* 5, no. 3 (1979): 47–59.

Exhibit 10-1

Spheres of Communication Excellence

of communication practices in the United States, Canada, and the United Kingdom. This project, called the "Excellence Study," was intended to identify the characteristics of "excellent" communication departments and determine the impact of excellence in communication management and public relations on organizational effectiveness.[5] Through a series of research methods, the study identified three spheres of communication excellence, shown in Exhibit 10-1.

The knowledge core deals with strategic management capabilities and draws on both two-way models of public relations: asymmetrical (persuasion-based) and symmetrical (understanding-based) communication. Excellent communication organizations are constantly engaged in research to better identify and understand their publics, and to refine how they communicate with those publics.

The second layer, shared expectations, concerns the public relations department's interactions with other power players in the organization. In excellent communication organizations, top management both appreciates the role of communication and relies on senior-management level input from the communication department.

The final layer, participative culture, deals with overall organizational culture. "Organizations with predominantly participative cultures infuse their employees

---

[5]David M. Dozier, with Larissa A. Grunig and James E. Grunig, *Manager's Guide to Excellence in Public Relations and Communication Management* (Mahwah, N.J.: Erlbaum, 1995).

with shared values, pulling employees together as a team to accomplish a common mission. Open to outside ideas, these organizations favor innovation and adaptation over tradition and domination."[6]

Defining Publics

The notion of diverse publics, all of which are critical to the organization's success, is key in public relations. A look at how public relations practitioners segment their publics helps to underscore the importance of two-way communication and corporate openness in communication success. Public relations personnel use traditional segmentation bases such as geographics, demographics, and psychographics in identifying publics, but they also look at a range of other issues. *Covert power segmentation* involves identifying those persons within a community who exert influence on a variety of issues or decisions; a public relations practitioner working as a government lobbyist might try to determine which congressional aides' opinions are listened to most frequently by lawmakers. *Position-occupant segmentation* looks at job categorizations instead of the individuals who hold those jobs. For example, a segment might be defined as financial industry analysts. *Reputation segmentation* deals with identifying people who are influential within social networks, such as opinion leaders and members of charitable society boards. *Membership segmentation* classifies people based on the organizations, professional associations, and clubs they belong to—Sierra Club members, for example. Lastly, segmentation based on *role in the decision process* looks to identify all those who play a part in decision making within an organization or industry; a public relations communication program might be targeted at decision influencers.[7]

Public Relations in IBC

This overview of the scope of public relations, the nature of communication excellence in the field, and the variety of approaches used to segment publics helps to explain why many public relations practitioners have been opposed to the inclusion of public relations in IBC. They feel that IBC reduces public relations' involvement in brand building to the press agentry/publicity or public information models, and focuses almost solely on the technical services provider role. As explained in one of the leading public relations textbooks: "Public relations historically has been relegated to a market-support function, concentrating on techniques instead of strategy. . . . Thus, many public relations practitioners prefer to remain in separate departments and coordinate, not integrate, with other functions such as advertising, direct mail, and marketing."[8]

---

[6]Ibid., p. 17.

[7]Glen M. Broom and David M. Dozier, *Using Research in Public Relations: Applications to Program Management* (Englewood Cliffs, N.J.: Prentice Hall, 1990).

[8]Dennis L. Wilcox, Phillip H. Ault, and Warren K. Agee, *Public Relations: Strategies and Tactics*, 5th ed. (New York: Longman, 1997), p. 21.

From a strategic perspective, IBC planning would seem to have a great deal to do with public relations, particularly the two-way symmetrical model of public relations. As we discussed earlier, IBC focuses on understanding the customer in order to develop better, more effective brand-building communication programs. Further, customer satisfaction often depends upon successful dealings with employees, government entities, stockholders, and the like. There is clearly an important role for public relations in brand communication efforts.

Brand Building or Business Building?

Like traditional advertising, public relations is generally considered to have long-term effects and to be primarily concerned with delivering messages. This places public relations efforts firmly in the brand-building category. Interestingly, the public relations industry has struggled with how to better measure and evaluate the effectiveness of its activities. A group of practitioners has developed standards for assessing both public relations outputs, or short-term results, and public relations outcomes, the longer-term impact.[9]

Outputs include media content analysis, Internet analysis, trade show participation, and event planning—specific activities that can be measured relatively easily. Outputs concern "how well an organization presents itself to others, the amount of attention or exposure that the organization receives."[10] In a sense, outputs concern how good a job is being done in the areas of press agentry/publicity and public information.

Outcomes concern measures of awareness and comprehension related to a firm's objectives, recall and retention of messages, and "possible opinion, attitude and behavior changes, resulting from the communications efforts."[11] Because measurement of outcomes necessarily involves conducting research among targeted publics, outcomes concern the firm's application of two-way asymmetrical and symmetrical communication.

Types of Public Relations Activity

As we noted at the beginning of this chapter, public relations encompasses a broad range of activities. The major areas are discussed below, with particular attention given to those used most frequently in brand communication campaigns.

Counseling

As the Excellence Study documents, public relations managers in the most successful communication programs serve a very important advisory role to senior

[9]Walter K. Lindenmann, "Setting Minimum Standards for Measuring Public Relations Effectiveness," *Public Relations Review* 23, no. 4 (1997): 391–408.

[10]Ibid., p. 392.

[11]Ibid.

management. They make recommendations on policy issues as well as decisions related specifically to communication. For example, corporate communication personnel at Mattel have been actively involved in ongoing discussions and lawsuits designed to protect the company's rights to the Barbie trademark. Magazine and newspaper articles on a variety of lawsuits Mattel has filed often quote Sean Fitzgerald, Mattel's vice president of corporate communications.[12] Part of Fitzgerald's job is not only speaking on the company's behalf, but also taking part in discussions on actions that should be taken in protecting the use of Barbie's name and likeness.

Research

Companies practicing either of the two-way models of public relations make extensive use of research to better understand and influence publics. Among the types of research used to measure attitudes and opinions are those discussed earlier in Chapter 7.

Media Relations

Press coverage is a critically important public relations output. Public relations specialists use publicity efforts (discussed below) to try to get coverage in the print and broadcast media. They also respond to requests for information or comment from journalists working on stories that concern their company or the company's products and services. Media relations activities might also include arranging press tours of manufacturing facilities, press conferences to announce new product introductions, and press coverage of the corporation's annual stockholders meeting.

Publicity

Publicity is defined by David Yale as "supplying information that is factual, interesting, and newsworthy to media not controlled by you."[13] A critical aspect of marketing public relations, publicity is described as "the process of planning, executing and evaluating programs that encourage purchase and consumer satisfaction through credible communication of information and impressions that identify companies and their products with the needs, wants, concerns and interests of consumers."[14] Marketing public relations involves activities related to persuading customers and prospects to buy (or continue to buy) the firm's products and services.

Among the tools used in publicity are press releases, fact sheets, press kits, and video news releases. Each is described briefly below.

---

[12]Aline McKenzie, "Why Mattel Is Suing to Guard Barbie Trademark," *Des Moines Register*, November 16, 1997, p. 7.

[13]David R. Yale, *The Publicity Handbook: How to Maximize Publicity for Products, Services, and Organizations* (Lincolnwood, Ill.: NTC Business Books, 1991), p. 2.

[14]Thomas L. Harris, *The Marketer's Guide to Public Relations.* (New York: Wiley, 1993), p. 12.

Press Releases

The press release is the basic building block of a publicity program concerned with story placement. This is where the important information about the product or service is summarized in a way that will catch the media's attention. Just as we would customize our advertising message for each target, we need to customize our press releases for the various media we contact. Exhibit 10-2 shows a press release sent out by Bristol-Myers Squibb about Science Horizons, an educational science program for middle school aged students.

Fact Sheets

A press release should be written so it can be used without any editing. That means all the relevant information must be included. Of course, there may be additional important information that doesn't really fit into the press release. That's where the fact sheet comes in. Fact sheets include more detailed information on the product, its origins, and its particular features. By providing fact sheets, we make it easier for the media to write a story about our product because the fact sheet can help to clear up misperceptions and answer reporters' questions, saving them a phone call or e-mail query.

Press Kits

The press kit pulls together all the press releases, fact sheets, and accompanying photographs about the product into one neat package. A comprehensive folder can serve as an attention-getter and keep the provided materials organized.

Video News Releases

The video news release (VNR) is the video equivalent of a press release. Prepared for use by television stations, the typical VNR runs about ninety seconds and can be used to highlight some important feature of the product. Exhibit 10-3 shows a Web page from TVN, Inc., outlining their VNR-related services for prospective clients. (TVN's URL is http://www.tvninc.com.)

Employee/Member Relations

An organization's employees are an extremely important internal public. Corporate public relations people often spend a great deal of time developing employee communication programs, including regular newsletters, informational bulletin boards, and intranet postings. In service organizations in particular, these kinds of activities can be used to help support brand communication efforts, for example, using the company newsletter to remind employees about the importance of prompt and polite customer service.

Exhibit 10-2
Bristol Myers Press Release

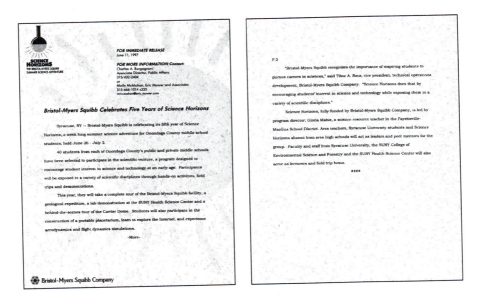

Community Relations

It is critical that companies maintain the role of good community citizen within the markets where they have offices and manufacturing facilities. Many companies actively encourage their employees to take part in community organizations, and local corporations are often major sponsors of community events and activities such as arts presentations, blood drives, and educational activities.

Public Affairs

Often, corporations are quite interested in decisions made in the public policy arena. After all, standards on family medical leave, environmental protection, and workplace safety, among others, all have the potential to affect how individual companies do business. The public affairs facet of public relations attempts to both influence and help the corporation adapt to public policy.

Government Affairs

Lobbying is probably the best-known aspect of government affairs. Most of the major national public relations agencies have offices in Washington, D.C., to work with legislators and federal regulators in an attempt to influence government decisions. Of course, government affairs activities take place at all levels of government: local, state, and national.

Issues Management

Issues management involves identifying issues that might have an effect on the corporation, determining the relative importance of those issues, and then assessing whether the corporation might be able to exert influence on those issues. For example, workers at a McDonald's restaurant in Macedonia, Ohio, recently went on strike to try to win better working conditions. The strike attracted a lot of attention, both in Macedonia and nationally. (The strikers were the subject of jokes on both Howard Stern's radio show and *The Tonight Show*.) McDonald's corporate management chose not to get involved in the strike, viewing it as a local issue unrelated to the chain's national operations. A *Washington Post* article on the incident quoted a McDonald's spokesperson as saying, "This is an isolated thing handled by a local owner-operator."[15] Obviously, the people responsible for issues management at McDonald's headquarters determined that this was a relatively unimportant issue, and one in which the corporation could have little influence. Had management chosen to react differently, perhaps by holding a press conference or the like, the story might have received even more attention and had a strong impact on the national brand image.

Financial Relations

Because so many major brand marketing organizations are publicly held companies, financial relations has become a key aspect of public relations activity in the United States. Downturns in company earnings quickly lead to declines in stock prices, and, frequently, to top executives losing their jobs. Financial relations people are responsible for establishing and maintaining relationships with the investment community, including industry analysts, stockbrokers, and journalists specializing in financial reporting. The financial relations specialist has the job of getting maximum press coverage for a company's financial successes and putting the best face possible on any financial losses. Financial relations personnel write the company's annual report as well as any other communications directed to stockholders.

Industry Relations

The primary public that industry relations specialists deal with is other businesses operating within the same industry, as well as trade associations. The recent travails of the tobacco companies help to underscore the importance of industry relations:

---

[15]Michael Colton, "Big Mac Attack," *Washington Post*, April 26, 1998, p. F01.

while the various companies are not in agreement on all issues, they have banded together in many instances to try to influence policy and legislation, with the thinking that there should be strength in numbers.

Development/Fund-Raising

This is a particularly important area for not-for-profit organizations such as arts organizations, educational institutions, and community service programs. These types of companies often rely on donations from the public, government, and other organizations to make up all or part of their operating budgets. Development specialists identify likely prospects for giving, prepare proposals to present to those prospects, and work to nurture ongoing relationships.

Multicultural Relations/Workplace Diversity

Specialists in this area help companies enhance opportunities for diverse populations within the company's employee and customer publics. Mistakes related to multicultural issues can create major publicity problems for corporations, such as the widely publicized charges against Denny's Restaurants related to the mistreatment of black and Asian customers. The company is now spending a great deal of time and money putting all of its employees through cultural sensitivity training programs and publicizing its efforts to solve past problems.[16]

Special Events

Event marketing is rapidly gaining popularity. The International Events Group estimates that more than 5,200 companies spent $6.8 billion on event sponsorships in 1998. Of that, about 65 percent goes to sporting event sponsorships, followed by 11 percent to entertainment tours (such as concerts and theater performances), and 9 percent to fairs and festivals.[17] Besides linking their brands to existing events, marketers are also creating events of their own designed to reach specialized targets. The event itself can serve as a compelling news angle for related publicity efforts, can be promoted through advertising, and can serve as a distribution point for sales promotion incentives. With a little creativity, events can serve as an important point of differentiation from competitors.

Chevy Trucks is the official sponsor of the U.S. Ski Team, giving the manufacturer the right to post banners at official U.S. Ski Team events, place its logo on skiers' apparel, and have its name appear in event programs. Chevy's goal is to have people think of Chevy trucks when they think of skiing, linking the brand to that lifestyle interest.[18] Since skiing is a rugged outdoor sport, its imagery fits nicely with the rough-and-tumble Chevy truck. Further, Chevy is likely to encounter much

[16]Leslie Stahl, *60 Minutes* segment on Denny's (April 26, 1998).

[17] Marguerite M. Plunkett, "Is Being a Sponsor Worth the Price?" *Palm Beach Post*, March 23, 1998, p. 16.

[18] Mark McGuire, "Moments on Slopes Are Golden to Sponsors," *Albany Times Union*, January 2, 1998, p. A1.

less competitive clutter at ski resorts than might be the case at other outdoor venues. Similarly, a number of companies are lining up to put their names on sports arenas, such as the FleetCenter in Boston (Fleet Bank), the United Center in Chicago (United Airlines), and Anaheim's Arrowhead Pond (Arrowhead Water). According to one observer, "Companies are profiting from their contracts, not just with national television exposure but with exposure at the event site and merchandising."[19] Stadium sponsorship often includes premium seating for the sponsoring organization, which can be used to reward employees or impress financial publics.

Event marketing does have its drawbacks, however. In addition to the time and effort required to work out the multitude of details associated with a major event, consumers may not make the connection between event and sponsor. For example, in a survey conducted after the Nagano Olympics, 73 percent of those surveyed identified Nike as an official sponsor. It was not. By comparison, only 63 percent were correct in identifying Kodak as a sponsor.[20]

Susan Sloves of the Heller Research Group has developed a list of questions an organization should ask to determine the effectiveness of their sponsorships:

1. Is the target group aware of your sponsorship?

2. If there is awareness, has that knowledge affected the target group's attitudes toward the sponsoring company and its products or services?

3. In what ways has sponsorship awareness affected attitudes and/or purchase behavior?

4. What are the sponsorship's most effective components?

5. Are the sponsorship's effects long-term or short-term?

6. What is the return on investment for the sponsorship dollars spent?

7. How are the answers to the above questions best used to increase the sponsorship payoff?[21]

The Internet and Public Relations

The Internet is both a boon and a challenge to public relations practitioners. The widespread availability of information, either through clearinghouses such as PR Newswire or companies' own Web sites, makes both the press agentry/publicity and public information aspects of public relations easier today than ever before. In addition, chat rooms and listserves, whether company-sponsored or independent, as well as interactive questionnaires on company Web sites, make it easier to monitor and assess public opinion—essential to both of the two-way models of public relations. However, chat rooms also make it possible for rumors and negative opinions

[19] Rick Westhead, "Companies Play the Name Game at Sports Stadiums," *Los Angeles Daily News*, January 20, 1998, p. B9.

[20] John Malmo, "Sponsorship a Tricky Way to Advertise," *Memphis Commercial Appeal*, February 23, 1998, p. B4.

[21] Susan Sloves, "Do Sponsorships Provide a Gold Mine or a Black Hole?" *Marketing News*, February 2, 1998, p. 9.

to spread more quickly. For example, there are several chat groups devoted to discussing the evils of McDonald's, Nike, and other corporate giants. In many of these companies, one or more public relations employees has the task of monitoring the various chat groups to learn just what is being said about the firm and its products.

Some Final Observations on Public Relations

Consumers understand the intent of advertising; they know the goal is to sell them something. As a result, everything said in advertising (and in sales promotion, direct marketing, and packaging) is viewed with at least some cynicism and sometimes with a great deal of mistrust. But in public relations, the media, rather than the company, become the information source. We can run a multimillion-dollar advertising campaign trumpeting the benefits of our product and never achieve the credibility that can come from a positive news story in a respected magazine or from an event tie-in.

Unfortunately, the increased credibility achieved through a mediated message is accompanied by a loss of control. In other forms of marketing communications, marketers pay for space or time to tell their message. As a result, they can say whatever they want within legal limits. In public relations, however, the marketer provides information to the media who construct the message. It's quite possible that issues the marketer feels are important will be ignored, watered down, or even used against the product in the resulting news story because the journalist acts as a gatekeeper, sifting through the information provided. Public relations can be an extremely frustrating business for just this reason. A great deal of time and effort goes into putting together publicity materials, but there is no guarantee that any of that material will ever be picked up by the media.

Despite these drawbacks, public relations in all its many forms is an essential part of most brand communication campaigns in today's marketplace. And, as consumers continue to grow more sophisticated, an even greater role for public relations is likely, particularly the two-way symmetrical approach that relies so heavily on developing a thorough understanding of the interests and needs of all of an organization's publics.

Summary

Public relations is a diverse field incorporating a wide variety of activities in support of both corporate and brand goals. In the IBC context, public relations activities such as product publicity and event marketing can help communicate brand-building messages to customer and consumer groups that might not be reached effectively through other marketing communications techniques. The greater credibility and often superior media placement gained through public relations efforts can be instrumental in building brand image.

11

Business Building

Trade Sales Promotion

The Importance of the Channel

As was discussed at the outset of this text, it is impossible for manufacturers to take the trade (wholesalers, retailers, and other channel members) for granted in the current marketplace. An ongoing trend toward consolidation and concentration has decreased the number of retail outlets, making individual retailers more important for manufacturers. Take the drugstore business, for example. In 1996, ten drugstore chains accounted for 10,500 store locations. In 1997, only three chains accounted for the same locations as the result of a series of mergers. Further, the sales volume from four chains—Walgreens, CVS, Rite Aid, and Eckerd—represents 70 percent of all drugstore industry sales.[1]

In addition, consumers demonstrate more store loyalty than they do brand loyalty. Retailers also know more about the manufacturer's product and its performance in their stores than ever before. Changes in information technology have changed the balance of power in the distribution channel, and today's retailers are not shy about flaunting their strength. As one industry observer put it when talking about the drugstore consolidation mentioned above, "'They are now in the business of selling stock on Wall Street, not selling toothpaste or lipstick. To increase the value of their stock, they have to create a better bottom line, and, to do that, they're asking manufacturers to take more and more of the responsibilities for the merchandise.'"[2]

---

[1]Marie Griffin, "Partners or Predators? Huge Consolidated Drug Chains Must Leverage Their Size, Technology and Buying Clout, but at What Cost to Their Suppliers?" *Drug Store News*, September 8, 1997, p. 1.

[2]Ibid.

UPCs and Scanners

Up until the early 1970s, most records of product shipment and movement were kept in gross measures only. For example, the manufacturer counted the cases of products shipped to the retailer but spent little time analyzing such things as package size, flavors, and the like. Retailers did much the same thing. The retailer knew what volume he or she had sold but did little analysis of why or how, relying primarily on experience and instinct for repurchase. Most manufacturers' information on what was moving, where it was moving to, pricing, competitive activity, and so on was based on estimations of activity in a sample of stores across the country. This was then projected to the whole. Retailers used some form of estimating procedure, as well.

In the mid-1970s, the Universal Product Code (UPC) was introduced. These bar codes have been placed on each specific item (SKU, for stockkeeping unit) stocked in the store. When passed over a scanner in a retail outlet, the UPC code identifies the product, brand, size, flavor, retail price, and so forth. Almost overnight, retailers began to know exactly what products were selling throughout their stores. Likewise, research organizations formed to gather this UPC code/scanner data from retailers and offered it, along with analysis, to the manufacturers. For the first time, manufacturers and retailers alike knew exactly what products were being sold, at what stores, at what time of year, in what volume, at what price, and so on. In addition, with some analysis, it became possible to measure the various combinations of sales promotion techniques and determine the optimal mix in terms of, for example, sales, volume, and return on investment.

With the development of more sophisticated computer analysis, retailers turned from looking simply at sales to examining the specific profit on each of the more than 10,000 items in the store. Known as Direct Product Profit (DPP), the analysis provided the retailer not just with sales volume, movement, and turns, but also with a record of the actual profit each product in the store provided. For example, although sugar has great overall sales volume, it is bulky, takes up a great deal of shelf space, has a low margin, and is easily damaged. So today, when a retailer looks at the sugar category, he or she knows the product must be stocked, but because the DPP is low, the amount of shelf space, the number of brands carried, and so on are reduced. Alternatively, a product such as a cold remedy takes up little space, has a high margin, and provides a substantial DPP (although it doesn't turn over as often as some other products). So the retailer expands the space for cold remedies and perhaps even the number of brands.

Category Management

Even more recently, retailers in many fields, but particularly in supermarkets, have embraced the concept of category management. In the category management system, the supermarket chain uses scanner data to analyze each product category sold in the store to determine what brands should be carried, in what sizes, and where they should be placed on the store's shelves.[3] Category management is being implemented by many supermarket chains, and it's changing the way both retailers and manufacturers do business. While the category management concept was intended to be consumer-focused, many retailers are using it as a way to cut their costs as much as possible by trimming less-profitable products regardless of consumer interest. And, while some manufacturers have pared down their product lines in response to category management, getting rid of poor performers, others have used the concept as an excuse for recommending that competitors' products be removed from the store in order to give more shelf space to the manufacturer's own brand.[4]

Those chains that have fully implemented category management are seeing positive results. For example, Supervalu stores, a Minneapolis, Minnesota–based grocery chain, saw a 12 percent reduction in SKUs (stockkeeping units, or number of items in the store) in its stores that participated in category management. At the same time, dollar sales increased by about 6.5 percent, unit sales by 4.7 percent, and gross profits by 7.1 percent, all over a two-year period of implementation.[5] Supervalu did this by carefully analyzing what products were selling best in each store and which combinations of products were bought together most often by shoppers. On the manufacturer side, Proctor & Gamble has cut its SKUs across product lines by 34 percent since 1991, eliminating poor-performing products or sizes that don't sell particularly well.[6]

Today, this is the sort of sophisticated analysis the retailer undertakes to determine which products and which brands will be stocked and promoted in his or her store. Brand managers must use similar complex, computer-based analyses in an attempt to influence the retailer either to increase the shelf space, display, or promotion of their individual brands. IBC planners must understand that planning sales promotion today is a very complex and sophisticated process—one that goes far beyond simply preparing a coupon drop or inserting a premium in the carton. The growing retailer insistence on customized products and promotional support makes the planner's job increasingly complicated.

What Is Trade Sales Promotion?

Trade sales promotion refers to the range of activities and incentives offered to retailers, wholesalers, distributors, and other channel members to encourage them to stock the manufacturer's brand and assist in promoting that brand to the end user. Specific trade sales promotion techniques are discussed later in this chapter. They include reducing the price of the product to the retailer and providing incentives to

---

[3]Ann Merrill, "Supervalu Seeks the Advantage; Goal Is to Streamline Food Delivery System," *Minneapolis Star Tribune*, October 6, 1997, p. 1D.

[4]Richard DeSanta, "When Push Comes to Shove; Category Management by Manufacturers, Suppliers and Retailers," *Supermarket Business*, May 1997, p. S3.

[5]Linda Purpura, "Supervalu Reporting SKU Drop, Sales Rise," *Supermarket News*, March 30, 1998, p. 39.

[6]Ken Cottrill, "The Supply Chain of the Future," *Distribution*, October 1997, p. 52.

Exhibit 11-1
Mott's *Rugrats* Advertisement

encourage the retailer to put up a manufacturer's display in the store. Exhibit 11-1 shows an ad from Mott's targeted at retailers to encourage them to stock up on Mott's Fruitsations. The appeal? A tie-in with the upcoming *The Rugrats Movie* that Mott's promises will generate higher sales for retailers. Increasing channel member profitability, most often by lowering costs, is the key element of most trade sales promotion offers.

According to *PROMO* magazine, 50 percent of manufacturers' marketing dollars went to trade sales promotion, compared to 24 percent spent on consumer-directed sales promotion and 26 percent spent on consumer-directed advertising.[7] Trade sales

---

[7]Betsy Spethmann, "Is Advertising DEAD?" *PROMO*, September 1998, pp. 32–36, 159–162.

promotion gets the largest share of dollars because manufacturers realize that without adequate distribution, consumer-directed marketing communications activities will be wasted.

Brand Building or Business Building?

In considering whether trade sales promotion efforts are brand building or business building, we need to look at both the brand marketer's and the channel member's point of view. For a brand marketer, most trade promotion activities are business building, in that they are concerned with delivering short-term incentives. The Mott's program illustrated in Exhibit 11-1 is clearly business building: it is for a specified period of time (Fall 1998), and is intended to convince retailers to increase their stock of Mott's, particularly the specially packaged products tied to the movie. When asked, marketers talk about trade promotion as being brand building; in a 1997 survey by Cannondale Associates, 81 percent of marketers versus 28 percent of retailers felt that trade promotion activities should build the brand.[8] And, in the sense that trade sales promotion helps hold on to shelf space, it can be viewed as brand building. Essentially, most brand marketers' trade sales promotion programs are made up of a series of business-building efforts that, in the aggregate, contribute to brand building.

From the channel member's perspective, particularly when that channel member is a retailer, trade sales promotion programs are very much brand building. It's just that the brand in question is the retailer's own brand, the retail store. Retailers use manufacturers' trade sales promotion offers as a way to differentiate their store from competitors. Looking again at the Cannondale results, 73 percent of retailers said that trade sales promotion helped to build consumer loyalty to their stores; only 16 percent of manufacturers agreed with this.[9] See the sidebar for an excerpt from an article that appeared in *Progressive Grocer*. The article describes how Safeway, a major grocery chain, is using trade sales promotion deals from manufacturers to set its stores apart.

Each week, retailers and other channel members sort through multiple trade sales promotion offers from brand manufacturers to pick the combination of incentives they will offer to their own customers. The retailer makes his or her decisions based on category management considerations, seasonality, profitability, and the need to promote the store's own private label products, which typically generate greater profit margins for the store than national manufacturers' brands. So, the retailer's goal is to maximize store profitability while the manufacturer's goal is to maximize brand sales. These two goals sometimes lead to conflict, as you'll see.

---

[8]Judann Pollack, "Trade Promo Luster Dims for Marketers, Retailers: Account-Specific Programs Are Hot Commodity in New Survey by Cannondale," *Advertising Age*, April 7, 1997, p. 18.

[9]Ibid.

Playing Safeway's Coupon Game

Safeway's main merchandising emphasis is on its monthly coupon book, and if manufacturers want to play the game, they have to ante up a lot of money. The promotion has been extremely successful, to the point where competitors have tried to emulate the idea, although their execution generally has not matched Safeway's.

While the coupon book may be the only game in town at Safeway, the entry price has soared beyond the reach of some manufacturers. The price keeps rising, says one supplier official. "Each time it does, manufacturers have to decide whether to continue to participate at all or to reduce their participation. The problem is there is no alternative with Safeway," he says.

The cost depends on the extent of participation and the strength of Safeway in a particular division. The most expensive division is northern California where top monthly participation (100 percent display and mention on radio ads) is estimated at close to $100,000. The cost to participate is lower elsewhere. In Seattle, which has lower sales than California, although it is probably the chain's most profitable division, participation costs only $30,000 or

$40,000. The price is the same whether one item or an entire line is involved.

Nobody actually gets 100 percent display, but that is not unique to Safeway, says one observer. And the chain performs better than others. "Traditionally, with chains, if you are getting 50–55 percent you are doing well," he says. "In northern California Safeways you get 70–80 percent participation, although the numbers are lower in other divisions."

In the Eastern division, a super coupon, with the best price and a weekly floor display, can cost more than $100,000, according to one broker. This would take in the lump sum plus the coupon value and redemption. He feels the high price is worthwhile, and even if manufacturers don't get their money back, some companies feel participation makes sense because "Safeway considers participation when they are looking at new items or considering reallocating shelf space," says one West Coast manufacturing sales manager.

Excerpted from Steve Weinstein, "The Price Is High: Safeway Inc. Charges Grocery Manufacturers Top Fees for Inclusion in Coupon Book," *Progressive Grocer*, January 1997, p. 27.

Major Goals of Trade Sales Promotion

In general, the goal of most sales promotion directed to the retailer or trade is to stimulate activity at the retail level in order to generate greater than normal product and sales movement. It is important here to understand what motivates the trade or retailer. If we think of the retail store as a big box that the retailer puts items into and the consumer takes items out of, several factors become clear. First, as with any type of container, there is a finite amount of space. Only a certain number of products can be stocked, so the retailer's choices are limited. If something new is to be added to the store, something else must come out. (In a typical year, 20,000 new grocery products come on the market; stores can't possibly take them all.[10])

Second, the retailer wants to put items in the store that customers will want. If the items aren't wanted, there will be no traffic and no sales. Because the retailer's largest single cost is usually inventory, he or she tries to find items that will sell quickly. This is *turnover*, or how fast the item moves through the store: the faster the inventory turnover, the more profit for the retailer (assuming, of course, a profit is made on the item). Third, the retailer wants to stock products that bring many people to the store. Most retailers rely heavily on impulse purchasing within the store, so the greater the store traffic generated, the greater the sales. Therefore, the retailer wants products that will help generate impulse purchases as the customers move through the store. Fourth, the retailer wants to stock items that give the greatest margin (or difference) between what he or she pays for the product and what it will sell for. So, the real goal of all retailers is to stock products with fast turnover and high margins.

To give the retailer an incentive to stock and promote a product, a manufacturer may (a) offer sales promotion activities that change the margin the retailer makes on the product, such as a price reduction or free goods offer; (b) promote events that bring traffic to the store, such as multiproduct promotions and demonstrations; and (c) sponsor activities that help improve the product's turnover. Typical trade or retail promotions that speed turnover include distributing consumer coupons and sharing the cost of advertising (co-op) or displays with advertisers.

One thing that some manufacturers have trouble understanding is that the goals of their promotion are quite different from those of the retailer. In most cases, the retailer really doesn't care which brand of a product he or she sells, assuming that the margins and turnover are about the same. The retailer is interested only in selling something to every person who enters the store. Because the retailer makes about the same profit on competing brands, there is little reward for his or her efforts to persuade consumers to switch.

Alternatively, the manufacturer is primarily interested in the sale of his or her particular brand. Therefore, most manufacturer marketing communications activities are designed to sell *the brand*, while most retailer activities are designed to generate store traffic and to sell *something*. These are the reasons for much of the conflict between manufacturers and retailers in the promotional area. Adding to the conflict is the fact that manufacturing operations are far more profitable than retail operations. In 1995, for example, manufacturers' average profit margins were 4.8 percent versus 1.9 percent for retailers.[11]

Manufacturers have three basic objectives or goals for most sales promotion that is directed against the retail trade:

1. To retain or gain more shelf space in the store.

2. To convince the retailer to build or maintain in-store displays on behalf of the promoted product.

[10]Sean Somerville, "High Price of Shelf Space," *Baltimore Sun*, June 1, 1997, p. 1D.

[11]Ken Partch and Richard DeSanta, "Slotting: The Issue That Won't Go Away," *Supermarket Business*, May 1997, p. 12.

3. To encourage the retailer to support the brand and/or promotion in the retailer's own advertising. Commonly, this sort of support consists of newspaper features, television advertising, and so forth.

The sort of support discussed above is important because the retailer's efforts to generate sales volume are many times more productive than those of the manufacturer. The sales impact of displays and featuring was alluded to in our discussion of consumer behavior and is illustrated in Exhibit 11-2.

Issues in Trade Sales Promotion

Despite, or perhaps because of, the amount of spending it accounts for, trade sales promotion issues are a source of contention between manufacturers and retailers. Several of the key points of disagreement are described below.

Slotting Allowances

Slotting allowances are fees manufacturers pay to retailers in order to get new products into stores. The fees are intended to cover the store's costs for filling the warehouse with the new product, rearranging the shelves to accommodate it, and inputting the UPC code into the store's computer system. Estimates of slotting fees vary widely. According to trade reports, Procter & Gamble does not pay slotting allowances; on the other hand, Frito Lay reportedly pays $100,000 per supermarket chain for each of its new products.[12] A *Supermarket Business* study reported that retailers and wholesalers charge between $10,000 and $20,000 per SKU for slotting.[13] That would mean that a juice manufacturer introducing two new flavor varieties, each in two different package sizes, would be charged up to $80,000 per chain in slotting fees.

Slotting fees make it particularly difficult for small, independent manufacturers to get new products into stores. Take the case of James Hajjar. He's a North Carolina manufacturer who makes Guido's Gourmet Salsa. As described in the Raleigh, North Carolina, *News and Observer*, "His product is in three Harris Teeter stores in Raleigh competing for a tiny slice of a $5.7 million local niche against the deep promotional budgets of salsa titans such as Tostitos and Pace. In the Raleigh-Greensboro area, Tostitos controls 37 percent of the Mexican sauces market; Pace has 22 percent, according to market research firm Information Resources Inc., of Chicago."[14] Hajjar has not moved to put Guido's in more large supermarkets because his budget will not allow for payment of slotting fees, let alone other trade sales promotion programs to compete with the big players.

---

[12]Somerville, "High Price of Shelf Space."

[13]Partch and DeSanta, "Slotting."

[14]Su-Jin Yim, "Shelf Shootout," *Raleigh News and Observer*, October 26, 1997, p. F1.

Exhibit 11-2
Impact of Displays and Featuring

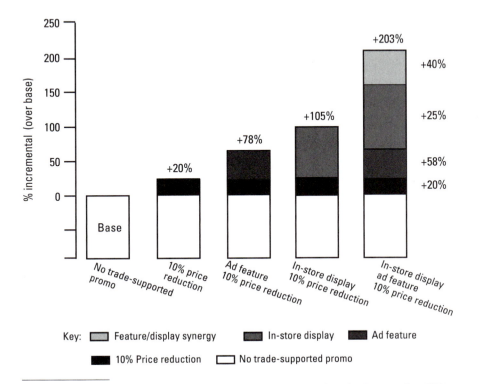

Key:
- Feature/display synergy
- In-store display
- Ad feature
- 10% Price reduction
- No trade-supported promo

Source: John C. Totten, "Health and Beauty Aids: A Sharp Pencil Is Needed," (Information Resources, Inc., 1985, unpublished paper), figure 9.

Forward Buying

The retailer who takes advantage of a manufacturer's short-term promotional offer or deal and buys a great deal more of a product than can be sold during the promotional period is "forward buying." In other words, the retailer buys enough to last well into the future. The retailer does this because the promotional offer is for a limited period of time. If the retailer buys now and warehouses the excess stock, he or she can take the full margin on the reduced-price merchandise by selling it at normal price over time. As long as the cost of warehousing and the value of invested capital are lower than the price paid by the retailer, it is profitable for the retailer to forward buy. Until there are some restrictions imposed by the manufacturer, forward buying will continue and manufacturers will find that less and less of their volume is sold anywhere close to the regularly established price. Indeed, some analysts estimate that as much as 80 percent of grocery store merchandise is bought on some sort of deal terms, while 40 percent is either forward bought or diverted.[15]

Diversion

Diversion is simply an extension of forward buying. In this case, however, retailers stock up with the intent of offering the reduced-price merchandise to another retailer, usually in another part of the country. Thus, the buyer for a supermarket chain in Tampa may buy twice as much of a promoted product as the chain's anticipated needs call for. He or she may then call another retailer in Buffalo and offer the merchandise at something over the manufacturer's reduced price. Because there is no lower price in the Buffalo area at that time, the Buffalo retailer can buy at a discount, which makes him or her more competitive in that market. The retailer in Tampa takes the shipment from the manufacturer, holds part of the inventory, and ships the balance to the retailer in Buffalo. The Tampa retailer then bills the Buffalo retailer at the slightly higher rate. Both retailers are happy, but the manufacturer isn't. The manufacturer offered the promotional price, assuming he or she would get activity in the Tampa stores. However, a large portion of the volume went to Buffalo, where the manufacturer may or may not get any sort of merchandising for the offered discount.

Both forward buying and diversion are major problems for manufacturers today. Although the IBC planner has little control over these types of activities, he or she should know that they exist and factor them into any type of merchandising or promotion plan that might be developed.

Types of Trade Sales Promotions

Because most of the emphasis in trade sales promotion is on gaining distribution and assisting the retailer in getting brand movement, trade sales promotion tactics usually involve either money off or money to help the retailer build his or her own local promotional program. The most common tactics are described below.

Price Deals

Price deals are usually special price concessions, over and above normal discounts, granted by the manufacturer for a limited period of time. These concessions may take the form of price-off or off-invoice allowances, which are simply additional reductions off the list price of a product. A second approach is that of free goods or extra cases of the product when a minimum amount is purchased—for example, one case free with twelve, or buy four cases, get one free. The hope is that the retailer will pass this reduced price along to the consumer, thus creating additional in-store demand for the brand.

[15]Ron Gable, "The History of Consumer Goods," *Manufacturing Systems*, October 1997, pp. 70–84.

Performance Deals

An alternative to the price deal is to add some sort of requirement for the retailer to "earn" the price reduction or bonus offer. For example, to receive a $3.00-per-case off-invoice allowance, the retailer must insert a mention of the product in his or her regular newspaper advertisement, build a display in the store, or give extra shelf space to the brand for a period of time. Generally, the retailer must provide some form of proof that the activity required was performed, such as a tear sheet of the advertisement or a picture of the display.

Allowances

In an attempt to get the retailer to support the brand in his or her advertising and promotion, the manufacturer may provide an allowance to help pay part of the cost for local advertising or for building a display. In general, these allowances are for advertising, display, or other in-store merchandising. Again, the retailer must provide some sort of evidence that the performance took place, such as an affidavit, a picture, or an advertisement tear sheet.

Cooperative Advertising

Realizing that retailer promotion works very well, particularly when it is location and price specific, many manufacturers have set up systems to share the cost of local advertising with the retailer. In these agreements, the manufacturer offers to share the cost (commonly up to 50 percent) of advertising that the retailer runs to support the brand at the local level. Most of these agreements cover newspaper advertising, but an increasing number are also available now for radio, television, and even circulars and flyers developed by the retailer. There are some problems with cooperative agreements, such as the advertising rate to be paid, the media to be used, and sometimes the aesthetics of the advertising itself. But more and more manufacturers are finding that localized advertising, especially when it offers some type of retailer promotion, is a very effective way of moving merchandise.

Point-of-Purchase Materials

The increasing emphasis on shelf shopping by consumers, which results in in-store brand-purchasing decisions, has contributed to the renewed interest in the whole area of point of purchase. The most common type of materials are developed and paid for by the manufacturer and shipped to the individual retailer for local display. These materials include such items as shelf-talkers, wire hangers, posters, and dump bins. Although there is much waste in this approach, because retailers cannot possibly use all the displays that come to them, its effectiveness (when combined with in-store support) in moving large amounts of the brand often makes it worthwhile.

Increasingly, point-of-purchase materials are becoming permanent store fixtures. For example, cigarette stands, case dividers, aisle and direction signage, and clocks

Exhibit 11-3
Gillette "Signedge" Advertisement

promote individual brands while serving a useful purpose in the store. In some cases, in-store displays such as shopping cart signs, checkout videos, and electronic price markings have actually become and are sold as regular media. As more and more consumer decisions are made in the store, it becomes increasingly important for the planner to find or devise ways to get customers' attention at the point of purchase to reinforce the brand message. Exhibit 11-3 is an ad from Gillette promoting their "Signedge" shaving center display system. Note how the ad focuses on benefits to the retailer from adopting the system.

Dealer Loaders

A dealer loader is designed to do exactly what the name implies—load the dealer with a product. One type of dealer loader packs the product in a display, such as a wheelbarrow, wagon, or other valuable premium. The premium (loader) and product are used as a display unit. When the product has been sold, the retailer keeps the premium.

Dealer loaders may take almost any form, from a small, impersonal gift to sporting goods, clothing, or even expensive foreign trips for the retailer and his or her family. Dealer loaders are often tied to a specific-size purchase, with the value of the loader being proportionate to the value of the offer. This type of promotion is frequently used to support a new advertising program, with the loader tied to the theme of the campaign.

Contests

Dealer contests have grown in size and importance over the years. A 1996 poll of manufacturers found that 80 percent offer dealer or salesperson incentive programs.[16] It is not unusual for retailers to have opportunities to win very expensive prizes, such as trips, cash, and other goods, in contests sponsored by manufacturers. Usually contests are tied to specific retailer achievements, such as purchases, total sales, sales based on quotas, sales increases over previous periods, or sales of a new or existing product line.

Contests often work better with independent retailers than with chain stores. Many chain store operations have very strict rules about contests, premiums, and gifts that may be given or awarded to their store managers. In these instances, clearance is required from the chain's headquarters before any type of contest can be conducted with employees. (The same survey cited above found that 46 percent of manufacturers said that some dealers refuse to take part in such programs.[17])

Push Money

Often called "spiffs" or "PM"—push money—is money the manufacturer pays directly to salespeople, usually those on the retail floor, to promote specific items in the product line. For example, Samsonite recently offered luggage store salespeople a spiff of up to $10 per suitcase for pushing some of the manufacturer's newer bags, compared to a category average of $1–2 per bag.[18] During the time the promotion is in effect, the retail salespeople are encouraged to personally promote that particular brand because they will be rewarded with an additional cash prize. Usually spiffs or PM work only for those products in which the retail salesperson is a key selling factor (such as for computers and home electronics). The device is not effective for products sold in self-service situations or those with a low selling price.

In nearly every case, the use of PM requires the cooperation and approval of the store manager or the headquarters office of the retail store. Because offering money to employees is regarded as an inducement, retail management must be consulted before the offer of such a program is made to their employees.

---

[16]Daniel McQuillen, Judy Quinn, and Vincent Alonzo, "Today's Dealers—One Tough Customer," *Incentive*, April 1996, pp. 22–26.

[17]Ibid.

[18]John F. Geer, Jr., "Same Old Bag," *Financial World*, November 1997, p. 36.

Sales Meetings

A final, widely used trade promotion tactic is the sales meeting conducted for retailers by the manufacturer's sales representative or the broker sales force. Sales meetings take many forms, from a simple meeting in a hotel room with a small group to a formal, traveling, professional show. The determining factor is the importance of the announcement to the manufacturer and the wholesaler. The advertising campaign is usually a key feature of a sales meeting program. Special emphasis often is given to the geographic areas represented by the retailers present. Thus, part of the development of many consumer product advertising campaigns is a brief outline of how the material will be presented to the retailers and the sales force.

Recent Trends and Developments in Trade Sales Promotion

The nature of the relationship between manufacturers and channel members, particularly retailers, continues to evolve. As the trend toward consolidation continues, and as we move closer to the consumer-dominated twenty-first-century marketplace, manufacturers and retailers will continue to experiment with more effective ways to work together to maximize profits and minimize costs.

Retailer/Marketer Alliances

One outgrowth of the category management trend discussed earlier in this chapter has been alliances between retailers and marketers who serve as category cocaptains. For example, Kmart has recently moved to introduce category management to its home video area, taking on Warner Home Video as its cocaptain. This means that Warner will advise Kmart on redesigning the layout of the home video section, as well as shelf space allocations and displays in the area. However, this move does not make Warner Home Video Kmart's exclusive video supplier; Kmart will also continue to buy from Buena Vista (Disney), Good Times, and Universal. In fact, Warner may sometimes have to recommend that competitors' videos receive better in-store placement than its own releases.[19]

Account-Specific Promotions

Increasingly, manufacturers are customizing promotional programs for specific retailer clients. The Cannondale survey discussed earlier highlights account-specific marketing as a growing area. This trend "involves personalized attention to a retail chain by devoting a team at the marketer to service that chain's needs, often including localized advertising and promotion that back both the brand and the

---

[19]Robert Scally, "Kmart to Launch Hard Lines Category Management," *Discount Store News*, April 6, 1998, p. 7.

retailer."[20] In the survey, 94 percent of the manufacturers expected to increase their account-specific spending over the next five years.[21]

Much of the interest in account-specific work probably results from Wal-Mart's success in making even the largest manufacturing organizations dance to its tune. Wal-Mart made news in trade circles in the early 1990s when Proctor & Gamble relocated a number of its employees to Bentonville, Arkansas (site of Wal-Mart's headquarters), just to insure close contact with the retailer.[22] That was a clear signal that Wal-Mart had taken firm control of the channel. More recently, Wal-Mart and its discount competitors (including Kmart, Target, and Home Depot) have begun making tough demands on suppliers, to the extent that some suppliers are backing out of the marketplace. Discount retailers are asking suppliers to provide a number of value-added services as part of their standard contract, including specially packed and palletized orders, special labels for each retailer customer, marking the product with the retailer's own price tags, attaching additional security tags, and confirming orders electronically.[23]

Here's how one manufacturer has responded to Wal-Mart's value-added demands. Manco, Inc., makes duct tape, and has been Wal-Mart's Vendor of the Quarter several times. The company uses electronic data interchange (EDI) to service Wal-Mart. How does it work? "Using sales data taken directly from retailers, the company has created a series of distribution zones in which product is allocated exactly where and when it is needed."[24] In other words, Manco has reorganized its distribution system to serve its retail customers' needs.

EDI is an outgrowth of the Efficient Customer Response (ECR) concept, which has also been adopted by a number of retailers and their manufacturer-suppliers. Another important aspect of ECR is just-in-time (JIT) deliveries, which allows retailers to reduce their warehouse stock (and warehousing costs) by getting more frequent deliveries from manufacturers. Grocery and discount stores track and forecast their inventory needs through data warehousing—individual item-level data that help the stores figure out what they need and when.[25] For example, one Michigan supermarket chain decided to continue to stock a brand of private-label chips because their trend data showed that the product sold well regardless of whether it was offered at a special price. The chain had planned to drop the product because of comments from delivery drivers, who claimed that the product did not sell well. In fact, the drivers' commission on that product was lower than on national chip brands, which may have affected their evaluation of the product.[26]

---

[20]Pollack, "Trade Promo Luster Dims for Marketers, Retailers."

[21]Ibid.

[22]Jay L. Johnson, "How Wal-Mart's People Make a Difference," *Discount Merchandiser*, August 1993, pp. 60–63.

[23]Robert J. Bowman, "Should You Just Say No to Wal-Mart?" *Distribution*, November 1997, p. 52.

[24]Ibid.

[25]Adam Blair, "Stocking Data: Building Data Warehouses, Supermarkets," *Supermarket News*, March 23, 1998, p. 19.

[26]Ibid.

Trade Sales Promotion Planning

Once the manufacturer starts to promote continuously by offering price discounts or other incentives on a regular basis, the retailer expects such events to continue. The retailer, like the consumer, becomes deal prone. He or she starts to buy and promote the product only when a deal is offered. In short, the special price soon becomes the normal price. The saying in the business is, "Trade promotion is easy to start but hard to stop." IBC planners should be wary of continuous or regularly scheduled promotional discounts, even though they do build business. These kinds of promotions can all too often take the place of brand-building activity.

Federal controls on all forms of trade promotion are spelled out in the Robinson-Patman Act and administered by the Federal Trade Commission. The Act requires that all trade promotion offers by a manufacturer or through a distributor for the manufacturer be made equally available and in proportionate value to all retailers in the market area. In other words, manufacturers must treat all retailers on an equal basis. Thus, if a volume discount is offered to a very large retail chain, a proportionate discount must be made to smaller retailers, as well. The Robinson-Patman Act has been defined as being applicable in individual market areas, commonly in the form of areas of dominant influence (ADIs), designated market areas (DMAs), and standard metropolitan statistical areas (SMSAs). Therefore, a manufacturer can offer one promotion in the Denver market and another in the Salt Lake City market. For the marketing communications planner, the key words in Robinson-Patman are "proportionately equal." This means that almost any promotion can be developed as long as it meets the "proportionately equal" test and is not in restraint of trade.

Summary

In the current marketplace, the retailer controls information via scanner data and thus controls the entire distribution channel. Trade sales promotion is the brand marketer's chief tool to both establish and maintain a competitive presence in the retail marketplace. As retailers continue to try to cut costs in order to improve their margins, they are likely to demand increasingly more value-added services from manufacturers, including more customized trade promotion programs as well as changes in delivery systems. The savvy IBC planner *must* understand the dynamics of the trade, and must plan both business-building and brand-building efforts accordingly.

12

Business Building

Consumer Sales Promotion

What Is Consumer Sales Promotion?

A shorthand definition of "sales promotion" might be "a short-term incentive to buy the product or service, created by changing the price/value relationship." Prompting immediate action is an important business-building goal of consumer sales promotion programs, but in today's marketplace there are also brand-building aspects associated with this marketing communications technique. We'll review both perspectives in this chapter.

PROMO magazine reported that marketers' 1997 spending on sales promotion-related activities totaled $79.4 billion; $6.2 billion of that was spent on coupons, while another $24.1 billion was spent on premiums.[1] Clearly, sales promotion accounts for a large part of brand marketers' communication investments.

Brand Building or Business Building?

Most consumer sales promotion activities are aimed primarily at business building: they are short-term incentives designed to generate an immediate sale. Many brand communication planners traditionally have regarded sales promotion as the quick fix in their communication toolbox. Run a coupon in the Sunday newspaper and watch sales shoot up the next week. Offer a premium tied to several purchases of the

[1]"The 1998 Annual Report of the Promotion Industry," PROMO, July 1998, p. S5.

product and see a longer-term increase in sales. But brand marketers are beginning to become more savvy in their approach to consumer sales promotion, as some of the examples in this chapter will illustrate. While sales promotion remains primarily a business-building activity, it is also being used by some to build brands. The logic behind this approach is not new; an argument in favor of the long-term impact of sales promotion appeared in *Advertising Age* in the late 1970s, and is discussed later.

Prentice's Consumer Franchise Building

Most marketers agree that continuous price promotion probably has some long-term effect on the brand image and the brand franchise. Robert M. Prentice has developed the concept of "consumer franchise building" or CFB. Prentice's position, which he has backed up with a fairly large number of in-market tests, is that some sales promotion techniques contribute to the value of the brand image and franchise while others tend to detract from or erode that image. Prentice's rationale for his CFB approach follows.

1. *To generate profit over an extended period, a brand must build a strong consumer franchise. It must establish a significant, lasting value in the minds of an important segment of consumers.*

2. *Value isn't enough. Consumers must believe that the brand's value is worth the price. If they don't, the marketer will have to reduce the price or increase the value to the point where they are willing to buy it—to the point where consumers believe that the value and price are in balance.*

3. *A brand's share of the market at any given time reflects how consumers perceive the brand's price-value relationship in comparison with other brands.*

4. *How does the consumer arrive at his or her perception of brand value? Obviously a lot depends on experience with the product, its unique performance, and the satisfaction it provides. But a lot also depends on the ideas the consumer gets about the brand which make it uniquely different in important respects from competitive brands. These ideas arise from the brand's name, its positioning, the package, and the various marketing activities that implant unique and important ideas about the brand in the mind.*

5. *What kinds of marketing activities do this? Prentice calls them consumer franchise-building activities. They include:*
   - *Advertising. Perhaps the most common way to register such ideas (although some advertising, we have to admit, does a fairly poor job in this respect).*
   - *Certain Types of Promotion. If they register unique and important selling ideas about the brand, including*
     - *Sampling. Because the package highlights the product's advantages, the proof of the pudding is in the eating, and a descriptive*

folder with a strong selling message (an ad, if you will), usually accompanies the sample.

— *Cents-Off Coupons. Distributed by the manufacturer by mail, in print ads, or in/on a package. These coupons can also register unique and important ideas about the brand, provided an effective selling message accompanies the coupon or appears on it.*

— *Demonstrations. Whether in the store or before users or other groups of consumers, demonstrations are CFB activities. Service, material, recipes, and so on, which enhance the image of a brand and register ideas of its unique superiority and value, are also CFB activities.*

All these activities perform two functions: (a) they build long-term brand preference; and (b) they generate immediate sales (often more effectively than many people realize).

6. *All other activities are classified as non-CFB activities. Their job is to accelerate the buying decision to generate immediate sales, but they generally do not implant unique and important ideas about the brand in the consumer's mind. Instead, they simply reduce the price or add temporary, extraneous value (as in the case of most premiums and contests) or help obtain retail distribution or cooperation. These are important and necessary functions, but they do not register important and unique ideas about a brand in the mind.[2]*

Although all marketing communications executives do not agree with Prentice's approach, he found that among the brands he studied, those who invested less than 50–55 percent of their combined advertising/sales promotion budget in CFB activities did not do as well in sales and profits as marketers who did so—a strong argument for the Prentice approach.

Major Goals of Consumer Sales Promotion

Most sales promotion programs targeted at consumers are trying to change consumer purchasing behavior in some way. There are three desirable behavior changes: purchase acceleration, stockpiling, and consumption increase.

Purchase Acceleration

In purchase acceleration, a consumer buys a product sooner than he or she normally would. For example, if I usually buy toothpaste once every six weeks, buying it after four weeks would be purchase acceleration. Usually, such a change in

---

[2]Robert M. Prentice, "How to Split Your Marketing Funds Between Advertising and Promotion," *Advertising Age*, January 10, 1977, p. 49.

purchasing behavior will be the result of a consumer sales promotion incentive. I buy earlier than I would have otherwise because I want to take advantage of a special offer, such as a coupon. While purchase acceleration does not lead to an overall increase in buying levels (I won't use the toothpaste any faster), it can provide a manufacturer with several benefits.

Consumers may accelerate their purchase *and* buy a different brand than they normally would. In this case, "normally" means in the absence of a sales promotion incentive. Not only has the manufacturer of the chosen brand succeeded in switching consumers to its brand, it may have lengthened the interval before the consumer will buy again, which hurts the consumer's regular brand (the manufacturer's competitor).

Purchase acceleration can also come in handy if a manufacturer knows (or suspects) that a competitor is about to launch its own sales promotion program. If the first manufacturer can entice consumers to buy its brand now, the competitor's action is more likely to fall flat. Thus, sales promotion programs aimed at accelerating purchase can be important defensive weapons, as well.

Stockpiling

When consumers purchase more units of a product at one time than they normally would, they are stockpiling. (Again, "normal" here means in the absence of a sales promotion offer.) For example, if usually I buy one bottle of Hidden Valley Ranch salad dressing at a time, but buy three bottles this week because I have a coupon that gets me a free bottle when I pay for two bottles, I am stockpiling. As with purchase acceleration, I probably won't buy more salad dressing over the course of a year than I normally would; I've just bought more this one time, and it'll be that much longer before I buy again.

Also, like purchase acceleration, stockpiling is a good defensive measure. Loading up consumers with one manufacturer's brand keeps them from buying competitors' brands. A stockpiling program can be especially effective when run just before a competitor introduces a new product. In today's marketplace, new products have to generate sales quickly to stay alive. Thus, if we've taken consumers out of the market through a stockpiling promotion, we're impeding the success of our competitor's new product.

Consumption Increase

Consumption increase is probably the most desirable goal of consumer sales promotion, because rather than the one-time shift in behavior that occurs with purchase acceleration and stockpiling, consumption increase results in an overall gain in the number of units of the brand the consumer buys and uses. In a consumption increase program, the manufacturer provides the consumer with incentives to regularly purchase a product. An example would be Hallmark's Gold Crown Card program. Every time a Gold Crown Card member makes a purchase in a Hallmark store and

Exhibit 12-1
Hallmark's Gold Crown Club Program

has her Gold Crown Card scanned as part of the transaction, she earns points. For example, each greeting card purchase earns fifty points and every dollar spent earns ten points. Each time the member accumulates 300 points during a three-month period, she receives a certificate for $1.00 off at a Hallmark store. Exhibit 12-1 shows some Hallmark Gold Crown Card promotional materials. A program like the Gold Crown Card not only encourages repeat purchasing, but probably also convinces Gold Crown Card members to shop at Hallmark stores more often than they otherwise might. Consumption increase programs require a long-term commitment from the manufacturer that can pay off in consumer loyalty.

Why Manufacturers Use Consumer Sales Promotion

In addition to purchase acceleration, stockpiling, and consumption increase, brand marketers usually have a number of other strategic goals that drive their use of sales promotion tactics aimed at consumers. Some of the more common of those goals are as follows:

Reach New Users

Sales promotion is often used to get trial purchases from new users or new customers. Often, the promotion is run when the product is expanded into a new retail channel.

Trade Up

Sales promotion can be used to encourage a consumer to move up to a brand that offers better quality or carries a higher price than his or her usual brand. Exhibit 12-2 shows a promotion for the Oreck XL vacuum cleaner. The promotion offers both a fifteen-day free trial period and the free gift of a Super Compact Canister vacuum. The Oreck XL is a more expensive, heavier-duty vacuum than most standard vacuum cleaners, so this promotion clearly is designed to encourage consumers to trade up.

Introduce a New Product

Because consumers don't know the benefits of a new product, sales promotion tactics often are used to reduce the cost of trial (couponing) or to encourage immediate trial (sampling).

Hold Current Users

In most product categories, the 80/20 rule seems to hold true, that is, 80 percent of the volume is purchased by 20 percent of the customers. Because current users are so important, sales promotion often is used to maintain that usage or to try to build purchase continuity.

Increase Usage

The "recipe" is the most common sales promotion technique employed to attempt to get consumers to use more of a food product. Many food product manufacturers offer recipe books featuring their products as premiums. Sales promotion tactics that show how to use the product, or how to use the product more often or in greater quantity, are important here.

Exhibit 12-2
Oreck XL Offer

Reinforce Advertising

Often, sales promotion is used simply to reinforce the brand's advertising. Over the years, Virginia Slims cigarettes has offered a number of premiums, all of which have related to, extended, and enhanced the independent feminine image that Slims has created through its advertising.

What Sales Promotion Can and Can't Do

As the techniques discussed earlier illustrate, sales promotion can be effective in changing consumers' buying behavior. Here, for example, are six things that sales promotion *can* do:

1. Sales promotion can help make a sale. By adjusting the price-value relationship, sales promotion can be used to generate immediate sales.

2. Sales promotion can help maintain present customers. Brand marketers have learned that their present customers are likely their best customers; therefore, there is increasing emphasis on activities that attempt to hold on to or build brand loyalty. The frequent shopper programs offered by many retailers are an excellent example of this effective use of sales promotion.

3. Sales promotion can increase purchase frequency. As we've already discussed, sales promotion is quite successful in persuading consumers to purchase and use the product more frequently.

4. Sales promotion can increase the size and number of items purchased by consumers.

5. Sales promotion can be used to support the brand's current image. It also can be used to reinforce the advertising messages that are being delivered. As we have discussed elsewhere, advertising and sales promotion must work together to present the same message and image for the product in all tactical activities. This is perhaps one of the most important factors that the marketing communications planner should consider.

6. Sales promotion can help generate sales channel support. As discussed in the previous chapter, sales promotion is a most effective approach to persuade retailers and others in the channel to promote and merchandise the product at the store level.[3]

In spite of these strengths, however, the IBC planner must recognize that there are some things that sales promotion alone *cannot* do:

1. Sales promotion cannot change negative attitudes. If the product is not well received or consumers' perceptions are negative, sales promotion can't solve these problems.

2. Sales promotion cannot reverse a declining sales trend. Although sales promotion may, on occasion, give sales a boost or help flatten or slow down a sales decline, it cannot reverse

---

[3]Adapted in part from Don E. Schultz and William A. Robinson, *Sales Promotion Management* (Chicago: Crain Books, 1982), pp. 51–67.

the sales trend. For example, no amount of sales promotion on behalf of vinyl albums would have prevented consumers from moving to the use of compact discs instead.

3. Sales promotion cannot create a brand image, with the exception of that of a promotional brand. Although sales promotion for Virginia Slims can help support and reinforce the liberated female image that has been established for that brand, sales promotion alone could not have created that image. It requires advertising, public relations, and other marketing communications techniques.

4. Sales promotion cannot compensate for inadequate advertising support. One of the most dangerous strategies a marketer can adopt (and an approach from which many prominent packaged goods companies are now retreating, as you'll see later in this chapter) is to convert a substantial amount of the available marketing funds to sales promotion and to ignore the other marketing communications options. It takes a combination of marketing communications techniques, including significant amounts of advertising, to build and maintain a brand. Advertising and sales promotion work hand in glove; therefore, as we have argued elsewhere, they must be planned and implemented together.

5. Sales promotion cannot overcome basic product problems. In fact, sales promotion, because of its ability to build purchase and trial, will do more to highlight product problems than almost any other promotional approach. If the product is no good, no one will want to buy it no matter how much promotional activity is used.[4]

Consumer Sales Promotion Tactics

As mentioned earlier, sales promotion provides an incentive to consumers by changing the price-value relationship associated with the product or service; sales promotion can either decrease the price of the product or increase the product's value to the consumer. In both situations, the result is an increase in the product's benefit to the consumer. It is hoped that the increased benefit will be strong enough to motivate a purchase. There are eight basic consumer sales promotion techniques available to IBC planners, and we'll look at each in terms of price and value.

Price Reduction Tactics

There are four major price reduction approaches: coupons, refunds, price-offs, and sampling. Coupons, refunds, and price-offs are business-building tactics primarily; sampling can be both business building and brand building.

Coupons

Coupons are an enormously popular type of consumer sales promotion; over $6 billion was spent on couponing in 1997.[5] Their popularity is at least partly due to their

---

[4]Ibid., pp. 68–74.

[5]"Couponing: The Undefeated," *PROMO*, July 1998, p. S14.

flexibility: The manufacturer can manipulate the face value of the coupon, the expiration date, and the delivery system, among other factors. Coupons signal consumers that something special is going on with the product. Further, they can provide an incentive to try a new product, as shown in the Hood Ice Cream coupon offer in Exhibit 12-3.

Most coupons (92 percent)[6] are distributed through free-standing inserts (FSIs) in newspapers. Although popular, FSIs are not a very selective way to get coupons to a particular target audience, and there is a great deal of wasted distribution inherent in the medium. For example, 1997 redemption rates for coupons averaged 1.7 percent, with FSI-distributed coupon redemption rates slightly lower than that average.[7] Direct mail, magazines, electronic cash register delivery, in- and on-package delivery systems, and even the Internet are all increasing in popularity.

Refunds

Unlike a coupon, the consumer does not see an immediate savings under a refund program. Instead, the savings come later when the consumer receives the refund in the mail. Refunds can be especially effective in getting trial for more expensive products because the promise of the refund reduces the risk to the consumer in buying the product. In addition, refund offers are particularly good at calling attention to the product on the store shelf.

Price-Offs

A price-off program involves flagging the product package to let consumers know that the recommended price of the product is lower than usual ("Price marked is 20 percent off regular price"). The flagging can catch the consumer's attention in the store, helping the promoted product to stand out on the shelf. And, since the manufacturer determines how many flagged packages are distributed, price-offs are an easy-to-control form of sales promotion.

Sampling

Sampling can be the ultimate price-reducing, risk-reducing sales promotion technique; brand marketers spent $925 million on sampling in 1997.[8] With a free sample, the consumer gets to try the product at no cost with no risk. So, while sampling programs can be very expensive, they are the absolute best way to generate trial for a new product or for an existing product in a new target market. The only risk is to the marketer: If the product is not better than competitive brands, sampling will trumpet that fact to consumers faster than any other form of sales promotion.

There are a number of ways to distribute product samples, including through the mail, door-to-door, at a central location (such as a grocery store) via a demonstrator,

---

[6]Ibid.

[7]Ibid.

[8]"Product Sampling: Sampling Continues to Stretch Out," *PROMO*, July 1998, p. S29.

Exhibit 12-3
Hood Ice Cream Coupon Offer

Exhibit 12-4
First Moments Sampling Program

TARGET THEIR FIRST MOMENTS...
AND GET THERE FIRST
SOLO AND CO-OP SAMPLING/COUPONING PROGRAMS

■ **NEW PARENTS**
Hand delivered by staff nurses to 3,700,000 new mothers in 3800 hospitals...over 90% of all births

■ **HISPANIC NEW PARENTS**
510,000 annual hospital bedside distribution...69% of all Hispanic births

■ **EXPECTANT PARENTS**
2,000,000 annual distribution through 10,000 childbirth educators...79% of all first births

■ **HISPANIC EXPECTANT PARENTS**
160,000 annual distribution through childbirth educators... 41% of all first time Hispanic parents

■ **SOLO SAMPLING PROGRAMS**
We will create and implement your own unique sampling or couponing program from concept to completion

All Programs Audited
As a further convenience, we offer contract packaging services
from our West, Central and East Coast production facilities.

Yes I am interested. Please forward information on:

☐ New Parents   ☐ Expectant Parents
☐ Hispanic New Parents   ☐ Hispanic Expectant Parents
☐ Solo Sampling Programs ☐ Contract Packaging

Name_____Title_____
Company _____Brand_____
Address _____City_____
State _____ Zip_____Telephone _____

Contact Steven Fleischer, Vice President Sales/Marketing
First Moments, Inc. • 55 Northern Blvd. • Greenvale, NY 11548
516-484-5740 • Fax# 516-484-2950

Circle No. 018 on Reader Service Card

or through a co-op or specialty service such as that offered by First Moments, Inc. Exhibit 12-4 shows an advertisement from First Moments outlining their sampling program. Magazines and newspapers also can carry samples, as can packages of other products (for example, General Mills distributed samples of Crispy Wheats and Raisins cereal inside boxes of Raisin Nut Bran). Some manufacturers will distribute coupons that can be redeemed for a free sample. And, in a variation on the free sample, some products are introduced through the use of smaller-than-usual, specially priced sample packages.

In a highly publicized sampling effort, Burger King introduced its reformulated french fries with Free FryDay. On the designated date (January 2, 1998), Burger King gave away a free small order of french fries to over 15 million consumers in the United States and Canada. No purchase was required—you just had to go to a Burger King restaurant and request the fries. Burger King spent about $70 million on the promotion, including $35–$45 million on television and radio commercials to let consumers know about the sampling day. In addition, the company sent mobile sampling units into forty-five markets across the country during the winter and spring to reach even more consumers with the new product. This was one in a series of Burger King efforts to compete more aggressively with McDonald's; in addition, the restaurant chain makes a better profit on french fries than it does on hamburgers, so selling more fries makes good business sense, justifying the cost of the sampling program.[9]

Value Enhancement Tactics

There are four major consumer sales promotion tactics that are used primarily to add value: special packs, continuity programs, sweepstakes and contests, and through-the-mail premiums. Continuity programs generally are both business and brand building; the others are largely business-building approaches.

Special Packs

Special packs include (a) bonus packs, in which the consumer receives more of the promoted product for the same price that he or she would normally pay for a lesser amount; (b) in-packs, on-packs, and near packs, which are means of delivering premiums (gifts) along with the product; and (c) reusable containers, where the product package itself is the premium. In each case, consumers are getting something extra when they buy the product.

Bonus packs are a nice way to reward current customers for their business, since they're the group most likely to be interested in receiving extra product. In-, on-, and near-pack premium offers are effective in generating interest among consumers in the store aisle. With an in-pack, the premium is carried inside the product package, and that fact usually is highlighted on the package. In the case of an on-pack, the premium is attached to the exterior of the package, which is attention-getting in itself.

---

[9]Betsy Spethmann, "French Fry Frenzy," *PROMO*, February 1998, p. 66.

Near-pack offers also deliver the premium at the time of purchase, but here the premium can't be put in or on the product package. Instead, it's usually located near the product, or, depending on the value of the premium, it may be kept at the cash register. Reusable containers are also attention-getters and can help to remind the consumer of the product in the future.

Doritos ran an in-pack premium promotion targeted at teens. A sell-in sheet describing the promotion is shown in Exhibit 12-5. Frito-Lay distributed 60 million guitar picks in 99-cent bags of Doritos. The picks featured different artists popular with teens to encourage multiple purchases. The promotional packs were available only in convenience stores, enhancing the appeal of the promotion with that class of retailers.

Continuity Programs

Continuity programs are growing quickly in popularity. As the name suggests, they are designed to generate purchase continuity, that is, to keep consumers coming back to the same brand over time. Hallmark's Gold Crown Card, discussed earlier, is an example of a continuity program, as are airline frequent flier programs and grocery store frequent shopper programs. Consumers earn the rewards of a continuity program as they accumulate product purchases. The reward may be free units of the product or some sort of premium. With continuity programs, it's important to keep in mind that the reward must be desirable enough to keep the consumer's attention during the time it takes to accumulate enough purchases to qualify.

Sweepstakes and Contests

The difference between a sweepstakes and a contest is an important legal distinction. A contest requires some demonstration of skill (answering a question, writing an essay, or the like) to win, while winning a sweepstakes is based on chance. Both give the manufacturer something to highlight in product advertising and at the point of sale. And, the more compelling the prize, the greater the consumer interest and excitement.

In an announced contest from Merit Ultra Lights, for example, the demonstrated skill was the ability to write an essay of twenty-five words or fewer on "your favorite place to enjoy a Merit." Five grand-prize winners were to get an eight-day/seven-night Alaskan cruise; ten first-prize winners would get a Panasonic Palmcorder, and ten second-prize winners would get an Alaskan king crab dinner for ten people. The large number of top prizes was intended to encourage entries. Merit also used this contest to gather information on smokers and build its database; the entry form noted that the contest was "limited to smokers 21 years of age or older" (participants were required to sign a statement certifying that they smoked and met the age requirement), and asked for the brand of cigarettes the entrant regularly smoked. Further, by entering the contest, participants agreed that they were "willing to receive cigarette coupons and branded incentive items in the mail."

Exhibit 12-5
Doritos Sell-In Sheet

Doritos

T2 "PICK YOUR MUSIC" Promotion

A teen-focused promotion to create incremental turns!

Timing: May 17 - August 8

An Original Program:
- Teen-focused promotion only available in c-stores, where teens consume more salty snacks than any other age group!
- 60MM collectible guitar picks featuring CD cover art of popular music groups in-packed in every bag of 99¢ DORITOS® brand Tortilla Chips.
- Guitar picks can be used to gain access to concerts and/or win music-based prizes in select markets.
- Instant win sweepstakes for large music-based prizes.
- Guitar pick collectibility drives repeat purchases!

A Teen-Focused Brand:
- All flavors of 99¢ DORITOS® brand Tortilla Chips

Consumer Marketing Support:
- Over $2MM in radio and Internet media - over 43% of total U.S. teens reached!*
- Extensive radio merchandising in top 26 national radio market to create more talk-value around the pick.
- Thematic packaging burst communicates offer on every bag of 99¢ DORITOS® brand Tortilla Chips .

In-Store Excitement:
- Cutting edge mini-weekender with compelling graphics to drive incremental turns and profits - $19.20 in profit per turn!
- High-visibility shelf danglers to clearly communicate the program with breakthrough, teen-focused imagery.

* Teen Frito-Lay Media Estimate, 1997.
DORITOS and DORITOS Logo are trademarks used by Frito-Lay, Inc. © Recot, Inc., 1998.

271

Chapter 12

Through-the-Mail Premiums

Like continuity programs, through-the-mail premiums offer delayed gratification. There are two forms of through-the-mail premiums: free-in-the-mail premiums and self-liquidating premiums. The premiums differ in who assumes the cost. Free-in-the-mail premiums, as the name suggests, cost the consumer nothing more than postage and handling and usually require some proof of product purchase. With self-liquidating premiums, however, the consumer pays for the premium, although usually at a lower cost than if the same item were bought at retail. Self-liquidators can, in fact, be very expensive specialty items.

Like all types of premiums, the through-the-mail variety is most effective when the item offered has some link to the promoted product. For example, consumers who buy a "Charlie the Tuna" telephone from StarKist are reminded of the product each time they see the telephone. That kind of link can play an important role in brand building.

Planning Sales Promotion

While sales promotion should be developed as part of an overall IBC program, there are some considerations involved in planning the promotion. The following is a fourteen-step outline commonly used to plan a successful sales promotion program.

Step one. Analyze the market situation. The IBC planner should look at category trends, economic trends, consumer behavior, and so on to determine the situation of the category and the brand. Most likely, this analysis already will have been done when planning other marketing communications activities, but it should be reviewed for changes or an impact that might be specific to sales promotion needs.

Step two. Evaluate the promotional environment. Look at what is happening in all marketing communications areas in the marketplace in general and particularly in the product category.

Step three. Assess competitive activity. How active are competitors in the area? What are they doing? What are they likely to do? How high are the promotional barriers that already have been erected in the brand category?

Step four. Identify the problem to be solved. Often, the problem is more complex than it first appears. We need to pinpoint the specific objectives that need to be achieved and make sure they can be accomplished through sales promotion.

Step five. Develop sales promotion objectives. As previously discussed, these must be clear-cut, specific, and measurable. We must be sure we're dealing with objectives and not tactics.

Step six. Identify the target audience(s) for the promotion. Who is to be reached and motivated by the promotional event? Is it the ultimate consumer, the sales force, distributors, or the trade? Be specific.

Step seven. Define the strategies that will be used. The major question is whether these strategies will meet the objectives that have been set.

Step eight. Outline the tactics. These should flow naturally from the objectives and strategies. Refer to the tactics discussed earlier in this chapter. Do they support the strategies?

Step nine. Develop a budget. Pull all the costs together and be sure to include redemption, handling, and other costs for ongoing programs. What will it cost to conduct the program outline? How does that compare to available funds?

Step ten. Create the "Big Idea." Here's where we consider all the executional alternatives. What is to be communicated? What is the tone? What involvement devices would help extend and expand the message? All these go into making sure that the sales promotion program really stands out in a very crowded marketplace.

Step eleven. Choose the promotional media. What media will be used for the sales promotion program—FSI, TV, magazines, point of sale, Internet, telemarketing, or direct mail? In other words, what is the most effective and efficient way to get the promotional program to the target market?

Step twelve. Pin down the promotional timetable. Cover all the important dates—including sell-in (when the promotion will be introduced to channel members), in-field date (when the promotion program will appear in the media and/or in the store), length of promotion (how long the offer will be valid), evaluation deadline (cut-off date for promotion redemptions/sales), and so on.

Step thirteen. Obtain a pretest evaluation. All major sales promotion programs should be pretested. Will it be done through market tests, consumer groups, or trade/dealer screens?

Step fourteen. Obtain a posttest evaluation. How will the results of the sales promotion event be measured? Will we use volume or share data, consumer response, attitude and awareness studies, executive judgment? It's important to determine in advance just how the program will be measured and evaluated.

With this checklist, any planner should be able to develop sound, effective sales promotion events. However, there are a few final planning questions that should be asked.

1. Are the objectives realistic?

2. Do strategies support the objectives?

3. Is the idea clear?

4. Can the sales promotion event be executed as planned?

5. Is the program cost efficient?

6. Will the event appeal to the target audience?

7. Is the creative approach unique enough to break through the clutter?

If we can answer yes to all these questions, our sales promotion program is likely not only to support the other marketing communications elements in our plan, but to enhance them as well.[10]

---

[10]Schultz and Robinson, *Sales Promotion Management*, pp. 139–44.

Sales Promotion and the Internet

The sales promotion industry has embraced the Internet with fervor, largely because of the medium's ability to deliver targeted messages. (Remember the low redemption rate for FSI coupons mentioned earlier? It's largely due to the lack of targeting available through most coupon distribution media.) While the entire interactive category (including telemarketing as well as Internet activities) made up only 1.1 percent of total sales promotion expenditures in 1997, interest in the medium is strong.[11] Marketers are using the Internet for contests, premium offers, and coupon offers, among others. Exhibit 12-6 is a coupon mailer one of the authors received by mail after filling out a simple questionnaire on Ragú's Web site http://www.eat.com. There are also services that offer barcoded coupons directly over the Web; for example, Catalina Marketing's SuperMarkets Online allows consumers to print out coupons that can be redeemed at a participating grocery store. Catalina charges brand marketers $52,000 for a year-long contract, which guarantees them category exclusivity.[12] As Catalina's service and that of other competitors prove themselves, more and more marketers are likely to sign up for this form of coupon distribution.

Besides couponing sites, at least two Web sites exist that offer Web surfers the chance to receive product samples. The service of FreeSampleClub.com is described in the sidebar. NetSampler, another product sample Web site, delivers samples to consumers within seventy-two hours. Finally, a number of product-themed Web sites offer contests, premiums, and other promotional deals. A sample page from http://www.icee.com is shown in Exhibit 12-7.

A Final Word on Sales Promotion Risks

In recent years, many major consumer products marketers have begun to agonize over their consumer sales promotion spending, particularly due to its effect on consumer shopping behavior. Have we created a nation of price-driven brand switchers?

To Coupon or Not to Coupon?

Not all brand marketers are fans of consumer sales promotion, at least, not as traditionally practiced. Procter & Gamble conducted a much-publicized couponing experiment, or, rather, lack-of-couponing experiment, in central New York State during 1996. Stating that their coupon offers were plagued by both low redemption rates and misredemption problems, P&G announced that they were going to test a program in which they would discontinue coupons and instead lower product prices overall. Other packaged goods companies followed suit, including Clorox, Colgate-Palmolive, Lever Brothers, Dial, DowBrands, Fort James, S. C. Johnson & Son,

---

[11]"Interactive: Stuck in Test Mode," *PROMO*, July 1998, p. S32.

[12]Robert Storace, "Bringing Online in Line," *PROMO*, April 1998, pp. 54 ff.

Exhibit 12-6
Ragú Coupon Mailer

Hungry From All That Net Surfing?
The Ragú® Brands Have What You're Looking For!
Try all our great tasting products available in several varieties:

RAGÚ®	CHICKEN TONIGHT®	PIZZA QUICK®
Pasta Sauces	*Cooking Sauces for Chicken*	*Pizza Sauces*
Hearty	Sweet & Sour	Traditional
Light	Cacciatore	Chunky Tomato
Chunky Gardenstyle	Country French	Chunky Mushroom
Old World Style®	Honey Mustard	Pepperoni
	Creamy Mushroom	

MANUFACTURER'S COUPON — EXPIRES DECEMBER 31, 1995

SAVE 35¢ on any
RAGÚ® HEARTY *Pasta Sauce*
Sautéed Onion & Mushroom
Flavored with Sautéed Beef
Parmesan
Hearty Italian Tomato

50094
5 36200 11035 0

MANUFACTURER'S COUPON — EXPIRES DECEMBER 31, 1995

SAVE 40¢ on any
CHICKEN TONIGHT® *Cooking Sauce for Chicken from Ragú®*
Cacciatore
Country French
Honey Mustard
Creamy Mushroom

51070
5 36200 40040 0

MANUFACTURER'S COUPON — EXPIRES DECEMBER 31, 1995

SAVE 40¢ on any
RAGÚ® PIZZA QUICK® *Pizza Sauce*
Chunky Tomato
Chunky Mushroom
Pepperoni

52036
5 36200 20040 2

MANUFACTURER'S COUPON — EXPIRES DECEMBER 31, 1995

SAVE 35¢ on any
RAGÚ® CHUNKY GARDENSTYLE *Pasta Sauce*
Super Mushroom
Super Vegetable Primavera
Chunky Garden Combination
Chunky Mushroom & Green Pepper
Chunky Mushroom & Onion
Chunky Green & Red Pepper

50095
5 36200 13035 8

MANUFACTURER'S COUPON — EXPIRES DECEMBER 31, 1995

SAVE 35¢ on any
RAGÚ® OLD WORLD STYLE® *Pasta Sauce*
Marinara
Flavored with Meat
Mushroom

50097
5 36200 14035 7

MANUFACTURER'S COUPON — EXPIRES DECEMBER 31, 1995

SAVE 35¢ on any
RAGÚ® LIGHT *Pasta Sauce*
Chunky Mushroom
Tomato & Herb No Sugar Added
Garden Harvest

50096
5 36200 12035 9

FreeSampleClub.com

Fast is what it's all about on the Internet. If it's not lightning-quick, the user is going to jump to someone else's page. That problem has sunk past online sampling efforts, which soured surfers with delivery times of up to six weeks. That's a lifetime in cyber-culture.

Those problems are in the past now, proclaims Sunflower ceo Dennis Garberg. His company's co-op FreeSampleClub.com delivers product via priority mail within five days and works like this: Customers initially have to "join" the club (providing name, address, and some demographic information), and receive a PIN number to use when popping in and out of the site. Once in, consumers can click and choose which products they want to try, like shopping in a virtual supermarket aisle.

"The site has relevant samples," says Garberg. "Customers can review one, some, or all of them."

FreeSampleClub.com gives clients two selection methods to choose from. With "Member Select," products are available to those consumers who simply choose to try them. The system only allows cyber-surfers to order half of featured products, limiting waste and cracking down on customers who may click on every product.

That spells added targetability, as online club members must prioritize and decide on which samples to receive. If they don't drink orange soda, they won't choose to receive some, and if they don't have a baby in the household, there shouldn't be an infant formula selection.

Option two is called "YOU Select," in which clients of the service can include their product as a bonus item to those members who fit predetermined demographic and geographic requirements.

Garber says the site is designed to be safe from scavengers. Club members must provide feedback on samples received before they can log back on and select additional items. False names are discarded before fulfillment. If the customer's initial e-mail address does not go through, the order is killed.

Ballpark pricing for the service ranges from 55 cents per item for Member Select to 85 cents per item for YOU Select, plus a discounted share of prevailing priority postal rates. Coupon inserts are also available at 40 cents per item. Minimum samples required to participate is 30,000.

Excerpted from Dan Hanover, "Clicking for Freebies," *PROMO*, December 1997, p. 86.

Pillsbury, and Reckitt & Colman. Consumers and consumer advocates in the affected markets were outraged, and their complaints led the state attorney general to sue the collected companies and Wegman's, one of the major supermarket chains in the area. The lawsuit was settled for $4.2 million, which was given back to consumers through running $2 coupons in local newspapers.[13] More than 35,000 consumers signed petitions complaining about the experiment. P&G claimed that prices on its brands dropped an average of 67 cents per case during the experiment;

---

[13]Jeff Harrington, "P&G Still Opposed to Coupons," *Cincinnati Enquirer*, September 11, 1997, p. B16.

Exhibit 12-7
WWW.ICEE.COM Home Page

Welcome to The ICEE Company Website.
Please click on ICEE Bear to enter the site.

that would net out to a reduction of only a few cents per item for consumers.[14] In settling the suit, none of the companies involved admitted any wrongdoing. P&G continues to test different ways to reduce prices that might cost the company less than couponing.

Price Sensitivity

One of the main results of the New York State test is the compelling evidence it provides of consumers' interest in and reliance on sales promotion offers in making purchasing decisions. This is very much in line with recent research findings by Mela, Gupta, and Lehmann. Their research is based on analysis of a database of purchases made in a single product category by 1,590 households over an eight-and-a-quarter-year period. They found two groups of consumers—a loyal group that was not particularly price-sensitive, and a nonloyal group that brand switched on the basis of price. The evidence suggested that the nonloyal group became even more sensitive to price as time went on, requiring larger inducements to generate a switch in brands. This negative effect of sales promotion was in contrast to a demonstrated positive effect of advertising, which appeared to decrease price sensitivity.[15]

[14]David Robinson, "WNYers Will Be Clipping Coupons for Years to Come," *Buffalo News*, September 14, 1997, p. 15B.

[15]Carl F. Mela, Sunil Gupta, and Donald R. Lehmann, "The Long-Term Impact of Promotion and Advertising on Consumer Brand Choice," *Journal of Marketing Research* 34 (Spring 1997): 248 ff.

Mela, Gupta, and Lehmann's findings bring us back to the point made at the beginning of this chapter that sales promotion, by and large, is a business-building activity. While the short-term sales gains achieved through promotional activity can be an important part of a marketing program, they are no substitute for brand-building activities. Sales promotion works best when used to enhance a brand-building communications strategy.

13

Business Building and Brand Building

Direct Response and Interactive Media

The twenty-first-century marketplace will approach brand communication from a consumer perspective. Given this, direct response and interactive media are likely to play increasingly important roles since they allow brand communicators to speak directly to very well-defined groups of consumers. In this chapter, we look at the fundamental traditional direct marketing approaches, as well as some of the newer interactive media, particularly the World Wide Web.

What Is Direct Marketing?

In a recent study commissioned to assess the economic impact of direct marketing in the United States, the Direct Marketing Association defined direct marketing as "any direct communication to a consumer or business recipient that is designed to generate 1) a response in the form of an order (*direct order*), 2) a request for further information (*lead generation*), and/or 3) a visit to a store or other place of business for purchase of a specific product(s) or service(s) (*traffic generation*)."[1] Direct marketing includes direct response advertising, direct sales, and telemarketing, among other elements.

Direct marketing differs from traditional advertising in a number of key ways, which are summarized in Table 13-1. Many of the characteristics of direct marketing

[1]Direct Marketing Association, "Economic Impact: U.S. Direct Marketing Today," 4th ed. (1998) (http://www.thedma.org).

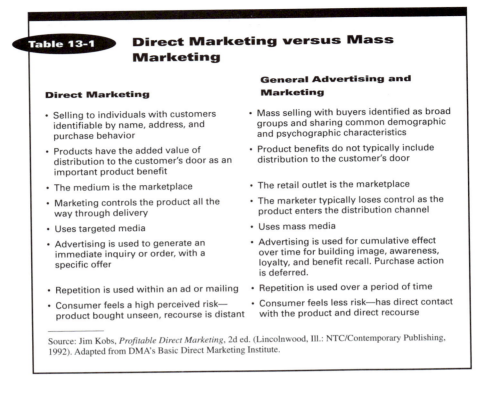

Table 13-1

Direct Marketing versus Mass Marketing

Direct Marketing	General Advertising and Marketing
• Selling to individuals with customers identifiable by name, address, and purchase behavior	• Mass selling with buyers identified as broad groups and sharing common demographic and psychographic characteristics
• Products have the added value of distribution to the customer's door as an important product benefit	• Product benefits do not typically include distribution to the customer's door
• The medium is the marketplace	• The retail outlet is the marketplace
• Marketing controls the product all the way through delivery	• The marketer typically loses control as the product enters the distribution channel
• Uses targeted media	• Uses mass media
• Advertising is used to generate an immediate inquiry or order, with a specific offer	• Advertising is used for cumulative effect over time for building image, awareness, loyalty, and benefit recall. Purchase action is deferred.
• Repetition is used within an ad or mailing	• Repetition is used over a period of time
• Consumer feels a high perceived risk—product bought unseen, recourse is distant	• Consumer feels less risk—has direct contact with the product and direct recourse

Source: Jim Kobs, *Profitable Direct Marketing*, 2d ed. (Lincolnwood, Ill.: NTC/Contemporary Publishing, 1992). Adapted from DMA's Basic Direct Marketing Institute.

listed in the table also apply to the World Wide Web and other forms of interactive advertising, with one critical exception: in almost all cases, the customer is not identifiable *in advance*. That is, while traditional direct marketing relies heavily on lists of specific customers and/or prospects about whom something is known before communications contact is made, Web users are identifiable (to some extent) only *after* they've made a visit to a Web site. That's an important distinction that we'll come back to later in this chapter.

Direct marketing is used extensively by brand communicators in the United States. In 1997, direct marketing media spending totaled $153 billion, which represented 57.8 percent of all U.S. advertising spending. Most of that money was spent in telemarketing ($58.1 billion in 1997) and direct mail ($37.4 billion), followed by television ($17.2 billion), newspaper ($15.1 billion), magazine ($7.8 billion), and radio ($5.3 billion).[2] In comparison, only $275 million was spent on interactive direct response advertising in 1997; of that, 64 percent was directed at business targets and 36 percent at consumers.

---

[2]Ibid.

Reasons for Direct Marketing Growth

Investments in direct marketing have grown phenomenally in the past four decades. The major reasons for this growth are as follows:

1. *Growth of computer capability.* Because direct marketing relies heavily on the capture, storage, and manipulation of large masses of information, such as names, addresses, and purchasing histories of customers and prospects, the increased capacity and capability of computers have been responsible for much of the growth. And, as computer technology and capability have grown, costs have declined. Therefore, it is now economically practical for marketers to make use of direct marketing capabilities, such as personalization, segmentation, and customer targeting.

2. *Advanced statistical techniques.* Partially as a by-product of increased computer technology, more advanced statistical techniques and procedures have been developed. These techniques allow direct marketers to accurately project the results of small-scale tests to larger population segments or databases. For this reason, direct marketing has become one of the more reliable methods of marketing communication.

3. *Measurability.* With reliable projections and known response rates, marketers are able to accurately measure the financial results of their efforts. In this era of accountability, measurability has great appeal. And, as you'll see later in this chapter, measurability has been touted as one of the hallmarks of Web-based marketing.

4. *Segmentation and personalization.* As former mass markets have been fragmented and segmented by marketers with niche products, there has been more emphasis on identification of target markets. With that identification has come the potential for personalization. New computer technology now permits direct marketers to identify, personalize, and print mail messages and responses targeted at individual segments of the population. On the interactive side, several firms have developed software that makes it possible to customize Web site information for individual users.

5. *Credit cards.* Widespread acceptance and use of credit cards as a medium of exchange has made distance purchasing possible and practical. By using a toll-free telephone number or a Web site ordering option, consumers can now purchase and pay for products easily and conveniently.

Although there are doubtless other factors, these five have been most responsible for the growth of direct marketing over the past twenty years or so. Further, they continue to drive the current growth of interactive marketing and advertising.

Business Building or Brand Building?

Direct marketing and interactive techniques can easily be used in support of an IBC program. There are four basic objectives for the direct marketing techniques used in most brand communication campaigns: building a marketer-customer relationship, inducing a product trial or a brand switch, developing a market through direct response, and building volume or usage of a brand. As that list might suggest, both business building (trial, direct response, volume building) and brand building (relationship development) efforts are possible with direct and interactive marketing.

Retaining Current Customers

Most direct marketing is based on the concept of building relationships between the marketer and the customer. The direct marketer believes that the ongoing relationship and continual purchases make direct marketing very different from traditional marketing. Therefore, the direct marketer is willing to invest heavily, often in excess of the first year's sales returns, to gain a new customer because he or she is building for repeat or future purchases. (This is the approach to communication investment we advocated in Chapter 8.)

As we have noted earlier, the 80/20 rule holds in most businesses. That is, about 80 percent of the company's sales are made to 20 percent of the customer base. Although the figures may vary somewhat, the relationship seems to hold in almost every category. In a marketplace such as ours, where there is little population growth, retaining present customers and building sales or volume over time is the key to successful direct marketing. That is what direct marketing teaches mass marketers today.

Continuity programs such as the one offered by BMG are an example of a customer retention effort. Consumers are encouraged to join BMG's music club through an attractive introductory offer that allows new members to pick seven CDs at no cost other than shipping and handling. Then, after buying one additional CD at regular price sometime in the next year, the member gets three more free CDs. Of course, BMG's hope is that customers will remain in the club and make many more purchases over time. BMG's introductory letter is shown in Exhibit 13-1. (Note the degree of personalization in the letter—the prospect's first name appears three times on the front page alone!)

Inducing Product Trial or Brand Switching

Direct marketing is an excellent tool to generate trial of a product or to encourage brand switching. Assuming something is known about the customer or prospect, specific direct marketing programs can be developed to build trial of the brand. For example, assume a list of persons known to have vegetable gardens is available. It would be a simple task for the marketer of a new type of fertilizer to mail a letter, a coupon, or even a sample to this group. One would naturally expect a high response from prospects who are known to have gardens. This is just one example of how direct marketers are able to deal with prospects, not just suspects. Alternatively, if a list of known users of competitive brands of facial bar soap were available, some type of trial offer could be made by a marketer of a competitive product to try to entice the consumer to switch to the marketer's brand.

Exhibit 13-2 is a spread from a brochure mailed to consumers to offer a free test drive of the Oldsmobile Intrigue. The offer was tied to the release of *The X-Files* feature film; consumers received six complimentary tickets to the movie for taking the

Exhibit 13-1
BMG Direct Mail Letter

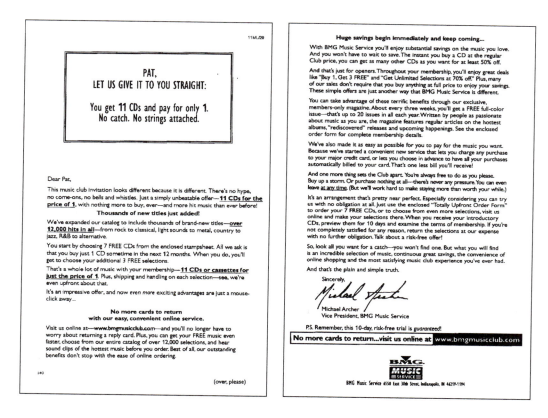

test drive. The brochure carried photos from the film, along with copy tied to the secrecy/conspiracy theme. The brochure arrived in a plain brown wrapper, with only the recipient's name and address on the front and a small *X-Files* logo on the back. (The mailing list for this offer appears to have come from subscribers to entertainment magazines such as *Entertainment Weekly*—people who would be likely to be familiar with *The X-Files* from television viewing and who might be interested in seeing the movie. And, in a nice bit of synergy, "X-File" Agents Mulder and Scully drive an Intrigue in the movie.)

Selling Through Direct Response

Direct marketing might also attempt to sell the product through direct response. Amazon.com has been very successful in selling books and related products over its Web site. Print ads in magazines and newspapers, television commercials, and even radio ads are other ways to sell products through direct response.

Exhibit 13-2
Oldsmobile Intrigue Brochure

Increasing Volume

Direct marketing is also used to build volume or usage of a brand. Book-of-the-Month Club rewards loyal customers by designating them as "Preferred Members." After every sixth purchase, the Preferred Member receives a certificate good for a free book (up to $25 in price). BOMC doesn't even charge shipping and handling on the free book. This encourages members to buy more books, and to buy more often to be able to qualify for more free books.

The key task for the IBC planner is to relate possible direct behavioral marketing objectives to the overall goals of the brand, product, or service for which the campaign is being developed. Based on an analysis of what the brand needs to accomplish, the direct behavioral marketing objectives can then be identified.

Forms of Direct Marketing

We'll look at four direct marketing approaches: direct response, direct mail, telemarketing, and the World Wide Web. Each can play an important role in a brand communication program.

Direct Response

Direct response seeks to achieve a direct, measurable response from the target audience. It can range from a mail-order house's magazine advertisement seeking to

Table 13-2	**Direct Response Media**	
Medium	**Pros**	**Cons**
Magazines	Both mass and segmented audiences available Greater exposure via large circulation Invited into home Excellent color reproduction A/B splits and regional editions allow testing	Limited format choices Long lead time Lack of Positioning control Relatively slow response
Newspapers	Immediate and authoritative Fast testing results Broad local coverage Broad reach with national papers Invited into home Inexpensive testing	Poor color reproduction Impersonal Positioning and format problems Nationally complex Little selectivity Overly localized
Freestanding inserts & Sunday magazines	Flexible formats Good color reproduction Exact timing Large reach potential Good for testing	Clutter Little selectivity
Billing and package inserts	Extends reach	Standard format and size Not a stand-alone medium
Television	Good for demonstration Broad format choices	Limited time available Viewer zapping Fleeting messages
Radio	Targeting through station format News value Good for fantasy and humor Immediacy	Fleeting messages Hard to build national reach No visuals; no response device Background medium

Source: Adapted from Susan K. Jones, *Creative Strategy in Direct Marketing* (Lincolnwood, Ill.: NTC Business Books, 1991), pp. 52–61.

generate catalog requests to build a list, to a business-to-business company's advertising in trade publications to generate sales force leads, to a magazine's direct mail package soliciting new subscribers.

Media choice is one of the more important decisions in developing a direct response program. Today, a variety of media are available for direct response use. Obviously, direct mail continues to be the most popular choice, and telemarketing also is widely used. But there are other options. Table 13-2 summarizes some advantages and disadvantages in terms of creative considerations of other traditional media for direct response. Whatever the media type used or the form of the offer made, customers and prospects respond by calling an 800 number, by returning a form by mail, or by using a computer modem.

Direct response programs can be one-step or two-step. In a one-step program, all the information needed to make the sale is included. In a two-step program, the prospect is first moved to request additional information and then to follow through by making a purchase. Whether a one- or two-step program is used, the goal in direct response is an immediate response from the target audience that ultimately results in the sale of the product or service. Exhibit 13-3 is an example of a two-step program offered by Mutual of Omaha, an insurance company. People who respond to the offer receive more information about specific types of insurance offered by Mutual of Omaha, tied to their birthdate.

Direct Mail

We classify all forms of direct contact with customers and prospects through the U.S. Postal Service as direct mail. This includes mass cooperative mailings of coupons, products, and other offers.

Direct mail can be highly selective, such as, a mailing to a list of the alumni of a specific college or, on a broader scale, a mailing to all automobile-owning households in the western half of the United States. In addition, direct mail need not require a specific response from the target audience. As with other forms of media, it may be used to build the image or impression of an organization with the hope of later purchasing activity. In other words, like any other advertising medium, direct mail can be used to send sales messages to customers and prospects. In most cases, the advantage of direct mail is that it can be highly targeted to predetermined and selected groups of people or companies.

There are five principle elements of a direct mail program: the list, the offer, the copy, the package, and the back-end response program. Each is reviewed in the following sections.

The List

Most direct marketing practitioners believe the list, or the names, addresses, titles, and so on to which direct marketing offers are made, is the key ingredient of the discipline. Some have gone so far as to say that the list is at least half the value of any direct marketing program.

There are a number of organizations involved with lists and list rentals. They can be categorized as follows:

List owners. List owners are the organizations that own a list of names, addresses, and additional customer or purchase information that they generate and maintain. Often, these lists are lists of the organization's customers. For example, Spiegel might offer a list of persons who have ordered from its catalog; *Reader's Digest* might offer a list of its subscribers; or VISA might furnish a list of its card members. In any case, the list is owned and maintained by the organization that, in turn, is willing to rent the list for direct marketing purposes.

There is another group of companies that do what is called "list enhancement." A list enhancer might take a list of names and addresses of persons who subscribe to a

Exhibit 13-3
Mutual of Omaha Letter

```
                    From                              MAIL IN THE ENCLOSED
                                                     POSTAGE-PAID ENVELOPE
              Mutual of Omaha Companies         PLEASE SEND ME MORE INFORMATION
              P.O. Box 2009                        ABOUT THE FOLLOWING!
Mutual of Omaha.  Syracuse, NY 13220-2009
Companies
                                                ☐  DISABILITY INCOME PROTECTION
                                                ☐  INDIVIDUAL HEALTH INSURANCE
                                                ☐  GROUP HEALTH INSURANCE
      B E Barnes                                ☐  HEALTH INSURANCE FOR PERSONS
                                                   AGE 65 OR OLDER
   |..||..||....|||...|..|..||.|.|..||.|..|||...||...|.||   ☐  LONG-TERM NURSING CARE
                                                ☐  LIFE INSURANCE
                                                ☐  MUTUAL FUNDS

   NAME_____              MY DATE OF BIRTH:
   ADDRESS_____
   CITY _____STATE ____ZIP_____    MY OCCUPATION IS:
   PHONE _____-_____-_____
```

IMAGINE LIFE WITHOUT
A PAYCHECK!

IF YOU FURNISH US WITH YOUR DATE OF BIRTH...

We will provide personal service in forwarding valuable information about our Disability Income Protection.

This plan, underwritten by Mutual of Omaha Insurance Company, can provide monthly benefits when a covered illness or injury prevents you from working. You do not have to be hospitalized to collect benefits.

I hope you will let us provide more facts about the benefits of Disability Income Protection. Requesting this information does not obligate you to buy insurance. Mail your reply today.

This policy provides disability income insurance only. It does NOT provide basic hospital, basic medical or major medical insurance as defined by the New York State Insurance Department. The expected benefit ratio for this policy is 55%. This ratio is the portion of future premiums which the company expects to return as benefits, when averaged over all people with this policy. Individual health insurance underwritten by: Mutual of Omaha Insurance Company. Group health insurance, life insurance and annuities underwritten by: Companion Life Insurance Company, Rye, NY Mutual funds distributed through: Mutual of Omaha Investor Services, Inc.

PLEASE REFOLD THIS LETTER SO THAT THE RETURN ADDRESS BELOW SHOWS THROUGH THE WINDOW IN THE ENCLOSED RETURN ENVELOPE. THANK YOU!

```
       Mutual of Omaha Companies         Phone (315) 461-4201
                                         Fax   (315) 461-4210
              P.O. Box 2009
          Syracuse, NY 13220-2009
AFN 28282-2-98
```

certain magazine and add or "overlay" additional information about each household to the original list. For example, National Demographics and Lifestyles processes warranty cards for a number of electronics products. When given a direct marketer's list, they can then add to it household file information, such as where and when certain products were purchased or used by the household. Thus, a marketer of 35mm film could enhance a customer list by adding or identifying persons who have recently purchased new 35mm cameras. This enhancement process has become very sophisticated. As a result, marketers can build very complex consumer behavior models that are used to target and predict the response of the list.

List brokers and managers. List brokers and managers act as the agents for the list owners. Generally, they are independent companies that arrange the rental of the list of names for the company developing a direct marketing campaign. Brokers receive a commission for each list they rent.

It should be noted that, in general, lists are rented, not sold. The list broker contacts a company that is interested in developing a direct marketing program. The broker works with the marketer to find the best list available from the group of companies whose lists the broker represents. The list selected is then rented to the direct marketing organization for a one-time-only use. The list owner has the right of approval of (a) the copy the direct marketer will use, (b) the timing of the list use and delivery dates, and (c) any selections the direct marketer might want to make from the list. For example, the marketer might want to rent only names in certain zip codes, or names of persons who have made purchases in the past six months. Under this agreement, the direct marketer rents the list on a cost-per-thousand-names basis. The list broker receives a commission on the rental, usually 10–20 percent of the total order paid by the list owner.

Service bureaus and letter shops. Service bureaus are organizations that deal primarily with lists, list maintenance (for example, changes and corrections), and merge-purge operations. (*Merge-purge* is a computer process by which two lists are combined and duplications of names and households or companies are noted and removed.) Service bureaus also print a list of the names on a set of labels or prepare the list of names on a magnetic tape to be sent to the direct marketing organization that rented the list for their mailing use.

Letter shops are organizations that print the direct mail materials, attach the labels to the mailing envelopes or pieces, assemble the entire direct marketing package, and deliver it to the post office for mailing.

Co-ops. A cooperative arrangement allows several direct marketing organizations to work together to mail packages with multiple direct response offers, manufacturer or retailer coupons, and the like. Perhaps of most interest to the brand planner is the mail order co-op, such as the Val-Pak Program offered by Cox Target Media. Val-Pak mails to more than 53 million homes and business in the United States and Canada. Advertisers can insert advertising, merchandising, and promotional materials in the mailing at a shared cost. Usually, this is much less expensive than an individual mailing. A study conducted for Val-Pak in 1997 found that 82 percent of consumers were aware of Val-Pak and that 90 percent of that group review every coupon in each Val-Pak mailing.[3] These types of co-op mailings are broadly used by packaged good companies to distribute coupons, rebate offers, or even product samples.

List Selection

The first step in most direct marketing/direct mail campaigns is to locate or identify the list of customers/prospects that will be used. As we noted earlier, a list of current customers is not available for many packaged goods companies (a 1996 survey

---

[3]"Val-Pak Tops in Consumer Awareness," August 14, 1997 (http://www.valpak.com).

found that 41 percent of packaged goods companies were in the process of building databases and an additional 24 percent had plans to start[4]). Because many consumer products are sold through some sort of distribution channel (such as a wholesaler, distributor, or retail store), or because the product or service is used by such a large number of people, developing a specific list of customers may not be economically practical or, in some cases, even possible.

Customer lists, which generally include names, addresses, some demographics, purchase histories, and perhaps some psychographic information, are commonly called "house lists" or "internal lists" because they have been developed and are maintained by the marketer. Assuming that the list is updated regularly, this is the best possible list. Using a customer list such as this, some direct marketers have been able to develop specific customer profiles. These profiles identify common traits among consumers, allowing the development of models of future customers; they single out factors that allow the selection of the best prospects from the general marketplace.

If a customer list is not available, however, or if the marketer is seeking to expand trial or usage or to encourage a brand switch among a new group of prospects, then "outside lists" are commonly used. Outside lists are names and addresses of persons who have some trait in common. For example, the list might be composed of magazine subscribers, members of the local opera guild, dog owners, or purchasers of automobile hobby kits. Just over half of the general population responds to direct marketing offers or sales efforts. Many direct marketers are willing to use this common trait—direct responsiveness—as the criterion for selecting names from the general population. (Note that Standard Rate & Data Service publishes a directory of available lists. It gives a general indication of the list membership, cost, and so on.)

List Segmentation

The broadest category of segmentation and list purchase is based on geographics, geodemographics, or zip codes. As we discussed in Chapter 7, organizations using U.S. census data, such as Claritas, have developed demographic profiles of all neighborhoods in the United States. Income levels, basic demographics, value of home, purchasing power, and so on can be identified for various areas of the country from this type of segmentation analysis. By tying these data to zip codes, marketers can target specific areas of the country that contain the best prospects for their product or service. Segmented lists based on these geodemographics can be purchased for mailing by the marketing organizations, or the lists can be developed through solo or cooperative programs with the list supplier.

Today, several organizations have taken basic geodemographic data a step further. Through surveys, these list companies have identified users of specific product categories and even brands. Therefore, the marketer is now able to purchase lists of category users or users of competitive brands. These lists offer the marketer a much

---

[4]"Database Use on Rise: Carol Wright Promotion Survey," *DIRECT newsline*, May 14, 1996.

more refined list of prospects than do lists based on geographics or demographics alone.

The next category of list segmentation is based on some trait or attribute that households or individuals share. Lists of these types include the following:

1. *Compiled lists.* These lists contain names identified with some common characteristic or interest. They are developed by organizations that gather the names, maintain the list, and offer it for sale to marketers. An example is the R. L. Polk list of automobile registrations. Leaders in this type of list development and rental are Metromail, R. L. Polk, and Donnelley Marketing.

2. *Inquiries or customer lists.* These are lists of other organizations' customers, users, responders, and so on. These lists include persons such as magazine subscribers or catalog users who have signified interest in the organization or its products or services. There are literally thousands of such lists available to the brand communication planner.

If an outside list is to be used, the rental of the list is usually negotiated through a list broker. There are rules about the use of the rented list:[5]

> Lists can be ordered directly from a list owner, but most list rental orders are placed through list brokers. The broker handles all the details with the list owner: clearances, order placement, follow up for order completion, billing, collecting, and payment to the list owner, less the usual 20 percent commission that accrues to the list broker.
>
> The rental of lists involves certain conditions:
>
> 1. The names are rented for one time use *only.* No copy of the list is to be retained for any purpose whatsoever.
>
> 2. Usage must be cleared with the list owner in advance. The mailing piece which is approved is the only one that can be used.
>
> 3. The mail date approved by the list owner must be adhered to.
>
> 4. List rentals are charged on a per-thousand-name basis.
>
> 5. Net name arrangements vary, but most list owners will specify the percentage (of the names supplied) for which the full list rental charge per M must be paid plus a specific running cost for the names not used.
>
> 6. Most list owners charge extra for selections such as: sex, recency, ZIP, state, unit of sale, or any segmentation available on the particular list. Prices vary.

Most lists are rented on the basis of a cost-per-thousand (CPM) names for one-time use. Customer list costs range from approximately $60 to $120 per thousand, plus selections, label costs, and other charges. Compiled lists typically rent for less than customer lists.

---

[5]Bob Stone, *Successful Direct Marketing Methods*, 5th ed. (Lincolnwood, Ill.: NTC Publishing, 1994), p. 221.

In making list selections for mailings, brokers usually develop "data cards" on each available list. These cards give the prospective list renter information and details of the list, its cost, who is included on it, how it was developed, and so on.

In most cases, prior to using the entire list, direct marketing planners make use of some form of list test response—a mailing or solicitation of a segment or portion of the list to see the response rate that is achieved. Most of these list tests consist of mailings of 5,000–10,000 names, considered an adequate sample.

If the marketer has a customer list, in order to avoid duplication or resolicitation of existing customers, most direct marketing experts recommend the use of the merge-purge technique described earlier. The list renter then pays the outside list supplier only for those unduplicated names or a percentage of names previously agreed upon.

The Offer

If the list is 50 percent of the success of a direct mail program, the offer contributes another 25 percent to the program's value. The offer, after all, is what we're trying to sell to the prospect. Offer elements include the description of the product or service, the price being charged, the terms of sale, any premiums used as an incentive to purchase, and the timing of the deal.

The Copy

Copy is 10 percent of the success of a direct mail program. The chief concern here is how the offer is described, particularly in the letter. As in traditional advertising, the copy needs to focus on customer benefits. An advantage that direct mail offers is that the copywriter generally has as much space as is needed to explain the benefits in detail and develop a convincing call for action.

The Package

This element involves the physical look and feel of the direct mail material and accounts for another 15 percent of the success of a program. It includes the outside envelope, the letter, the response device, inserts, personalization, and even the type of postage chosen (bulk rate or stamped).

Exhibit 13-4 shows elements from a subscription renewal package for *VIBE* magazine. Note the "urgent" message on the outer envelope, and the large "final notice" heading on the letter. The order form includes "Yes" and "Maybe" stickers; using the "Maybe" sticker continues the subscription with an option to cancel later.

The Back-End Response Program

This element is concerned with conversion, retention, and generation of repeat sales. Two critical back-end elements are fulfillment and customer service, that is, delivering the product on time and in a reliable manner and then following up with service after the sale. Obviously, if problems occur, customers are likely to become unhappy and either not place an order in the first place, cancel their order, or order

Exhibit 13-4
VIBE Subscription Package

once but never again. A solid back-end program helps retain customers, increasing the return on the investment made to attract those customers.

Telemarketing

The use of toll-free telephone numbers (800-, 888-, etc.) and telemarketing is growing at a rapid rate. The following are some of the more common uses of telemarketing:

1. *Direct ordering.* Through the use of inbound toll-free telephone number programs, the customer usually can order products and services from major catalog houses and other direct marketing organizations twenty-four hours a day, seven days a week. With the growth and acceptance of nationwide credit cards and those of individual organizations, this system has become more attractive to customers.

2. *Additional information or customer service.* Through the use of a toll-free telephone number, questions about the product, repair services, product add-ons, and so forth can be handled easily and quickly by a manufacturer.

3. *Lead qualification.* Often, telemarketing is used to qualify leads for the sales force on either an inbound (customer calls marketer) or outbound (marketer calls customer) basis.

4. *Outbound telemarketing.* In some instances, particularly business-to-business areas, telemarketing is used as a sales call on customers who cannot be visited regularly by the sales force, or as a way to take orders for products that are repurchased regularly. In these situations, the calls are generated by the telemarketer on a regular basis to a list of prospects or customers.

Over the past several years, IBM has slowly shifted some of its sales effort to direct marketing, achieving direct marketing-based sales of $13 billion in 1997. Most of the direct marketing effort is telemarketing targeted at small- and medium-sized companies worldwide, where personal sales calls would be very costly and inefficient. Customers can order hardware and software over the telephone, either in response to a catalog or other direct mail offer, or as the result of an outbound call from an IBM telesales representative. Telemarketing lets IBM quickly and economically serve a much wider customer base than before.

No matter how telemarketing is used, though, there are certain costs associated with any program. The chief cost is that of personnel and training. Telemarketing is very labor intensive, and turnover among telemarketing representatives is high. In addition, there is the cost of telephone equipment and service and office facilities.

Telemarketing offers some compelling advantages. The telephone is a very personal and interactive medium, and a trained operator can persuasively address consumer questions and concerns. The give-and-take between the seller and prospective buyer is an example of the flexibility of telemarketing. The sales script can be written to encourage maximum communications effectiveness. Once the original order has been taken, the operator can encourage the buyer to purchase other items or receive additional information. Finally, with telemarketing, the marketer gets immediate feedback on the attractiveness of the offer.

There are also some strong drawbacks to telemarketing, however. It is very expensive—even more expensive than direct mail. Also, there is no permanence to the telephone conversation, so prospects can easily disregard the information presented to them. Further, the lack of visual capability can make telemarketing inappropriate for many products and services. Most critically, many consumers view telemarketing, particularly outbound telemarketing, as a major nuisance and a serious intrusion on their privacy.

The preceding discussion is by no means comprehensive, but it helps guide our thinking on the use of direct marketing techniques as part of a brand communication program. In summary, "The 30 Timeless Direct Marketing Principles" developed by Bob Stone, one of the leaders in making direct marketing what it is today, are shown in Exhibit 13-5.

Distributing the Direct Marketing Offer

Beyond creative considerations, key ingredients in the selection of distribution methods of direct marketing support programs include the following:

1. *Cost per thousand* (CPM). The cost of distributing direct marketing offers usually is based on the cost of distributing 1,000 copies, or the CPM rate. The CPM may range from a few dollars in the mass media to hundreds of dollars for direct mail sent to very specific target markets, such as physicians and chief executive officers.

2. *Response rate*. Response rates usually are calculated as a percentage of the number of replies received based on the total number distributed. Some forms of direct marketing media traditionally generate greater response rates than do others. As a rule of thumb, the more targeted the mailing list, the greater the response. Thus, some business-to-business direct marketing programs generate a 40 percent response or more. Generally, mass media direct mail or marketing offers made through newspapers and magazines and even freestanding inserts (FSIs) have response rates in the 3–6 percent range.

3. *Cost per order* (CPO). Although knowing the cost per thousand to distribute the direct marketing offer is helpful, and estimating the response rate is a closer measure of the value of the media, the calculation that is most important to direct marketers is that of CPO. This calculation takes the total cost of the direct marketing or mail program and divides it by the number of responses received from that media distribution system. For example, a direct mail–delivered package might have a CPO of $6.50, while a newspaper-delivered offer might have a CPO of $15.00. In this case, even though the newspaper might have a lower CPM and a higher response rate than direct mail, it is the actual CPO or cost per lead or cost per redemption, rather than the gross cost of media or the response rate, that is important to the planner in a direct marketing program.

Exhibit 13-5

Bob Stone's 30 Timeless Direct Marketing Principles

Direct marketing is in the forefront of new technology, but the knowledge base that is the heritage of direct marketers has not diminished in value. Following are 30 principles that have stood the test of time:

1. All customers are not created equal. Give or take a few percentage points, 80 percent of repeat business for goods and services will come from 20 percent of your customer base.

2. The most important order you ever get from a customer is the second order. Why? Because a two-time buyer is at least twice as likely to buy again as a one-time buyer.

3. Maximizing direct mail success depends first on the lists you use, second on the offers you make, and third on the copy and graphics you create.

4. If, on a given list, "hotline" names don't work, the other list categories offer little opportunity for success.

5. Merge/purge names—those that appear on two or more lists—will outpull any single list from which these names have been extracted.

6. Direct response lists will almost always outpull compiled lists.

7. Overlays on lists (enhancements), such as lifestyle characteristics, income, education, age, marital status, and propensity to respond by mail or phone, will always improve response.

8. A follow-up to the same list within 30 days will pull 40–50 percent of the first mailing.

9. "Yes/No" offers consistently produce more orders than offers that don't request "No" responses.

10. The "take rate" for negative option offers will always outpull positive option offers at least two to one.

11. Credit card privileges will outperform cash with order at least two to one.

12. Credit card privileges will increase the size of the average catalog order by 20 percent or more.

13. Time limit offers, particularly those that give a specific date, outpull offers with no time limit practically every time.

14. Free-gift offers, particularly where the gift appeals to self-interest, outpull discount offers consistently.

15. Sweepstakes, particularly in conjunction with impulse purchases, will increase the order volume 35 percent or more.

16. You will collect far more money in a fund-raising effort if you ask for a specific amount from a contributor. Likewise, you will collect more money if the appeal is tied to a specific project.

Exhibit 13-5
Bob Stone's 30 Timeless Direct Marketing Principles (continued)

17. People buy benefits, not features.

18. The longer you can keep someone reading your copy, the better your chances of success.

19. The timing and frequency of renewal letters is vital. But I can report nothing but failure over a period of 40 years in attempts to hype renewals with "improved copy." I've concluded that the product—the magazine, for example—is the factor in making a renewal decision.

20. Self-mailers are cheaper to produce, but they practically never outpull envelope-enclosed letter mailings.

21. A preprint of a forthcoming ad, accompanied by a letter and response form, will outpull a postprint mailing package by 50 percent or more.

22. It is easier to increase the average dollar amount of an order than it is to increase percentage of response.

23. You will get far more new catalog customers if you put your proven winners in the front pages of your catalog.

24. Assuming items of similar appeal, you will always get a higher response rate from a 32-page catalog than from a 24-page catalog.

25. A new catalog to a catalog customer base will outpull cold lists by 400 percent to 800 percent.

26. A print ad with a bind-in card will outpull the same ad without a bind-in up to 600 percent.

27. A direct response, direct sale TV commercial of 120 seconds will outpull a 60-second direct response commercial better than two to one.

28. A TV support commercial will increase response from a newspaper insert up to 50 percent.

29. The closure rate from qualified leads can be from two to four times as effective as cold calls.

30. Telephone-generated leads are likely to close four to six times greater than mail-generated leads.

Source: Bob Stone, *Successful Direct Marketing Methods,* 6th ed. (Lincolnwood, Ill.: NTC Business Books, 1997), pp. 7–9.

Interactive Media and Marketing

Difficult though it may be to believe, at the time the previous edition of this book was written, almost no one had heard of the World Wide Web. E-mail was beginning to catch on, and Netscape was just a dream in the minds of its creators. Today, the interactive realm is getting attention from brand marketers across a spectrum of products and services. The growth of this new communication form has been phenomenal. *MediaWeek* notes that "radio took 38 years, TV 13 years, and cable 10 years, to reach the elusive 50-million-households mark. But in the one-equals-seven, dog-years world of the Web, the Internet is on pace to reach that same coveted position a scant eight years after its birth in 1994 as a consumer medium."[6]

As might be expected for a new medium, figures on numbers of users and revenue vary widely depending on the source. Jupiter Communications estimated online advertising spending at $301 million in 1996, and projects it will grow to $7.7 billion in 2002. Many Web sites are direct marketing vehicles, allowing for online information requests and product purchasing. Direct marketing revenue from online sources was $13 million in 1996, and should grow to $1.3 billion by 2002.[7]

Another industry analyst group, Forrester Research, put 1997 online advertising spending at $550 million, making online spending .3 percent of all U.S. advertising spending. The biggest spenders currently are computer companies, consumer products firms, telecommunications companies, financial services providers, and new media companies. Most online spending is split among banner ads, electronic billboards that encourage users to click on the ad in order to be connected to the advertiser's own site, and sponsorships of individual sites.[8]

Companies from a wide range of both consumer and business-to-business product categories are developing Web sites to provide product information, build brand name awareness, enhance both brand and company image, and, in many cases, to sell products and services. While the number of online households still is small, Jupiter Communications believes that almost 55 percent of U.S. households and 32 percent of European households will be online by 2002.[9] Online households tend to be better educated and higher income than the national average. And, while early users were predominately male, women now make up 42 percent of online users.[10] That's an important statistic for advertisers, since women are the primary target for many products and services.

Web Measurement

One of the biggest hurdles to continued growth of the Web as an advertising medium is the problem of measuring audiences. As we noted at the outset of this chapter, the

[6]Evan Neufeld, "Where Are Audiences Going? The Internet as a Mass Medium," *MediaWeek*, May 5, 1997, p. 2.

[7]Doug Henschen, "Report Sees Online Ad/DM Convergence," *DM News*, August 25, 1997, p. 18.

[8]"Whither Ad Revenues? Underlying Problems with the Online Ad Model," *Min's New Media Report*, July 20, 1998.

[9]"Consumer Internet Economy," July 31, 1998 (http://www.jup.com).

[10]George Hunter, "Advertisers Flock to Net: Ad Agencies Increase Cyberspending by 271% in Just a Year," *The Detroit News*, July 24, 1998, p. B1.

Web differs from traditional direct marketing in that we don't know who will see our message until he or she logs into our Web site. Remember that the bulk of direct marketing programs use either direct mail or telemarketing, starting with a list of either current customers or likely prospects about whom something is known. In Web marketing, we can learn about the people who visit our site, but only after they've made their first visit.

A number of research firms are working to develop measurement programs for the Web that will record not only the number of visitors to a site, but also information about who those people are. Among the firms currently providing data on Web use are PC Data, Inc., A. C. Nielsen, Media Metrix, NetRatings, Inc., and RelevantKnowledge, Inc.[11] Most of these companies recruit panels of Web users who are questioned periodically about their behavior (recall our discussion of panel research in Chapter 5). Valid usage data are essential so that advertisers can make cost-per-thousand and demographic composition comparisons between the Web and traditional media.

Other companies provide software that individual site owners can use to learn who and how many are accessing their site. Major players in this area include I/Pro and Andromedia. I/Pro also offers independent auditing of Web site traffic counts, as do the Audit Bureau of Circulation and BPA International. Auditing gives a prospective advertiser third-party verification. In other words, the prospective advertiser doesn't have to simply take the site owner's word for how much traffic the Web site attracts.[12]

Banner Advertising Basics

DoubleClick, one of the leaders in the growth of effective online advertising, tells its clients that the four most important factors for online advertising success are the creative execution of the ad, careful placement to maximize appropriate targeting, determining the optimal frequency for banner exposure (DoubleClick's research shows that banners burn out after the fourth exposure), and choosing the right surrounding editorial content for the ad.[13]

Where banner appearance and placement are concerned, DoubleClick advises clients to ask a question in the banner to encourage interaction, to use bright colors (especially blue, green, and yellow), to negotiate placement on the first page of a site or at the top of succeeding pages, to use animation, and to include a call to action.[14] (Search engines attract the majority of Web traffic, making them very appealing locations for advertising.) "Click Here" buttons are a frequently-used call to action. Some banner messages change every few seconds, providing more information about online offerings.

[11]Pete Barlas, "Rivals Vie to Be 'Nielsen of the Net,'" *Investor's Business Daily*, July 9, 1998, p. A9.

[12]Marla Matzer, "Advertising & Marketing: New Study Casts Doubt on Web Advertising Data," *Los Angeles Times*, July 30, 1998, p. D6.

[13]DoubleClick, "Research Findings: Effectiveness Influencers" (http://www.doubleclick.net/learning_center/research_findings/influencers.htm).

[14]DoubleClick, "Research Findings: Banner Effectiveness Tips" (http://www.doubleclick.net/learning_center/research_findings/effectiveness.htm).

Web Site Content

If you've spent any time on the Web, you know that site content varies widely. Here's a brief example of one site that illustrates the Web's ability to aid in both brand building through message delivery and business building through incentive offers.

Ragú might seem like an unlikely prospect for cyberspace innovation. But the Ragú Web site (at http://www.eat.com) is an excellent example of how to use the Web to enhance brand image. Ragú's site is "Mama's Cucina," an Italian grandmother's warm, welcoming home. Exhibit 13-6 shows the opening page for the site, featuring Mama herself. As you can tell from the headings, the site includes recipes (all using various Ragú products, of course), product and coupon offers ("Goodies"), and a sweepstakes. But there's much more. If you move into Mama's dining room (Exhibit 13-7), you can get travel information on Italy ("Mama's favorite places") and even learn to speak Italian (a great collection of phrases, most of which have something to do with eating Ragú products).

Other parts of the Ragú site allow you to request e-mail notification of changes to the site, biweekly e-mail with new recipes, and coupons for Ragú products. You also can complete a questionnaire with your comments on the site. The content of the site lets Ragú provide a wealth of information to visitors. Much of the brand sell is tongue-in-cheek; there's no sense of hard sell here. And, the Italian-ness of the site (admittedly, an American stereotype of what's Italian) likely helps to improve visitors' perceptions of the authentic taste of Ragú products. Most of "Mama's Cucina"

Exhibit 13-6
"Mama's Cucina" Home Page

Exhibit 13-7
"Mama's Dining Room"

is designed to build the brand, with a few business-building incentives thrown in to keep visitor interest.

Customizing Web Site Content

Several firms are offering companies the opportunity to customize their Web site content for specific groups of users. The application of this technology makes it possible for one Web site to serve multiple purposes very effectively. While both Microsoft and Netscape provide tools that work with their Web servers to be used to construct such a customized site, Eprise Corporation offers its customers an "out-of-the-box" product to build a customized Web site quickly and easily.

Exhibit 13-8 shows two Web screens illustrating the customization concept. The top screen is the standard page any visitor to the Web site would see. It contains basic information about each of the host company's partner organizations. The bottom screen is the page a Hewlett-Packard prospect would see. It goes into more detail on the host company's relationship with Hewlett-Packard, and does not include information on the host's other partners.

In the Eprise system, access to specific content is controlled by the host organization. Visitors to the Web site are asked to register; the registration information identifies their relationship to the host company—employee, channel member/

Exhibit 13-8
Eprise Web Pages

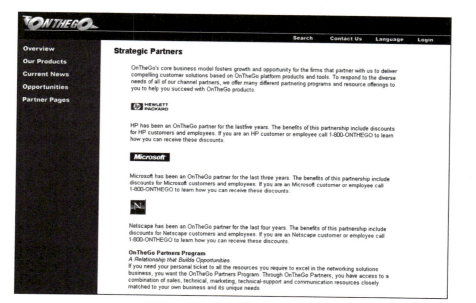

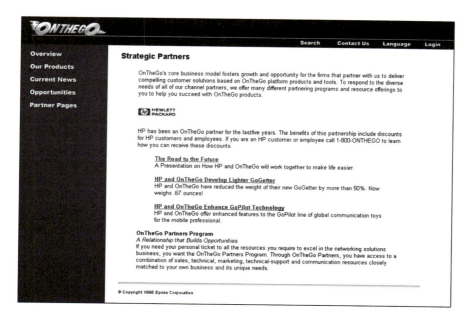

trading partner, end user, and so on. They then receive the Web site content appropriate to that relationship. (The incentive to register is the access to useful, targeted information not available to unregistered visitors.) For example, a channel member might have access to detailed price lists that an end user wouldn't see. One of Eprise's clients, American Express, uses the system to better organize the flow of information available to employees in its worldwide travel offices. Eprise's package allows access to the American Express site in a variety of languages, but also goes beyond that translation of content. For example, a travel office manager has access to more information on the Web site (corporate financial data, for example) than does one of that manager's employees.

This customization approach to the Web fits with how most marketers conduct their other communication operations: they identify target audiences and focus their communication on the needs of those audiences. Web site customization eliminates a lot of the communication "noise" that is found in one-size-fits-all sites—the nonrelevant information that people see and have to process (or ignore) to get to the information that is relevant to them.

Under current applications, such customization of content helps manufacturers improve their relationships with a variety of publics, particularly channel members. As more and more companies adopt this approach to Web site design, it's likely that current customers might see different content than highly qualified prospective customers, who might see different content than prospects who are just browsing. The degree of targeting made possible by such systems holds intriguing possibilities for IBC planners.

Privacy

One major concern for both traditional direct marketers and those making use of the World Wide Web to market products is the very hot topic of consumer privacy. The United States differs from most other countries in that there is very little existing legislation limiting either the collection or sale of consumer information. Privacy concerns among consumers and the government have escalated as more and more companies turn to direct marketing as a way to increase both the efficiency and effectiveness of their communications efforts, and as more households go online. Some 8,500 bills related to privacy issues were introduced in state legislatures across the country in 1997.[15] That number may be a response to the fact that 600 million credit reports on individual consumers were sold in 1997, developed by companies such as Experian Inc., Equifax Inc., and Trans Union Corporation. A credit report includes name, age, social security number, address and address changes, and credit and payment history[16]—very useful information for a direct marketer, but not necessarily something a consumer wants spread around. Also, there has been much publicity about some Web sites' use of "cookies" (electronic tracking markers) to track user movement through the Web, recording which sites are visited.

[15]Robert O'Harrow, Jr., "Data Firms Getting Too Personal?" *Washington Post*, March 8, 1998, pp. A1, A18.

[16]Ibid.

The Direct Marketing Association has long had some consumer protection devices in place, including a Mail Preference Service that allows consumers to request removal from mailing lists and a Telephone Preference Service that offers the same option for telemarketing. But neither service is foolproof, and compliance has been voluntary for DMA members. In response to the recent spate of state bills and increasing discussion at the federal level, the DMA is currently involved in a program to make compliance mandatory for all of its members and to develop additional programs to protect consumer privacy. For example, DMA members who market online are now required to get permission from a parent before collecting information from children under age thirteen. In addition, the DMA is developing an e-mail version of its preference services, which would let consumers opt out of receiving unsolicited e-mail.[17]

The DMA provides members with a "Fair Information Practices Checklist" that can be used to evaluate an organization's performance on data privacy issues.[18] An outline of the checklist is shown in Exhibit 13-9.

A quick review of the checklist shows that most concerns are related to how customer data are collected and how those data are maintained and used. The DMA stresses that customer data should not be gathered without the customer's approval and knowledge, and that customers must be told that the data will be used for future decision making as well as the particular purpose for which they are being collected. Data accuracy is another critical point; there are plenty of horror stories of consumers who were denied credit or had belongings repossessed because of a data mix-up that saddled them with someone else's credit history.

As we noted in our discussion of direct mail, list rental is a big business. The DMA encourages its members to give consumers included on their house lists the chance to request that their name and other information not be rented to outside companies. Further, DMA members are urged to monitor how their lists are used, as well as to institute security measures to limit internal access to customer data.

As is the case for traditional advertising, the direct marketing industry would greatly prefer self-regulation to government-mandated restrictions. The simplest message is this: treat consumers, and their personal information, as you would like to be treated yourself. Consumers are likely willing to accept some loss of privacy in exchange for more information and better service, but marketers must be sensitive to how they use the information collected.

---

[17]James Crowe, "Privacy's Hot, Hot Summer," *DMA News*, July 29, 1998.

[18]"Fair Information Practices Manual" (New York: Direct Marketing Association, 1994).

Exhibit 13-9
Fair Information Practices Checklist

Section I: Data Collection
    I-A   Data Should Be Collected by Fair and Lawful Means

    I-B   Only Data Appropriate and Necessary for Direct Marketing Should Be Collected

Section II: Data Use
    II-A   Consumer Data Should Be Used by Direct Marketers Only for Direct Marketing Purposes

    II-B   Data Should Be Accurate and Complete

Section III: List Rental Practices
    III-A   A Company Should Provide Notice of Its List Rental, Sale, and Exchange Practices and of the Opportunity for the Consumer to Opt Out (For Companies That Exchange Data Only)

    III-B   Name-Removal Procedures (For Companies That Do Not Rent, Sell, or Exchange Marketing Data)

    III-C   The Company Should Subscribe to the Direct Marketing Association's Mail and Telephone Preference Services

    III-D   List Owners, Brokers, and Compilers Should Not Permit the Sale or Rental of Their Lists for Any Promotion or Use That Is in Violation of Any of the DMA Ethical Guidelines

Section IV: Data Protection and Security
    IV-A   The Company Should Employ Security Measures to Protect Its Consumer Data

Source: "Fair Information Practices Manual" (New York: Direct Marketing Association, 1994).

Summary

Direct marketing, whether through traditional means such as direct mail and telemarketing or through newer interactive channels, offers the IBC planner a way to communicate with very specific customers and customer groups. Direct marketing efforts usually are intended to spark a behavioral response and are easily measurable—two critical aspects of the overall IBC process. As a result, direct marketing is likely to play an increasingly important role in IBC plans.

Campaign Evaluation: Issues in
Campaign Management

14

Using Media to Deliver Brand Messages and Incentives

Selecting and Implementing Brand Communication Tactics

The third step in the IBC planning process is to identify, select, and develop the various functional communication elements that will be used to implement our brand communication program in the marketplace. As shown in the IBC process chart in Exhibit 14-1, this involves the selection of various types of advertising, sales promotion, direct marketing, events, public relations, and other programs that might be used—the elements we reviewed in the previous chapters. At this point, we need the skills and capabilities of true functional specialists. For example, if we decide a general media advertising program is called for, we will need that specialist's functional skills in developing and delivering effective advertising programs, and likewise for public relations, direct marketing, and so on.

As shown, the selection of the various tactical activities to support the IBC and behavioral marketing objectives really frees the planner to select the best mix of activities and elements to achieve the goals that have been set. Rather than being confined to developing an advertising program when some types of sales promotion elements are needed, the IBC planner is free to develop the type of program that will influence the income flow from the customers or prospects for which the plan is being developed. Thus, we move from functional elements in the IBC process to a new approach that we call relevance and receptivity, illustrated as Exhibit 14-2.

Exhibit 14-1
IBC Planning Process, Steps 3-5

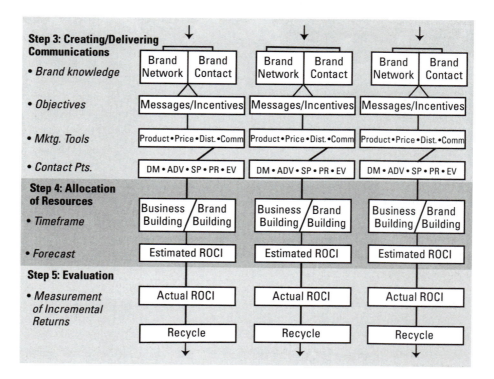

Step 3: Creating/Delivering Communications
- *Brand knowledge*
- *Objectives*
- *Mktg. Tools*
- *Contact Pts.*

Step 4: Allocation of Resources
- *Timeframe*
- *Forecast*

Step 5: Evaluation
- *Measurement of Incremental Returns*

This approach follows the IBC process described previously. We start with how customers or prospects might be exposed to our IBC program or how they might encounter various forms of communication activities. We look at how customers and prospects might come in contact with our brand, in any form. We don't want to go looking for customers and prospects or try to drive them to the place we want to deliver our messages or incentives. Instead, we want our brand communication programs to be where our customers and prospects are.

Our first decision point, then, is to determine the most relevant message or incentive we could deliver on behalf of the brand. Knowing and understanding customers and prospects is key to this endeavor. The relevance of our message, of course, is related to the goals of our brand communication program. We also must try to find the time and place at which our message or incentive might be most relevant to the customer's decision about our product or service. The most relevant time is

Exhibit 14-2
The Integrated Message Delivery System

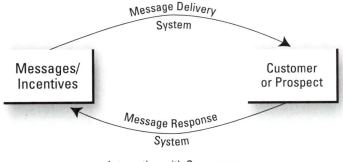

Interacting with Consumers

likely when the customer or prospect is either in need of our message or incentive, or when he or she would like to access it.

As shown in Exhibit 14-2, we approach this decision from the point of view of the customer or prospect. We try to determine when he or she would like to hear from us—not when we would like to make the contact. In addition, we try to determine when customers or prospects might be most receptive, that is, when they would like to receive or gain the information concerning the brand. Ideally, we want them to be listening—not simply hearing us talk. Thus, it is relevance and receptivity that will guide our message development and delivery systems. This brings a whole new view of when and how brand communication programs should be delivered.

Media planning and buying are critical in delivering relevant messages at times of maximum receptivity. Indeed, media issues come into play for most of the forms of marketing communication we've reviewed: advertising, public relations, sales promotion, and direct and interactive marketing. While we will give some attention to the fundamentals of media planning (gross rating points, cost per thousand, reach, frequency, and the like), our primary focus is more qualitative in nature, in keeping with relevance and receptivity concerns.

We believe that in many advertising agencies today media planning is all too often hampered by the planners' inability to see the forest for the trees. Because of day-to-day job demands, it's easy to get caught up in the terminology and statistics of media planning to the point where the relationship the media build with the consumer gets lost. The IBC planner, however, seeks to use media planning to build a solid relationship with consumers and prospects.

Efficiency Versus Effectiveness: The Continuing Debate

Efficiency

Traditionally, much of advertising agency media planning and buying has been driven by an emphasis on efficiency. Efficiency means buying media that deliver the greatest number of people for the least amount of money, that is, trying to keep cost per thousand (CPMs) as low as possible. The people in the audience may or may not all be part of the target, depending on the medium and the type of analysis used. All of the various cost-ranking programs offered by media research providers, such as SMRB, MRI, and others, are set up to deliver efficiency goals, as are the computer-based optimizer programs currently gaining popularity among U.S. agencies. Vehicles within a medium compare themselves to one another based on audience size and CPM. New magazine titles and new cable television networks have to reach minimum audience levels even to be measured by the syndicated research services. Numbers are the name of the game.

An efficiency focus does have its merits. In this age of tight (and shrinking) budgets, no agency wants to be accused of wasting its clients' money. With many media buying assignments moving either in-house or to specialized media buying firms (some of them spun off from full-service advertising agencies), everyone involved in the industry—client, agency, and medium—has a strong sense of cost and a desire to keep that cost reasonable. Nonetheless, an emphasis on efficiency to the exclusion of other considerations is dangerously shortsighted because it all but ignores the issues of relevance and receptivity.

Effectiveness

In effectiveness-driven media planning, the emphasis is on results rather than relative cost levels. True effectiveness planning starts by examining how the consumer interacts with the various media under consideration. Which media and media vehicles do the consumers use regularly? Which do they trust? Which do they turn to for information or entertainment? Obviously, these are questions that address receptivity levels.

An effectiveness approach makes intuitive sense, but we don't want to understate how difficult it is to put into practice. Many highly effective media, such as direct mail and targeted magazines to name only two examples, are quite expensive, particularly on a cost-per-thousand basis. Including these media in a recommendation requires the planner to throw conventional wisdom to the winds and step away from the various computerized media planning programs that have found a place in the industry, since those programs emphasize efficiency almost exclusively. Further, in some cases choosing the effectiveness approach means planning without the research "net" that most media departments have come to rely on. Since most audience measurement services were developed to look at numbers and aggregate measures of behavior, a focus on individual interactions with media pushes the planner instead toward qualitative data, or even "gut" reactions.

We believe that the ongoing changes in media offerings, particularly the continuing move toward media vehicle specialization and the industry's emphasis on integration, will lead to the development of new audience research methods. But in the short run, media departments are faced with a choice between business as usual (that is, efficiency) and taking a chance on a different means of evaluation (effectiveness). This is particularly true in those advertising agencies in which the media department is asked to lead the way in developing forays into other forms of marketing communication.

Importance of Venue

As we already noted, effectiveness looks at where the consumer comes into contact with the medium. A current media trend is the growth of "place-based" media, or media offerings developed to capitalize on knowledge of consumer behavior and relevance issues. One basic consideration is whether the message is delivered inside or outside the consumer's home. Traditionally, television, magazines, newspapers, and direct mail have been considered in-home media, while radio, outdoor, and transit deliver their messages outside the home. There are, of course, exceptions to these generalizations. For example, the Internet doesn't fit neatly into either of these categories since it can be accessed anywhere that a computer and a dataport are available.

Several companies have taken the idea of venue a step further by first identifying a location at which consumers might be considered to be "captive" audiences and then developing media vehicles to take advantage of that location. Turner Broadcasting's Turner Private Networks division is having success with CNN Airport Network, capitalizing on reaching the traveling public, particularly business travelers. Likewise, Primedia's Channel One offers advertisers a way to reach junior high and high school students in the classroom. Because both companies' efforts reflect an understanding of relevance and receptivity, we'll discuss each in some detail.

CNN Airport Network

CNN Airport Network is currently in thirty-one U.S. airports, including most of the largest hubs. At large airports, CNN pays for the installation of the necessary audio/video equipment and negotiates advertising revenue rate-sharing with the airport. Smaller airports that want to provide the service must pay for the equipment themselves and sell local advertising time to help make up the costs. (For a small airport, the equipment installation cost may be as high as $50,000.) CNN helps the airport get equipment at a good price, however, and provides training on ad sales and insertion.[1]

CNN Airport Network screens are located at departure gates primarily. The captive audience? Those travelers waiting for outgoing flights. A recent survey of advertisers targeting business audiences ranked airport advertising third most

---

[1]"Some Smaller Airports Invest in CNN Airport Network: What's in It for Them?" *World Airport Week*, February 24, 1998, p. 125.

desirable in terms of quality, impact, and audience value. (Weekly and daily business publications ranked first and second, respectively, and airport advertising was followed by various inflight media.)[2]

CNN Airport works for all involved: travelers get information/entertainment programming to watch while waiting for their flight; CNN gets a very appealing, upscale audience to market to national advertisers, as well as more visibility for the CNN name in general; and airports get a new source of revenue (from local advertising sales) while providing their customers with a service.

In some markets, media firms are going beyond CNN Airport to take full advantage of the variety of media now available linked to the airport venue. For example, Washington, D.C.-based Magazine Group is offering advertisers a $35,000 package that includes both print and electronic media advertising. The package: a full-page, four-color ad in each issue of *Washington Flyer Magazine* (a bimonthly specialty publication available at both Reagan National and Dulles Airports); four ads daily on CNN Airport Network at National and Dulles; and eight ads daily on National's Arrival TV, a closed-circuit system located at baggage carousels.[3] Any advertiser buying the package is guaranteed exposure to the business traveler audience.

Primedia's Channel One

For many marketers, students are an important target group. Channel One was developed to reach students at the junior high (middle school) and high school levels. Participating schools are given TV sets and VCRs for every classroom; the schools agree to have Channel One's daily news broadcast (with advertising) on in 80 percent of their classrooms on 90 percent of school days. The program is a twelve-minute newscast; national advertisers pay $200,000 for a thirty-second commercial. Channel One's current audience is about 8 million students.[4]

Bringing commercials into the classroom has generated a great deal of controversy, and Channel One has many critics. (A recent study estimated that Channel One costs $1.8 billion a year in classroom time.) But Channel One claims that 99 percent of its subscribers renew each year, and the programming has won a Peabody Award for excellence.[5] For an advertiser who wants to reach a teenaged audience, Channel One offers a unique opportunity to do so.

What place-based media such as CNN Airport Network and Primedia's Channel One have in common is delivery of a specific group of consumers under specific circumstances. In Channel One's early years, those advertisers who customized their messages for the teenaged audience saw the greatest response from that audience. With place-based media, the consumer, the exposure situation, and the message all come together with a resulting synergy that increases effectiveness. We'll come back to that synergy later in this chapter.

---

[2]"One-on-One with Sky Sites CEO," *World Airline News*, October 14, 1997.

[3]"National Airport Launches Hi-Tech Advertising," *World Airport Week*, September 2, 1997.

[4]"TV News in Schools Costs $1.8 Billion in Class Time, Study Says," *New York Times*, April 1, 1998, p. B11.

[5]Ibid.

Which Comes First—Media or Creativity?

In traditional advertising planning, creative considerations frequently drive media planning. For example, there's often a bias toward television advertising because of its aura of glamour, an aura that tempts many clients and agencies. However, in an effectiveness-based planning approach, or in relevance- and receptivity-based planning, the media must be the driving factor. Where can we come into contact with the consumer we're trying to influence? More specifically, where are the optimal contact points in relation to buying behavior? Knowing which media the consumer uses and how those media fit into the consumer's lifestyle should make the creative process simpler by giving us more insights to use in developing executions.

Relevance and Receptivity in Media Planning

The changes that have beset the advertising industry in recent years probably have been felt most sharply in media departments.[6] The staff of the media department is expected to make sense of the television audience data explosion that came with people meters, to sort through the ever increasing media options available to decide which to recommend to clients, and to guide agency thinking in marketing communication areas outside of advertising. When we consider that these new expectations are added to the daily demands of developing, updating, and checking client plans, it's not surprising that most agency media departments find themselves operating somewhere behind the learning curve when it comes to understanding marketplace changes.

That's not to say that agencies aren't trying to make sense of the current status of media. A number of agencies, among them Leo Burnett, Saatchi & Saatchi, and DDB Needham Worldwide, devote considerable energy to media research activities. In this section, we'll look at some key concepts emerging from DDB Needham's efforts to better understand how consumers interact with media.

The Personal Media Network

DDB Needham defines Personal Media Network (the name is copyrighted), or PMN, as "the combination of media vehicles which a customer individually selects to satisfy his or her individual needs."[7] Notice the emphasis on the individual, which immediately moves us away from the traditional focus on aggregate numbers and behaviors. Here's some more of the thinking behind this concept:

> *Consumers make media choices based on their needs, their interests, and their moods at each moment. Because these constantly change, the consumer*

---

[6]Much of the material in this section comes from the Media Department of DDB Needham Worldwide, Chicago, where Dr. Barnes worked as a faculty media intern during the summers of 1991 and 1992. The authors thank the Media Department, particularly Mike White, Beth Uyenco, and Helen Katz, for their assistance and insights.

[7]*1995/6 Media By the Numbers* (Chicago: DDB Needham Worldwide, 1993), p. 3.

is led to specific vehicles (not broad media), and these vehicles cross from one medium to another, sometimes in rapid succession. . . . The challenge for the advertiser is to map that pattern for key prospects.[8]

In developing PMN for a specific target audience, DDB Needham looks at media use as it relates to daily activities. For example, what type(s) of media does a consumer use before breakfast, on the way home from work in the afternoon, and in the evening before going to bed? Tying media use to a person's daily routine allows for insights on other activities he or she might be involved in while using the medium, other thoughts he or she might be having, and his or her mood. In other words, PMN allows the planner to think about the target's relationship with the medium. To help in that analysis, the PMN system also looks at whether the consumer is using the medium primarily for information, for entertainment, or, in the case of television and radio, as a background to other activities.

Table 14-1 shows a PMN grid for the target group of women aged twenty-five to fifty-four. This particular PMN analysis is for weekdays (as weekend media use can be very different from weekday use, the two are analyzed separately) and is expressed in percentages. So, 32 percent of women aged twenty-five to fifty-four reported watching television "Shortly after waking up/before breakfast." Twenty-two percent of the women watched television for information during this period, 6 percent watched for entertainment, and 3 percent used the television as background. (The percentages add to 31 percent rather than 32 percent because of rounding.) Interestingly, and perhaps surprisingly, the grid shows that in this age group, newspaper and magazine usage is highest in the evening after dinner.

Personal Media Network information is based on DDB Needham's proprietary research. Reported media usage levels are consistent with those found by syndicated services, which underscores the validity of the PMN approach. As the agency notes,

> *Where differences [between PMN and other sources] exist, they are linked to PMN's use of activity-based measurement periods rather than traditional clock-time periods. These differences help to underscore the uniqueness of the PMN approach in its ability to paint a clearer picture of how the various media fit into consumers' lifestyles. For while the PMN system matches media use to the consumer, the syndicated audience measurement services attempt to fit the consumer to the media.[9]*

While the data used to develop PMN profiles are proprietary, any planner should be able to adapt the principles behind PMN in developing media recommendations. We must think about the consumer's use of media throughout the day and then decide which potential contact points are optimal for our product's message, a concept we'll revisit in our discussion of media objectives.

---

[8]*PMN: Personal Media Network* (Chicago: DDB Needham Worldwide, 1993), pp. 2–3.

[9]*A Comparison of PMN with Other Sources of Audience Data* (Chicago: DDB Needham Worldwide, July 1991) pp. 10–11.

Table 14-1

PMN Grid

Women, 25-54

Weekdays	Watched Television				Listened to Radio				Read Newspaper			Read Magazines		
Total in target: 1899	Any	Info.	Entr.	Bkgd.	Any	Info.	Entr.	Bkgd.	Any	Info.	Entr.	Any	Info.	Entr.
Shortly after waking up/before breakfast	32	22	6	3	43	22	13	8	21	20	2	5	2	2
During breakfast	22	13	6	3	25	10	10	5	19	18	2	3	2	0.9
Mid to late morning	18	2	13	3	42	6	22	13	12	11	0.9	6	3	3
During lunch	21	7	12	2	26	4	14	8	8	6	2	7	3	4
Early to mid afternoon	20	1	18	1	35	3	19	14	5	4	0.6	7	3	4
Late afternoon/before dinner	43	15	24	4	33	7	18	9	18	17	2	7	4	4
During dinner	39	14	20	5	11	2	5	4	4	4	0.9	2	1	1
After dinner/ mid to late evening	73	6	64	3	14	2	9	4	22	19	3	17	8	9
In bed/ just before going to sleep	44	11	29	3	14	2	6	6	4	3	0.9	17	5	12

Source: DDB Needham Worldwide, Inc.

Core Audience Concept

Looking at the relationship consumers develop with media types and media vehicles suggests differences in the intensity of those relationships. The "core audience" concept examines the existence of loyal vehicle users and the realization that "the people that make up these loyal audiences bring more than just a superficial interest in subject matter to the medium."[10]

For a weekly television program, the core audience would be defined as viewers who watched at least three of the previous four episodes of the program. Similar definitions can be developed for audiences of daily television programs, radio stations, and magazines. Through their more consistent exposure to the media vehicle, core audience members have more involvement in the vehicle's editorial content and interact differently with advertising in the vehicle than do noncore audience members. Research suggests that, especially in magazines, the core group is more likely to see advertising in the vehicle, to spend more time with the vehicle, to recall vehicle advertising, and to use ideas obtained from the vehicle.[11]

At a basic level, the core audience concept suggests that planners should give careful consideration to the editorial environment in which their ads will be seen. It

---

[10]*The Core Audience Concept: A Media Position* (Chicago: DDB Needham Worldwide, February 1983), p. 2.

[11]Ibid., p. 12.

also calls into question the usefulness of traditional measures such as pass-along audience (i.e., readers in addition to the person who paid for the copy of the magazine), which has been widely used by magazines and newspapers as a way of augmenting their circulation figures. If the noncore audience is less interested in the vehicle and advertising within the vehicle than the core group, their value to the advertiser may also be lower.

Media Involvement in Communications Effectiveness

Researchers David W. Lloyd and Kevin J. Clancy reviewed nearly seventy previous studies of the effect of audience involvement with television program environment on advertising response. Their analysis showed that in natural viewing situations, greater audience involvement with programming results in significantly better advertising performance in terms of standard measures such as recall, credibility, purchase interest, and behavioral change.[12] While Lloyd and Clancy looked only at television advertising, it seems reasonable to assume that a similar pattern would hold for other media types, again underscoring the importance of considering how the target interacts with the media vehicles being evaluated.

Relevance and Receptivity-Driven Media Objectives

Developing media objectives from a customer perspective involves answering questions in three basic areas:

1. How many consumers do we need to contact with our message and how often should they be contacted?
2. What should the timing of those contacts be?
3. What Consumer Aperture® considerations can we capitalize on?

If we can answer these questions, we're well on our way to developing an effective media plan.

Reach and Frequency

The question of how many and how often addresses the traditional media concerns of reach and frequency and the trade-off between the two. The reach objective for the media plan is the proportion of the target audience we need to contact in order to achieve the overall goals for our campaign; this should come directly from the communication objectives we've established. Because the media plan deals with the

---

[12]David W. Lloyd and Kevin J. Clancy, "Television Program Involvement and Advertising Response: Some Unsettling Implications for Copy Research," *Journal of Consumer Marketing* 8, no. 4 (1991): 61–74.

tactical execution of the marketing communication program, we may have different reach goals for mass media advertising, sales promotion programs, product publicity, and so forth. How many people need to be exposed to the message to achieve the desired behavioral objective?

Closely related to this concern is the idea of frequency: How many times does the target need to see or hear the message for the desired behavior to happen? The standard is to state reach and frequency goals for a four-week period; for example, 60 reach and 2 frequency for four weeks means that we want 60 percent of our target to see our message at least twice during the four weeks. Appropriate frequency levels vary widely depending on the product and the target group. For example, if we're marketing a soft drink and have an objective of retaining current customers as well as stealing users from our competitors, we might set a frequency goal of two exposures per week because soft drinks are purchased often (sometimes daily from vending machines) and are a highly competitive category. Two exposures per week could be required to keep our name in the front of the consumer's mind. On a four-week basis, that would result in a frequency goal of eight or more exposures.

Alternatively, suppose that our product is a vacuum cleaner. Vacuums are bought far less frequently than soft drinks, and there's less competitive clutter, so a lower frequency goal would be appropriate. Maybe putting a message in front of potential purchasers once a month would be enough to generate recognition for our brand. The point is, although frequency decisions are often reduced to a one-size-fits-all formula, they should be made based on a thorough understanding of audience receptivity as it relates to the product.

The traditional view of the trade-off between reach and frequency has been that we can't shoot for a lot of both unless we have a substantial budget. That remains true to a certain extent, but careful integration of marketing communication techniques can come into play here. For example, product publicity and event marketing are both good reach builders (at a relatively low cost in the case of publicity), although not especially good at developing frequency. Outdoor and transit advertisements are useful for bumping up frequency at the local level. Freestanding-insert coupon distribution can add reach to a sales promotion program. In short, marketers need to keep in mind that they can mix and match marketing communication techniques to attain campaign reach and frequency goals.

Recent research by John Philip Jones at Syracuse University suggests that continuity of advertising exposure is a key element in a brand's sales success. Looking at a year's worth of single-source data (including data on sales, advertising, and sales promotion) for seventy-eight leading brands of repeat-purchase packaged goods, Jones was able to identify situations in which brands saw an immediate effect on sales from advertising exposure. Gaps in advertising exposure led to a decrease in sales.[13]

GRPs

Reach and frequency multiplied together equal gross rating points or GRPs. (That is, a four-week reach of 60 at a frequency of 4 is 240 GRPs.) GRPs are a usual

---

[13]John Philip Jones. *When Ads Work: New Proof That Advertising Triggers Sales.* (New York: Lexington, 1995).

shorthand for looking at the weight of a media schedule. If you know that your competitor is running 300 GRPs during the same period that you're running 240 GRPs, you know that their media schedule is heavier than yours. Of course, that 300 GRPs could mean the competitor is reaching 60 percent of its target five times, or 30 percent of its target ten times.

Timing/Scheduling

Timing considerations also are related to consumer behavior because they deal chiefly with seasonality issues. Ideally, we would want to advertise our product at a consistently high rate throughout the year. But that approach can be both cost prohibitive and unnecessary. Instead, we look first at when people buy our product. Obviously, it's most important to reach the target with messages close to the time when the product purchase is being considered. That's why there isn't much charcoal advertising during the winter months in the northern part of the country.

There are a number of possible timing patterns for a brand communication campaign. The three major patterns are continuity, flighting, and pulsing. In continuity, advertising is run throughout the year and at a consistent level. (This is the approach suggested by Jones's research.) For example, a continuity plan might call for running 150 GRPs each week for a total of 7,800 GRPs for the year. A continuity plan keeps the advertising in front of the target all the time. But, as we noted above, you may not need to advertise consistently—your product may be seasonal. Or, you may not have the budget to run a continuity plan that has sufficient weight to get noticed.

In that case, flighting may be a good alternative. In a flighting plan, periods of advertising are interspersed with periods of no advertising. Let's say you decided to advertise every other month—six flights during the year. With the same 7,800 GRPs we used earlier, each of those flights could be at a level of 300 GRPs a week. So, while we would be out of the market every few weeks, our advertising would be more noticeable during the weeks that we were advertising.

But maybe you can't afford to be out of the market for a month at a time, or even a week at a time, because your competition's just too intense. In that case, a pulsing schedule might be most appropriate. In pulsing, you advertise continually, but at varying levels. For example, you could run twenty-six weeks of advertising at 200 GRPs a week and drop down to 100 GRPs a week every other week. Total GRPs still come to 7,800, but now you're maintaining a presence throughout the year (rather than not advertising at certain times under the flighting schedule) and your presence is stronger half the time (the 200 GRP weeks) than it was under the continuity schedule.

Finally, timing decisions should take other marketing communication activities into consideration. For example, periods of advertising inactivity might be compensated for through event marketing, or a publicity push might be used to lead into an advertising burst. Whatever the mix that results, coordination of marketing communication efforts leads to greater effectiveness across the board.

Consumer Aperture

Another DDB Needham concept, Consumer Aperture, considers "when, where, and under what circumstances is the customer's mind most receptive to the selling message."[14] To answer the Aperture question, we need to add the product to the relationship between the consumer and the media. For example, the breath mint category traditionally relies primarily on television advertising. But television reaches consumers at home, whereas breath mints are most often used in social or work situations. Although the consumer might be receptive to a breath mint message seen on television, there are other times when he or she is likely to be more receptive; for example, when the consumer is on his or her way back to work after having eaten a cheesesteak with grilled onions for lunch. In this case, transit advertising using exterior displays on buses might get the message across.

Aperture considerations should not start with media, but with the consumer. Once we've identified the ideal time, place, and circumstances for effective communication to take place, our task is to determine which available medium or media come closest to meeting those conditions. Using the breath mint example, the question would be, "How could we best reach someone on their way back to work from lunch?" That sort of thinking guides effective media choices.

Choosing Which Media to Use

In today's marketplace, one thing media planners don't lack is choice. There are the traditional media, including broadcast television, newspapers, consumer magazines, radio, outdoor, and transit options. There are newer, fast-growing media types including direct mail, syndicated and cable television, and the Internet. And, as our earlier discussion of venue indicates, new media options are emerging all the time. Many of the newer options are handicapped by a lack of audience research data, but many advertisers who are desperate to reach specialized audiences are giving these newcomer media types a try.

In major advertising agencies, most media recommendations focus on television and consumer magazines, with attention given to radio, outdoor, the Internet, and other choices, depending on the client. Television and magazines are old standbys in building national reach and are structured to work effectively with national agencies. Things become more complicated when dealing with radio, outdoor, and newspapers, however, because these media types are largely localized and must be explored on a market-by-market basis. As far as newer media are concerned, they face the twin tasks of first making agencies and clients aware of their existence and then persuading the advertiser to include them in the plan.

Three major areas need to be considered when choosing which media types to use: the consumer (what media do they use and when?), the product (where is this type of product typically promoted?), and the message (what kind of creative support does the benefit need?). And, of course, cost also plays a role.

---

[14] *1995/6 Media By the Numbers*, p. 3.

Where consumers are concerned, primary research can be used to determine media usage. But, if there's no time for primary research, SMRB and MRI both provide information on media patterns. Quintile and tercile data can be used to select media types: if the index numbers are high for quintiles 1 and 2 (or for tercile 1), the medium is a good means to reach the target audience. Quintile and/or tercile data are available for magazines, newspaper, outdoor, radio (in different dayparts), broadcast television (in different dayparts), cable television, and Yellow Pages.

Once the media types have been determined, SMRB and MRI can also be used to select vehicles. Data are available for a number of magazines, television programs, cable networks, and radio station formats and networks. If you're using the P (product) volumes of SMRB or MRI, the percentage in column B is a coverage figure, indicating what percent of the target market uses the vehicle. The column C percentage is a composition figure, showing what percentage of the vehicle's audience is made up of target market members. So, column B can be used as a reach figure, while column C gives a sense of how much wasted circulation would be associated with the vehicle. For Example, Table 14-2 shows an excerpt of SMRB data indicating readership of *Better Homes & Gardens* and *Good Housekeeping* magazines by female homemakers who buy gel-type toothpaste. The percentages in column B indicate that 31.5 percent of all female homemakers who are gel-type toothpaste users read *Better Homes & Gardens*, while 26.2 percent of the product users read *Good Housekeeping*. The percentages in column C tell us that, for both of these magazines, 38.0 percent of their readers are female homemakers who buy gel-type toothpaste. So, if our target market is female homemakers who use gel-type toothpaste, we could reach 31.5 percent of the target by advertising in *Better Homes & Gardens* and 26.2 percent of the target by advertising in *Good Housekeeping*. We also know that 62 percent of the readers of either magazine would not be in our target audience (100 percent – 38 percent = 62 percent), so that portion of each magazine's circulation would be considered wasted circulation for our purposes.

There are, of course, other sources of reach data for specific vehicles. While SMRB and MRI are commonly used for magazines, Nielsen is used for national, spot, and cable television ratings (or reach), and Arbitron for local radio. Most media planning texts include detailed discussions of where to find and how to use these numbers.

Costs

The standard efficiency-based means of comparing vehicles is to calculate the cost per thousand (CPM). The formula is simple: [(Cost of an ad in the vehicle) × 1,000]/(Audience delivered by the vehicle). Optimizer programs are designed to rank media vehicles by CPM, from lowest (that is, most people delivered for the least money) to highest. In general, broadcast media CPMs are lower than those for print media.

Depending on the type of data available, cost per rating point (CPP) may be more useful than CPM. The CPP is the cost to reach one percent of the target market one time. For example, the average spot radio CPP for adults aged twenty-five to

	Table 14-2	Toothpaste—Forms Used (Female Homemakers)				

			Use Gel Form		
	TOTAL U.S. '000	**A '000**	**B % DOWN**	**C ACROSS %**	**D INDX**
Female homemakers	09592	32554	100.0	36.0	100
Better Homes & Gardens	26968	10247	31.5	38.0	106
Good Housekeeping	22463	8536	26.2	38.0	106

Source: Excerpted from *The Study of Media and Markets* (New York: Simmons Market Research Bureau, Spring 1997).

fifty-four during drivetime in the top 100 markets was $5,979 in 1996.[15] If you know that the average rating for drivetime spot radio among your target is 8.5, you can estimate the cost of a spot by multiplying the rating (8.5) times the CPP ($5,979). The estimated cost would be $50,821.50. (The media cost guides developed by major advertising agencies, as well as *The Marketer's Guide to Media*, a reference published by *Adweek*, regularly report average CPPs for different media and different broad targets.)

Media Types

In the following brief discussion of each of the major media types, the focus is on the relationship between medium and user.

Television

In the marketing communication industry, we make distinctions between broadcast, cable, syndication, spot, and so forth. But viewers don't make those distinctions. As of 1997, the average television household could receive 49.2 television stations, up from 27.7 in 1988.[16] Given that degree of choice, a viewer doesn't sit down and say, "Should I watch a broadcast network, a cable network, or a syndicated program?" Viewers choose programs that interest them, and it's up to the media planner to figure out what those programs might be for the specific target audience in which he or she is interested.

---

[15]Ibid., p. 60.

[16]*1998 Report on Television* (New York: Nielsen Media Research, 1998), p. 19.

Television in any form is unique because it offers a combination of high-quality sight and sound. This makes it an ideal choice for products that need to be demonstrated or that are working to create an image appeal. And television is unmatched in its ability to generate excitement. Even with fragmented audiences, there still are major television events, like the Super Bowl, the Academy Awards, and the Olympics, that draw large audiences and can serve as a showcase for advertisers.

Television does have its drawbacks, however. Messages are fleeting and must fight against viewer disinterest and the clutter of other commercials (an increasing problem as advertisers move to fifteen-second commercials as a way to stretch budgets). Nonetheless, for impact, television remains the most attractive media choice available.

Magazines

Consumer magazines have gone through tough times in recent years, with drops in ad pages coupled with increased printing and postage costs that have driven some titles out of business. However, magazines remain an excellent way to reach specialized audiences, particularly for products whose target is defined largely in terms of lifestyle. Editorial prestige also is a hallmark of many publications, drawing upscale readers who are appealing to advertisers and making magazines a preferred choice for product publicity as well. Magazines' superior color reproduction makes them an attractive showcase for prestige products, and the printed page gives the opportunity to explain a product in some detail. Further, the long "shelf-life" of magazines, particularly monthly magazines, increases the chances that an ad will be seen, perhaps repeatedly. This permanence feature also makes magazines an attractive option for distribution of sales promotion offers.

Magazines are a key advertising and publicity medium for business-to-business marketers, who use magazine advertising and product announcements to generate leads for their sales forces or to attract new distributors. And farm publications are important enough to merit their own SRDS (Standard Rate & Data Service, a comprehensive listing of media options) category, serving a large, but very specialized, group of businesses.

Radio

Radio is often overlooked by national advertisers. Although there are a number of programmers offering network radio packages, radio remains primarily a local medium. In addition to the problems related to dealing with station representatives in multiple markets, radio is hindered by a lack of solid audience research data. Like magazines, radio stations offer advertisers very specialized audiences who are attracted by the particular station's format. Radio blends this audience selectivity with a sense of immediacy, aided by its ability to reach consumers outside their homes. (This feature can make radio an excellent option for a variety of aperture considerations.) Good radio advertising tends to be very, very good, capitalizing on the medium's advantages through the use of humor or imagination. This is important because radio is often used as a background medium, which means that advertising must quickly capture the listener's attention in order to be heard.

Newspapers

Newspapers remain the number one media choice for local advertisers and rank with television as the most widely used advertising medium in the United States. In some ways, newspapers probably have been the medium to suffer most from changes in audience behavior. Declining literacy rates have sapped newspapers' claim to broad reach within a market. Rising printing costs and alternative methods of news delivery (particularly all-news television stations and the Internet) call into question the long-term viability of newspapers, at least in their current form. Many newspapers have established on-line versions as a means of increasing their competitive strength. Newspapers continue to face a major challenge to attract national advertiser support, however, because of concerns related to production standardization and audience measurement.

Still, newspapers are one of the top advertising media for good reasons. Their local credibility is unmatched by other media types, and their short closing dates make them ideal for marketers who need to get either advertising or sales promotion messages out quickly (witness what happens whenever there's an airline price war). And, because they exist to convey news and information to their readers, newspapers can lend an air of authority to the advertisements they carry. The news and information appeal also makes newspapers an ideal delivery vehicle for product publicity. Concerns about poor color reproduction are largely a thing of the past thanks to *USA Today*'s insistence that its local printing plants meet strict quality standards. (Even the *New York Times* now carries color photographs!) The newspaper industry is moving to make itself even more attractive to national advertisers by developing buying networks and working toward greater standardization of production requirements.

Outdoor and Transit

Like radio and newspapers, outdoor and transit are used primarily to add local reinforcement to a national campaign. They are excellent reminder media because commuters tend to see the same message at the same time day after day. As with radio, humor and imagination can be used to great advantage in these media, although message space is limited, especially in the case of outdoor. Particularly if the target is a working, urban audience, outdoor and transit can be valuable additions to a media plan.

Direct Mail

Traditionally, direct mail efforts have been handled by agencies specializing in direct response rather than by traditional advertising agencies. That's because direct mail is in many ways a vastly different medium than the mass media we have reviewed.

As we discussed in Chapter 13, direct mail is *not* mass, it's personal. It requires a different creative approach, as well as an understanding of the intricacies of mailing lists. But, if an appropriate list is available, direct mail imposes no space boundaries or limitations on imagination. It is an appropriate distribution vehicle for advertising, sales promotion offers, and event marketing announcements.

Interactive Media

Like direct mail, interactive media, particularly the World Wide Web, are not mass media. Unlike many other media types, consumers do not encounter Web sites by chance; they have to make the effort to seek out the site and the information it contains. As we saw in Chapter 13, this presents a very different set of challenges to advertisers. And yet, if your target audience is technology-savvy, you likely can't afford *not* to be on the Web.

Other Media

The options in this category increase every day. "Other" media forms include aerial advertising, in-flight ads, movie theater advertising (growing quickly in popularity in the United States), stadium advertising, ads on the sides of tractor-trailers, ads in bathrooms stalls, even ads on the sides of cows grazing in fields alongside heavily traveled highways; the list goes on and on. Perhaps the best way to approach these other media options is from an Aperture perspective: What are the optimal circumstances for reaching the target, and where/when can we come closest to that time? In today's marketplace, if there isn't already a medium that fits a marketer's needs, he or she should consider creating one.

Media Planning Versus Media Buying

Although media planners can use the ideas discussed in this chapter to bring an effectiveness focus to their recommendations, it's important to recognize that media buying is almost entirely efficiency based. Buyers are trained to negotiate for the lowest possible price for their clients and prefer to have as much flexibility as possible when entering into a negotiation. For example, a planner might recommend that a particular product, such as Kool-Aid, be advertised on Nick at Nite. Kool-Aid emphasizes its history, the fact that the product has been around for quite a while, and that today's mothers probably drank Kool-Aid when they were children. Nick at Nite's nostalgia programming attracts the right demographic group for Kool-Aid, and the tone of the programming fits the product. A nice effectiveness-based recommendation, right? But telling a buyer that we want time only on Nick at Nite doesn't allow him or her much room to negotiate an attractive price. The buyer would prefer a group of television networks to choose from so as to get the best deal. In this situation, efficiency and effectiveness may well be working at cross purposes.

For some products, it may be relatively simple to develop a list of acceptable substitutes for each recommended media vehicle. However, as the planner's focus shifts more and more to effectiveness and decisions are made based on relevance and receptivity considerations, lines of communication between planners and buyers will have to be strengthened to insure that buyers understand why media vehicle substitutions aren't appropriate. Also, such a change may mean that agencies will have to more clearly delineate who has the ultimate decision-making authority in developing a media schedule—an authority that currently rests with the buyers in many agencies. A focus on relevance and receptivity can thus result in paying higher prices for desired media vehicles, but those higher prices should be justified by the increased return generated by the marketing communication effort.

Summary

Careful media selection is critical to the effectiveness of the IBC plan. The mix of communication techniques chosen to deliver messages and/or incentives must be matched to appropriate media choices. In evaluating the wealth of available media options, the IBC planner should be guided by the issues of relevance, that is, what messages, incentives, and media are of greatest importance to the consumer, and receptivity. Receptivity is concerned with identifying when the consumer will be most open to our message or our incentive offer. Close and deliberate consideration of these two factors should lead to effective media decisions.

15

Measuring the Results of IBC Programs

The Importance of Measurement

In most marketing and communication texts, the chapter on measurement or evaluation is typically quite short or, in some cases, not even included. The reason? Historically, most advertising, marketing, and marketing communication attention has been focused on planning, developing, and implementing communication programs, that is, the "what and how we are going to say what we want customers and prospects to know." Thus, most communication efforts have focused on measuring "outputs," or what the organization sent out—not on "outcomes," or what the firm got back.

As we have stressed throughout this text, measurement and evaluation will be watchwords for all marketers now and into the future. For example, the ability to measure results or returns will be just as important for those operating in the historical and current marketplaces (review Exhibit 1-2, the Evolution and Revolution diagram) as it will be for those entering the twenty-first-century marketplace. The reason for this increased attention to measurement and evaluation is quite simple. If the brand and the customer are the primary assets the organization will manage, rather than plants or factories or facilities or even R&D, the firm simply must know when it is building value and when it is improperly allocating the finite resources that it has available. Today and tomorrow, there will be less and less margin for error, particularly in a rapidly changing, response-driven arena in which competitors can quickly take advantage of any misstep or missed opportunity. Indeed, the proper allocation of finite corporate resources will be one of the primary skills required of the brand, marketing, and communication manager of the future.

It is important for the IBC planner to know what has gone before and to understand the approaches and methodologies still in practice. This background also provides the basis for the brand communication measurement approach we advocate. Following a review of current practice, we describe what is needed or required to develop an effective brand communication measurement system. Next, we provide an ROI (Return on Investment) or, in our preferred terminology, ROCI (Return on Customer Investment) process that is based on the strategy planning approach presented in Chapter 5. We describe our process in some detail so that the reader can develop and implement this approach in actual practice. We move next to a discussion of the new areas of measurement, that is, how to measure both internal and external brand communication programs. Most traditional brand communication evaluation systems focus only on external communication—on programs delivered to or against consumers or end users. We argue, however, that successful brand communication programs must involve both internal and external audiences. Therefore, we devote some attention to the measurement of internal brand communication among employees, channel members, and other stakeholders. Finally, we end the chapter with a discussion of the future of brand communication measurement when the twenty-first-century marketplace is fully developed.

Historical Methods of Measuring Brand Communication Impact

To understand the development of the present methods of marketing and marketing communication measurement, it is important to understand the restrictions and limitations that previous planners and evaluators faced. One must remember that many of the things we take for granted today—the massive amounts of customer data obtained through scanner or other POS (point-of-sale) systems, the Internet and the World Wide Web, the development of databases, the ability to conduct large-scale research projects over WATS-line telephones, and the ability to access substantial amounts of syndicated data—are fairly recent inventions or developments in the field of marketing and communication. For example, computing power sufficient to develop and manage extensive databases became practical and economically feasible only in the late 1980s. Extensive availability of scanner and POS data, beyond samples and test markets, became practical only in the early 1980s, while the Web is just a few years old. So, in truth, the historical methods of marketing and marketing communication measurement are in place not because brand planners and researchers were not capable of thinking more broadly and extensively, but because they were the methods possible with the technology and tools available.

In addition, one must recall that mass media advertising as we know it today sprang from mass communication, which was developed in the 1930s and 1940s. Advertising was really a tagalong to communication measurement research and therefore appropriated the research methodologies. As a result, much of the marketing and communication measurement methodologies that are in use today were based on what was developed in other fields. In other words, if it worked for other disciplines, we tried—not always successfully—to adapt it to marketing, advertising, and marketing communication.

Measuring Communication Effects

In Chapter 5, we discussed the development and use of Lavidge and Steiner's hierarchy of effects model and the resulting advertising measurement approach developed by Colley called DAGMAR (Designing Advertising Goals for Measured Advertising Results), which was first published by the Association of National Advertisers. Both approaches were published in 1961, and, while they seem somewhat archaic and perhaps even irrelevant in today's financially driven marketplace, one must remember that they were developed because they were the best that could be done in that time frame. That is, researchers in the 1960s were not trying to avoid relating marketing and marketing communication to actual marketplace financial results. They simply didn't have the tools or techniques that were required to do that job. Thus, they did what they could with the tools at hand. In fact, this borrowing or adapting of approaches and techniques from other fields led to current evaluation approaches that rely on the use of sampling and projection. That is, the researcher takes what is believed to be a representative sample of the population to be studied and then projects the results of the study or evaluation of that sample to the whole using various types of statistical techniques. Remember, when the present methodologies were developed in the 1950s and 1960s, capturing even a sample of the population was a significant achievement. To capture data on the entire population and their behaviors was simply unthinkable. Because many researchers still believe that it is simply impractical to attempt to survey the entire population and capture their actual behaviors, researchers and analysts have used attitudes, which could usually be obtained rather easily through various sampling techniques, and then projected them to the whole to represent the marketplace.

The same approach has commonly been used with customer behaviors. Even if we were able to capture all the actual behaviors by customers in the marketplace, we simply could not have manipulated that amount of data to make any sense out of it. Thus, advertisers, who typically accounted for the majority of most marketing and communication research investments, accepted and adapted various types of social science research techniques and applied them to commercial communication. In fact, most of our communication measurements today are based on awareness, recall, and attitudinal change—all topics that have been studied in some detail by social scientists. The approach we propose is an improvement that has become possible in the last three to five years as the result of technology, primarily in the form of computer capacity, data capture and storage, and various new manipulation techniques. Current advertising, marketing, and communication measurement approaches are not "wrong." Indeed, many still are relevant. But because technology allows us to do different things better, faster, and more effectively now, we can think differently. That is the message of the new brand communication evaluation process.

The marketplace challenge of today is not to get more or better or less expensive attitudinal measurements; it is the need for behavioral data. Behaviors can be translated into financial results that accrue to the organization as a result of brand communication programs. Therefore, simply knowing that awareness of an advertising campaign has improved or grown or diffused quickly has little real value to the organization, unless one can relate that awareness in some way to what the organization invested and tie that back to greater returns than would have been achieved without the investment. As we have stated repeatedly throughout this text, we invest dollars to develop, implement, and deliver brand communication activities; therefore, we must find some way to connect our results to dollar returns back to the organization. Dollars out. Dollars returned. This is the backbone of our brand communication measurement and evaluation system, which uses income flows as the system's yardstick for measurement.

The Drive for Financial Measurement

In the 1950s and 1960s, awareness and attitudinal change were likely important to advertisers and marketers and marketing communication planners. Generally, marketing and communication was far less costly and risky in those days. For example, an organization could make a marketing or communication mistake and not have competitors, or sometimes even customers, notice it. Of course, times have changed. Today's marketplace is extremely competitive, with no leeway for marketing mistakes and great emphasis on accountability. In our view, four major factors demand financial evaluations of brand communication programs now and into the future.

1. *The Move from Product to Brand Value.* When marketers competed on product innovations and improvements, such new developments were important differentiating factors. People paid attention to them. Today, however, most marketers operate in a commodity-like arena. Products and services often are essentially the same; therefore, competition occurs among brands, not among products or services. Indeed, the value of the brand is one of the major assets of most organizations. Because the brand is an intangible asset, knowing how much to invest and how to measure the resulting return from the investment becomes a critical financial issue for the organization. As we move from product competition to distribution competition to customer competition, evaluating the results of brand communication programs becomes key to management success.

2. *Complex Channels.* When marketing organizations distributed their products through relatively simple channel systems, financial returns on those channel investments were easy to measure. The marketer provided the channel partner with a promotional program. The channel either implemented the program or didn't, and results were fairly easy to observe. But, as distribution systems have become more complex, it has become increasingly difficult for the marketing organization to determine what is working and what is not, particularly with the end user. Indeed, as the marketer has had less contact with the ultimate end users or consumer, the need to understand where and under what conditions and circumstances marketing and communication programs have had any impact has become more important. In other words, today the risk of

poor communication programs is higher and the impact of improper decisions has longer-lasting effects. In short, simple attitudinal or awareness measures often have little or no relevance in the complex distribution system through which most marketing organizations operate today.

3. *Competition.* Closely related to the development of complex distribution systems is the rise of major competitors. Historically, most marketing organizations could identify their competitors and could predict how they would react to marketplace activities. Organizations competed in fairly stable, vertical silos in which competitors were known and understood. As new forms of competition have entered the marketplace, however, the general assumptions on which competitor activities and reactions were based have given way to a rapidly changing arena in which affiliations, alliances, and agreements have changed the competitive landscape. Yesterday's competitor has become today's business partner and vice versa. So, as competition, often on a global scale, has become more intense, the traditional measures of results are too simplistic for application in today's and tomorrow's organizations. They simply don't yield information that is relevant to current needs.

4. *Communication Overload.* In the mid-1960s, an advertiser could buy a television commercial during prime time on each of the three major television networks and reach over 90 percent of American households. Today, network television, depending on how one defines "networks," generally attracts less than 55 percent of U.S. households on an accumulated basis and is headed south. The explosion of communication alternatives, which literally inundate households today, is almost beyond comprehension. Some estimates have suggested that the typical U.S. consumer is exposed to more than 3,000 commercial messages each day, and there is no end in sight. Marketing organizations are determined to find every available delivery system for their messages and incentives. As we discussed in the previous chapter, simply evaluating brand communication on the basis of delivery or OTS (Opportunities to See) or CPM or gains in awareness or changes in attitudes seems somewhat irrelevant when the actual goal is to provide or deliver messages that result in behaviors. Thus, we must move beyond the measurement systems of the past and develop some type of system that enables the marketing organization to determine the amount of financial returns being provided as a result of brand communication investments.

In the balance of this chapter, we provide a description of the ROI or ROCI process that we have developed. We begin with the required elements needed to develop this type of evaluation.

What's Needed for Effective Brand Communication Measurement?

Much of what is discussed in this section has already been emphasized throughout this text. The structure and format of the measurement system proposed is dependent on these elements, however, so we cover them briefly here as a review.

A Process, Not a Group of Functions

Proper measurement of a brand communication program requires a process. It is not simply a group of functional activities tied together in some way, with someone trying to make sense of the combinations. Instead, the ROCI measurement approach is a planned, systematic approach that is used repeatedly. The brand communication approach we advocate is summarized in the process development chart and the strategic planning programs that appeared in Chapters 4 and 5. These now-familiar process charts appear as Exhibit 15-1 and 15-2 and are the basis for the evaluation system.

Closed-Loop Methodology

The closed-loop approach, which was described in some detail in Chapter 5, is vital to the measurement process as well. The general model is illustrated in Exhibit 15-3. Indeed, knowing the value of a customer or prospect (income flows) is key in the measurement process. If we know the current value of a customer, and we know what we have invested in that customer, then we should be able to measure the results of that program. In other words, we can measure the Return on Investment or the Return on Customer Investment that we have made.

Incremental Value

In Chapter 4, we discussed the concept of incremental value. The measurement system is based on incremental value, that is, the return to the organization from investing in brand communication programs over and above what it would have received had the investment not been made. The concept is shown in Exhibit 15-4. To add value, an investment in a brand communication program must increase the return that the organization would receive if it had not invested the funds at all, or it must be greater than the cost of the investment itself. This is a critical element in evaluating brand communication programs.

Financial Time Frames

Here, we introduce a new element in the brand communication measurement approach: financial time frames. For the most part, marketing and communication programs have been evaluated on the basis of communication results. That is, marketing and communication managers tried to determine when the communication program would have an impact or effect and what it might be. Generally, most findings were that advertising worked over time, and thus the concepts of "lagged effects" and "consumer response rates" and the like were developed. These measures may still be applied by many of today's marketing communication planners; however, they have little relationship to how the organization actually operates in the marketplace.

Exhibit 15-1 IBC Five-Step Planning Process

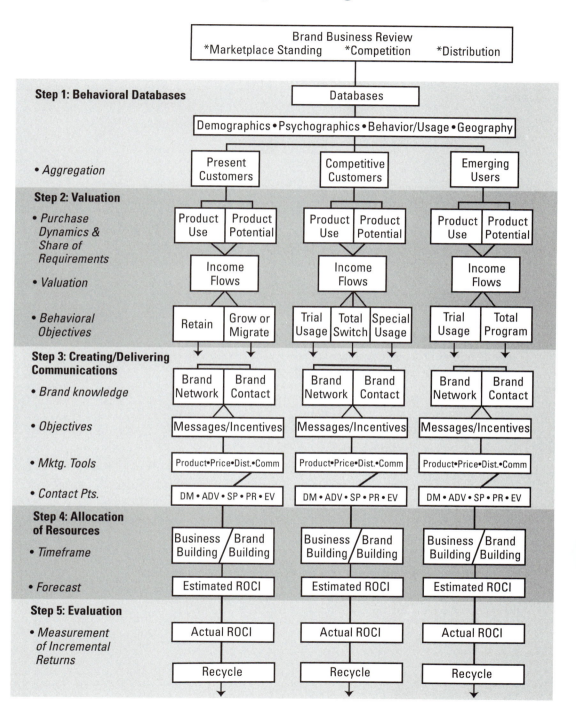

Exhibit 15-2
IBC Strategy Development Process

Step One—Customer Definition

1. What is the customer group we want to communicate with? (Current customers, competitive users, new/emerging users, etc.)

2. What does this group buy now? How do they buy and use the product(s)?

3. What do we know about the consumers in this group? (Demographics, lifestyles, psychographics)

Step Two—Customer Behavior

1. What income flow does this group generate to the category? To our product?

2. What is our share of requirement from this customer group?

3. What is the current value of this customer group? What is their potential value?

4. How does this group perceive the products in the category?

5. What is the key group insight?

Step Three—Customer Strategy

1. What is our strategy for this group? Grow? Retain? Migrate? Capture? Trial?

2. Given this strategy, what is the competitive frame? Why?

3. What do those competitors now communicate to the consumer?

4. How are the competitors perceived by the consumer?

5. How is competition likely to retaliate against our strategy?

Step Four—Investment Strategy

1. Review the current value of this group to our brand.

2. How much are we willing to invest in brand-building activities against this group?

3. How much are we willing to invest in business-building activities against this group?

4. What is the time frame for this investment?

Step Five—Communication Strategy

1. Do we need to deliver a message or an incentive (or both) to this group?

2. If a message, what is the strategy for this group (grow, retain, etc.)?

3. If an incentive, should it decrease the product's price or increase the product's value to the consumer?

Exhibit 15-2
IBC Strategy Development Process (continued)

Step Six—Delivery Strategy

1. Which marketing communication technique(s) should be used to deliver the message and/or incentive? Why?

2. Which message/incentive delivery systems are most relevant to this communication strategy?

3. Which message/incentive delivery systems are consumers in this group most receptive to?

Step Seven—Action Objectives

1. What action do we want the consumer to take as a result of the communication? (Trial? Increased usage? Request more information?)

2. What main point do we want the consumer to take away from the communication?

Exhibit 15-3
The Closed-Loop Process

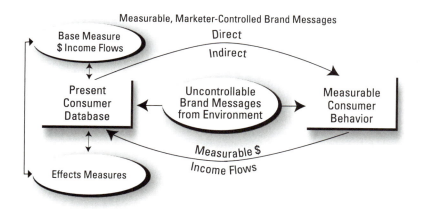

Exhibit 15-4
The Concept of Incremental Value

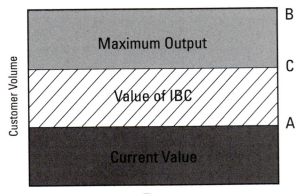

All business organizations operate according to an accounting schedule. The company opens its books on a given date and closes its books generally one year later. It is this fiscal time frame that drives the organization—not the marketing or communication time frame on which many brand communication programs are developed and implemented. Because organizations are bound to financial time frames, the evaluation of brand communication programs must reflect the fiscal time frame—not a marketer's communication time frame.

Expenses that are incurred during a given fiscal year are accounted for during that fiscal year. The organization must look at its expenses and investments and evaluate returns for that fiscal year. An organization may choose to take an expense as an investment and treat it as an asset. In doing so, it characterizes that expenditure as a long-term investment, generating long-term returns. Likewise, short-term expenses are taken in the year they are incurred. How an organization's accountants choose to treat an expenditure from a financial standpoint determines the evaluation method to be used.

In Chapter 3, we presented the concept of a communication matrix. That is reproduced as Exhibit 15-5. As you know, organizations can choose to deliver either messages or incentives. These can be defined in terms of when it is believed they will generate returns to the organization. If short term, returns will be generated during the organization's current fiscal year; if long term, returns will come in a subsequent year or over multiple years.

In the measurement process that follows, we will define our estimated returns as shown:

Short-term returns, or those obtained during the current fiscal year = Business Building.

Long-term returns, or returns generated over multiple future years = Brand Building.

Exhibit 15-5
Brand Communication Planning Matrix

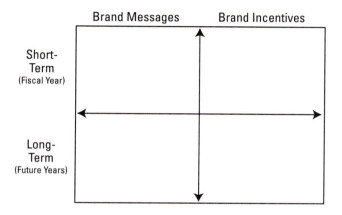

These are fundamental to the evaluation system we will use to measure the return on brand communication investment.

In the next section, we describe the short-term, or business-building, approach using a spreadsheet methodology.

The Spreadsheet Approach to Measuring the Return on Business-Building Brand Communication Programs

The key element required to effectively measure the Return on Customer Investment is the ability to separate business-building from brand-building brand communication.[1] While the line between the two activities will not always be distinct, the basis for separation between short-term (returns within the organization's fiscal year) and long-term (returns over periods longer than the fiscal year) is critical because of current accounting standards.

This measurement process is designed to work primarily with customer or prospect groups. While it would be wonderful if we could estimate or calculate the ROCI for every individual customer, presently that approach has limited practicality. So, though our approach can accommodate one-to-one brand communication

---

[1]This and the following sections have been adapted from Don E. Schultz and Jeffrey S. Walters, *Measuring Brand Communication ROI* (New York: Association of National Advertisers, 1997). Used with permission.

calculations, we focus on customer groups in this section since that is a relevant measure for the majority of marketing organizations in the foreseeable future.

We illustrate our measurement process through a basic spreadsheet approach. An important part of this process is that it can be used either to calculate the actual return or to estimate the return in advance using various "what if" scenarios. The approach is illustrated in Table 15-1.

The Basic Concept

The basic business-building ROCI spreadsheet is shown as Table 15-1. The spreadsheet can be changed or adapted as needed by the organization. It simply provides a standardized framework that can be used across the organization for the process of calculating the ROCI.

As shown in the horizontal column heading in Table 15-2, customers or groups have been aggregated by their behavior. For the brand or organization, these groups can be as broad or as narrow and as many or as few as needed. Along with each customer group we have specified the behavioral goal that we hope to have achieved in the measurement period. Examples of behavioral goals would be to *acquire* new customers, *retain* the business of existing customers, or to *grow* the share of business we are obtaining from that group. There are even times we may want to *divest* ourselves of certain high-maintenance, low-profit customers, but that would need to be done in such a way that it does not damage our reputation or reduce our volume level such that economies of scale are affected.

The spreadsheet is divided into five sections that provide the basis for the ROCI calculation. In the first section we estimate the customer's total category demand in dollars spent at the factory level. Next, in the second section we determine our share of that requirement, and then our base income flow and contribution margin. The next two sections adjust our share and contribution margin estimates under alternate levels of communication investment. From this comparison, we isolate the incremental change in revenue attributed to the communication efforts. From that we calculate our ROCI. As mentioned before, this calculation is based on the incremental gain or, in some cases, the loss on our investments.

Each of these five sections is discussed in more detail below.

Category Requirement Assumptions

This section estimates the customer's entire demand, or requirement, within a given category, spread across all available vendors.

Line 1: Estimated Category Demand is based on historical or "what if" data about customer purchase behavior. In Table 15-1, we show this only as a single line entry, but this estimate can become quite sophisticated and complex. It is also possible to use historical data to adjust these calculations to take into account changes in demand due to environmental factors, competitive activity, and so on. For now, however, the point is that potential total demand for the current period is the basis for our calculation, and it is expressed in dollars, not units, shipments, or other non-financial measures.

Table 15-1

Business-Building Return on Brand Communication Investment, or Return on Customer Investment

	Aggregated Customer Group:	Group A	Group B	Group C
Category Requirement Assumptions				
1 Estimated Category Demand	Historical Data/Estimate	$	$	$
Base Income Flow Assumptions				
2 Base Share of Requirement	Historical Data/Estimate	%	%	%
3 Base Income Flow to Us	Line 1 × Line 2 =	$	$	$
4 Noncommunication Costs (Product, Fixed, G&A, etc.)	Operating Estimate	%	%	%
5 Contribution Margin %	100% – Line 4 =	%	%	%
6 Contribution Margin $	Line 3 × Line 5 =	$	$	$
Scenario A: No Communication Investment				
7 Change in Share of Requirement	Estimate	±%	±%	±%
8 Resulting Share of Requirement	Line 2 + (Line 7 × Line 2) =	%	%	%
9 Resulting Customer Income Flow to Us	Line 8 × Line 1 =	$	$	$
10 Less: Noncommunication Costs (Product, Fixed, G&A, etc.)	– (Line 9 × Line 4) =	–$	–$	–$
11 Less: Brand Communication Cost	$0	—	—	—
12 Net Contribution	Line 9 + (Line 10 – Line 11) =	$	$	$
Scenario B: Communication Investment				
13 Brand Communication Efforts (a–m)	Estimate			
14 Brand Contact Points (n)	Estimate			
15 Total Brand Communication Investment	Estimate	$	$	$
16 Change in Share of Requirement	Estimate	±%	±%	±%
17 Resulting Share of Requirement	Line 2 + (Line 16 × Line 2)=	%	%	%
18 Resulting Customer Income Flow to Us	Line 17 × Line 1 =	$	$	$
19 Less: Noncommunication Costs (Product, Fixed, G&A, etc.)	– (Line 18 × Line 4)=	–$	–$	–$
20 Less: Brand Communication Cost	– Line 15	–	–	–
21 Net Contribution	Line 18 + (Line 19 – Line 20) =	$	$	$
ROI Calculation				
22 Incremental Gain/Loss vs. "No Investment" Scenario	Line 21 – Line 12 =	$	$	$
23 Incremental ROCI	Line 22/Line 15 =	$	$	$

Base Income Flow Assumptions

This section combines basic assumptions about the brand's share-of-customer requirement and brand cost dynamics. These factors are then applied under alternative scenarios calling for differing levels of communication spending.

Line 2: Base Share-of-Customer Requirement represents the proportion of the customer's total category requirements that our brand gained in the past or that we estimate for the future in a given time period. In most cases, the base is the firm's fiscal year. These base numbers are supported by historical or scenario data. As with all other measures in the process, this reflects dollars, not units. So, our share-of-requirement reflects the proportion of the customer's dollar spending that comes to our brand, not the proportion of units they acquire. In categories with wide variances in prices between competitors, this distinction between dollars and units could be an important one.

Line 3: Base Income Flow to Us is the estimated category demand multiplied by the percentage of that demand that comes to our brand. In other words, this is the income flow in dollars to our brand that the customer or group represents.

Line 4: Noncommunication Costs is a cost factor subtracted from the Base Income Flow. This covers all fixed and variable costs of running the business *excluding* brand communication costs or dollars taken as profit. For the sake of simplicity, we have shown this as a simple percentage of the Base Income Flow. While this single percentage approach will be adequate for many organizations, it should be acknowledged that the dynamics of fixed and variable expenses in some companies may require a more complex, volume-sensitive calculation. However a company factors its expenses, we want to isolate all costs other than brand communication and profit to generate the Contribution Margin line.

Line 5: Contribution Margin Percentage is equal to 100 percent minus the percentage used above in Line 4 to account for nonbrand communication costs. In our system, we define Contribution Margin as only profits and brand communication funds. Here, we are estimating that margin as a percentage of the Income Flow from each customer or customer group.

Line 6: Contribution Margin $ is the brand Contribution Margin expressed in dollars. It is obtained by multiplying Line 3, Base Income Flow, by Line 5, Contribution Margin Percent. In other words, it is what is left over after all fixed and variable costs (other than those for brand communication and profit) have been removed from the customer income flow. If there were no communication efforts against the customer, then this figure would equal our net contribution to the organization's bottom line for the period. However, to the extent that funds were, or might be, spent on brand communication programs during the period, this line reflects the combined total of those expenditures plus the organization's profit. At this point we do not need to specify just how much was spent on communication in the past. So, will the brand be better off by making an investment in communicating with its customers? That key question is addressed in the next two sections of the spreadsheet.

Scenario A: No Communication Investment

This section establishes a "baseline" of profitability if the brand made no further communication investment. If there were no communication efforts—no advertising, no direct mailings, no telemarketing—how much business would the brand receive from each of its customers or customer groups? It is, of course, unlikely that the brand would lose 100 percent of its customer base support without brand communication in the fiscal year. However, some change in demand or share would likely occur. In this section we calculate or estimate just what that impact might be, that is, somewhere between 0 and 100 percent, and then reproject the brand's income flow, costs, and net contribution based on the factors established in the previous section.

Line 7: Change in Share of Requirement represents the estimated or actual results of what would or did happen to the brand's Share of Requirement (SOR) in the measurement period if there were no brand communication investments. How much would the brand decline from what it presently receives from each customer or customer group? For simplicity, we assume that even though we are not communicating actively, the customer likely will maintain the same overall category requirement. A mother with an infant will still need approximately the same number of disposable diapers each day whether or not the brand is actively communicating to her. What will likely change, however, is the Share of Requirement the brand receives, expressed as a percentage decrease or increase in customer Share of Requirement. In most cases this will result in a negative number, such as a –15 percent (decrease) in the SOR.

The question for many organizations will be how to develop an accurate estimate of their change in requirement. Companies with a great deal of historical data probably can extrapolate from past experiences. Others may have done paired market tests (as discussed in Chapter 7) that could provide a starting point. And, in many cases, there may be nothing other than the manager's own best professional judgment and insight based on experience. In truth, assumptions about what would happen if we did no communications are made every day, albeit indirectly. Managers often maintain levels of communication spending because they are afraid to change them. Or they underspend because they have never closely examined the impact that an additional communication investment could make. The value of this process is that it forces the manager to focus on the issue(s) to be resolved and to make viable and supportable decisions, not just maintain the status quo or continue the traditional spending patterns.

Line 8: Resulting Share of Requirement is the result of adjusting the initial Share of Requirement in Line 2 by the factor increase or decrease specified in Line 7. For example, if the brand's initial Share of Requirement was 50 percent, but we felt that our share would decrease by 25 percent without communication support, our resulting share of requirement would be [.50 + (.50 × –.25) = 37.5 percent].

Line 9: Resulting Customer Income Flow to Us multiplies the adjusted Share of Requirements from Line 8 by the Estimated Category Demand in Line 1. Recall that we did not alter the customer's overall need for products in the category. Rather, we estimated how much of that business we expected to get or calculated what we got. This line, then, represents what would happen to our income flow for the period if we made no brand communication expenditures.

Line 10: Less: Noncommunication Costs (Product, Fixed, G&A, etc) applies the percentage allocated to cover all noncommunication costs and profits from Line 4 to the adjusted income estimate in Line 9. Remember, this should include all costs, with the exception of brand communication and expected/required profit.

Line 11: Less: Brand Communication Cost is $0 in this scenario because there are no marketing communication expenditures.

Line 12: Net Contribution is what remains after the costs associated with Lines 10 and 11 are subtracted from the income flow estimate in Line 9. This is our calculation, or estimate, of the brand contribution level under a scenario in which no funds are invested in brand communication. It is this figure that is the basis for estimating the incremental gain, if any, that is to be achieved when we invest in brand communication programs, as in Scenario B, which follows.

Scenario B: Communication Investment

The next step is to estimate how the value of each customer group would change if we conducted a brand communication program directed toward it.

Line 13: Brand Communication Efforts (a–m) are identifiable and generally controllable brand communication programs that the organization can direct to specific groups of customers or prospects. There can be as many or as few efforts directed to each group as needed.

Line 14: Brand Contact Points (n) are simply the number of times each of the above Brand Communication Efforts we use are expected to result in Brand Contacts with the target segment.

As was discussed in earlier chapters, the real value of brand communication is in creating brand contacts with customers or prospects. These can come in any number of ways; that is, they need not be only media-delivered, which is how we have traditionally tried to measure advertising results, nor direct mail- or telemarketing-delivered, which is how most direct marketing is measured. We want to be able to accommodate any and all forms of brand communication activities that can be either a brand message or a brand incentive for the customer or prospect.

Business-building brand contacts can, in fact, occur multiple times within the context of a customer relationship or time period. As a result, we talk about brand contact points, not just a single point. This allows us to accommodate communication activities that may create multiple impressions or occur multiple times with no additional cost or investment by the organization. For example, a point-of-purchase display may deliver multiple brand contacts to the same customer once it is erected in a retail store. There is an initial cost of development and installation, but from then on, the cost has been absorbed although the brand contacts continue.

Line 15: Total Brand Communication Investment represents our total investment in brand communication through all brand contacts with this group of customers. As was discussed earlier, in this process no attempt is made to determine the ROCI of the individual communication effort, such as one advertising insertion versus another, or a direct mail campaign against a public relations program, or a cross-media comparison. In a robust communication environment, there is too much synergy between efforts and activities to accurately measure the impact of each with any accuracy. However, using the process described here, we can measure our total investment against a specific group of customers and compare that to the resulting change in the income flow to the brand.

Line 16: Change in Share of Requirement estimates what percentage increase (or decrease) we can expect in our Share of Requirement as a result of the brand communication program.

Lines 17, 18, and 19 recalculate our revised Share of Requirement, income flow, and noncommunication costs based on the factor used in Line 16.

Line 20: Less: Brand Communication Costs is equal to the Total Brand Communication Investment figure in Line 15. It is repeated here as a negative so that it can be subtracted from income flow along with the noncommunication costs in order to produce the result in Line 20.

Line 21: Net Contribution is the net income after all communication and noncommunication expenses have been deducted.

Line 22: Incremental Gain/Loss vs. "No Investment" Scenario compares the two net contribution estimates developed in Lines 12 and 21. Note, these are incremental gains (or losses) to the brand as a result of the brand communication program. Further, we can use this same process to estimate or calculate the return to the organization from a customer income flow retention program.

Line 23: Incremental ROCI is the total Incremental Gain/Loss (Line 22) divided by the investment made in Line 15.

This provides an overview of the process that is used to estimate or calculate the return on a business-building brand communication program. While there will be many adaptations necessary for various types of organizations, this illustrates how the process works and how it might be used in brand communication program evaluation.

ROCI: An Example

Table 15-2 illustrates the process of developing a brand communication program Return on Customer Investment using a consumer product example. We also expand upon the basic ROCI model used earlier to incorporate more real-world situations.

The situation on which Table 15-2 is based is the same computer supply product used in the IBC Strategy Development Process example in Chapter 5. This will highlight the relationship between strategy development and IBC evaluation. While our strategy focused on one aggregated customer group, the loyal buyers, the evaluation spreadsheet in Table 15-2 looks at three additional groups: switchers, new/emerging customers, and problem customers.

As described in Chapter 5, the Loyals for this product are long-term customers who give the brand 60 percent of their category business. The demand from this group is not growing significantly, but we obviously need to maintain what we have. Our goal is to retain their income flow at the same level as in the past.

The second group is Switchers, a set of customers who switch between our brand and the competitor quite often. While the 40 percent SOR they currently purchase from us is significant, we feel we can strengthen our brand relationship and capture a greater proportion of their share of requirement.

The third group is an Emerging group of customers just now coming into the market. This group is expected to expand rapidly, and even though our brand currently receives only 10 percent of their business, the goal is to acquire more of their income flow.

The last group of customers is our Problem group. In some cases this group gives our brand only a small percentage of its business. In others, the group's requirements are very low, and in still others, the group consistently shops on price only. In

Table 15-2   **Consumer Product ROCI Example**

Aggregated Customer Group:	Loyals	Switchers	New or Emerging	Problem
Behavioral Goal:	Retain	Grow Share	Acquire	Divest
Category Requirement Assumptions				
1 Historical Category Demand	$1,000.00	$1,000.00	$1,000.00	$1,000.00
2 Environmental Changes in Demand	2%	5%	20%	–20%
3 Demand Adjusted for Environmental Changes	$1,020.00	$1,050.00	$1,200.00	$800.00
4 Impact of Competitive Activities	–1%	–5%	–5%	–5%
5 Demand Adjusted for Competitive Activities	$1,009.80	$997.50	$1,140.00	$760.00
Base Income Flow Assumptions				
6 Base Share of Requirement	60%	40%	10%	15%
7 Base Income Flow to Us	$605.88	$399.00	$114.00	$114.00
8 Noncommunication Costs (Product, Fixed, G&A, etc.)	75%	80%	80%	90%
9 Contribution Margin %	25%	20%	20%	10%
10 Contribution Margin $	$151.47	$79.80	$22.80	$11.40
Scenario A: No Communication Investment				
11 Change in Share of Requirement	–20%	–20%	–30%	–20%
12 Resulting Share of Requirement	48%	32%	7%	12%
13 Resulting Customer Income Flow to Us	$484.70	$319.20	$79.80	$91.20
14 Less: Noncommunication Costs (Product, Fixed, G&A, etc.)	$(363.53)	$(255.36)	$(63.84)	$(82.08)
15 Less: Marketing Communications Cost	$—	$—	$—	$—
16 Net Contribution	$121.18	$63.84	$15.96	$9.12
Scenario B: Communication Investment				
17 Brand Communication Effort A	$3.00	$4.00	$4.00	$5.00
18 Brand Contact Points N	2	1	1	0
19 Brand Communication Effort B	$2.50	$3.75	$3.50	$4.00
20 Brand Contact Points N	2	1	2	0
21 Brand Communication Effort C	$2.00	$2.50	$2.75	$1.00
22 Brand Contact Points N	2	2	1	0
23 Brand Communication Effort D	$1.50	$1.75	$2.00	$3.50
24 Brand Contact Points N	2	1	1	1
25 Brand Communication Effort E	$1.00	$1.00	$1.00	$1.00
26 Brand Contact Points N	0	1	1	1
27 Total Brand Communications Investment	$18.00	$15.50	$16.75	$4.50
28 Change in Share of Requirement	0%	10%	40%	1%
29 Resulting Share of Requirement	60%	44%	14%	15%
30 Customer Income Flow to Us	$605.88	$438.90	$159.60	$115.14
31 Less: Noncommunication Costs (Product, Fixed, G&A, etc.)	$(454.41)	$(351.12)	$(127.68)	$(103.63)
32 Less: Marketing Communication Costs	$(18.00)	$(15.50)	$(16.75)	$(4.50)
33 Net Contribution	$133.47	$72.28	$15.17	$7.01
ROI Calculation				
34 Incremental Gain/Loss vs. No Investment Scenario	$12.29	$8.44	$(0.79)	$(2.11)
35 Incremental ROCI	68%	54%	–5%	–47%

addition, this group requires a great deal of support, and customer service costs to maintain them are quite high. Demand from this group is expected to decline in the coming period. We would like to reduce our brand communication investment in this group and actually divest some of these customers, but we can't afford to alienate them, as it could damage our reputation with other, more valuable customers. In some instances, we need this group's purchase volume to maintain our economies of scale in manufacturing.

On Line 1, we have arbitrarily set dollar volume income flows at the factory level for each group at the same rate during the measurement period, that is, $1,000. Most likely, this would never be the case in the marketplace, but it is done to illustrate the dynamics of the process so that comparisons can be made.

Since this is a retail-driven consumer product, we ignore retail pricing. We are not interested in how much the customer actually spent to buy the product; we want to know the potential income that each group of customers can, or did, generate for our brand at the factory level.

Lines 2 through 5 are used to explain and adjust the value of each of the groups as a result of observations of activities in the marketplace during the measurement period (the fiscal year of the organization). Line 2 reflects changes in demand driven by environmental factors. Within some groups, customers are purchasing increasing amounts of the product or service simply because they are interested, or have increasing needs. An example might be computer software. Category revenue is growing at a rate of approximately 5 percent per year, while unit sales are growing at approximately 12 percent per year.[2] But even as customer consumption increases, product prices are generally falling. Thus, customers are buying more but paying less.

In our example, our group of Loyal customers is expected to grow by only 2 percent, while the projected growth rates for the other groups are 5 percent and 20 percent. Our Problem group is declining by 20 percent. So, after growth factors are taken into account, our initial demand or available income flow of $1,000 becomes $1,020 for the Loyals, $1,050 for our Switchers, $1,200 for our Emerging group, and $800 for our Problem segment.

Having provided a way to deal with the broad category or environmental changes during the measurement period, we also must provide some way to deal with competitive activities. Line 4 shows that competitive activities have only a slight negative impact on the income flow of the Loyals group. It might be that those customers are very brand loyal or have some other reason not to react to competitive pricing tactics. However, competitive activities do have an impact on each of the other groups. As shown, each of the other groups' income flow is driven down by 5 percent as a result of competitive price discounting or other income-flow-reducing activity.

Line 5, therefore, is simply an adjusted income flow for each of the groups after taking into account environmental factors and competitive activities that will either increase or decrease each group's income flow. In effect, it is the actual amount spent by each of the groups in our product category once the adjustments have been

---

[2]"NPD SofTrends Reports Moderate Sales Increases for Consumer Software; Stronger Unit Growth Points to Downward Pricing Shift," *PR Newswire*, April 25, 1997.

made (i.e., the available income flow from each group at the factory income level). Thus, our adjusted estimated requirement for Loyal customers becomes $1,009.80; $997.50 for the Switchers; $1,140.00 for the Emerging group; and $760.00 for the Problem segment.

With overall category demand established, we can move on to determining the base value each customer group represents to our brand. Line 6 details our share of requirement. In this case, we have been receiving 60 percent of the income flow our Loyals group spent or will spend in the category. This results in an income flow of $605.88. The Switchers give our brand 40 percent of their business, so we receive $399.00 from them. The group of Emerging customers' income flow of 10 percent SOR is $114.00. And the Problem segment is using our brand for 15 percent of their requirement, which results in $114.00 income flow.

Next, we must estimate our costs other than those from brand communication and profit. This is our allocation for all fixed and variable costs such as those related to product manufacturing and distribution, staff salaries, and general and administrative costs. Typically there will be some justifiable variation in costs attributed to different groups. For example, new customers generally incur greater administrative costs as accounts are established, promotional offers extended, and so on. Established customers, on the other hand, are often the easiest and most efficient to serve. They understand the product, require less hand-holding, are acquainted with our products and services and can explain easily and quickly what they want or need, and are commonly receptive to our communication efforts.

In our example, we determined that 75 percent of the total income flow will be needed to cover all these noncommunication costs for our Loyals group. As shown on Line 8, they cost somewhat less to service than the Switchers and the Emerging group, both of which have more churn and therefore greater ongoing administrative expenses. Finally, as explained earlier, the Problem group requires an even higher level of customer service.

These cost factors give us the contribution margin available for each customer group in Line 9. This is obtained by subtracting the percentage factor in Line 8 from 100 percent. Line 10 expresses the contribution margin in terms of dollars. (Recall, contribution margin in this approach includes funds available for brand communication and profit only.) It ranges from $151.47 for the Loyals group, to $79.80 for the Switchers, to $22.80 for the Emerging group, to $11.40 for the Problem customers.

To regroup, what we have just done is determine the value of the four groups of customers at the contribution margin line based on their income flows to the organization. If we could generate these income flows without investing any funds in brand communication, we might be able to justify serving each of them. However, even if we were able to drive our share of their requirement up substantially—getting, say, 70–80 percent of the Switchers or Emerging categories—we still would have limited funds available for brand communication programs. This is the challenge that every IBC manager faces when using this type of ROCI analysis. There are some customers against which finite resources simply can't be invested, or if the investment is made, it must be through some type of very efficient, low-cost communication activity that commonly limits its power and impact. This is not to say that these types of brand communication programs are not possible or useful, but it does suggest that targeting and focusing on best customers, or at least on those who provide the greatest opportunity for returned income flows, is the first requirement of any brand communication program.

With this analysis of customer value, we can move to the next step in the process: identifying the incremental value created by brand communication programs. We do this by first estimating the impact on income flows if no brand communication investment was made. This is then compared with the results achieved when we develop and implement various brand communication programs. The results often are surprising.

First we create the "No Investment" scenario. This is done by estimating or calculating how much the customer group would decline or how much our share of their requirement would fall if we suspended communication activity during the measurement period. In our example, we stated earlier that this is a competitive category with low loyalty and much competitive brand communication activity. On Line 11, we estimate that we would lose 20 percent of the share we receive from our Loyals, Switchers, and Problem groups if no brand communication programs were conducted. Even though Loyals are familiar with our products, they have many alternatives and need to hear our brand messages to remind them of our products' value and to distinguish us from the crowd. Switchers and Problems, without messages or incentives to encourage them, have little reason to consider our brand. The market tests that gave us those data indicated that the Emerging group is even more vulnerable. We could expect our SOR there to decrease by 30 percent during the measurement period.

You may recall from the earlier discussion that the customer's total demand or income flow in the category does not change as a result of our diminished communication activity. Only the proportion that we receive is impacted.

Lines 12 through 16 recalculate all the components that lead to the net contribution:

- Since the share of requirement among Loyals falls by 20 percent, the resulting SOR goes from 60 percent to 48 percent. Multiplying this by their category demand of $1,009.80 produces an income flow of $484.70. From this we subtract $363.53 to cover the 75 percent provision for product, administrative, and other noncommunication costs. This generates a net contribution of $121.18 from the group.

- The share of requirement among Switchers falls 20 percent as well, to an adjusted share of 32 percent. Given their category demand of $997.50 and the expected decline without brand communication, we now have an income flow of $319.20, 80 percent of which ($255.36) is allocated for noncommunication expenses. This generates a net contribution of $63.84.

- As was noted earlier, the Emerging group was more impacted by the lack of communication. They are newer to the category, have little previous experience with our products, and, in some cases, are still experimenting with products and brands. Without brand communication, their share of requirement drops by 30 percent. We can expect to receive only 7 percent of their income flow dollars, or $79.80. Subtracting allocated costs of $63.84 provides a net contribution of $15.96 to our brand.

- Finally, we expect a 20 percent decrease in share from the Problem group. Thus, our adjusted share of requirement is 12 percent. This produces an income flow of $91.20. When allocated noncommunication costs of $82.08 are deducted, we find a net contribution of $9.12.

The net contribution income flow shown for each group becomes the basis against which we will measure the incremental gain or loss resulting from brand communication.

The next step in our analysis is to estimate or calculate the alternative scenario using one or more brand communication efforts against each group. Again, this example is only for illustrative purposes, but it will provide a view of the process. Those conducting an analysis within their own organizations will have to adjust and adapt this particular chart to accommodate either more or fewer brand communication elements and activities than shown here.

In this illustration, we have five brand communication efforts, Lines 17 through 26. Some of these efforts have been targeted to each group, although messages and delivery systems may be different. Others we sent to only one or two groups. As part of our analysis, we must determine the cost of each of these brand communication efforts.

As can be seen, we have two lines for each brand communication effort. One is the identification of the program and the cost, and the second is the number of times the activity was used. For example, as shown on Line 17, brand communication effort A costs $3.00 to implement against the Loyals group. However, it costs $4.00 to implement against the Switchers and Emerging customers and, had it been used to reach the Problem segment, it would have cost $5.00. The costs of delivery are based on message delivery systems that differ according to the ease or difficulty of reaching each group.

Line 18 shows the number of times brand communication effort A was used against each group. It was used twice against Loyals, once against the Switchers and Emerging groups, and not used with the Problem group.

Lines 19 through 26 repeat this process for brand communication efforts B through E. As can be seen, there is a mix of communication efforts going against all of the four groups with varying levels of intensity, based on the planned brand communication program.

Line 27 is a summary of investments against each customer group during the measurement period. This is simply an addition of the cost of each brand communication effort multiplied by the number of times it was used. For example, for the Loyals group, we used brand communication effort A twice at a cost of $3.00 each or a total of $6.00. We used that same communication effort once with Switchers at a cost of $4.00.

If we total all the brand communication efforts and the number of times they were used, we arrive at Line 27. For example, we invested $18.00 against Loyals, $15.50 against Switchers, $16.75 against Emerging customers, and $4.50 against the Problem group.

In the previous section we asked, "What if we made no communication investment whatsoever; what would happen to our share of requirement? And what would happen to our brand?" In this section we turn the question around asking, "What happens to our share of requirement and our brand if we invest all this money in these customers and prospects? How much—if any—will our business increase? And will our profits increase as a result?"

Just as in the "No Communication Investment" scenario, the key is to estimate or calculate the change in share of requirement that results from a planned brand communication effort. This estimate uses historical behavioral data, such as the responsiveness of customers and prospects to messages, incentives, and delivery programs. As was discussed in an earlier section, we are not trying to evaluate each functionally specific communication effort. Instead, we are attempting to determine the synergistic effect produced by all elements of a brand communication program.

Once we determine how much, if any, our share of requirement will change as a direct result of our brand communication program, we then can recalculate all of the income, costs, and net contribution for each group.

- Even though we invested $18.00 in communicating with the Loyals, there was no impact on share of requirement. However, since our original intention had been to maintain our current SOR level, our objective has been achieved. Our income flow remains at $605.88, with 75 percent ($454.41) of this allocated to noncommunication costs. However, we must now deduct our $18.00 communication expenditure to arrive at our net contribution of $133.47.

- We estimate that our share of requirement among Switchers will increase by 10 percent, giving us a total share of their income flow of 44 percent. This would produce an income flow of $438.90. While income has increased; so have our costs; 80 percent ($351.12) of the income is allocated to noncommunication costs. After we subtract our brand communication investment of $15.50, we have a net contribution of $72.28.

- Emerging customers are very receptive to our messages, and we are able to increase our share of requirement by 40 percent, giving us a new share of 14 percent of their income flow. This produces an adjusted income flow of $159.60, 80 percent of which ($127.68) is required for noncommunication expenses. When we subtract the $16.75 brand communication investment, we are left with a net contribution of $15.17.

- The Problem segment unfortunately had a very slight change in share of requirement as a result of the brand communication program. The $4.50 we invested in them produced a 1 percent increase in our share of requirement. Our income flow becomes $115.14, with $103.63 in noncommunication costs. After deducting our $4.50 communication investment, we are left with a net contribution of $7.01.

We now can develop the actual calculation of the Return on Customer Investment. Only three lines are used in that calculation:

Line 16, our net contribution under the "No Communication Investment" scenario.

Line 33, our net contribution under the "Communication Investment" scenario.

Line 27, the total amount of communication spending occurring under the communication investment scenario.

For each group, we look at the incremental gain or loss in net contribution under the two scenarios. This is simply Line 33 minus Line 16. Because we are comparing net contribution values after all communication spending has been deducted, we are looking at the change in profitability that each group of customers or prospects can contribute.

The Return on Investment is calculated by taking the incremental gain/loss (i.e., the "return") in Line 34 and dividing it by Line 27, total brand communication investment.

- Our Loyals group received the largest portion of our communication spending, $18.00. That investment created no impact on our share of requirement versus our historical level. However, the alternative was to suspend communication, and in that event we likely would have lost 20 percent of our share among this key group. By spending the $18.00, we maintained our share and added to our profitability in the amount of $12.29 (i.e., $133.47 versus $121.18). Our Return on Investment is 68 percent [($133.47 − $121.18)/$18.00].

- Switchers increased their net contribution from $63.84 under the "No Communication Investment" scenario to $72.28. This is an incremental gain of $8.44 which, when divided by the communication investment of $15.50, produces an ROI of 54 percent.

- Communication dollars against the Emerging customer groups did not have as much impact. The net contribution actually fell from $15.96 to $15.17. While we were able to increase our share of requirement, the additional income was not sufficient to offset the communication costs. There is a loss of $0.79, and a negative ROI of minus 5 percent. This illustrates why it is often true that new customers are expensive to acquire and their value often occurs over time. In many cases, organizations are better off trying to nurture the business they have established from existing customer relationships before investing significant amounts to acquire new customers. The true value of customer acquisition usually cannot be reflected in a business-building model such as this, as the time frame is limited. There is, however, long-term value in acquiring new customers, which we'll discuss in more detail when we look at brand-building.

- Communication to the Problem group also produced a negative impact on the bottom line. While share of requirement has a slight increase, net contribution went from $9.12 to $7.01, an incremental loss of $2.11 and a negative ROI of minus 47 percent.

While this illustration is based on a real-world example, it has been adapted to illustrate the process. In other industries in which this process has been used, similar results have been found.

What Is a Good ROCI?

The questions often raised in this type of brand communication ROCI calculation are "What is a good ROCI?" and "What is a bad ROCI?" Obviously, brand communication managers want some sort of comparison with like organizations or with competitors. Unfortunately, such yardsticks or rules-of-thumb do not exist, or they are of little value. All organizations are different. They have differing strategies and in expectations from management and stockholders. Thus, whether an ROCI number is "good" or "bad" depends on the financial requirements of the organization.

We have worked with clients who have set hurdle rates—that is, required returns—for brand communication programs in the 200–300 percent range, for this is the return they believe they can get with other uses of the organization's finite resources. Other organizations are pleased with returns in the 20–40 percent range, and still others with much more modest goals. The true determination of whether the ROCI is good or bad is to compare it to the return that could be expected from investing those same funds in other corporate activities. If R&D is expected to return 40 percent, for example, then that is a relevant comparison number. If new plant investments will return 18 percent, that is the relevant ROCI to use in comparing communication ROCI. Again, it all depends on the organization and the other uses to which the corporate resources might be put. It is within this framework that brand communication must function now and into the future.

With this example of how to develop a business-building return-on-brand-communication investment analysis, we are ready to move on to a discussion of how to measure the return on a brand-building investment.

Measuring the Return on Brand-Building Communication Programs

Our definition of brand-building communication investment is that which is developed and adequately sustained to have longer-term impact on customers and the marketplace than those investments identified as business building. We have separated brand-building and business-building communication programs primarily according to accepted accounting procedures that require returns to be measured within the organization's fiscal year. Thus, if a brand communication program investment is expected to have a life span or value of more than one fiscal year, we classify it as brand building.

As before, we acknowledge that this differentiation between business building and brand building is not as precise as we would like. It does, however, broadly separate the two activities for measurement and analysis. The success of this separation depends to a great extent on management consensus and the support of accounting and financial managers. Of course, this agreement on the process, separation, and classification of brand building and business building will vary with the needs and values of each specific organization. Thus, while we can define and illustrate the concept and the approach, the actual calculation of returns must be organization specific. As the organization works with the concepts of brand building and business building over time, managers generally develop standards and guidelines to differentiate one activity from the other.

Customer-Brand Value

To review, the goal of our proposed process is to understand how customers value the brand and to determine that value currently and over time. By being able to measure customer-brand value and changes in that value, we can either relate or define the manner in which investments in brand communication have impacted customer value. This then allows us to calculate the return on our brand-building communication spending.

Throughout this book, we have emphasized that the critical value of brand communication lies with the customer or consumer of the brand. It is the customer who responds to brand communication through increased usage, brand loyalty, advocacy, or another measurable activity. It is the current or continuing flow of income from customers that is critical in understanding the true value of the brand, that is, how and when that value increases and how and when it declines. A number of measures to identify changes in customer brand value in the marketplace can be used. Some of those measurement tools include levels of brand loyalty, retention and repurchase rates, customer willingness to pay price premiums, customer switching costs, erection of cost barriers to category entry by competitors, and the level and value of customer brand advocacy. While these values are determined using specific measurement tools and methodologies that are widely available in the marketplace, they do not help us truly understand how total customer brand value might be measured. That requires a new approach, outlined in the following section.

The Conceptual Model of Brand-Building Communication Investments

From a theoretical standpoint, we can treat brand-building communication investments differently from those of business building. We can do the same from an accounting and financial standpoint. Unfortunately, given the present accounting conventions in the United States, and the various federal and state tax codes, translating these theoretical concepts into practice is not quite so easy. In this section, we describe the theoretical underpinnings of the brand-building communication investment measurement approach. Following that, we illustrate a methodology that is being used in the marketplace today.

Much of our measurement approach is based on the marketing concept of Lifetime Customer Value (LTV). LTV is the ongoing relationship and resulting income flows that come from brand customers who continue to purchase products and services over time.

Unfortunately, as powerful as is the concept of LTV, at present there is no way to handle future customer income flows (income flows beyond the organization's fiscal year) using current financial and accounting procedures. So, even though the organization has customers whom it is fairly confident will continue to purchase its products and services and provide business relationships and income flows now and into the future, there is no way to reflect that anticipated value except to lump it into corporate goodwill. This is what makes it so difficult to determine brand value or to estimate whether the value of the brand is increasing or decreasing. Brand value simply becomes a part of the summary goodwill holdings of the firm. These holdings include its relationships with a host of groups, organizations, employees, and the like, all of which are treated as part of the assets of the organization. Efforts are being made to remedy this nebulous brand value situation through new accounting procedures such as activity-based and cash-flow accounting, and even the use of economic valuation analysis (EVA). For the foreseeable future, however, current expenses and current revenue and tangible assets will rule, and LTV is something marketers can only talk about.

In spite of the accounting and tax difficulties in measuring and valuing customers and brands into future accounting periods, it is useful to explain how these concepts might be used in determining customer-brand values.

There are two key elements in this brand-building approach. One is that the customer value of the brand will provide future income flows to the organization (the concept of lifetime customer value). The second is that these future income flows have current and future value to the organization. In truth, the current and future customer income flows for many organizations are the true value of the firm. Today, income flows make up substantial portions of many organizations' assets. One only need look at most types of service organizations to see this concept in action. Prime examples of the income flow–driven organization are various forms of communications agencies, such as advertising, direct marketing, and public relations. These organizations have few tangible assets, yet they generate large income flows from clients. Indeed, it is the income flows from those clients now and into the future that are the true value of the organization—not the tangible assets, which generally are quite small. The same is true of many traditional marketing organizations such as Nike or Coca-Cola or Pepsi-Cola. For example, Nike outsources most of its manufacturing and thus has no plants or factories loading its balance sheet. Yet Nike has high income flows, and thus asset value based on its brand's ongoing value to its customers. The same is true of Coke and Pepsi. They have very low tangible assets in relation to their customer income flows, since they make only the syrup concentrate for the product and provide that to their bottlers. It is the bottlers who own most of the tangible assets, invested in plants, equipment, and delivery trucks. Examples of income-flow-as-assets organizations can be found in many other areas such as media firms, law partnerships, credit card companies, and franchise fast-food organizations such as McDonald's and Burger King. Given this, let's assume that relationships with customers and the future income flows those customers will provide comprise the value of many organizations.

Assume that a brand's customer value can be measured in the form of income flows. Assume, too, that customer value can be converted into financial value with defined returns into the future, that is, lifetime customer value. Further, assume that the customer value of a brand is continuously declining, because indeed, in most cases it is. While some brands are doubtlessly increasing in value due to growth of the product category and other reasons, many of our most valuable marketplace brands have customer values that are static or declining. The reason is that brands are continuously being challenged in the marketplace: present customers die, move away, or change their lifestyles; competitors create new products or mount aggressive marketing and communication programs to draw customers away; technology or other factors render the brand's product value obsolete in real terms. Consequently, value is decreasing, unless the organization invests in maintaining or enhancing the brand. Finally, assume that there is some ideal or optimal brand value among customers in the marketplace.

With these assumptions, we can construct a method of valuing the brand as an asset of the organization. That is, we can define actual, tangible value of the brand in the marketplace. This comes as a result of present and future income flows from present and future customers. As an asset with tangible income flow values, the brand could be capitalized and placed on the firm's balance sheet. With this capitalization process, we could then view the brand as a depreciating asset and accrue for replacement or replenishment of the brand value in the marketplace. Since the brand is continuously declining, we would likely want to continuously invest in building brand value to maintain the income flows from customers and prospects. As a result, we would likely be continuously replenishing the brand value by making brand-building investments in marketing and brand communication. (Recall how the calculation/estimation of the brand value decline was done in the business-building section. If no brand communication is used during a period, the income flow was expected to decline or remain static. This same process forms the basis for brand replenishment over a longer period of time.) One could argue, however, that an accrual fund, based on the replenishment of the brand at some level, might be a financially feasible alternative approach.

Brand investments in the form of various brand communication programs could be considered a capital expenditure and not a current period expense. Therefore, those investments would be treated differently from an accounting standpoint.

One could then take the final step and start to treat the brand as an actual organizational asset, such as intellectual property. This approach would be based on the premise that the brand is the physical manifestation of the relationship between the organization and its customers. It is this relationship that must be nurtured and maintained if the income flows are to continue into the future. Thus, the organization should treat the brand as intellectual property and account for it in the same manner as any other intellectual property asset on its books and financial records.

While this conceptual argument has intuitive appeal, it faces a great many challenges under today's accounting and financial codes and conventions. Nonetheless, it does provide a basis on which we must begin to calculate the return on brand-building investments.

Measuring the Return on Internal Brand Communication Programs

As has been discussed in several other areas of this text, in an IBC program, it is essential that the entire organization support the brand initiatives. For example, if the organization develops a superb external brand communication program but is unable to support the brand promise or fulfill the brand value proposition with customers on an ongoing basis, generally those funds are wasted. Customers or prospects will come to the brand with certain expectations. When they are not met, the customers will leave and are unlikely to return. Therefore, a measurement system to evaluate the return on internal brand communication investments is likely as critical as one for external communication.

The Challenges of Internal Brand Communication Evaluation

Commonly, most persons who will be responsible for fulfilling the promises of the brand to customers and prospects are not under the supervision of the marketing or communication manager. Often, those communication responsibilities fall on human resources, operations, or other departments. Therefore, it is critical for the IBC planner to determine who and through what means internal communication occurs. Frequently, it is through employee newsletters, departmental meetings, chat-lines, and even the inevitable internal grapevine. Thus, one of the primary tasks of the IBC manager must be to identify the key internal gatekeepers who are responsible for these internal communication systems. In truth, identification of these key communication gatekeepers is no different than the process we used to identify and value external customers, consumers, and end users. In fact, the same type of process that was described in Chapter 4 works very well for this purpose.

Internal Brand Communication Audits

The first step in an internal brand communication evaluation system is to determine which employees, channels, and associates have the most impact on customers and prospects. In other words, who comes in contact with the customer and how does that contact occur? This determination can be made the same way an external brand communication audit is conducted, as discussed in Chapter 3. It is important to determine what and how employees are communicating to customers and the satisfaction of customer contacts. Often, we can find much of this information in customer satisfaction studies and by interviewing customer service representatives, tech support people, and the like. How we are presently communicating and how effective that process is are key to developing an internal brand communication program.

From Audit to Influence

Once the brand audit has been conducted and a determination is made as to who communicates about the brand and what the impact of that communication is, we can start to value those brand contacts. Here, we will need to look at two levels. First, who are the most important internal customer brand contacts who impact external customers? Second, who controls or influences those contacts?

The first is fairly easy. For example, FedEx knows that its couriers and its customer service personnel are the prime brand contact it has with its customers. For other organizations, it may be the telephone operator or the retailer or the shipping clerk in a direct marketing organization. Businesses touch their customers in different ways, and it is important for the brand planner to know who makes those contacts and the circumstances surrounding the contacts. With this knowledge, the planner can move up the hierarchical line to determine who is responsible for the contacts. Key people are those who influence the behaviors of those who report to them. It is these managers whom the brand planner wants to influence to make sure that the brand communication program is explained fully to the managers' employees.

Measure over Time

By knowing what brand contacts currently are, by defining what brand contacts should be, and by knowing who influences the behavior of the persons who deliver those brand contacts, the brand planner can start to develop and define a brand contact program. Measurement in this case is relatively simple. The brand planner has defined the importance of the brand contact, that is, he or she has prioritized the various brand contacts and can therefore define the optimum brand contact that could be delivered. Thus, having some objective measures such as "Answering help line calls in three rings," or "All employees should be familiar with current brand communication external programs so they can discuss them with customers and prospects" allows for fairly easy monitoring. The real key is to set up some type of process and then follow through with it.

As before, evaluation of internal brand communication is based on a determination of what is to be accomplished, the value of accomplishing that objective, and the return to the organization if the objective is satisfactorily achieved.

A Summary View of Evaluation in the Twenty-First Century

Today, most of our evaluation tools are quite crude and unwieldy. As organizations move toward the brand relationships we have discussed throughout this text, evaluation of results will not be a separate activity—it will be part of the ongoing relationship between the organization and its customers. Evaluation will therefore be continuous. As the marketing company begins to understand the value of customers, it will become a simple matter to identify those who are most important and those who have lesser value. Thus, allocation of resources will not be so much a planning process as it will be a customer management and customer relationship process. It will be simple for the organization to know which customers to invest in and to determine if the marketing and brand communication program worked.

Summary

Measurement and evaluation are not carried out in many brand marketing and communication organizations today simply because they are difficult tasks to do well, given the accounting environment and the tools at hand. Ideally, we can build those systems into the brand communication process, helping managers to know what is working and what isn't. As a consequence, measurement and evaluation will be so closely integrated with other aspects of brand communication, they will no longer be regarded as tasks set apart, warranting treatment in a separate chapter in future editions of this text.

16

Selling Management on the IBC Plan

One of the biggest jobs the IBC planner may face in developing a brand communication program is presenting that plan to management. After all, the IBC planning approach takes a different view of the marketplace than that assumed in traditional marketing communication planning, particularly an advertising campaign. As a result, if everyone involved in the planning process—the people at the client organization and throughout the various marketing communication agencies—is not familiar with and committed to the principles of IBC planning, the planner may run into roadblocks in trying to get the plan approved at various internal levels.

At best, winning management approval is often difficult even when a traditional planning process is followed, but because an IBC plan requires a change in thinking and the process commonly threatens the status quo, we have found that IBC plans are subject to additional challenges. We discuss those challenges as we highlight some of the points on which the IBC approach differs from traditional marketing communication planning.

Reasons for Resistance to IBC Planning

Focus on the Future

IBC planning isn't restricted to the typical one-year marketing communication planning horizon. Instead, it requires a consideration of the organization's future and a focus on what the company and the brand might become. If the planner's vision of the future doesn't agree with that of higher management, the entire plan might be immediately challenged. Given the tensions that exist within corporate America, where regular promotions are seen as a sign of success and decisions tend to be made hierarchically, the planner's superiors may view future projections as their domain and think the planner is overstepping the bounds of his or her job.

We should also recognize that some marketing communication planners themselves will be reluctant to make the move to IBC planning and projecting results into the future. On the client side, brand managers are rewarded for playing it safe, for keeping the product out of trouble. If a brand manager expects to be in his or her job for only a year or so, there is little incentive to develop future plans. Likewise, on the agency side, brand planning has traditionally been the domain of the client. Many account executives might be reluctant to make recommendations to their clients on anything beyond the next year's plan for the brand. In addition, IBC planning requires marketing and communication people to understand enough about the finance and accounting areas of the brand to be able to speak persuasively to people in senior management. Those skills are not always in the repertoire of today's agency planners, however, and, as a result, some additional study may be required.

The psychological mindset that supports the status quo over change may well be the most difficult barrier for the IBC planner to overcome. Successful IBC planning requires a commitment that begins with top management and works its way down through the organization. While more companies may develop the tools that make IBC planning possible, those tools will not be used to their full extent. We believe that it may well be the next generation of planners, the readers of this text, who will bring about the organizational changes needed for IBC planning to take hold. So, we must recognize the barriers we face, but view them as hurdles rather than roadblocks.

Understanding Behavior

The IBC approach requires an examination of current customer behavior and the use of that understanding as the basis for the plan. This means that consumer research and consumer analysis—important elements in any planning approach—become paramount. If the IBC planner can convince management that he or she understands the consumer inside and out, then a major part of the job of winning management over to IBC has been done. While the database plays an important role in developing consumer understanding, we must move beyond a recitation of facts and figures to make the consumer come alive for corporate decision makers. We may want to consider bringing the voice of the consumer into the presentation through tape recordings or videos made during research activities. Or perhaps we can develop profiles of representative consumers to be presented as part of the plan.

Conveying a sense of consumer understanding should be an area in which the various agencies shine. After all, advertising campaigns traditionally have focused on communication goals, and effective communication requires consumer understanding. Further, the recent addition of account planners to many U.S. advertising agencies fits nicely with the IBC emphasis on consumer expertise. Account planning reaffirms the advertising agency's consumer expertise, relying on traditional consumer research techniques such as observation, depth interviews, motivational research, and focus groups to learn about the consumer.

Behavioral Segmentation

A major difference between IBC planning and traditional marketing communication planning is that IBC segments are identified based on their behavioral differences, while traditional market segments are typically described in terms of demographic and psychographic characteristics. Demographics, in particular, have long been the preferred currency of brand managers, account executives, and media planners. A smart IBC planner will recognize that making a complete break from demographics and psychographics isn't feasible. Instead, once the appropriate behavioral segments have been identified, we can use the information in the database to determine the demographic and psychographic characteristics of each segment. That way, while our emphasis will be on behavior, we'll also be able to mollify doubters who are tied to the traditional bases of segment identification. Interestingly, we might find that there may not be major demographic differences between heavy and light users or between loyal users and switchers for a given product. In that case the lack of demographic and psychographic differences may serve to strengthen our argument in favor of the move to behavioral segmentation.

Customer Valuation

The IBC planning approach asks the planner to determine customer value for different aggregated groups. While the concept of valuation may seem strange, the underlying principles have been accepted by marketers for some time (the often-mentioned 80/20 rule is an example of this principle). When differential customer value is presented in terms of resource allocation and profit potential, the reasons for the approach quickly become clear.

Emphasis on Behavioral Objectives

Like customer valuation, IBC planning's emphasis on behavioral objectives can be supported easily by presenting the objectives in terms of bottom-line results, or, more appropriately, ROCI (Return on Customer Investment). A behavioral objective that calls for an increase in loyalty can be translated into increased sales at a non-promotional price. An increase in purchase volume can lead to a corresponding sales increase. With the growing corporate emphasis on results, setting objectives according to behavioral goals makes good business sense.

ROCI-Based Spending and Evaluation

One thing that should be clear from the preceding discussion is that IBC planning can be justified through an emphasis on profitability. That should make corporate management, particularly the financial people, happy. However, there may be an education task involved in converting to an ROCI-based allocation approach. Imagine the task faced by the financial people at a multibrand, multimarket company such as Procter & Gamble. They review and justify expenditures on a wide variety of brands and programs. Their job is simplified if they are fairly sure budgets will not change greatly from year to year. But that assumption can't be made in IBC planning, particularly during the transition period from a traditional approach to the IBC approach.

Unfortunately, there is no simple way to get over this hurdle because IBC planning cannot work if the planner is not allowed sufficient resources. However, if the rest of the plan has been prepared carefully and supported adequately, the budget request should speak for itself. IBC planning depends on data availability; once the necessary information is available, we must use it to its full extent in order to justify our investment requests. (By the way, it's quite possible that IBC spending may be lower than in the past for many products because of the greater efficiency realized through more precise targeting. Think how happy that will make the management people!)

How to Get Started with IBC Planning

There are several steps the would-be IBC planner can take to introduce the IBC process into his or her company. The first, and, likely, the most important one, is to identify a management champion. Find someone in the senior management ranks whom you believe will be amenable to a change in planning approach. Explain to that person the IBC process and approach and the benefits that commonly result. As we noted at the outset of this chapter, the important points to communicate about the IBC process are the emphasis on ROCI, the strategic rather than tactical view of marketing communication, and the focus on investing in customers. These are benefits that should be appreciated by most senior managers.

Second, demonstrate the financial value of the IBC process to corporate decision makers. When marketing communication activities are regarded as strategic tools that will deliver targeted returns on the investment made in them, the value of the IBC process becomes clear to management.

Third, capture the brand. By this, we mean that ultimate responsibility for the brand should be given to the organization's communication people because the communication people are the keepers of the customer, and, by extension, the keepers of the brand. If you accept the basic IBC premise that it is customers who determine brand value, the essential need to place brand stewardship in the hands of the IBC planner becomes obvious. This transition is likely to take time, particularly in firms in which the brand has long been the responsibility of the brand manager and communicators have been viewed as service providers or tacticians. Brand managers still have an important role to play; they must coordinate all the marketing activities on behalf of the brand. The difference is that they do so working with the IBC planner, so that the likely impact of those activities on the relationship between the customer and the brand will always be considered as part of the planning and coordination process.

Finally, start small. Select one project and approach it from the IBC perspective. This will give you a concrete way to demonstrate how the process works and, more importantly, the strategic and financial benefits derived from using the process. Once your management sees that it is possible to determine what the company gets back for the dollars it spends against various customer segments, your management champion will have ample ammunition to use in winning others over to your side.

Presentation Tips

In marketing communication, style often is as important as substance, at least when it comes to making presentations designed to win a new client or gain support for a proposed plan. There are numerous books that take readers through the intricacies of preparing a business presentation, so we won't go into those details here. Yet there are some lessons to be learned from people who have been involved in new business or new plan presentations in the past.

Advertising Age periodically runs columns offering lists of mistakes that agencies make when pitching new business. The main point that comes through time after time is a lack of understanding about what the client really needs, what the problems really are. This probably happens because an agency's focus is often on what it can do well, which may or may not fit the client's situation. Generally, in IBC planning this translates to an emphasis on what the planner wants to do versus the concerns of those with greater decision-making authority. When developing a presentation, we must try to think about the points we'll be covering from the audience's point of view. What's really important? What's likely to raise questions? Just as effective IBC planning requires an understanding of the consumer, effective IBC presentation requires an understanding of the audience.

Understanding the audience also means realizing we're requiring a substantial time commitment from them when we make a presentation. It's not as though people in the communication and marketing fields have tremendous amounts of free time just waiting to be filled by our presentation. We need to stick to our time limit, present the facts coherently and succinctly, and allow time for interaction through questions and answers. In other words, prepare. Don't wing it. That doesn't mean we have to stick to a script and give a canned presentation. It does mean, however, that we should have a good idea of what we're going to say before we walk into the meeting.

Preparation also includes having the appropriate materials to back up the points we intend to make. Clear, easy-to-read visuals that document the relevant statistics, an ROCI spreadsheet with alternate scenarios, and a flowchart that shows not only media scheduling, but also dates for other marketing communication activities, are basic to a successful presentation. There are a number of computer software packages available designed specifically to produce presentation-quality materials. The extra effort we put into this part of the presentation is a strong indication of the quality of thinking and the level of interest we bring to our recommendations. (Having said that, we should also caution that a presentation that's all flash and no substance won't get us too far with most decision makers.)

Selling ideas is the heart of marketing communication, and we have to make it through various layers of approval before we get the chance to sell our ideas to consumers. In advertising agencies, the selling process frequently revolves around creative executions. Keith Reinhard, chairman of DDB Needham Worldwide, addressed the difficulty of selling "breakthrough creative" ideas to clients. His observations apply to any selling situation and may be especially pertinent for planners trying to gain approval for IBC plans since they, like breakthrough creative, involve taking chances. The following are Reinhard's points with our interpretations after each:

1. You can't sell breakthrough creative to a client who's fired you. *At the end of the day, it's the client who pays the bills and makes (or doesn't make) the profit. It's their brand, and we're only offering recommendations. We must learn to recognize when we've pushed things as far as we can.*

2. You won't succeed at selling breakthrough creative or anything else by telling clients they're wrong or implying their intelligence is inferior. *Again, it's their brand, not ours. While we may have spent weeks living with the brand situation, the client has likely spent years with the brand. We can disagree with someone without implying that our way is the only right way.*

3. Breakthrough creative must also be right. A good question to ask is: "Would I invest my own money in this idea?" *If we wouldn't back it up with our money, why should we expect the client to support it? Recognize that there's often more than one way to interpret research results or to approach a problem.*

4. You won't succeed at selling breakthrough creative unless you have at least looked through client eyes at what is being proposed. Methodically anticipating client concerns and working out answers in advance is essential. *This is where doing our homework comes into play. We empathize with the consumer in developing the IBC program and with the client in presenting it.*

5. The braver the creative idea, the more trust is required. Clients don't buy much of anything from people they don't trust. *Trust comes more easily if recommendations are backed up with solid data.*

6. "Digging in" and "taking a stand" are concepts alien to salesmanship. They suggest a kind of arrogance and confrontation that is hardly in keeping with the art of persuasion. *Know when to say when. If the IBC planner feels himself or herself becoming confrontational or senses that the conversation isn't moving forward (that is, it's just a rehash of the same points over and over), it's time to step back and regroup.*

7. Enlisting the client's early involvement in strategy development helps create ownership of the breakthrough creative ideas which result.[1] *IBC planning works best when everyone with a stake in the decision making is involved from the beginning of the planning process.*

---

[1]Keith Reinhard, "Any Wednesday" (DDB Needham Worldwide, Chicago, May 6, 1992, in-house memorandum).

What can the IBC planner take from Reinhard's advice? To recap the point made at the beginning of this chapter, we need to recognize that IBC planning may seem foreign to many people who have been in the marketing communication business for a considerable length of time. We may find ourselves in the minority when it comes to arguing in favor of an IBC approach. But for our own future success, as well as that of the brand entrusted to us, we can't use information as an excuse for arrogance. Just because the people we work with (and report to) haven't been trained in IBC concepts doesn't mean they cannot understand them or will not appreciate the perspective. Opinions and recommendations need to be presented with appropriate support and include an appreciation of the way the brand has been marketed in the past. IBC planning stems from advances in technology and is evolutionary, not revolutionary. If we can show how our plan builds on past efforts and generates positive ROCI for the firm, we're well on the way to winning approval for the next steps.

Index